T0326292

MATHEMATICS
FOR
ACTUARIAL STUDENTS

MATHEMATICS
FOR
ACTUARIAL STUDENTS

by

HARRY FREEMAN, M.A., F.I.A.

PART II

Finite Differences, Probability &
Elementary Statistics

CAMBRIDGE

Published for the Institute of Actuaries

AT THE UNIVERSITY PRESS

1952

CAMBRIDGE
UNIVERSITY PRESS

University Printing House, Cambridge CB2 8BS, United Kingdom

Cambridge University Press is part of the University of Cambridge.

It furthers the University's mission by disseminating knowledge in the pursuit of
education, learning and research at the highest international levels of excellence.

www.cambridge.org
Information on this title: www.cambridge.org/9781316606995

© Cambridge University Press 1952

First edition 1939
Reprinted 1940, 1945, 1946, 1947, 1948, 1949, 1952
First paperback edition 2016

A catalogue record for this publication is available from the British Library

ISBN 978-1-316-60699-5 Paperback

Cambridge University Press has no responsibility for the persistence or accuracy
of URLs for external or third-party internet websites referred to in this publication,
and does not guarantee that any content on such websites is, or will remain,
accurate or appropriate.

CONTENTS

MEMORANDUM

If the modern student, who aspires to be an Actuary, is faced with a wider range of actuarial subjects and a more searching test of his understanding of actuarial principles than was the student of an earlier generation, he has this compensation—that the means to acquire such understanding are more readily available and put into a form which may more readily be assimilated.

This book is such an example of the help afforded to the actuarial student, and he is fortunate to have the opportunity to study a work of this merit at the very beginning of his Course. A complete grasp of its principles will not only assist him to satisfy his examiners as to his proficiency in the mathematical problems by which he will be tested, but when he has so satisfied them he will have laid such foundation for his future work that he will ever have cause to be grateful to the author of this treatise.

H. J. P. O.

NOTATION

$P_n(x)$ a polynomial (i.e., a rational integral function) of degree n in x.

$n_{(r)}$ $\dfrac{n(n-1)(n-2)\ldots(n-r+1)}{r(r-1)(r-2)\ldots 3.2.1} = \dfrac{n^{(r)}}{r!}$, where n may be positive or negative, integral or fractional.

This is represented in other works by the symbols $\dbinom{n}{r}$ or n_r; see *J.I.A.* vol. LXIII, p. 58.

$n^{(r)}$ $n(n-1)(n-2)\ldots(n-r+1)$.

There seems to be no recognized symbol for the more general factorial $n(n-h)(n-2h)\ldots(n-\overline{r-1}h)$. It may sometimes be convenient to represent this by the same symbol $n^{(r)}$, but in that case the symbol must be specially defined and consistently used. Cf. *post*, p. 19.

$n^{(-r)}$ $\dfrac{1}{(n+1)(n+2)\ldots(n+r)} = \dfrac{1}{(n+r)^{(r)}}.$

A different notation is employed in certain other works—see *post*, p. 19.

$\underset{bc\ldots}{\triangle^t u_a}$ the divided difference of order t. This notation is explained and reference is made to other notations in Chapter III.

Paragraphs and examples marked with an asterisk, thus *, are intended for the advanced student only, and need not be read by students preparing for Part I of the Institute Examinations.

REFERENCES

J.I.A.   *Journal of the Institute of Actuaries.*
T.F.A.   *Transactions of the Faculty of Actuaries.*
J.S.S.   *Journal of the Institute of Actuaries Students' Society.*

AUTHOR'S PREFACE

As explained in the Preface to Part I of this book, the revision of the syllabus for the Examinations of the Institute of Actuaries rendered it necessary to divide *An Elementary Treatise on Actuarial Mathematics* into two parts and to make additions to that part of the book intended for students who were reading for the first Part of the Examinations. The opportunity has been taken to revise thoroughly the Chapters on Finite Differences and Probability and to bring the book up to date. While little alteration has been made in a few Chapters of *Actuarial Mathematics* the majority have been entirely rewritten, and it is therefore advisable to refer to each Chapter of the present book in detail.

Chapters I and II do not differ markedly from the first two Chapters on Finite Differences in *Actuarial Mathematics*. Chapter III, on Interpolation with Unequal Intervals, has been rewritten. The introduction of Dr Aitken's notation has simplified the general problem of divided differences, and as a result a more logical exposition of the theorems connected with these differences has been given. The earlier parts of Chapter IV, on Central Differences, have been remodelled, and much new matter inserted. With regard to Chapter V as given in *Actuarial Mathematics* it was thought that the treatment of the principles of Inverse Interpolation was to a certain extent incomplete. Dr Aitken suggested lines on which improvement might be made and the initial paragraphs have therefore been redrafted. Considerable alterations have been made in the Chapter on Summation: the first few paragraphs have been recast, a new section dealing with the application of operators to the summation of algebraic series has been introduced and paragraphs on the operator $[n]$ have been inserted. Chapter VII, on Miscellaneous Theorems, has been enlarged by the introduction of new material and a fuller treatment has been given of the matter in the previous book. Chapter VIII is entirely new. It was considered that there was now an opportunity to collect in one Chapter a number of modern methods and special devices which have recently appeared from the pens of Mr Lidstone and Dr Aitken, but which are scattered over the pages of various Journals. The Chapter on Approximate Integration has been amended in order to clarify certain proofs and theorems, but is otherwise unaltered.

In view of the introduction of Elementary Statistics into the syllabus for Part I of the Examinations it was considered advisable to approach the study of Probability from a slightly different angle. As a consequence, Chapter X has been largely rewritten. New Chapters on Elementary Statistics have been introduced: these Chapters do not deal exhaustively with the subject, but are, it is hoped, sufficient to enable the student to solve simple types of problem met with in practical work. Little alteration has been made in the Chapter dealing with Mean Value and the application of the Calculus to Probability.

The Examples are mainly those which have already appeared in *Actuarial Mathematics*. Examples 11 and 12 contain exercises in Statistics and the Miscellaneous Examples contain many new questions.

In the preparation of this Part of the book I have received much help from various sources. I have had access to the notes written for the Actuarial Tuition Service and some of the Lessons on Probability and Statistics (prepared originally by P. M. Marples) have proved of value. My thanks are due to Mr H. Tetley and Mr O. C. J. Klagge for helpful suggestions on certain points.

It is, however, to Dr A. C. Aitken and Mr G. J. Lidstone to whom I am most indebted. Dr Aitken generously put at my disposal his notes on various subjects connected with Finite Differences. In particular, his suggestions on Inverse Interpolation, the divided difference notation and the methods of cross-means have been such that I was able to adopt them with little alteration. Throughout the preparation of the book, from the earliest stages to the final proof-reading, Mr Lidstone has been my constant guide and mentor. A great deal of the work has been inspired by him and his comments and criticisms on all points have been invaluable. He has read through and annotated the whole of the book with that thoroughness for which he is justly famous, and I am deeply grateful to him for his help.

H. F.

March 1939

FINITE DIFFERENCES

CHAPTER I

DEFINITIONS AND FUNDAMENTAL FORMULAE

1. The function $y = a + bx + cx^2 + \ldots + kx^n$ is a rational integral function of the nth degree in x, where the indices are positive integers, n being the greatest, and $a, b, c \ldots k$ are constants, of which $k \neq 0$ but the others are unrestricted.

A rational integral function is also called a polynomial, and it is convenient to represent a polynomial of the nth degree as $P_n(x)$.

Consider the simple polynomial $y = u_x = 1 + x + x^2$. It is quite easy to obtain the value of y corresponding to any value of x by substituting that value of x on the right-hand side of the equation. For example

x	0	1	2	3	4	5	6	7	8
y	1	3	7	13	21	31	43	57	73

It will be found that for successive integral values of x in the above table the values of y have interesting properties. If from each value of y the previous value of y be subtracted, we obtain a new set of figures:

$$(\alpha) \quad 2 \quad 4 \quad 6 \quad 8 \quad 10 \quad 12 \quad 14 \quad 16$$

and if the subtraction be performed on these figures in the same way the new differences are

$$(\beta) \quad 2 \quad 2 \quad 2 \quad 2 \quad 2 \quad 2 \quad 2$$

The sequence of 2's in (β) is not a mere coincidence: it will be shown later that when y has the value supposed all the terms in (β) have the same value, 2, however far the series extends.

This leads us to another method of obtaining values of y. Suppose that we write down the original table in a different form, and include in the table the two sets of figures (α) and (β) thus:

x	y	(α)	(β)
0	1		
		2	
1	3		2
		4	
2	7		2
		6	
3	13		2
		8	
4	21		2
		10	
5	31		2
		12	
6	43		2
		14	
7	57		2
		16	
8	73		

We can now find any further value of y by extending the columns (α) and (β). We must however work from (β) to (α) and then to y instead of from y to (α) and then to (β) as has already been done. For example, to obtain the value of y when x has the value 9, i.e. to obtain u_9, a new 2 must be inserted in the (β) column: the new value in the (α) column will be $16 + 2 = 18$, and the required value of y will be $73 + 18 = 91$. To find u_{10} the process is continued. Any value of y corresponding to an integral value of x can be obtained in a similar manner.

2. The above is a particular instance of a far more general set of operations. We have used the simplest possible numerical values of x, namely the natural numbers, and we have evolved our example from a known quadratic function $y = u_x = 1 + x + x^2$. As a general rule the form of the function is not known and the given values of x are not necessarily consecutive integers.

3. Now suppose that instead of numerical values of x differing by unity we have the following consecutive values of x:

$$a, \ a+h, \ a+2h, \ a+3h, \ \dots,$$

where the values of x differ by a quantity h instead of by unity.

Then if the function be still $y = u_x$ the values of y corresponding to the above values of x will be

$$u_a, \ u_{a+h}, \ u_{a+2h}, \ u_{a+3h}, \ \ldots.$$

In order to form a column similar to column (α) above we shall have to write down

$$u_{a+h} - u_a, \ u_{a+2h} - u_{a+h}, \ u_{a+3h} - u_{a+2h}, \ \ldots.$$

These are called the *first differences* of the function $y = u_x$ and are denoted by

$$\Delta u_a, \ \Delta u_{a+h}, \ \Delta u_{a+2h}, \ \ldots,$$

where Δ is not a quantity but a symbol representing an "operation".

Column (β), being the differences of column (α), will be

$$(u_{a+2h} - u_{a+h}) - (u_{a+h} - u_a),$$
$$(u_{a+3h} - u_{a+2h}) - (u_{a+2h} - u_{a+h}),$$
$$\ldots\ldots\ldots\ldots\ldots\ldots\ldots$$

or, more shortly,

$$\Delta u_{a+h} - \Delta u_a,$$
$$\Delta u_{a+2h} - \Delta u_{a+h},$$
$$\ldots\ldots\ldots\ldots\ldots\ldots$$

These are called the *second differences* of u_x and are denoted by

$$\Delta^2 u_a, \ \Delta^2 u_{a+h}, \ \Delta^2 u_{a+2h} \ \ldots,$$

where, it must be emphasized, the symbol Δ^2 does not represent the square of a quantity but denotes the repetition of the operation Δ.

Similarly, third, fourth, ... nth differences, formed in exactly the same way, are denoted by

$$\Delta^3 u_a, \ \Delta^4 u_a \ \ldots \ \Delta^n u_a.$$

4. Before forming a *difference table* similar to that in paragraph 1, it is convenient to introduce alternative names for x and y in our equation $y = u_x$. Where our ultimate object is to obtain numerical values of x or y, the independent variable is often termed the *argument*, and the corresponding value of y the *entry*.

In a table of logarithms the number itself is the argument and the logarithm the entry. The converse holds in a table of antilogarithms, where the logarithm is the argument. Similarly in a table of $\sin \alpha$, α is the argument and the sine the entry, whereas α is the entry in a table of $\sin^{-1} \alpha$.

5. Our new difference table is therefore

Argument	Entry	First differences	Second differences	Third differences
a	u_a			
		Δu_a		
$a+h$	u_{a+h}		$\Delta^2 u_a$	
		Δu_{a+h}		$\Delta^3 u_a$
$a+2h$	u_{a+2h}		$\Delta^2 u_{a+h}$	
		Δu_{a+2h}		$\Delta^3 u_{a+h}$
$a+3h$	u_{a+3h}		$\Delta^2 u_{a+2h}$	
		Δu_{a+3h}		$\Delta^3 u_{a+2h}$
$a+4h$	u_{a+4h}		$\Delta^2 u_{a+3h}$	
		Δu_{a+4h}		
$a+5h$	u_{a+5h}			

The first term in the table (u_a) is called the *leading term*, and the differences which stand at the head of the respective columns, namely Δu_a, $\Delta^2 u_a$, $\Delta^3 u_a$ ..., are called the *leading differences*.

6. Although we have expressed the terms in the difference table by the use of Δ symbols, it is quite easy to obtain any difference in terms of the function alone.

For example, $\Delta^3 u_a$ is the difference between $\Delta^2 u_{a+h}$ and $\Delta^2 u_a$, or $\Delta^3 u_a = \Delta^2 u_{a+h} - \Delta^2 u_a$.

Again, $\Delta^2 u_a$ is the difference between Δu_{a+h} and Δu_a, or

$$\Delta^2 u_a = \Delta u_{a+h} - \Delta u_a,$$

and as $\Delta u_a = u_{a+h} - u_a,$

we have $\Delta^3 u_a = \Delta^2 u_{a+h} - \Delta^2 u_a$

$$= (\Delta u_{a+2h} - \Delta u_{a+h}) - (\Delta u_{a+h} - \Delta u_a)$$

$$= \Delta u_{a+2h} - 2\Delta u_{a+h} + \Delta u_a$$

$$= (u_{a+3h} - u_{a+2h}) - 2(u_{a+2h} - u_{a+h}) + (u_{a+h} - u_a)$$

$$= u_{a+3h} - 3u_{a+2h} + 3u_{a+h} - u_a.$$

7. It is a simple matter to construct a difference table from a given set of data.

Consider the following examples:

Example 1.

Construct a difference table from the following values, where y is a function of x:

x	y	Δy	$\Delta^2 y$	$\Delta^3 y$
1	1			
		7		
2	8		12	
		19		6
3	27		18	
		37		6
4	64		24	
		61		6
5	125		30	
		91		6
6	216		36	
		127		
7	343			

Example 2.

Show that, in the following table of annuity-values, third differences are practically constant:

Argument x	Entry a_x	Δa_x	$\Delta^2 a_x$	$\Delta^3 a_x$
35	14·298			
		−·154		
36	14·144		−·004	
		−·158		+·001
37	13·986		−·003	
		−·161		·000
38	13·825		−·003	
		−·164		+·001
39	13·661		−·002	
		−·166		+·001
40	13·495		−·001	
		−·167		
41	13·328			

It will be observed that in Ex. 1 third differences are invariably the same. In the second example, however, third differences are not quite constant, although the error in assuming them to be so is very small.

The difference in the two examples lies in the fact that, while the first function is $y = x^3$, the table of annuity-values from which the data in the second example have been taken does not conform to a simple mathematical law and, further, the values do not naturally terminate with the third decimal place, but are rounded off at that place.

Example 3.

Assuming third differences constant, find the values of u_2 and u_3 from the data:

x	4	5	6	7	8
u_x	·35	·88	1·71	2·90	4·51

Construct the difference table from the given values, and fill in the vacant spaces in the $\Delta^3 u_x$ column with the constant third difference, thus:

x	u_x	Δu_x	$\Delta^2 u_x$	$\Delta^3 u_x$
2	− ·05			
		·11		
3	+ ·06		·18	
		·29		·06
4	+ ·35		·24	
		·53		·06
5	+ ·88		·30	
		·83		·06
6	+ 1·71		·36	
		1·19		·06
7	+ 2·90		·42	
		1·61		
8	+ 4·51			

8. Now it has been stated above that a convenient method for expressing the difference between two successive values of a function u_{a+h} and u_a is by the symbol Δ prefixed to u_a, so that $\Delta u_a = u_{a+h} - u_a$. It will be seen therefore that to find Δu_a we perform two operations: we change u_a to u_{a+h} and subtract u_a from it. The new function u_{a+h} resulting from the first of these operations is denoted symbolically by Eu_a, and the double operation may be written

$$\Delta u_a = Eu_a - u_a.$$

This gives

$$Eu_a = u_a + \Delta u_a.$$

Eu_a may therefore otherwise be expressed as the sum of u_a and its first difference.

Suppose that in either of the above relations the u_a which occurs in each of the terms be omitted. Then we can state that the two operations denoted by "E" and "Δ" are connected by the symbolic identity

$$E \equiv 1 + \Delta.$$

It must be distinctly understood that we have not "factorized out" u_a in the relation $Eu_a = u_a + \Delta u_a$, and that we must relate the symbols to the functions on which they operate. If, therefore, we were using the equivalence $\Delta \equiv E - 1$, and we operated on the function $\sin x$, it would be wrong to say that $\Delta \sin x = E \sin x - 1$. The correct statement is $\Delta \sin x = E \sin x - \sin x$. When we are dealing with symbols of operation we cannot treat any of them as quantities, and on forming the algebraic or trigonometrical identity the function must be included in all three terms. In other words, in the identity $E \equiv 1 + \Delta$ the 1 is a symbol of operation just as are E and Δ, and its meaning is that the function on which it operates is to be taken once without alteration.

9. In the same way as Δ^2 denotes, when operating on a function, the difference of the difference of the function, i.e. the second difference, so E^2 denotes the operation of repeating E. That is to say

$$E^2 u_x = E \cdot E u_x = E u_{x+h} = u_{x+2h},$$

$$E^3 u_x = u_{x+3h},$$

$$\cdots\cdots\cdots\cdots\cdots$$

and, generally, $\quad E^n u_x = u_{x+nh}.$

Care must be taken not to confuse the expression $E^2 u_x$ with $(Eu_x)^2$. For example,

$$E^2(x^2) = (x + 2h)^2 = x^2 + 4hx + 4h^2,$$

but $\qquad (Ex)^2 = (x + h)^2 = x^2 + 2hx + h^2.$

10. It is evident that the first difference of a function of the form cx, where c is a constant, is constant: for $\Delta cx = c(x + h) - cx = ch$, which is constant.

Let us consider the effect of differencing a function of x of higher degree than the first.

Example 4.

Difference successively the functions (i) $y = bx^2$ and (ii) $y = ax^3$.

(i) $\Delta bx^2 = b(x+h)^2 - bx^2 = 2bhx + bh^2$,

$\Delta^2 bx^2 = \Delta(2bhx + bh^2) = 2bh(x+h) + bh^2 - 2bhx - bh^2 = 2bh^2$,

and since $2bh^2$ is constant all higher differences will be zero.

(ii) $\Delta ax^3 = a(x+h)^3 - ax^3 = 3ahx^2 + 3ah^2x + ah^3$,

$\Delta^2 ax^3 = 6ah^2x + 6ah^3$,

and $\Delta^3 ax^3 = 6ah^3$, higher differences vanishing.

Collating the above results, we have that

the first differences of functions of the form cx are constant,

the second   ,,   ,,   ,, bx^2 ,,

the third   ,,   ,,   ,, ax^3 ,,

It follows therefore that third differences of $ax^3 + bx^2 + cx + d$ are constant, for before we reach the third differences the terms bx^2, cx and d will have been eliminated.

11. The above considerations lead us to the following important proposition:

If u_x be a polynomial of the nth degree in x, then the nth difference of the function is constant.

Let the function be

$$u_x = ax^n + bx^{n-1} + cx^{n-2} + \ldots + s;$$

then $\quad \Delta u_x = a(x+h)^n + b(x+h)^{n-1} + c(x+h)^{n-2} + \ldots + s$

$$\quad - ax^n - bx^{n-1} - cx^{n-2} - \ldots - s$$

$$= anx^{n-1}h + b'x^{n-2} + c'x^{n-3} + \ldots + r',$$

where b', c', ... r' are coefficients involving h but not x.

Similarly,

$$\Delta^2 u_x = an(n-1)x^{n-2}h^2 + b''x^{n-3} + c''x^{n-4} + \ldots + q'',$$

and so on.

Each time that we difference we lower the degree of the function by unity. After differencing n times no terms after the first will appear, and we shall be left with

$$\Delta^n u_x = an\,(n-1)\,(n-2)\,(n-3)\,\ldots\,2\,.\,1\,.\,h^n \text{ or } an!\,h^n,$$

which is independent of x and is therefore constant.

As a corollary we may note that $\Delta^{n+1} u_x = 0$, a property of a polynomial of the nth degree which is of value in the practical application of the work.

The converse proposition is of importance: if the $(n+1)$th difference of a function is the first to become zero, the function is a polynomial of not more than the nth degree.

12. It should be remembered that we are dealing here with a particular form of function. Should the function be other than a polynomial the nth difference will not vanish however great n may be. Thus, we have

Example 5.

Find the nth difference of e^x.

$$\Delta e^x = e^{x+h} - e^x = e^x\,(e^h - 1),$$

$$\Delta^2 e^x = (e^h - 1)\,(e^{x+h} - e^x) = e^x\,(e^h - 1)^2.$$

Similarly, $\quad \Delta^3 e^x = e^x\,(e^h - 1)^3,$

$$\ldots\ldots\ldots\ldots\ldots\ldots$$

Generally, $\Delta^n e^x = e^x\,(e^h - 1)^n$, which is still a function of x, and is therefore not constant.

13. Although it has been said that the symbols Δ and E are in no sense algebraic quantities, our definitions, namely that Δ^n denotes the operation of differencing the function n times, and that E^n denotes the operation of obtaining a new function when the argument is increased by n unit differences, enable us to apply to these symbols the ordinary algebraic laws. For example,

$$\Delta\,(u_x + u_y) = u_{x+h} + u_{y+h} - u_x - u_y \text{ or } u_{x+h} - u_x + u_{y+h} - u_y,$$

which is $\Delta u_x + \Delta u_y$. This relation is exactly similar to the ordinary algebraic identity $3\,(x+y) = 3x + 3y$.

The three simple algebraic laws are the laws of (i) distribution, (ii) commutation, (iii) indices.

(i) $\Delta (u_x + v_x + w_x + ...)$

$$= (u_{x+h} + v_{x+h} + w_{x+h} + ...) - (u_x + v_x + w_x + ...)$$
$$= (u_{x+h} - u_x) + (v_{x+h} - v_x) + (w_{x+h} - w_x)$$
$$= \Delta u_x + \Delta v_x + \Delta w_x + ...$$

Similarly,

$$E (u_x + v_x + w_x + ...) = Eu_x + Ev_x + Ew_x + ...$$

(ii) The symbols Δ and E are commutative in their operation as regards constants. For if c be a constant,

$$\Delta cu_x = cu_{x+h} - cu_x = c (u_{x+h} - u_x) = c\Delta u_x,$$

and $\qquad Ecu_x = cu_{x+h} \qquad = cEu_x.$

(iii) The application of indices to the symbols Δ and E may be shown thus:

If m be a positive integer, then Δ^m represents the operation of differencing u_x m times.

$$\Delta^m u_x = (\Delta\Delta\Delta\Delta \, ... \, m \text{ times}) \, u_x,$$
$$\Delta^n (\Delta^m u_x) = (\Delta\Delta\Delta\Delta \, ... \, n \text{ times}) (\Delta\Delta\Delta\Delta \, ... \, m \text{ times}) \, u_x$$
$$= (\Delta\Delta\Delta\Delta \, ... \, \overline{m+n} \text{ times}) \, u_x$$
$$= \Delta^{m+n} u_x.$$

Similarly, $\qquad E^m u_x = u_{x+mh},$

$$E^n (E^m u_x) = E^n u_{x+mh} = u_{x+mh+nh} = E^{m+n} u_x.$$

14. In connection with the law of indices we must be careful to define Δ^m, Δ^n, E^m, ... when m and n are not positive integers. So far, the symbols Δ^m and E^m are intelligible only when we can actually perform the operations defined above and obtain the values of the new functions. We have not yet defined these symbols when the indices are negative. Consider for example the symbol Δ^{-1}. Since we have assumed that the symbol Δ obeys the ordinary algebraic laws, Δ^{-1} must be such that $\Delta (\Delta^{-1}u_x)$ gives $\Delta^0 u_x$, i.e. u_x.

Let m be a positive integer. Then we define $\Delta^{-m}u_x$ as a function such that if it be operated on by Δ^m the result will be $\Delta^{m-m}u_x,$

i.e. u_x. In the same way we have a meaning for $E^{-m}u_x$, namely, that E^m operating on $E^{-m}u_x$ produces u_x. But if m be a positive integer, E^m operating on u_{x-mh} produces $u_{x-mh+mh}$, i.e. u_x. Therefore the same result is obtained by operating with E^m on $E^{-m}u_x$ as on u_{x-mh}. In other words just as $E^m u_x$ gives u_{x+mh} so $E^{-m}u_x$ gives u_{x-mh}.

The symbols E and Δ may be manipulated in a manner similar to algebraic quantities provided that it is always remembered that they are operators and that they have no actual values. There are, however, two important points in which algebraic precedent cannot be safely followed. These are:

(1) Operators are not commutative with regard to variables. E.g., $\Delta(u_x v_x)$ does not as a rule equal $u_x \Delta v_x$.

(2) It is fundamental in algebra that if a function vanishes, then one of its factors must vanish. It is not true that if the result of a series of operations on u_x is equivalent to $0.u_x$ (i.e. zero), then some one of the operations on u_x must produce $0.u_x$. For example, if $x^2 = 0$, then $x = 0$; it does not necessarily follow, however, that if $\Delta^2 \equiv 0$, then $\Delta \equiv 0$.

In many problems it is convenient to use operators alone and to omit the functions on which they operate. Where this practice is followed the sign $\equiv$ (is equivalent to) should be adopted in place of $=$ (equals). Thus, $Eu_x = (1+\Delta)u_x$, but $E \equiv (1+\Delta)$.

For further information on the difficulties connected with the use of operators the student may refer to *J.S.S.* vol. II, pp. 237 *et seq.* (S. H. Alison).

15. Proceeding from the definition of differencing, it has been shown that

$$u_{x+h} = u_x + \Delta u_x,$$
$$u_{x+2h} = u_{x+h} + \Delta u_{x+h}$$
$$= u_x + \Delta u_x + \Delta(u_x + \Delta u_x)$$
$$= u_x + 2\Delta u_x + \Delta^2 u_x,$$
$$u_{x+3h} = u_{x+2h} + \Delta u_{x+2h}$$
$$= u_x + 2\Delta u_x + \Delta^2 u_x + \Delta(u_x + 2\Delta u_x + \Delta^2 u_x)$$
$$= u_x + 3\Delta u_x + 3\Delta^2 u_x + \Delta^3 u_x.$$

The coefficients of the various terms in these expansions are the coefficients of x in the expansions of $(1+x)$, $(1+x)^2$, $(1+x)^3$ by the binomial theorem. If we assume, for positive integral values of n, that the general relation between u_{x+nh} and u_x and its differences follows the same law, we can prove the truth of the assumption by the method of mathematical induction.

Assume therefore that

$$u_{x+nh} = u_x + n_{(1)}\Delta u_x + n_{(2)}\Delta^2 u_x + \ldots + n_{(r)}\Delta^r u_x + \ldots + \Delta^n u_x$$

is true for the value n.

Then, since $\quad u_{x+(n+1)h} = u_{x+nh} + \Delta u_{x+nh}$,

we have

$$u_{x+(n+1)h} = u_x + n_{(1)}\Delta u_x + n_{(2)}\Delta^2 u_x + \ldots + n_{(r)}\Delta^r u_x + \ldots + \Delta^n u_x$$
$$+ \Delta\,(u_x + n_{(1)}\Delta u_x + n_{(2)}\Delta^2 u_x + \ldots + n_{(r)}\Delta^r u_x + \ldots + \Delta^n u_x)$$
$$= u_x + \Delta u_x\,(n_{(1)}+1) + \Delta^2 u_x\,(n_{(2)}+n_{(1)}) + \ldots$$
$$+ \Delta^r u_x\,(n_{(r)}+n_{(r-1)}) + \ldots + \Delta^{n+1} u_x.$$

But $\qquad\qquad n_{(r)}+n_{(r-1)} = (n+1)_{(r)}$,

therefore

$$u_{x+(n+1)h} = u_x + (n+1)_{(1)}\Delta u_x + (n+1)_{(2)}\Delta^2 u_x + \ldots + (n+1)_{(r)}\Delta^r u_x$$
$$+ \ldots + \Delta^{n+1} u_x,$$

which is of the same form in $(n+1)$ as was the original expression in n.

Therefore if the assumption is true for n it is true for $n+1$.

But the theorem holds when $n=1, 2, 3$.

Therefore it is true when $n=4, 5, \ldots$ and for all positive integral values.

Therefore, for positive integral values of n,

$$u_{x+nh} = u_x + n_{(1)}\Delta u_x + n_{(2)}\Delta^2 u_x + n_{(3)}\Delta^3 u_x + \ldots + n_{(r)}\Delta^r u_x + \ldots + \Delta^n u_x.$$

16. When the relation between the operators Δ and E was discussed it was stated that our definition of these operations enables us to apply the ordinary algebraic laws to these symbols. We may therefore use the equivalent relation

$$E \equiv 1 + \Delta,$$

and if we operate on the function u_x we shall have

$$u_{x+nh} = E^n u_x = (1+\Delta)^n u_x$$
$$= (1 + n_{(1)}\Delta + n_{(2)}\Delta^2 + \ldots + n_{(r)}\Delta^r + \ldots + \Delta^n)\, u_x.$$

If we introduce the fact that the symbols follow the algebraic distributive law, we may write

$$u_{x+nh} = u_x + n_{(1)}\Delta u_x + n_{(2)}\Delta^2 u_x + \ldots + n_{(r)}\Delta^r u_x + \ldots + \Delta^n u_x,$$

which is the relation proved above for positive integral values of n.

This result is true whatever the form of the function so long as n is a positive integer. If n be other than a positive integer we cannot adopt the binomial expansion without further investigation. For the purposes of this chapter it will be sufficient to assume that the relation $E^n \equiv (1+\Delta)^n \equiv 1 + n_{(1)}\Delta + n_{(2)}\Delta^2 + n_{(3)}\Delta^3 + \ldots$ holds without restriction. The conditions of the validity of the expansion will be discussed at a later stage (see Chap. II)

17. We are now in a position to state that if $n+1$ consecutive values of a polynomial of the nth degree are given, then, by the method of finite differences, we can obtain the actual function in the form

$$u_x = u_0 + x_{(1)}\Delta u_0 + x_{(2)}\Delta^2 u_0 + \ldots + x_{(n)}\Delta^n u_0,$$

or
$$u_x = A + Bx_{(1)} + Cx_{(2)} + \ldots + Kx_{(n)},$$

where the coefficients A, B, C, ... K are obtained by inspection of a table of differences.

Now if we are given $n+1$ corresponding values of x and u_x it does not immediately follow that u_x is a polynomial of the nth degree.

For example, suppose that we have the following data:

x	0	1	2	3	4	5
u_x	1	4	9	16	25	36

Since six values are given there are the following possibilities:

(i) they may be actually given as values of the function $(1+x)^2$;

(ii) they may be given as values of a polynomial of the *second degree* in x, and it may be required to find the function;

(iii) they may be given as values of a polynomial of the *nth degree, where n is less than* 6, and it may be required to find the function;

(iv) they may be given as values of a polynomial without any information as to degree;

(v) no information regarding the nature of the function may be available.

The answer to (ii) and (iii) is obviously $u_x = (1 + x)^2$.

The answer to (iv) is $u_x = (1 + x)^2 + \dfrac{1}{6!} x (x - 1) \dots (x - 5) F_x$ or $(1 + x)^2 + x_{(6)} F_x$, where F_x is a polynomial in x which does not become infinite at any of the points 0, 1, 2, 3, 4, 5. The function

$$\frac{1}{6!} x (x - 1) \dots (x - 5) F_x$$

will then obviously vanish for these values.

The answer to (v) is the same as to (iv) except that F_x need not be a polynomial.

It is of importance to realize that we can always find a value for F_x which will make the function $u_x = (1 + x)^2 + x_{(6)} F_x$ agree with any additional value whatever. For example, if $u_{4\cdot5} = 19\cdot75$ the function $u_x = (1 + x)^2 + x_{(6)} 2^9$ will agree with the given values and also with the additional value which has been inserted at the point $x = 4\cdot5$.

Conversely we can say that whatever be the complete form of the function of which the six given values are samples, the value at any other point is the value of the function $(1 + x)^2$ at that point with an error $x_{(6)} F_x$. Whether the value is a good approximation or not depends on the magnitude of F_x, and we may or may not have reason to suppose that F_x is so small that it can be neglected. It should be understood that we are not at liberty to say that $(1 + x)^2$ gives an approximate value at the point in question unless we can give such a reason, based either on theory or on experience.

The matter is further investigated in later paragraphs, but it may be said that in most practical cases F_x is of the same order of magnitude as $\Delta^{n+1} u_x$ for some value of x in the range under consideration. It may in fact be shown that $F_x = \dfrac{d^6 u_\xi}{d_\xi^6}$, where ξ is a quantity falling in the range which includes x and the given values of u. (See Chap. III, paragraph 17.)

18. If instead of writing $E^n \equiv (1+\Delta)^n$ and expanding this by the binomial theorem, we write $\Delta^n \equiv (E-1)^n$ and expand, a new series is obtained:

$$\begin{aligned}
\Delta^n u_x &= (E-1)^n\, u_x \\
&= [E^n - n_{(1)} E^{n-1} + n_{(2)} E^{n-2} - n_{(3)} E^{n-3} + \ldots + (-1)^r n_{(r)} E^{n-r} \\
&\qquad\qquad\qquad\qquad\qquad\qquad\qquad\qquad + \ldots + (-1)^n]\, u_x \\
&= u_{x+nh} - n_{(1)} u_{x+(n-1)h} + n_{(2)} u_{x+(n-2)h} - \ldots \\
&\qquad\qquad\qquad + (-1)^r n_{(r)} u_{x+(n-r)h} + \ldots + (-1)^n u_x.
\end{aligned}$$

Just as the relation established in paragraph 15 enables us to obtain the value of u_{x+nh} in terms of u_x and its leading differences, so the above relation gives any required difference of the function u_x in terms of successive values of the function.

19. A few simple illustrations of the use of these two formulae are given below.

Example 6.

Find u_6, given $u_0 = -3$, $u_1 = 6$, $u_2 = 8$, $u_3 = 12$; third differences being constant.

The leading differences are easily found to be $\Delta u_0 = 9$; $\Delta^2 u_0 = -7$; $\Delta^3 u_0 = 9$.

$$\begin{aligned}
u_6 &= (1+\Delta)^6\, u_0 = (1 + 6\Delta + 15\Delta^2 + 20\Delta^3)\, u_0 \\
&= u_0 + 6\Delta u_0 + 15\Delta^2 u_0 + 20\Delta^3 u_0 \\
&= -3 + 54 - 105 + 180 = 126.
\end{aligned}$$

Note. There is no need to continue the expansion beyond third differences, as further differences are zero.

Example 7.

Find u_2, given $u_4 = 0$, $u_5 = 3$, $u_6 = 9$; second differences being constant.

Here the initial term of the known series is u_4, so that in order to find u_2 we must use the relation

$$u_2 = u_{4-2} = E^{-2} u_4 = (1+\Delta)^{-2}\, u_4 = (1 - 2\Delta + 3\Delta^2)\, u_4,$$

as far as second differences.

$$u_2 = u_4 - 2\Delta u_4 + 3\Delta^2 u_4$$
$$= 0 - 6 + 9 = 3,$$

since $\qquad \Delta u_4 = 3 \quad \text{and} \quad \Delta^2 u_4 = 3.$

Example 8.

From the following values of u_x, calculate $\Delta^5 u_0$:

$$u_0 = 3, \quad u_1 = 12, \quad u_2 = 81, \quad u_3 = 200, \quad u_4 = 100, \quad u_5 = 8.$$

Since we require only one value of $\Delta^5 u_x$, we do not need to form a difference table, but may write at once

$$\Delta^5 u_0 = (E - 1)^5 u_0$$
$$= (E^5 - 5E^4 + 10E^3 - 10E^2 + 5E - 1) u_0$$
$$= E^5 u_0 - 5E^4 u_0 + 10E^3 u_0 - 10E^2 u_0 + 5E u_0 - u_0$$
$$= u_5 - 5u_4 + 10u_3 - 10u_2 + 5u_1 - u_0$$
$$= 755.$$

Note. Before we can find the fifth difference six terms of the series must be given.

20. Separation of symbols.

In obtaining the value of $E^n u_x$ in terms of u_x and its differences we have used the symbolic relation $E \equiv 1 + \Delta$ and have expanded $(1 + \Delta)^n$ by the binomial theorem without introducing the function u_x until the last stage. This method, in which in fact u_x is omitted from both sides of the identity, is known as the method of *separation of symbols*, and enables many relations involving u_x and differences of u_x to be readily established. It must however be remembered that the operators cannot really stand alone and that the operand u_x is always understood.

Example 9.

Show that

$$u_0 + u_1 + u_2 + \dots + u_n$$
$$= (n+1)_{(1)} u_0 + (n+1)_{(2)} \Delta u_0 + (n+1)_{(3)} \Delta^2 u_0 + \dots + \Delta^n u_0.$$

$$u_0 + u_1 + u_2 + \ldots + u_n$$

$$= u_0 + Eu_0 + E^2u_0 + \ldots + E^nu_0$$

$$= (1 + E + E^2 + \ldots + E^n)\, u_0$$

$$= \frac{E^{n+1} - 1}{E - 1}\, u_0, \text{ or substituting } 1 + \Delta \text{ for } E,$$

$$= \frac{(1 + \Delta)^{n+1} - 1}{\Delta}\, u_0$$

$$= \frac{1}{\Delta}\left[1 + (n+1)_{(1)}\Delta + (n+1)_{(2)}\Delta^2 + (n+1)_{(3)}\Delta^3 + \ldots + \Delta^{n+1} - 1\right]u_0$$

$$= \left[(n+1)_{(1)} + (n+1)_{(2)}\Delta + (n+1)_{(3)}\Delta^2 + \ldots + \Delta^n\right]u_0$$

$$= (n+1)_{(1)}u_0 + (n+1)_{(2)}\Delta u_0 + (n+1)_{(3)}\Delta^2 u_0 + \ldots + \Delta^n u_0.$$

Example 10.

Prove by the method of separation of symbols that

$$u_x = u_{x-1} + \Delta u_{x-2} + \Delta^2 u_{x-3} + \Delta^3 u_{x-4} + \ldots + \Delta^{n-1}u_{x-n} + \Delta^n u_{x-n}.$$

$$u_x - \Delta^n u_{x-n} = u_x - \Delta^n E^{-n}u_x = \left\{1 - \left(\frac{\Delta}{E}\right)^n\right\}u_x = \frac{E^n - \Delta^n}{E^n}\, u_x$$

$$= \frac{1}{E^n}\left\{\frac{E^n - \Delta^n}{E - \Delta}\right\}u_x, \quad \text{since } E - \Delta \equiv 1,$$

$$= E^{-n}\left(E^{n-1} + \Delta E^{n-2} + \Delta^2 E^{n-3} + \ldots + \Delta^{n-1}\right)u_x$$

$$= \left(E^{-1} + \Delta E^{-2} + \Delta^2 E^{-3} + \ldots + \Delta^{n-1}E^{-n}\right)u_x$$

$$= u_{x-1} + \Delta u_{x-2} + \Delta^2 u_{x-3} + \ldots + \Delta^{n-1}u_{x-n}.$$

$$\therefore \quad u_x = u_{x-1} + \Delta u_{x-2} + \Delta^2 u_{x-3} + \ldots + \Delta^{n-1}u_{x-n} + \Delta^n u_{x-n}.$$

Since this is true for all values of n we have the convenient formulae

$$u_x = u_{x-1} + \Delta u_{x-1} \text{ (which is otherwise evident)},$$

$$u_x = u_{x-1} + \Delta u_{x-2} + \Delta^2 u_{x-2},$$

$$u_x = u_{x-1} + \Delta u_{x-2} + \Delta^2 u_{x-3} + \Delta^3 u_{x-3},$$

and so on.

Example 11.

Obtain a formula based on u_n similar to that given by the relation

$$E^x u_0 = (1 + \Delta)^x\, u_0.$$

$$E^x u_0 = u_x = E^{x-n} u_n = \left(\frac{\mathrm{I}}{E}\right)^{n-x} u_n = \left(\frac{E-\Delta}{E}\right)^{n-x} u_n, \quad \text{since } E - \Delta \equiv \mathrm{I},$$

$$= \left(\mathrm{I} - \frac{\Delta}{E}\right)^{n-x} u_n$$

$$= (\mathrm{I} - \Delta E^{-1})^{n-x} u_n$$

$$= [\mathrm{I} - (n-x)_{(1)} \Delta E^{-1} + (n-x)_{(2)} \Delta^2 E^{-2} - \ldots] u_n;$$

$$\therefore \quad u_x = u_n - (n-x)_{(1)} \Delta u_{n-1} + (n-x)_{(2)} \Delta^2 u_{n-2} - \ldots.$$

It will be found that this is an ordinary formula which could be obtained by using the values in the reverse order u_n, u_{n-1}, u_{n-2}, ... u_0. There is as much justification for using one order as the other. It should be noticed that the same numerical values appear in the table of differences, but that they are in the reverse order with a change of sign for the odd differences. This should be tested by a numerical example.

If $x > n$, we may use the general relation

$$(n-x)_{(t)} = (-\mathrm{I})^t (x-n+t-\mathrm{I})_{(t)}$$

and write the formula as

$$u_x = u_n + (x-n)_{(1)} \Delta u_{n-1} + (x-n+\mathrm{I})_{(2)} \Delta^2 u_{n-2} + \ldots,$$

where the coefficients are positive and are those in the expansion of $(\mathrm{I} - \Delta E^{-1})^{-(x-n)} u_x$.

Example 12.

Find the value of

$$\Delta x^m - \tfrac{1}{2} \Delta^2 x^m + \frac{\mathrm{I} \cdot 3}{2 \cdot 4} \Delta^3 x^m - \frac{\mathrm{I} \cdot 3 \cdot 5}{2 \cdot 4 \cdot 6} \Delta^4 x^m + \ldots \text{ to } m \text{ terms.}$$

Since $\Delta^{m+1} x^m$ and higher differences of x^m are zero, the sum of the series to m terms is the same as the sum to infinity.

Omitting the function x^m, and working on symbols alone, we have

$$\Delta - \tfrac{1}{2}\Delta^2 + \frac{\mathrm{I} \cdot 3}{2 \cdot 4}\Delta^3 - \frac{\mathrm{I} \cdot 3 \cdot 5}{2 \cdot 4 \cdot 6}\Delta^4 + \ldots \equiv \Delta\left(\mathrm{I} - \tfrac{1}{2}\Delta + \frac{\mathrm{I} \cdot 3}{2 \cdot 4}\Delta^2 - \frac{\mathrm{I} \cdot 3 \cdot 5}{2 \cdot 4 \cdot 6}\Delta^3 + \ldots\right)$$

$$\equiv \Delta\left(\mathrm{I} - \tfrac{1}{2}\Delta + \frac{\frac{1}{2} \cdot \frac{3}{2}}{2!}\Delta^2 - \frac{\frac{1}{2} \cdot \frac{3}{2} \cdot \frac{5}{2}}{3!}\Delta^3 + \ldots\right)$$

$$\equiv \Delta (\mathrm{I} + \Delta)^{-\frac{1}{2}} \equiv \Delta E^{-\frac{1}{2}}.$$

The value of the given series is therefore

$$\Delta E^{-\frac{1}{2}} x^m = \Delta (x - \tfrac{1}{2})^m = (x + \tfrac{1}{2})^m - (x - \tfrac{1}{2})^m,$$

if the interval of differencing be taken as unity.

Further examples of the application of the method of separation of symbols to the operators Δ and E and to other operators will be found in Chapters VI and VII.

21. Factorial notation.

For many purposes it is useful to use a notation for the product of m factors of which the first is x and the successive factors decrease by a constant difference.

Generally,

$$x^{(m)} \equiv x\,(x-h)\,(x-2h)\,(x-3h) \ldots (x-\overline{m-1}h).$$

For convenience in working we shall take $h = 1$. Then, if

$$x^{(m)} = x\,(x-1)\,(x-2)\,(x-3) \ldots (x-\overline{m-1}),$$
$$\Delta x^{(m)} = (x+1)\,x\,(x-1) \ldots (x-\overline{m-2}) - x\,(x-1)\,(x-2) \ldots (x-\overline{m-1})$$
$$= mx\,(x-1) \ldots (x-\overline{m-2})$$
$$= mx^{(m-1)}.$$

Similarly $\qquad\qquad \Delta^2 x^{(m)} = m\,(m-1)\,x^{(m-2)},$

and, eventually, $\qquad\qquad \Delta^m x^{(m)} = m\,!.$

Again, from the definition of $x^{(m)}$,

$$x^{(m)} = (x-m+1)\,x^{(m-1)}.$$
$$\therefore \text{ when } m = 0, \quad x^{(0)} = (x+1)\,x^{(-1)}.$$

By convention, $\qquad\qquad x^{(0)} = 1.$

$$\therefore \quad 1 = (x+1)\,x^{(-1)}$$

or $\qquad\qquad\qquad x^{(-1)} = \dfrac{1}{x+1}.$

When $m = -1$

$$x^{(-1)} = (x+2)\,x^{(-2)},$$

so that $\qquad\qquad x^{(-2)} = \dfrac{x^{(-1)}}{x+2} = \dfrac{1}{(x+1)\,(x+2)}.$

Generally $\quad x^{(-m)} = \dfrac{1}{(x+1)\,(x+2) \ldots (x+m)} = \dfrac{1}{(x+m)^{(m)}}.$

This notation, adopted by Aitken and Milne-Thomson, differs from that used in Boole's *Finite Differences*, Steffensen's *Interpolation* and Freeman's *Actuarial Mathematics*. It has the advantage that, for any value of x, the relation $\quad x^{(r)} (x-r)^{(m)} = x^{(m+r)}$

is valid for all integral values of r and m, whether negative, zero or positive, provided that division by zero is not involved.

By proceeding as above it can be shown that

$$\Delta x^{(-m)} = -mx^{(-\overline{m+1})}; \quad \Delta^2 x^{(-m)} = m\,(m+1)\,x^{(-\overline{m+2})},$$

and so on.

It should be noted that the result of differencing $x^{(-m)}$ is to increase the degree of the denominator, and that, as a result, $\Delta^m x^{(-m)}$ is not constant.

A special case of $x^{(m)}$ is where x is a positive integer. We have then that

$$x^{(m)} = x\,(x-1)\,(x-2)\,\ldots\,(x-m+1) = x!/(x-m)! \quad \text{or} \quad {}^x P_m.$$

It is also of interest to note that the result of differencing $x^{(m)}$ is analogous to that of differentiating x^m. We have

$$\Delta x^{(m)} = mx^{(m-1)} \quad \text{and} \quad Dx^m = mx^{m-1},$$

$$\Delta^m x^{(m)} = m! \quad \text{and} \quad D^m x^m = m!.$$

Similarly we have

$$\Delta^r x_{(m)} = x_{(m-r)} \quad \text{and} \quad \Delta^m x_{(m)} = 1.$$

These relations are very important.

Note. In the demonstrations above Δx has been taken as unity. If $\Delta x = h$, then $\Delta x^{(m)} = mh\,x^{(m-1)}$, $\Delta^2 x^{(m)} = m\,(m-1)\,h^2 x^{(m-1)}$, and so on. The general principles are the same.

Example 13.

Express $2x^3 - 3x^2 + 3x - 10$ and its differences in factorial notation.

Let

$$u_x = 2x^3 - 3x^2 + 3x - 10 = Ax\,(x-1)\,(x-2) + Bx\,(x-1) + Cx + D.$$

Putting $x = 0, 1, 2$ in succession, we obtain easily that

$$D = -10; \quad C = 2; \quad B = 3.$$

By equating coefficients of x^3 on both sides of the identity we find that $A = 2$.

$$\therefore \quad 2x^3 - 3x^2 + 3x - 10 = 2x^{(3)} + 3x^{(2)} + 2x^{(1)} - 10.$$

$$\Delta u_x = 6x^{(2)} + 6x^{(1)} + 2,$$

$$\Delta^2 u_x = 12x^{(1)} + 6,$$

and

$$\Delta^3 u_x = 12.$$

22. An alternative method for expressing $P_n(x)$ in the factorial notation is by use of *detached coefficients*. By this method any such function can be written down in the form

$$Ax^{(n)} + Bx^{(n-1)} + Cx^{(n-2)} + \ldots + K$$

with very little trouble.

The principle can best be illustrated by an example.

Example 14.

Write down $11x^4 + 5x^3 + 2x^2 + x - 15$ in factorial notation.
Let

$$u_x = 11x^4 + 5x^3 + 2x^2 + x - 15 = Ax^{(4)} + Bx^{(3)} + Cx^{(2)} + Dx^{(1)} + E$$
$$= Ax(x-1)(x-2)(x-3) + Bx(x-1)(x-2)$$
$$+ Cx(x-1) + Dx + E.$$

If we divide u_x by x, the quotient will be

$$11x^3 + 5x^2 + 2x + 1$$

and the remainder $\qquad -15 \qquad\qquad = E.$

Divide $11x^3 + 5x^2 + 2x + 1$ by $x-1$:

$$
\begin{array}{r|l|l}
x-1 & 11x^3 + 5x^2 + 2x + 1 & 11x^2 + 16x + 18 \\
& \underline{11x^3 - 11x^2} & \\
& 16x^2 + 2x & \\
& \underline{16x^2 - 16x} & \\
& 18x + 1 & \\
& \underline{18x - 18} & \\
& 19 & = D.
\end{array}
$$

Divide $11x^2 + 16x + 18$ by $x-2$:

$$
\begin{array}{r|l|l}
x-2 & 11x^2 + 16x + 18 & 11x + 38 \\
& \underline{11x^2 - 22x} & \\
& 38x + 18 & \\
& \underline{38x - 76} & \\
& 94 & = C,
\end{array}
$$

and so on.

The above processes may be appreciably shortened by adopting the following procedure:

(i) omit the x^4, x^3, x^2, ... and work on coefficients alone;

(ii) change the sign of the constant term in $x-1$, $x-2$, $x-3$, ..., so that addition takes the place of subtraction.

The required remainders can then be easily obtained. Thus:

1	11	5	2	1	-15
	0	11	16	18	
2	11	16	18	19	
	0	22	76		
3	11	38	94		
	0	33			
4	11	71			
	0				
	11				

$$\therefore u_x = 11x^4 + 5x^3 + 2x^2 + x - 15 = 11x^{(4)} + 71x^{(3)} + 94x^{(2)} + 19x^{(1)} - 15.$$

This short method is the method of detached coefficients and is of particular advantage in solving certain problems in summation of series (see Chap. VI).

23. It is often simpler, and in some cases more practically useful, to express $P_n(x)$ in terms of $x_{(r)}$, $x_{(r-1)}$ ... rather than in terms of $x^{(r)}$, $x^{(r-1)}$ .... This can easily be done by evaluating $u_0, u_1, u_2, ...,$ forming a difference table and then using the formula given in paragraph 15. Thus, using the polynomial in Example 14, we have

x	u_x	Δu_x	$\Delta^2 u_x$	$\Delta^3 u_x$	$\Delta^4 u_x$
0	-15				
		19			
1	4		188		
		207		426	
2	211		614		264
		821		690	
3	1032		1304		
		2125			
4	3157				

whence $u_x = 264x_{(4)} + 426x_{(3)} + 188x_{(2)} + 19x_{(1)} - 15$. The arithmetic can be made even simpler by using ... u_{-2}, u_{-1}, u_0, u_1, u_2 ... and inserting the constant difference for the purpose of obtaining the leading differences of u_0. In the case of the polynomial considered above, the constant difference will be $\Delta^4 u_x$, and it is instructive for the student to rework the example on these lines.

EXAMPLES 1

By constructing difference tables, find:

1. The sixth term of the series 8, 12, 19, 29, 42, ...

2. The seventh and eighth terms of the series 0, 0, 2, 6, 12, 20, ...

3. The first term of the series whose second and subsequent terms are 8, 3, 0, −1, 0, ...

4. The entry corresponding to the argument 3 from the table:

x (argument)	5	6	7	8	9	10
y (entry)	10·1	18·1	29·5	44·9	64·9	90·1

5. The tenth term of the series 3, 14, 39, 84, 155, 258, ...

6. Given that $y = x^3 - x^2 + x + 10$, verify by constructing a difference table that the value of y when $x = 10$ is 920. Use the following values of x: 1, 2, 3, 4, 5, 6 and the corresponding values of y.

7. Prove that $u_4 = u_3 + \Delta u_2 + \Delta^2 u_1 + \Delta^3 u_1$.

8. Find $\Delta^3 u_x$, where $u_x = ax^3 + bx^2 + cx + d$ and the interval of differencing is h.

9. u_x is a polynomial in x, the following values of which are known: $u_2 = u_3 = 27$; $u_4 = 78$; $u_5 = 169$. Find the function u_x.

10. Obtain $\Delta^{10} [(1 - ax)(1 - bx^2)(1 - cx^3)(1 - dx^4)]$.

11. Find Δab^{cx} and $\Delta^2 ab^{cx}$. Hence sum the first ten differences of ab^{cx}.

12. What are the functions whose first differences are (1) x; (2) c^x; (3) $9x^2 + 3$?

13. $u_x = (5x + 12)/(x^2 + 5x + 6)$. Find Δu_x and $\Delta^2 u_x$.

14. $u_x = -(x - 1)^{-1}(x - 2)^{-1}$. Find Δu_x.

15. $u_1 = (12 - x)(4 + x)$; $u_2 = (5 - x)(4 - x)$; $u_3 = (x + 18)(x + 6)$; $u_4 = 94$. Obtain a value of x, assuming second differences constant.

16. Find $\Delta^n u_x$, where u_x is (1) $ax^n + bx^{n-1}$, (2) e^{ax+b}.

17. Show that $u_4 = u_0 + 4\Delta u_0 + 6\Delta^2 u_{-1} + 10\Delta^3 u_{-1}$ as far as third differences.

18. The first four terms of a series are 0, 5, 16, 30. Find the sixth term, using the relation in Qu. 17.

19. Find the value of $\Delta^2 \left[\dfrac{a^{2x} + a^{4x}}{(a^2 - 1)^2} \right]$.

20. Obtain the function whose first difference is
$$x^3 + 3x^2 + 5x + 12.$$

By means of the relation $u_x = (1 + \Delta)^x u_0$, find

21. u_{12} given $u_0 = 3$; $u_1 = 14$; $u_2 = 40$; $u_3 = 86$; $u_4 = 157$; $u_5 = 258$.

22. u_6 given $u_0 = 25$; $u_1 = 25$; $u_2 = 22$; $u_3 = 18$; $u_4 = 15$; $u_5 = 15$.

23. u_9 given $u_0 = 1$; $u_1 = 11$; $u_2 = 21$; $u_3 = 28$; $u_4 = 29$.

24. The tenth term of the series 1, 37, 61, 77, ...

25. The eleventh term of the series 1, 4, 13, 36, 81, 156, 269, ...

26. Prove that the rth difference of a polynomial of the nth degree is a polynomial of the $(n-r)$th degree if $r < n$. What happens when (1) $r = n$, (2) $r > n$?

27. Define the functions $x^{(m)}$ and $x^{(-m)}$. Obtain their nth differences, distinguishing between the cases when $n \lessgtr m$.

28. Represent the function $x^4 - 12x^3 + 42x^2 - 30x + 9$ and its successive differences in factorial notation.

29. Find $\Delta^n u_x$ where u_x is

(i) $(ax+b)(a.\overline{x+1}+b)(a.\overline{x+2}+b) \dots (a.\overline{x+m}+b)$ given $m > n$.

(ii) $[(ax+b)(a.\overline{x+1}+b)(a.\overline{x+2}+b) \dots (a.\overline{x+m}+b)]^{-1}$.

30. Obtain $\Delta \sin x$, $\Delta \tan x$ and $\Delta (x + \cos x)$ where the interval of differencing is α.

31. Explain the difference between $\left(\dfrac{\Delta^2}{E}\right) u_x$ and $\dfrac{\Delta^2 u_x}{E u_x}$ and find the values of these functions when $u_x = x^3$.

32. $u_x = \sin x$. Show that $\Delta^2 u_x = kE u_x$ where k is constant.

33. Prove that $\Delta (\tan^{-1} x) = \tan^{-1} \left\{ \dfrac{h}{1 + xh + x^2} \right\}$, where h is the interval of differencing.

Use the method of separation of symbols to prove the following identities:

34. $u_1 x + u_2 x^2 + u_3 x^3 + \dots$
$$= \frac{x}{1-x} u_1 + \frac{x^2}{(1-x)^2} \Delta u_1 + \frac{x^3}{(1-x)^3} \Delta^2 u_1 + \dots.$$

35. $\Delta^n u_{x-n} = u_x - n_{(1)} u_{x-1} + n_{(2)} u_{x-2} - n_{(3)} u_{x-3} + \dots.$

36. $u_{x+n} = u_n + x_{(1)} \Delta u_{n-1} + (x+1)_{(2)} \Delta^2 u_{n-2} + (x+2)_{(3)} \Delta^3 u_{n-3} + \dots.$

37. $u_0 + x_{(1)}\Delta u_1 + x_{(2)}\Delta^2 u_2 + x_{(3)}\Delta^3 u_3 + \ldots$
$$= u_x + x_{(1)}\Delta^2 u_{x-1} + x_{(2)}\Delta^4 u_{x-2} + \ldots.$$

38. $u_0 + \dfrac{u_1 x}{1!} + \dfrac{u_2 x^2}{2!} + \dfrac{u_3 x^3}{3!} + \ldots$
$$= e^x \left[u_0 + x\Delta u_0 + \frac{x^2}{2!}\Delta^2 u_0 + \frac{x^3}{3!}\Delta^3 u_0 + \ldots \right].$$

39. $u_x - u_{x+1} + u_{x+2} - u_{x+3} + \ldots = \dfrac{1}{2}\left[u_{x-\frac{1}{2}} - \dfrac{1}{8}\Delta^2 u_{x-\frac{3}{2}} \right.$
$$\left. + \frac{1 \cdot 3}{2!}\left(\frac{1}{8}\right)^2 \Delta^4 u_{x-\frac{5}{2}} - \frac{1 \cdot 3 \cdot 5}{3!}\left(\frac{1}{8}\right)^3 \Delta^6 u_{x-\frac{7}{2}} + \ldots \right].$$

40. $u_{2n} - n_{(1)} \cdot 2u_{2n-1} + n_{(2)} \cdot 2^2 u_{2n-2} - \ldots + (-2)^n u_n = (-1)^n (c - 2an)$,
where $u_x = ax^2 + bx + c$.

41. $u_x - \dfrac{1}{8}\Delta^2 u_{x-1} + \dfrac{1 \cdot 3}{8.16}\Delta^4 u_{x-2} - \dfrac{1 \cdot 3 \cdot 5}{8.16.24}\Delta^6 u_{x-3} + \ldots$
$$= u_{x+\frac{1}{2}} - \tfrac{1}{2}\Delta u_{x+\frac{1}{2}} + \tfrac{1}{4}\Delta^2 u_{x+\frac{1}{2}} - \tfrac{1}{8}\Delta^3 u_{x+\frac{1}{2}} + \ldots.$$

42. Find the relation between α, β, γ in order that $\alpha + \beta x + \gamma x^2$ may be expressible in one term in factorial notation.

43. Sum to n terms
$$1 . 2\Delta x^n - 2 . 3\Delta^2 x^n + 3 . 4\Delta^3 x^n - 4 . 5\Delta^4 x^n + \ldots.$$

44. If u_x be a polynomial in x of the third degree and $\Delta x = 1$, prove that
$$u_x = u_0 + x\Delta u_0 + \frac{x^{(2)}}{2!}\Delta^2 u_0 + \frac{x^{(3)}}{3!}\Delta^3 u_0.$$

45. Prove that
$$u_0 + n_{(1)} u_1 x + n_{(2)} u_2 x^2 + n_{(3)} u_3 x^3 + \ldots$$
$$= (1+x)^n u_0 + n_{(1)} (1+x)^{n-1} x\Delta u_0 + n_{(2)} (1+x)^{n-2} x^2 \Delta^2 u_0 + \ldots.$$

46. If n be a positive integer, prove that u_n is the difference between the two series:
$$n_{(1)} u_1 + (n+1)_{(3)}\Delta^2 u_0 + (n+2)_{(5)}\Delta^4 u_{-1} + \ldots$$
and $\qquad (n-1)_{(1)} u_0 + n_{(3)}\Delta^2 u_{-1} + (n+1)_{(5)}\Delta^4 u_{-2} + \ldots.$

CHAPTER II

INTERPOLATION WITH EQUAL INTERVALS

1. Interpolation may be defined as the operation of obtaining the value of a function for any intermediate value of the argument, being given the values of the functions for certain values of the argument. The process has been picturesquely described by Thiele as "the art of reading between the lines of a table". Where the form of the function $y = u_x$ is known or can be deduced from the given values, the ordinary algebraic process of substitution can be used and the required value obtained with little difficulty. In actuarial work the relation connecting the function and the independent variable is seldom simple or evident, and it is then that recourse must be had to finite difference methods.

2. Before proceeding to examine the practical aspect of interpolation the question of negative and fractional values of n in the expression $(1 + \Delta)^n u_x$ must be considered. The proof of the identity $u_{x+nh} = (1 + \Delta)^n u_x$ by means of operators or by induction, as in the previous chapter, ceases to have a meaning if n is negative or fractional, since the reasoning assumes that the argument x advances by steps of h at a time. The assumption that, so long as the ordinary algebraic rules are followed, the expansion is true for all values of the quantities involved and not only for certain specified values, is not necessarily true, and an analogy can be drawn between the application of the binomial theorem to algebraic quantities and to operators. For example, the expansion $(1 + x)^n$ is only convergent, i.e. is arithmetically intelligible, for negative values of n, provided that x is numerically less than unity.

Thus $(1 - x)^{-2} = 1 + 2x + 3x^2 + 4x^3 + \ldots + rx^{r-1} + \ldots$ leads to an absurd result if we put $x = 2$, for then we should have

$$(-1)^{-2} = 1 + 4 + 12 + 32 + \ldots$$

which is impossible, since

$$(-1)^{-2} = 1/(-1)^2 = 1.$$

Similarly, in some cases there is no possibility of expanding $(1+\Delta)^n u_x$ by the use of the binomial theorem.

Consider the two following series of corresponding values of x and u_x:

(i)

x	0	1	2	3	4	5
u_x	1	4	9	16	25	36

Then to find the value of, say, $u_{\frac{1}{2}}$ we shall have

$$u_{\frac{1}{2}} = E^{\frac{1}{2}} u_0 = (1+\Delta)^{\frac{1}{2}} u_0$$

$$= u_0 + \tfrac{1}{2}\Delta u_0 + \frac{\tfrac{1}{2}(\tfrac{1}{2}-1)}{2!}\Delta^2 u_0 + \ldots.$$

The leading differences are $\Delta u_0 = 3$ and $\Delta^2 u_0 = 2$, higher differences being zero.

$$\therefore\; u_{\frac{1}{2}} = 1 + \tfrac{1}{2}\cdot 3 + \frac{\tfrac{1}{2}(\tfrac{1}{2}-1)}{2!}\cdot 2$$

$$= 1 + \tfrac{3}{2} - \tfrac{1}{4} = \tfrac{9}{4},$$

which is otherwise evident, since u_x is $(1+x)^2$, and, for the value $x = \tfrac{1}{2}$, $u_x = (\tfrac{3}{2})^2 = \tfrac{9}{4}$.

(ii)

x	0	1	2	3	4	5
u_x	1	5	25	125	625	3125

This is evidently a geometrical progression and the function from which the values are derived is $y = u_x = 5^x$. If we attempted to express u_x as a polynomial in x so that

$$u_x = a + bx + cx^2 + dx^3 + \ldots,$$

and then applied the relation $E^n u_0 = (1+\Delta)^n u_0$, for the value $n = \tfrac{1}{2}$, we should obtain as above

$$u_{\frac{1}{2}} = E^{\frac{1}{2}} u_0 = (1+\Delta)^{\frac{1}{2}} u_0$$

$$= u_0 + \tfrac{1}{2}\Delta u_0 + \frac{\tfrac{1}{2}(\tfrac{1}{2}-1)}{2!}\Delta^2 u_0 + \ldots.$$

Here the leading differences are 1, 4, 16, 64, 256, ... and tend to become successively larger. But $u_{\frac{1}{2}} = 5^{\frac{1}{2}} = 2\cdot 24$ approximately, and this cannot be the same as the divergent series found by expanding $(1+\Delta)^{\frac{1}{2}} u_0$.

Hence unless the function is capable of being expressed as a polynomial in x we cannot use the relation $E^n \equiv (1+\Delta)^n$ for the value $n=\frac{1}{2}$.

3. Let us now consider the problem more generally. If u_x be a polynomial of degree k in x, we may write

$$u_x = a + bx + cx^2 + \dots + px^k.$$

If we adopt the binomial expansion of $(1+\Delta)^n$ for expressing u_x in terms of u_0 and the leading differences of u_0, namely,

$$u_x = u_0 + x_{(1)} \Delta u_0 + x_{(2)} \Delta^2 u_0 + \dots + x_{(r)} \Delta^r u_0 + \dots$$

we have two series for u_x which are equivalent for more than k values of the variable, since they are true for all positive integral values of x.

Hence by a well-known algebraic theorem, they are true for all values of x, positive or negative, integral or fractional.

Therefore so long as u_x is a polynomial in x the binomial expansion is valid for all values of x. It is not necessarily valid for other forms of function, and we are led to the conclusion that we can expand u_{x+nh} in terms of Δu_x, $\Delta^2 u_x \dots \Delta^r u_x \dots$ for all forms of the function if n be a positive integer, but for other values of n only if u_{x+nh} is a polynomial. (Cf. Chap. I, paragraph 17.)

4. All finite difference formulae which are employed for the purpose of interpolation are based on the hypothesis that the functions in question can be represented by polynomials, i.e. by rational integral functions, with sufficient accuracy for the purpose in hand. This assumption is the justification for extending the formulae to fractional intervals: the processes to be explained in this and subsequent chapters are simply various methods of carrying out the calculations based on these assumptions. One special advantage of these methods is that it is unnecessary to fix in advance the degree (n) of the polynomial; the interpolation formulae will be in such a form that to increase n will merely involve the introduction of a fresh term without affecting the other terms. The introduction of additional terms however will not necessarily improve the approximation or justify the assumption, although it will generally do so. Fortunately, in actuarial work the functions with which we deal are usually such that the assumption is sufficiently accurate for our purpose.

5. In applying the formula in paragraph 3 to a given set of data the following points should be noted:

(a) If the basic curve is $y = a + bx + cx^2 + \ldots + kx^{n-1}$ there will be n constants, and in order to determine these constants n equations are necessary. For there to be n equations, values of y corresponding to n values of x must be given. Therefore either n points on the curve, or n other corresponding relations between x and y, must be known. In that event the curve will be of degree $n - 1$, and nth and higher differences are zero.

(b) Our investigation has been confined to equidistant values of the argument. If the given values are not equidistant a formula slightly different in form from the expansion $(1 + \Delta)^x u_0$ can be developed with a modified method of differencing (see Chap. III).

With regard to the statement (a) above that for a curve of degree $n - 1$ there must be n facts given, it is not essential that n points on the assumed curve must be known. We may have given, for example, three points and two values of the differential coefficient $\frac{du_x}{dx}$. Here we have five facts; we assume therefore a fourth degree curve, so that fifth and higher differences are zero.

6. Newton's formula.

The formula $u_{x+nh} = u_x + n_{(1)} \Delta u_x + n_{(2)} \Delta^2 u_x + \ldots$ is known as Newton's formula, and is the fundamental formula for interpolation when the given values are at equidistant intervals. The expansion can be applied to solve many forms of the problem of interpolation.

The following variations of the problem may arise:

(i) Where there are n equidistant terms and it is required to find an intermediate term.

(ii) Where there are n equidistant terms of which $n-1$ are known and it is required to find the missing term.

(iii) Where there are n equidistant terms of which $n-r$ are known and it is required to find the r missing terms.

Note. Some modern writers have adopted the name "Newton-Gregory formula" for the above expansion, as the first publication appears to have occurred in a letter from James Gregory to John Collins on 23 Nov. 1670. The letter is given and the question of Newton's priority is fully discussed by D. C. Fraser in *J.I.A.* vol. LII, pp. 117–35.

7. Examples of the variations referred to above are given below: they are all solved by assuming the last difference constant.

Example 1.

The values of annuities by a certain table are given for the following ages:

Age	x	25	26	27	28	29
Annuity-value	a_x	16·195	15·919	15·630	15·326	15·006

Determine the value of the annuity at age $27\frac{1}{2}$.

Five values are given: we must therefore assume that fourth differences are constant. The difference table is

x	a_x	Δa_x	$\Delta^2 a_x$	$\Delta^3 a_x$	$\Delta^4 a_x$
25	16·195				
		−·276			
26	15·919		−·013		
		−·289		−·002	
27	15·630		−·015		+·001
		−·304		−·001	
28	15·326		−·016		
		−·320			
29	15·006				

The leading differences correspond to the argument $x = 25$ and we require the entry for age $27\frac{1}{2}$. Our formula is therefore

$$a_{27\frac{1}{2}} = E^{2\frac{1}{2}} a_{25} = (1 + \Delta)^{2\frac{1}{2}} a_{25}$$

$$= \left[1 + 2 \cdot 5\Delta + \frac{2 \cdot 5 \times 1 \cdot 5}{2} \Delta^2 + \frac{2 \cdot 5 \times 1 \cdot 5 \times \cdot 5}{6} \Delta^3 \right.$$

$$\left. + \frac{2 \cdot 5 \times 1 \cdot 5 \times \cdot 5 \times (- \cdot 5)}{24} \Delta^4 \right] a_{25}$$

$$= a_{25} + 2 \cdot 5 \Delta a_{25} + 1 \cdot 875 \Delta^2 a_{25} + \cdot 3125 \Delta^3 a_{25} - \cdot 03906 \Delta^4 a_{25}$$

$$= 16 \cdot 195 - \cdot 6900 - \cdot 0244 - \cdot 0006 - \cdot 00004$$

$$= 15 \cdot 480.$$

Note. Since the data are given to three places of decimals, sufficient figures have been used to give three places only in the result. Since our interpolation is based on an assumption, namely, that fourth differences are constant, a result to more than this number of decimal places would be unjustifiable.

Example 2.

From the following data find the value of u_{47}:

$$u_{46} = 19{\cdot}2884; \quad u_{48} = 19{\cdot}5356; \quad u_{49} = 19{\cdot}6513; \quad u_{50} = 19{\cdot}7620.$$

We cannot form a difference table, since the given terms are not equidistant. As however four terms are available we may assume that third differences are constant, and that as a consequence fourth differences are zero.

If the function is $y = u_x$ we assume therefore that $\Delta^4 u_x = 0$ whatever the value of x. We may write

$$\Delta^4 u_{46} = 0,$$

i.e.
$$(E-1)^4 u_{46} = 0,$$

or
$$(E^4 - 4E^3 + 6E^2 - 4E + 1)\, u_{46} = 0,$$

i.e.
$$u_{50} - 4u_{49} + 6u_{48} - 4u_{47} + u_{46} = 0,$$

so that
$$19{\cdot}7620 - 78{\cdot}6052 + 117{\cdot}2136 - 4u_{47} + 19{\cdot}2884 = 0,$$

from which
$$u_{47} = 19{\cdot}4147.$$

Note. As mentioned above, all the given terms are not equidistant. The method however depends upon the fact that the term required makes up in all five equidistant terms.

Example 3.

Complete the following table:

x	2·0	2·1	2·2	2·3	2·4	2·5	2·6
u_x	·135		·111	·100		·082	·074

This is similar to Ex. 2. Instead of using the assumption once that $\Delta^5 u_x = 0$, we write down two equations of the same form, thus

$$\Delta^5 u_{2{\cdot}0} = 0, \quad \text{so that} \quad (E-1)^5 u_{2{\cdot}0} = 0,$$

and
$$\Delta^5 u_{2{\cdot}1} = 0, \quad \text{,,} \quad (E-1)^5 u_{2{\cdot}1} = 0.$$

Our two equations then become

$$u_{2{\cdot}5} - 5u_{2{\cdot}4} + 10u_{2{\cdot}3} - 10u_{2{\cdot}2} + 5u_{2{\cdot}1} - u_{2{\cdot}0} = 0,$$

and
$$u_{2{\cdot}6} - 5u_{2{\cdot}5} + 10u_{2{\cdot}4} - 10u_{2{\cdot}3} + 5u_{2{\cdot}2} - u_{2{\cdot}1} = 0,$$

since the interval of differencing is 0·1.

Inserting the known values of u_x and solving, the required values are easily found to be $u_{2\cdot1} = \cdot123$ and $u_{2\cdot4} = \cdot090$.

Note. The function in this question is $y = e^{-x}$ and the tabular value of $u_{2\cdot4}$ is $\cdot091$ correct to three decimal places. This difference is due to the fact that our assumption that the curve $y = u_x$ is a polynomial of the fourth degree in x is only approximately true.

8. Change of origin and scale.

If we had plotted the curve $y = u_x$ on which the values of u_x in, say, Example 2 were assumed to lie, we should have had values of y corresponding to values of x at 46, 48, 49, 50. Precisely the same curve would result, however, if we changed the origin of our co-ordinates so that 46 was represented by the value $x = 0$, 48 by $x = 2$, 49 by $x = 3$ and so on, the unit of x being unaltered. This process of changing the origin simplifies our notation considerably. In the examples above we could have changed the origin alone, or both the origin and scale, and could have altered the questions to read:

Ex. 1. Origin at age 25   Given u_0, u_1, u_2, u_3, u_4
       Unit of differencing 1 year of age   Required $u_{2\frac{1}{4}}$.

Ex. 2. Origin at $x = 46$ Given u_0, u_2, u_3, u_4
       Unit of differencing $x = 1$ Required u_1.

Ex. 3. Origin at $x = 2\cdot0$ Given u_0, u_2, u_3, u_5, u_6
       Unit of differencing $x = 1$ Required u_1 and u_4.

9. If in Newton's formula

$$u_{x+nh} = u_x + n_{(1)}\Delta u_x + n_{(2)}\Delta^2 u_x + n_{(3)}\Delta^3 u_x + \dots$$

we put $h = 1$, $x = 0$, and replace n by x, we obtain the series

$$u_x = u_0 + x_{(1)}\Delta u_0 + x_{(2)}\Delta^2 u_0 + x_{(3)}\Delta^3 u_0 + \dots.$$

This is generally called the *advancing difference* formula, and gives u_x in terms of u_0 and its leading differences, where the interval of tabulation is treated as the unit abscissa.

If, however, we wish to obtain u_x in terms of u_{-m} and its leading differences, we may write the formula

$$u_x = u_{-m+(m+x)} = E^{m+x}u_{-m} = (1 + \Delta)^{m+x}u_{-m}$$
$$= u_{-m} + (m+x)_{(1)}\Delta u_{-m} + (m+x)_{(2)}\Delta^2 u_{-m} + \dots$$
$$+ (m+x)_{(r)}\Delta^r u_{-m} + \dots.$$

It is often more convenient to use this formula than to obtain u_x in terms of u_0 and differences of u_0, the advantage being that thereby we can make use of values of the argument on either side of x.

In some cases, particularly when dealing with the summation of certain series, it is expedient to represent the first term by u_1 rather than by u_0. If in Newton's formula we put $h=1$, $x=1$ we have

$$u_x = u_1 + (x-1)_{(1)}\Delta u_1 + (x-1)_{(2)}\Delta^2 u_1 + \ldots$$

or $\qquad u_{1+x} = u_1 + x_{(1)}\Delta u_1 + x_{(2)}\Delta^2 u_1 + \ldots,$

and these formulae can be used for the summation of the series $u_1 + u_2 + u_3 + \ldots$. (See Chap. VI, paragraph 2.)

10. Subdivision of intervals.

A frequent problem in actuarial work is the interpolation for values of u_x at intervening points given every fifth or tenth value of the function. For example, the problem may be to complete the series u_0, u_1, u_2, u_3, ... from the known values u_0, u_5, u_{10}, u_{15}, ... or from u_0, u_{10}, u_{20}, u_{30}, ...

A simple method for obtaining the intervening values where quinquennial values are known is given below.

Let δu_x denote the difference for *unit* intervals of x and Δu_x denote the difference for *quinquennial* intervals.

Then u_{x+5} may be expressed as either $(1+\delta)^5 u_x$ or as $(1+\Delta) u_x$.

Symbolically $\qquad (1+\delta)^5 \equiv 1+\Delta,$

i.e. $\qquad (1+\delta) \equiv (1+\Delta)^{\frac{1}{5}},$

or $\qquad \delta \equiv (1+\Delta)^{\frac{1}{5}} - 1.$

From this relation we can find easily that

$$\delta u_x = (\cdot 2\Delta - \cdot 08\Delta^2 + \cdot 048\Delta^3 - \ldots) u_x.$$

Hence $\qquad \delta^2 u_x = (\cdot 2\Delta - \cdot 08\Delta^2 + \cdot 048\Delta^3 - \ldots)^2 u_x$

$$= (\cdot 04\Delta^2 - \cdot 032\Delta^3 + \ldots) u_x.$$

Similarly $\qquad \delta^3 u_x = (\cdot 008\Delta^3 - \ldots) u_x.$

The same principle can be adopted if decennial values are known. In that event Δu_x, $\Delta^2 u_x$, ... will represent differences for decennial intervals, and the individual differences will be found from the identity $\delta \equiv (1+\Delta)^{\frac{1}{10}} - 1$.

An example will show the application of the method.

Example 4.

From the following table of yearly premiums for policies maturing at quinquennial ages, estimate the premium for policies maturing at all ages from 45 to 50 inclusive:

Age x	45	50	55	60	65
Premium	2·871	2·404	2·083	1·862	1·712

The leading differences for quinquennial intervals are

Δu_x	$\Delta^2 u_x$	$\Delta^3 u_x$	$\Delta^4 u_x$
−·467	+·146	−·046	+·017

The formulae required are

$$\delta u_x = (\cdot 2\Delta - \cdot 08\Delta^2 + \cdot 048\Delta^3 - \cdot 0336\Delta^4)\, u_x = -\cdot 1078592,$$

$$\delta^2 u_x = (\cdot 04\Delta^2 - \cdot 032\Delta^3 + \cdot 0256\Delta^4)\, u_x = +\cdot 0077472,$$

$$\delta^3 u_x = (\cdot 008\Delta^3 - \cdot 0096\Delta^4)\, u_x = -\cdot 0005312,$$

$$\delta^4 u_x = \cdot 0016\Delta^4 u_x = +\cdot 0000272,$$

assuming fourth differences constant.

We have therefore by completing the table of differences,

Age	u_x	δu_x	$\delta^2 u_x$	$\delta^3 u_x$	$\delta^4 u_x$
45	2·871				
		−·10786			
46	2·763		+·007747		
		−·10011		−·0005312	
47	2·663		+·007216		+·0000272
		−·09290		−·0005040	
48	2·570		+·006712		+·0000272
		−·08618		−·0004768	
49	2·484		+·006235		
		−·07995			
50	2·404				

Note. Since we require the value of the premium to the nearest penny, three decimal places will be required in the u_x column. In this example, for results correct to three figures, four decimal places will be needed: δu_x must therefore be given to five decimal places, $\delta^2 u_x$ to six and $\delta^3 u_x$ to seven, since errors in higher differences accumulate rapidly.

EXAMPLES 2

Given the following data (a), find the missing term or terms (b):

1. (a) $u_0 = 580$, $u_1 = 556$, $u_2 = 520$, $u_4 = 385$; (b) u_3.

2. (a) $u_1 = 386$, $u_3 = 530$, $u_5 = 810$; (b) u_2; u_4.

3. (a) $u_0 = 150$, $u_1 = 192$, $u_2 = 241$, $u_4 = 374$; (b) u_3.

4. (a) $u_1 = 94$, $u_3 = 265$, $u_5 = 415$; (b) u_2; u_4.

5. (a) $u_0 = 6021$, $u_1 = 5229$, $u_2 = 4559$, $u_3 = 3979$; (b) $u_{\frac{1}{2}}$.

6. (a) $u_{50} = 92345$, $u_{51} = 91556$, $u_{52} = 90748$, $u_{55} = 88204$; (b) u_{53}; u_{54}.

7. (a) $u_{-1} = 202$, $u_0 = 175$, $u_1 = 82$, $u_2 = 55$; (b) $u_{\frac{1}{2}}$.

8. (a) $u_0 = 0$, $u_1 = 3$, $u_2 = 10$, $u_3 = 34$, $u_5 = 209$, $u_8 = 1002$; (b) u_4; u_6; u_7.

9. (a) $u_0 = 192 \cdot 1$, $u_1 = 187 \cdot 5$, $u_2 = 184 \cdot 7$, $u_3 = 184 \cdot 6$, $u_4 = 194 \cdot 6$, $u_5 = 199 \cdot 4$, $u_7 = 212 \cdot 7$, $u_9 = 224 \cdot 3$; (b) u_6; u_8.

10. (a) $u_0 = 98203$, $u_1 = 97843$, $u_2 = 97459$, $u_3 = 97034$; (b) $u_{2 \cdot 25}$.

11. The numbers of members of a certain Society are as given in the following table:

Year	Number	
1910	845	
1911	867	
1912		Make the best estimate
1913	846	you can of the
1914	821	numbers in 1912 and
1915	772	1916
1916		
1917	757	
1918	761	
1919	796	

12. Find p_{53} if $p_{50} = \cdot 98428$, $p_{51} = \cdot 98335$, $p_{54} = \cdot 98008$, $p_{55} = \cdot 97877$.

13. If u_0, u_1, u_2, ... u_6 be consecutive terms of a series, prove that, if fifth differences are constant,

$$u_3 = \cdot 05 u_0 - \cdot 3 u_1 + \cdot 75 u_2 + \cdot 75 u_4 - \cdot 3 u_5 + \cdot 05 u_6.$$

Supply the missing term:

$u_0 = 72795$	$u_4 = 67919$
$u_1 = 71651$	$u_5 = 66566$
$u_2 = 70458$	$u_6 = 65152.$

14. $u_{235} = 2\cdot37107$ $u_{237} = 2\cdot37474$

$u_{236} = 2\cdot37291$ $u_{238} = 2\cdot37658.$

Find $u_{235\cdot63}$.

15. Given $u_0 = -\cdot5$, $u_1 = -\cdot484$, $u_5 = 0$, $u_6 = \cdot256$, find the missing terms.

16. Given the following data: $u_0 = 0$, $u_{10} = 15$, $u_{20} = 50$; estimate u_{15}.
If you were given in addition $u_5 = 35$, how would your estimate be revised? Illustrate your answer by a diagram.

17. Find the value of an annuity at $5\frac{3}{8}$ per cent. given the following table:

Rate per cent.	Annuity-value
4	17·29203
4½	16·28889
5	15·37245
5½	14·53375
6	13·76483

18. Obtain approximations to the missing values:

x	50	51	52	53	54	55	56
$f(x)$	3·684			3·756	3·780	3·803	3·826

19. The area A of a circle diameter d is given for the following values:

d	80	85	90	95	100
A	5026	5674	6362	7088	7854

Find approximate values for the areas of circles of diameters 82 and 91 respectively.

20. Calculate the value of $\sin 33^\circ\ 13'\ 30''$ from the following table of sines:

angle x°	30	31	32	33	34
$\sin x^\circ$	·5000	·5150	·5299	·5446	·5592

21. $u_{75} = 2459$; $u_{80} = 2018$; $u_{85} = 1180$; $u_{90} = 402$. Calculate the values of u_{82} and u_{79}.

22. From the data in Qu. 21 complete the table for values of u_x corresponding to individual values of x from 75 to 85.

23. Four values of a function at decennial points are given. Express δu_x, $\delta^2 u_x$, $\delta^3 u_x$ (the differences for unit intervals) in terms of the differences of the function for decennial intervals.
Find the values u_1 to u_9 inclusive, given $u_0 = 0$, $u_{10} = \cdot174$, $u_{20} = \cdot347$, $u_{30} = \cdot518$.

24. $u_0 = 23 \cdot 1234$; $u_6 = 23 \cdot 7234$; $u_{12} = 24 \cdot 6834$; $u_{18} = 26 \cdot 1330$. Complete the series u_0 to u_6.

25. If you were asked at very short notice to obtain approximate values for the complete series $f(0)$, $f(1)$, $f(2)$, ... $f(20)$, being given that $f(0) = \cdot 013$, $f(10) = \cdot 248$, $f(15) = \cdot 578$, and $f(20) = \cdot 983$, what methods would you adopt, and what value would you obtain for $f(9)$?

26.
$$u_0 + u_8 = 1 \cdot 9243 \qquad u_2 + u_6 = 1 \cdot 9823$$
$$u_1 + u_7 = 1 \cdot 9590 \qquad u_3 + u_5 = 1 \cdot 9956.$$
Find u_4.

27. Tables are available giving premiums at age 40 at the following rates per cent.:

Rate per cent.	3	$3\frac{1}{2}$	4	$4\frac{1}{2}$	5	6
P_{40}	$\cdot025891$	$\cdot024654$	$\cdot023517$	$\cdot022470$	$\cdot021509$	$\cdot019811$

It is desired to obtain P_{40} at $5\frac{1}{2}$ per cent. Obtain this, using

(α) two of the above values; (β) four of the above values; (γ) six of the above values.

28. Given
$$\sum_{1}^{10} f(x) = 500426, \ \sum_{4}^{10} f(x) = 329240, \ \sum_{7}^{10} f(x) = 175212 \text{ and } f(10) = 40365,$$
find $f(1)$.

29. $u_1 = 1$; $u_2 + u_3 = 5 \cdot 41$; $u_4 + u_5 + u_6 = 18 \cdot 47$;
$$u_7 + u_8 + u_9 + u_{10} + u_{11} + u_{12} = 90 \cdot 36.$$
Find the value of u_x for all values of x from 1 to 12 inclusive.

30. If you were given u_0, u_1, u_2 and $\overset{x=10}{\underset{x=1}{\Sigma}} u_x$ how would you complete the table of u_x up to u_{10}?

31. Given $u_0 = 117 \cdot 7$; $u_2 = 110 \cdot 5$; $u_4 = 102 \cdot 7$; $u_{10} = 75 \cdot 4$, obtain the values of u_x for all integral values of x from 0 to 10.

32. Obtain the following relation between nine terms of the series represented by $u_1, u_2, \dots u_9$:
$$u_5 = \tfrac{4}{5}(u_4 + u_6) - \tfrac{2}{5}(u_3 + u_7) + \tfrac{4}{35}(u_2 + u_8) - \tfrac{1}{70}(u_1 + u_9),$$
and find u_5, given
$$u_1 = \cdot 74556; \quad u_2 = \cdot 55938; \quad u_3 = \cdot 42796; \quad u_4 = \cdot 32788; \quad u_6 = \cdot 18432;$$
$$u_7 = \cdot 13165; \quad u_8 = \cdot 08828; \quad u_9 = 0.$$

33. It is asserted that a quantity, which varies from day to day, is a rational and integral function of the day of the month, of less than the fifth degree, and that its values on the first seven days of the month are

30,   30,   28,   25,   22,   20,   20.

Examine whether these assertions are consistent. If so, assume them to be true, and find (1) the degree of the function, (2) its value on the sixteenth of the month.

34. Extrapolation may be defined as the process of obtaining further terms of a series as opposed to interpolation, which is the process of finding intermediate terms.

The values of a certain function, corresponding to the values 4, 6, 8, 10 of the argument are 914, 742, 605, 500 respectively. Extrapolate to calculate the value of the function corresponding to the value 11 of the argument.

35. Given $u_0 = 1876$, $u_1 = 777$, $u_3 = 19$, $u_6 = -218$, interpolate the values of u_2, u_4 and u_5, and find the form of the function, assuming it to be a rational integral function.

36. Show that Newton's formula

$$u_x = u_0 + x_{(1)}\Delta u_0 + x_{(2)}\Delta^2 u_0 + x_{(3)}\Delta^3 u_0 + x_{(4)}\Delta^4 u_0 + \ldots$$

can be put into the form

$$u_x = u_0 + x\Delta u_0 - xa\Delta^2 u_0 + xab\Delta^3 u_0 - xabc\Delta^4 u_0 + \ldots,$$

where $a = 1 - \frac{1}{2}(x+1)$, $b = 1 - \frac{1}{3}(x+1)$, $c = 1 - \frac{1}{4}(x+1)$ etc.

Hence show that the successive coefficients converge slowly and tend eventually to numerical equality.

CHAPTER III

INTERPOLATION WITH UNEQUAL INTERVALS

1. In the previous chapter formulae have been developed on the assumption that the argument proceeded by equal intervals. Although in actuarial problems the data are generally given at equidistant intervals of the independent variable, it sometimes happens that we are required to interpolate when values of the function are known for unequal intervals. In other words, instead of values of u_x for arguments $x+h$, $x+2h$, $x+3h$, ... being given, the known values correspond to the arguments a, b, c, ..., where $a-b$, $b-c$, ... are not necessarily equal.

2. Divided differences.

Since we cannot use the differences as hitherto defined, we adopt a special process involving the argument as well as the entry. The differences obtained by this process are called "divided" differences, and are found in the following manner.

Let $f(x) \equiv u_x$ be given for the values $x=a$, $x=b$, $x=c$, $x=d$ ..., where the intervals need not be equal.

Then we have

(i) First divided differences:

$$\frac{u_b - u_a}{b-a}; \quad \frac{u_c - u_b}{c-b}; \quad \frac{u_d - u_c}{d-c}; \quad \dots$$

which may be written as

$$f(b, a); \quad f(c, b); \quad f(d, c); \quad \dots.$$

(ii) Second divided differences:

$$\frac{f(c, b) - f(b, a)}{c-a}; \quad \frac{f(d, c) - f(c, b)}{d-b}; \quad \dots$$

or
$$f(c, b, a); \quad f(d, c, b); \quad \dots.$$

(iii) Third divided differences:

$$\frac{f(d, c, b) - f(c, b, a)}{d - a}; \ \ldots \ \text{ or } \ f(d, c, b, a); \ \ldots.$$

3. Notation for divided differences.

There seems to be at present no universally recognized notation for divided differences. There are objections to the many forms in practice. For example, $\Delta' u_a$, representing $(u_b - u_a)/(b - a)$ (Freeman's *Actuarial Mathematics*, p. 57, and Henry's *Calculus and Probability*, Chap. VIII), has the disadvantage that the dash is apt to be confused with the index (cf. $\Delta'^2 u_a$ and $\Delta'^{12} u_a$). A preferable form $\Delta(a, b)$, $\Delta^2(a, b, c) \ldots$ is clearer, but departs from the recognized symbolical notation in that the function u_x on which the divided difference symbol operates is not present; this renders the notation unsuitable for elementary work. The method adopted in paragraph 2 above is simple, and where there is no ambiguity with $f(x, y)$, representing a function of two variables, there is no objection to its use. This notation does not, however, conform with the Δ notation for differencing when the intervals are equal and to that extent it is hardly satisfactory.

The following are some alternative notations that have been used:

	Arguments	Function	Divided differences
(1)	$a, b, c \ldots$	$u_a, u_b, u_c \ldots$	$\Delta(a, b), \Delta(b, c), \Delta^2(a, b, c) \ldots$
(2)	$a, b, c \ldots$	$u_a, u_b, u_c \ldots$	$(a, b), (b, c), (a, b, c) \ldots$
(3)	$x_0, x_1, x_2 \ldots$	$f(x_0), f(x_1), f(x_2) \ldots$	$f(x_0, x_1), f(x_1, x_2), f(x_0, x_1, x_2) \ldots$
(4)	$x_0, x_1, x_2 \ldots$	$f(x_0), f(x_1), f(x_2) \ldots$	$[x_0, x_1], [x_1, x_2], [x_0, x_1, x_2] \ldots$
(5)	$a_0, a_1, a_2 \ldots$	$A_0, A_1, A_2 \ldots$	$\theta A_0, \theta A_1, \theta^2 A_0 \ldots$

(1) D. C. Fraser, (2) W. F. Sheppard, (3) J. F. Steffensen, (4) Milne-Thomson, (5) De Morgan.

The notation that we shall adopt is due to Dr A. C. Aitken (*Proc. Roy. Soc. Edin.* vol. LVIII, pp. 169 and 175) and has all the advantages possessed by the ordinary difference symbol.

The convention and definition are

$$\underset{b}{\triangle}u_a = (u_a - u_b)/(a-b)$$

$$= \frac{u_a}{a-b} + \frac{u_b}{b-a}.$$

$$\underset{bc}{\triangle^2}u_a = \underset{c}{\triangle}\left(\underset{b}{\triangle}u_a\right)$$

$$= \frac{1}{a-c}\left\{\frac{u_a}{a-b} + \frac{u_b}{b-a}\right\} + \frac{1}{c-a}\left\{\frac{u_c}{c-b} + \frac{u_b}{b-c}\right\}$$

$$= \frac{u_a}{(a-b)(a-c)} + \frac{u_b}{(b-c)(b-a)} + \frac{u_c}{(c-a)(c-b)}.$$

Similarly it may be shown that

$$\underset{bcd}{\triangle^3}u_a = \frac{u_a}{(a-b)(a-c)(a-d)} + \frac{u_b}{(b-c)(b-d)(b-a)}$$

$$+ \frac{u_c}{(c-d)(c-a)(c-b)} + \frac{u_d}{(d-a)(d-b)(d-c)}.$$

The symmetry of these differences is apparent and suggests that the property holds for a divided difference of any order. This is in fact true and the general proposition may be proved in many different ways.

It may be proved by induction, by actually arranging the coefficients or, incidentally, in establishing another important proposition, namely that if u_x is of the form $P_n(x)$ then $\triangle^n u_x$ is constant (see paragraph 6).

An elegant and succinct proof, based on the permutability of the arguments, is due to Dr Aitken, and is given below.

*4. By definition

$$\underset{a}{\triangle}u_x = (u_x - u_a)/(x-a)$$

$$= (u_a - u_x)/(a-x) = \underset{x}{\triangle}u_a.$$

The suffix of the operator and the argument of the operand are therefore interchangeable. Also, if u_x is of the form $P_n(x)$, by the remainder theorem $x-a$ is a factor of $u_x - u_a$ and it follows that $\underset{a}{\triangle}u_x$ is of the form $P_{n-1}(x)$.

For divided differences of higher orders the definitions are

$$\underset{b}{\triangle} (\underset{a}{\triangle} u_x) = \underset{ab}{\triangle^2} u_x$$

$$\underset{c}{\triangle} (\underset{ba}{\triangle^2} u_x) = \underset{abc}{\triangle^3} u_x,$$

and so on.

A divided difference of any order, e.g. $\underset{abc}{\triangle^3} u_x$, is unaltered by any permutation of the arguments. For, since the suffix of any $\triangle$ operator and the argument of the operand are interchangeable, we have such interchanges as

$$\underset{b}{\triangle} (\underset{a}{\triangle} u_x) = \underset{b}{\triangle} (\underset{x}{\triangle} u_a) = \underset{a}{\triangle} (\underset{x}{\triangle} u_b)$$

$$= \underset{a}{\triangle} (\underset{b}{\triangle} u_x) = \underset{x}{\triangle} (\underset{b}{\triangle} u_a)$$

$$= \underset{x}{\triangle} (\underset{a}{\triangle} u_b).$$

All permutations can be obtained by successive single interchanges. Thus, in the illustration above,

$$bax \to bxa \to axb \to abx \to xba \to xab.$$

These interchanges are obviously possible for divided differences of any order and it follows therefore that a divided difference is a symmetrical function of all the arguments involved.

Note. The proof given above depends entirely on the symmetrical property of the differences. It does not follow that if $u_x = v_y$ then $\underset{a}{\triangle} u_x = \underset{a}{\triangle} v_y$. In passing from, say, $\underset{a}{\triangle} (\underset{b}{\triangle} u_x)$ to $\underset{a}{\triangle} (\underset{x}{\triangle} u_b)$ the student should satisfy himself that the equivalence holds by writing down

$$\underset{a}{\triangle} (\underset{b}{\triangle} u_x) = \frac{1}{x-a} \left\{ \frac{u_x - u_b}{x-b} - \frac{u_a - u_b}{a-b} \right\}$$

$$= \frac{u_x}{(x-a)(x-b)} + \frac{u_b}{(b-x)(b-a)} + \frac{u_a}{(a-b)(a-x)},$$

$$\underset{a}{\triangle} (\underset{x}{\triangle} u_b) = \frac{1}{b-a} \left\{ \frac{u_b - u_x}{b-x} - \frac{u_a - u_x}{a-x} \right\}$$

$$= \frac{u_b}{(b-x)(b-a)} + \frac{u_x}{(x-a)(x-b)} + \frac{u_a}{(a-b)(a-x)}.$$

5. The method of forming a divided difference table is best illustrated by an actual example.

Example 1.

Take out the divided differences of u_x given the following table:

x	1	2	4	7	12
u_x	22	30	82	106	206

The table is

x	u_x	$\triangle u_x$	$\triangle^2 u_x$	$\triangle^3 u_x$	$\triangle^4 u_x$
1	22				
		$\dfrac{30-22}{2-1}=8$			
2	30		$\dfrac{26-8}{4-1}=6$		
		$\dfrac{82-30}{4-2}=26$		$\dfrac{-3\cdot6-6}{7-1}=-1\cdot6$	
4	82		$\dfrac{8-26}{7-2}=-3\cdot6$		$\dfrac{\cdot51-(-1\cdot6)}{12-1}=\cdot192...$
		$\dfrac{106-82}{7-4}=8$		$\dfrac{1\cdot5-(-3\cdot6)}{12-2}=\cdot51$	
7	106		$\dfrac{20-8}{12-4}=1\cdot5$		
		$\dfrac{206-106}{12-7}=20$			
12	206				

Note. When the arguments and their order are fixed, we may use the shortened notation $\triangle u_x$, $\triangle^2 u_x$, $\triangle^3 u_x$ ... for the leading divided differences of u_x, as in the example above.

It is essential to arrange the work systematically if error is to be avoided. The numerators and denominators must be set out, either in parallel columns or in the form of fractions. Where there is ample space the columnar arrangement is better, especially where the divisors are cumbrous. It should be noted that while the numerators are the first ordinary differences of the preceding divided differences, the denominators are all formed directly from the arguments, differencing first in the ordinary way, then in pairs, then in triplets, and so on. It will also be seen that the divisor is always the difference between the values of x for the last and first u_x involved in the difference.

6. Newton's divided difference formula.

Let the given values of u_x be

$$u_a,\ u_b,\ u_c \dots u_k,\ u_l.$$

Then, by definition,

$$u_x = u_a + (x-a)\,\underset{r}{\triangle}u_a,$$

$$\underset{x}{\triangle}u_a = \underset{b}{\triangle}u_a + (x-b)\,\underset{bx}{\triangle^2}u_a,$$

$$\underset{bx}{\triangle^2}u_a = \underset{bc}{\triangle^2}u_a + (x-c)\,\underset{bcx}{\triangle^3}u_a,$$

$$\dots\dots\dots\dots\dots$$

$$\underset{bc\dots kx}{\triangle^n}u_a = \underset{bc\dots kl}{\triangle^n}u_a + (x-l)\,\underset{bc\dots lx}{\triangle^{n+1}}u_a.$$

Hence, by successive substitution of each identity in the one preceding it, we have

$$u_x = u_a + (x-a)\,\underset{b}{\triangle}u_a + (x-a)(x-b)\,\underset{bc}{\triangle^2}u_a + \dots$$

$$+ (x-a)(x-b)\dots(x-k)\,\underset{bc\dots l}{\triangle^n}u_a + (x-a)(x-b)\dots(x-l)\,\underset{bc\dots lx}{\triangle^{n+1}}u_a.$$

Thus

$$u_x = U_x + R_{n+1}(x),$$

where U_x represents the sum of all the terms except the last and $R_{n+1}(x)$ the last.

$R_{n+1}(x)$ may be written as

$$(x-a)(x-b)\dots(x-l)\,\underset{abc\dots l}{\triangle^{n+1}}u_x$$

by permuting the arguments of the divided difference.

It should be noted that the term preceding R is

$$(x-a)(x-b)\dots(x-k)\,\underset{bc\dots l}{\triangle^n}u_a,$$

involving n factors in the coefficient. In R there is an additional factor $x-l$.

If we put x equal to $a, b, c \dots$ in succession, the R term vanishes and we have the following results which are identities, analogous to those obtained for equal intervals in Chapter I:

$$[U_x]_{x=b} = u_b = u_a + (b-a)\,\underset{b}{\triangle}u_a,$$

$$[U_x]_{x=c} = u_c = u_a + (c-a)\,\underset{b}{\triangle}u_a + (c-a)(c-b)\,\underset{bc}{\triangle^2}u_a,$$

$$[U_x]_{x=d} = u_d = u_a + (d-a)\,\underset{b}{\triangle}u_a + (d-a)(d-b)\,\underset{bc}{\triangle^2}u_a$$
$$+ (d-a)(d-b)(d-c)\,\underset{bcd}{\triangle^3}u_a.$$

$$\dots\dots\dots\dots\dots$$

It is seen that R is the only term involving u_x; it vanishes if x takes any of the values $a, b, c \dots l$, or for any value of x if $\triangle^{n+1}u_a = 0$.

It follows therefore that U_x is that polynomial of the nth degree in x which takes the $(n+1)$ given values u_a, u_b, u_c ... u_l, when $x = a, b, c ... l$ respectively. If therefore u_x is itself a polynomial of the nth degree in x it must be the polynomial U_x; i.e. R vanishes for all values of x. We have therefore that

$$\underset{abc...l}{\triangle^{n+1}} u_x = 0 \quad \text{and} \quad \underset{bc...l}{\triangle^{n}} u_x \text{ is constant.}$$

U_x is thus the *unique* polynomial of degree n which represents u_a, u_b, ... Therefore the coefficient of x^n does not depend on the order in which $a, b, c, ...$ are taken. Since this coefficient is $\triangle^n u_x$, it follows that the divided difference is a symmetrical function of all the arguments involved. (See paragraph 3 above.)

If u_x is not a polynomial of the nth degree in x, we have only the relation

$$u_x = U_x + R_{n+1}(x),$$

where the R term itself involves u_x, and if the expression $U_x + R_{n+1}(x)$ be worked out by expanding the coefficients all that we obtain is the identity $u_x = u_x$. Thus our results do not help us to find u_x unless we have some knowledge of or may make some assumption with regard to the value of $R_{n+1}(x)$. It may be said in fact that $R_{n+1}(x)$ plays the same part as does F_x in Chap. I, paragraph 17. As in the case of ordinary differences it is assumed that $R_{n+1}(x)$ is negligible and may be put equal to zero, giving finally

$$u_x = U_x$$
$$= u_a + (x-a) \underset{b}{\triangle} u_a + (x-a)(x-b) \underset{bc}{\triangle^2} u_a + ...$$
$$+ (x-a)(x-b) ... (x-k) \underset{bc...l}{\triangle^n} u_a,$$

which is Newton's formula for interpolation with divided differences.

For the method of obtaining the limits between which $R_{n+1}(x)$ lies, see paragraphs 16 and 17 below.

7. Sheppard's rules.

If, as in the paragraph above, the arguments are $x, a, b, c ... k, l$, where u_x is to be found and the $n+1$ values u_a, u_b, u_c... u_k, u_l are given, we may put Newton's formula into a more compact form by the use of a notation due to Mr D. C. Fraser. This notation is as follows:

$$x - a \equiv A,$$
$$x - b \equiv B,$$
$$x - c \equiv C,$$
$$\cdots\cdots$$

The arguments a, b, c ... involved in the divided differences and the factors A, B, C ... are in the same order, with the exception that the small letters are always one in advance of the capitals, thus:

Arguments,	a	ab	abc	$abcd$	$abcde$ ....
Capitals,	1	A	AB	ABC	$ABCD$ ....

Newton's formula thus reads

$$u_x = u_a + A \underset{b}{\triangle} u_a + AB \underset{bc}{\triangle^2} u_a + ABC \underset{bcd}{\triangle^3} u_a + \dots + ABCD \dots K \underset{bc\dots l}{\triangle^n} u_a.$$

Dr W. F. Sheppard has given very convenient rules, embodying the same principle, and by means of these rules formulae may be written down at sight for any intervals. As expanded by Mr G. J. Lidstone [*J.I.A.* vol. LVIII, p. 65 and references there given] these rules are as follows:

"(i) We start with any tabulated value of u.

(ii) We pass to the successive differences by steps, each of which may be either upward or downward";
[each step involving a new u whose subscript will be numerically the next lower/higher if the step is up/down, and the u's are arranged in the numerical sequence of the variables.]

"(iii) The new suffix [of u] which is introduced at each step determines the new factor (involving x) for use in the next term."

[That is, each divided difference of the nth order has for its coefficient the product of n factors of the form $(x - a_k)$ where a_k represents a value of the variable, and has to be given all the n values that were involved in the last preceding difference.

These rules apply whether the intervals are equal or unequal; if they are equal the divided differences are of the form $\Delta^n u/n!$.]

These rules are familiarly known as the "zig-zag rules" for reasons which will now be explained. If we are given a set of u's and their differences as in the following scheme

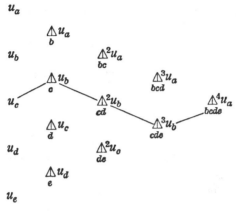

and use them to interpolate for u_x, it is not necessary to use the formula involving u_a and its leading differences. We may begin with *any* of the u's and at each step move either upwards or downwards in proceeding to the next column in the difference table, so that we may if we like follow a "zig-zag" route; in fact with n values we have a choice of 2^{n-1} different routes. [Cf. Sheppard, *J.I.A.* vol. L, p. 89.]

Suppose we wish to begin with u_c. The next term may be either $\underset{c}{\triangle u_b}$ or $\underset{d}{\triangle u_c}$, since both of these involve u_c: let us take $\underset{c}{\triangle u_b}$ involving u_c and u_b. We may next take either $\underset{bc}{\triangle^2 u_a}$ or $\underset{cd}{\triangle^2 u_b}$, since both of these also involve u_c and u_b: let us take $\underset{cd}{\triangle^2 u_b}$. We may then move to $\underset{bcd}{\triangle^3 u_a}$ or $\underset{cde}{\triangle^3 u_b}$ and we select the latter. We then have no further choice and we move to $\underset{bcde}{\triangle^4 u_a}$. Our formula thus brings in the small letters in the order

$$c, b, d, e, a$$

and therefore the factors of the coefficients will enter in the order

$$\text{I}, C, B, D, E.$$

Thus we may write down at once the required formula

$$u_x = u_c + C \underset{c}{\triangle} u_b + BC \underset{cd}{\triangle^2} u_b + BCD \underset{cde}{\triangle^3} u_b + BCDE \underset{bcde}{\triangle^4} u_a$$

or

$$u_x = u_c + (x-c) \underset{c}{\triangle} u_b + (x-b)(x-c) \underset{cd}{\triangle^2} u_b + (x-b)(x-c)(x-d) \underset{cde}{\triangle^3} u_b$$

$$+ (x-b)(x-c)(x-d)(x-e) \underset{bcde}{\triangle^4} u_a.$$

Sheppard's rules are of the utmost importance, and a clear understanding of them will save the student much trouble.

8. The following is an alternative proof of the property of divided differences which was established in paragraph 6.

If u_x be a polynomial of the nth degree in x, then the nth divided difference of u_x is constant.

It will be sufficient to consider the function $y = x^n$. Then, if the values of the argument x be a, b, c ..., the first divided difference $\underset{b}{\triangle} a^n$ is

$$(b^n - a^n)/(b-a) = b^{n-1} + b^{n-2}a + b^{n-3}a^2 + \ldots + a^{n-1}.$$

This is a symmetrical function of the $(n-1)$th degree in a and b, and is the coefficient of x^{n-1} in the expansion of

$$(1 + bx + b^2x^2 + \ldots)(1 + ax + a^2x^2 + \ldots),$$

i.e. in the expansion of $\dfrac{1}{1-bx} \cdot \dfrac{1}{1-ax}$.

Thus $\underset{c}{\triangle} b^n$ is the coefficient of x^{n-1} in $\dfrac{1}{1-cx} \cdot \dfrac{1}{1-bx}$ and therefore $\underset{bc}{\triangle^2} a^n$ is the coefficient of x^{n-1} in

$$\frac{1}{c-a}\left(\frac{1}{1-cx} \cdot \frac{1}{1-bx} - \frac{1}{1-bx} \cdot \frac{1}{1-ax}\right),$$

i.e. in $x \left(\dfrac{1}{1-cx} \cdot \dfrac{1}{1-bx} \cdot \dfrac{1}{1-ax}\right)$, or the coefficient of x^{n-2} in

$$\frac{1}{1-ax} \cdot \frac{1}{1-bx} \cdot \frac{1}{1-cx}.$$

Proceeding in this way, we find that $\underset{bc\ldots}{\triangle^r} a^n$ is the coefficient of

x^{n-r} in $\dfrac{1}{1-ax} \cdot \dfrac{1}{1-bx} \cdot \dfrac{1}{1-cx} \dots$, where there are r factors in the product. This coefficient is evidently symmetrical in $a, b, c \dots$.

Finally, $\underset{bc\dots}{\triangle^n a^n}$ is the coefficient of x^0 in a similar expression, and this coefficient is unity.

Thus, the nth divided difference of a polynomial of the nth degree in x is constant and equal to the coefficient of the highest power of x; and higher divided differences vanish. Also, it has been proved incidentally that a divided difference is a symmetrical function of the variables involved; for the expression obtained for $\underset{bcd\dots}{\triangle^r a^n}$ is symmetrical in $a, b, c \dots$.

9. Newton's divided difference formula is quite easy to apply in practice, as the following example will show.

Example 2.

From the data in Ex. 1, find u_8.

Assuming fourth divided differences constant, the formula gives

$$u_8 = u_1 + (8-1)\,\triangle u_1 + (8-1)\,(8-2)\,\triangle^2 u_1$$
$$+ (8-1)\,(8-2)\,(8-4)\,\triangle^3 u_1 + (8-1)\,(8-2)\,(8-4)\,(8-7)\,\triangle^4 u_1$$
$$= u_1 + 7\triangle u_1 + 42\triangle^2 u_1 + 168\triangle^3 u_1 + 168\triangle^4 u_1$$
$$= 22 + 56 + 252 - 268 \cdot 8 + 32 \cdot 3$$
$$= 93 \text{ to the nearest integer.}$$

10. Relation between divided differences and ordinary differences.

If the arguments $a, b, c \dots k, l$ are spaced at equal intervals h, we shall have
$$h = b - a = c - b = d - c = \dots = l - k.$$

Hence in forming $\triangle u$ the divisors will all be equal to h.

Thus $\qquad\qquad \underset{b}{\triangle} u_a = \Delta u_a / h \text{ etc.}$

Similarly in forming $\triangle^2 u$ the divisors $c - a$, $d - b \dots$ will all be equal to $2h$.

$\therefore \qquad\qquad \underset{bc}{\triangle^2} u_a = \Delta^2 u_a / 2!\, h^2.$

In forming $\triangle^3 u$ the divisors $d - a$, $e - b \dots$ will all be equal to $3h$.

$\therefore$ $\underset{bcd}{\triangle^3 u_a} = \Delta^3 u_a / 3\,!\,h^3.$

In general $\underset{bcd\ldots}{\triangle^n u_a} = \Delta^n u_a / n\,!\,h^n.$

If therefore the common interval $h \lesseqgtr$ unity, the divided differences will diminish much more rapidly than the ordinary differences. In interpolation formulae this is counterbalanced by the denominators of the form $n!$ which appear in the coefficients of the ordinary differences but not in the coefficients of the divided differences.

The formula for u_x in terms of u_a and its leading divided differences is

$$u_x = u_a + (x-a)\underset{b}{\triangle}u_a + (x-a)(x-b)\underset{bc}{\triangle^2}u_a + \ldots$$
$$+ (x-a)(x-b)\ldots(x-k)\underset{bc\ldots l}{\triangle^n}u_a.$$

This becomes, on putting $x - a = nh$,

$$u_{a+nh} = u_a + nh\underset{b}{\triangle}u_a + nh\,[nh - (b-a)]\underset{bc}{\triangle^2}u_a + \ldots.$$

If now $b - a = h,\ c - a = 2h \ldots$

$$u_{a+nh} = u_a + \frac{nh\Delta u_a}{h} + \frac{nh\,(nh - h)\,\Delta^2 u_a}{2\,!\,h^2}$$
$$+ \frac{nh\,(nh - h)\,(nh - 2h)\,\Delta^3 u_a}{3\,!\,h^3} + \ldots$$

from the relations proved above;

i.e. $u_{a+nh} = u_a + n_{(1)}\Delta u_a + n_{(2)}\Delta^2 u_a + n_{(3)}\Delta^3 u_a + \ldots,$

which is Newton's formula for advancing differences.

It is easily seen therefore that in order to pass from the divided difference formula

$$u_x = u_a + (x-a)\underset{b}{\triangle}u_a + (x-a)(x-b)\underset{bc}{\triangle^2}u_a + \ldots$$

to the advancing difference formula (when the intervals are the same) we may replace $\triangle$ by Δ, drop the subscripts and insert factorial denominators thus:

$$u_x = u_a + (x-a)\Delta u_a + \frac{(x-a)(x-a-1)}{2\,!}\Delta^2 u_a + \ldots.$$

11. Lagrange's interpolation formula.

On the same assumption as has been made hitherto, namely that the function concerned is a polynomial in x, an interpolation formula can be evolved which is equivalent to the process of splitting up an algebraic fraction into its partial fractions.

Let n values of the function $y = u_x$ be given, so that u_x is supposed to be a polynomial of the $(n-1)$th degree in x, and let the given values of x be $a, b, c, \dots, j, k$.

Then we may write

$$u_x = A(x-b)(x-c)\dots(x-k) + B(x-a)(x-c)\dots(x-k) + \dots$$
$$+ K(x-a)(x-b)\dots(x-j),$$

where there are n terms each of degree $n-1$ in x.

This is true for all values of x involved. Put therefore $x = a$.

Then
$$u_a = A(a-b)(a-c)\dots(a-k),$$
$$\therefore A = \frac{u_a}{(a-b)(a-c)\dots(a-k)}.$$

Similarly, by putting $x = b$,

$$B = \frac{u_b}{(b-a)(b-c)\dots(b-k)}.$$

In like manner all the coefficients can be found.

$$\therefore u_x = u_a \frac{(x-b)(x-c)\dots(x-k)}{(a-b)(a-c)\dots(a-k)} + u_b \frac{(x-a)(x-c)\dots(x-k)}{(b-a)(b-c)\dots(b-k)} + \dots$$
$$+ u_k \frac{(x-a)(x-b)(x-c)\dots}{(k-a)(k-b)(k-c)\dots},$$

or otherwise

$$\frac{u_x}{(x-a)(x-b)\dots(x-k)} = \frac{u_a}{(a-b)(a-c)\dots(a-k)} \cdot \frac{1}{x-a}$$
$$+ \frac{u_b}{(b-a)(b-c)\dots(b-k)} \cdot \frac{1}{x-b} + \dots.$$

It is evident that this is exactly the same as splitting the fraction

$$\frac{u_x}{(x-a)(x-b)\dots(x-k)}$$

into partial fractions.

This alternative expression is due to Euler and was given earlier than Lagrange's formula.

It is interesting to note that Euler's form, when written as

$$\frac{u_x}{(x-a)(x-b)\ldots}+\frac{u_a}{(a-x)(a-b)\ldots}+\frac{u_b}{(b-x)(b-a)\ldots}+\ldots=0$$

is an expression for the divided difference $\underset{abc\ldots}{\triangle^n u_x}$. It follows therefore that Euler's formula (and consequently Lagrange's) can be evolved from the divided difference formula by equating the nth divided difference to zero. Also, since the expansion is symmetrical in x, a, b, c ... k, the divided difference is independent of the order in which the arguments are taken, as stated in paragraph 3 above.

12. Lagrange's formula is usually laborious to apply in practice and requires close attention to sign; it is generally simpler to employ other finite difference methods. Where the intervals are equal an advancing difference formula may be used, and for unequal intervals it is preferable to use divided differences.

The principles on which this formula has been developed are the same as those assumed for the difference formulae, namely that n values of the function being given, nth differences are assumed zero. The following examples show the application of the formula:

Example 3.

Given the data in Ex. 1, obtain u_8 by the use of Lagrange's formula.

$$\frac{u_8}{(8-1)(8-2)(8-4)(8-7)(8-12)}=\frac{u_1}{(1-2)(1-4)(1-7)(1-12)}\cdot\frac{1}{(8-1)}$$
$$+\frac{u_2}{(2-1)(2-4)(2-7)(2-12)}\cdot\frac{1}{(8-2)}$$
$$+\frac{u_4}{(4-1)(4-2)(4-7)(4-12)}\cdot\frac{1}{(8-4)}+\ldots,$$

i.e. $\dfrac{u_8}{7.6.4.1.(-4)}=\dfrac{22}{(-1)(-3)(-6)(-11).7}+\dfrac{30}{1.(-2)(-5)(-10).6}$
$$+\frac{82}{3.2.(-3)(-8).4}+\frac{106}{6.5.3.(-5).1}$$
$$+\frac{206}{11.10.8.5.(-4)}.$$

$\therefore\ u_8=-10\cdot666\ldots+33\cdot6-95\cdot666\ldots+158\cdot293\ldots+7\cdot865$

$=93$ (to the nearest integer) as in Ex. 2.

Example 4.

Find the form of the function $y = u_x$ given that

$$u_0 = 8, \quad u_1 = 11, \quad u_4 = 68, \quad u_5 = 123.$$

By Lagrange's formula:

$$\frac{u_x}{x(x-1)(x-4)(x-5)} = \frac{8}{(-1)(-4)(-5)} \cdot \frac{1}{x} + \frac{11}{1(-3)(-4)} \cdot \frac{1}{x-1}$$

$$+ \frac{68}{4 \cdot 3(-1)} \cdot \frac{1}{x-4} + \frac{123}{5 \cdot 4 \cdot 1} \cdot \frac{1}{x-5}$$

$$= -\frac{2}{5} \cdot \frac{1}{x} + \frac{11}{12} \cdot \frac{1}{x-1} - \frac{68}{12} \cdot \frac{1}{x-4} + \frac{123}{20} \cdot \frac{1}{x-5}$$

$$= \frac{1}{20} \frac{115x + 40}{x(x-5)} - \frac{1}{12} \frac{57x - 24}{(x-1)(x-4)}$$

$$= \frac{23x + 8}{4x(x-5)} - \frac{19x - 8}{4(x-1)(x-4)}.$$

$$\therefore \quad u_x = \tfrac{1}{4}[(23x + 8)(x^2 - 5x + 4) - (19x - 8)(x^2 - 5x)]$$
$$= x^3 - x^2 + 3x + 8.$$

It is useful to work out this example by divided differences, adopting two different orders for the values of x, thus illustrating the principle that, if the same u's are involved, the order is indifferent.

(a)

x	u_x	$\triangle u_x$	$\triangle^2 u_x$	$\triangle^3 u_x$
0	8			
		$3 \div 1 = 3$		
1	11		$16 \div 4 = 4$	
		$57 \div 3 = 19$		$5 \div 5 = 1$
4	68		$36 \div 4 = 9$	
		$55 \div 1 = 55$		
5	123			

$$\therefore \quad u_x = 8 + 3x + 4x(x-1) + 1x(x-1)(x-4) = x^3 - x^2 + 3x + 8.$$

(b)

x	u_x	$\triangle u_x$	$\triangle^2 u_x$	$\triangle^3 u_x$
5	123			
		$-115 \div -5 = 23$		
0	8		$-8 \div -1 = 8$	
		$+60 \div +4 = 15$		$-4 \div -4 = 1$
4	68		$+4 \div +1 = 4$	
		$-57 \div -3 = 19$		
1	11			

$$\therefore \quad u_x = 123 + 23\,(x-5) + 8\,(x-5)\,x + 1\,(x-5)\,x\,(x-4)$$
$$= 123 + 23x - 115 + 8x^2 - 40x + x^3 - 9x^2 + 20x$$
$$= x^3 - x^2 + 3x + 8.$$

Here, for example,

$$\underset{4}{\triangle} u_1 = \underset{1}{\triangle} u_4 = 19,$$

$$\underset{1,4,5}{\triangle^3} u_0 = \underset{0,4,1}{\triangle^3} u_5 = 1.$$

13. The following examples are instructive:

Example 5.

$u_0 = -18,\ u_1 = 0,\ u_3 = 0,\ u_5 = -248,\ u_6 = 0,\ u_9 = 13104.$

Find the form of u_x, assuming it to be a polynomial in x.

Now since $u_1 = 0,\ u_3 = 0,\ u_6 = 0$, the function must be of the form $(x-1)\,(x-3)\,(x-6)\,\phi\,(x)$, where $\phi\,(x)$ is a polynomial in x of the second degree.

$$\therefore \quad \frac{u_x}{(x-1)\,(x-3)\,(x-6)} = \phi\,(x).$$

I.e. $\dfrac{u_0}{(-1)\,(-3)\,(-6)} = \phi\,(0) \quad \therefore \quad \phi\,(0) = 1$, since $u_0 = -\quad 18$

            $\dfrac{u_5}{4.2\,(-1)} = \phi\,(5) \quad \therefore \quad \phi\,(5) = 31,\ \text{,,}\ u_5 = -\quad 248$

and $\dfrac{u_9}{8.6.3} = \phi\,(9) \quad \therefore \quad \phi\,(9) = 91,\ \text{,,}\ u_9 = \quad 13104$

Whence, from the divided difference table,

x	$\phi\,(x)$	$\triangle\phi\,(x)$	$\triangle^2\phi\,(x)$
0	1		
		6	
5	31		1
		15	
9	91		

$$\phi\,(x) = \phi\,(0) + x\,\triangle\phi\,(x) + x\,(x-5)\,\triangle^2\phi\,(x)$$
$$= 1 + 6x + x\,(x-5)$$
$$= x^2 + x + 1;$$
$$\therefore \quad u_x = (x-1)\,(x-3)\,(x-6)\,(x^2+x+1)$$
$$= x^5 - 9x^4 + 18x^3 - x^2 + 9x - 18.$$

Example 6.

Given $u_5 = 23$, $u_{11} = 899$, $u_{27} = 17315$, $u_{34} = 35606$, $u_{42} = 68510$, construct a table of divided differences and extend the table to include arguments $x = 3$ repeated as many times as may be necessary to find u_x in powers of $(x - 3)$.

From the data we have

x	u_x	$\triangle u_x$	$\triangle^2 u_x$	$\triangle^3 u_x$
5	23			
		146		
11	899		40	
		1026		1
27	17315		69	
		2613		1
34	35606		100	
		4113		1
42	68510		a	
		b		1
3	c		d	
		e		1
			f	
				1

Now

$$a = \quad 100 - 24 \times 1 = \quad 76$$
$$b = \quad 4113 - 31 \times a = \quad 1757$$
$$c = 68510 - 39 \times b = - \quad 13$$
$$d = \quad a \quad - 31 \times 1 = \quad 45$$
$$e = \quad b \quad - 39 \times d = \quad 2$$
$$f = \quad d \quad - 39 \times 1 = \quad 6$$
$$\therefore \quad u_x = c + (x-3)\, e + (x-3)^2 f + (x-3)^3 \times 1$$
$$= -13 + 2(x-3) + 6(x-3)^2 + (x-3)^3.$$

14. Newton's formula with divided differences may be considered as the basic formula in finite differences. It has been shown that, by making the intervals equal, the ordinary advancing difference formula follows, and that Lagrange's formula can be evolved from the divided difference formula by equating the nth divided difference to zero. Moreover, by taking the limiting values when the intervals tend to zero, Taylor's theorem can be obtained.

The formula is of the utmost importance analytically and

historically, and the advanced student may be recommended to read Mr D. C. Fraser's "Newton's Interpolation Formulas" (*J.I.A.* vol. LI, pp. 77–106 and pp. 211–32, and vol. LVIII, pp. 53–95) and the same author's "Newton and Interpolation" (an article in *Newton*, 1727–1927, a memorial volume published by the Mathematical Association).

*15. Adjusted differences.

There is a system of differences which may be considered as the connecting link between ordinary differences and divided differences. These differences, which are called *adjusted differences*, were used by Newton and re-discovered by Sheppard.

When the successive arguments are $a, b, c \ldots$ the relation between adjusted differences and ordinary differences is as follows:

Order of differences	Divisor of difference for divided differences	Divisor of difference for adjusted differences
First	$a-b$	$a-b$
Second	$a-c$	$\frac{1}{2}(a-c)$
Third	$a-d$	$\frac{1}{3}(a-d)$
Fourth	$a-e$	$\frac{1}{4}(a-e)$
$\vdots$	$\vdots$	$\vdots$

Ordinary differences are adjusted differences and both sets can be used in the same scheme.

An interesting account of the Newton-Sheppard system of adjusted differences will be found in *J.I.A.* vol. LVIII, pp. 60–74 (D. C. Fraser).

*16. An expression for the nth divided difference.

The results of paragraph 5 may be written in the form

$$R_{n+1}(x) = u_x - U_x,$$

where $R_{n+1}(x)$ vanishes for $n+1$ values of x, say $a, b, c \ldots l$. Hence, by repeated application of Rolle's Theorem (Part I, Chap. IV, p. 62), it follows that, in the interval which includes these values, the first differential coefficient of R with respect to x vanishes at least n times, the second differential coefficient vanishes at least

$n-1$ times, and finally, the nth differential coefficient vanishes at least once, say where $x = \xi$.

$$\therefore \quad 0 = \left[\frac{d^n}{dx^n} R_{n+1}(x) \right]_{x=\xi}$$

$$= \left[\frac{d^n}{dx^n} (u_x - U_x) \right]_{x=\xi}.$$

Now U_x is of the form $P_n(x)$, and since the nth differential coefficient of $P_n(x)$ with respect to x is $n!$ times the coefficient of x^n, it follows that

$$\frac{d^n}{dx^n} U_x = n! \underset{bc\ldots l}{\triangle^n} u_a.$$

$$\therefore \quad 0 = \left[\frac{d^n}{dx^n} u_x \right]_{x=\xi} - n! \underset{bc\ldots l}{\triangle^n} u_a,$$

or

$$\underset{bc\ldots l}{\triangle^n} u_a = \frac{1}{n!} \left[\frac{d^n}{dx^n} u_x \right]$$

for some value of x (ξ) within the range which includes $a, b, c \ldots l$, and x.

*17. Remainder term in the divided difference formula.

If in the proof above we bring in another term u_x, we have

$$\underset{bcl\ldots x}{\triangle^{n+1}} u_a = \left[\frac{d^{n+1}}{d\xi^{n+1}} u_\xi \right] \Big/ (n+1)!,$$

where $\dfrac{d^{n+1}}{d\xi^{n+1}} u_\xi$ is written for $\left[\dfrac{d^{n+1}}{dx^{n+1}} u_x \right]_{x=\xi}$.

This is the divided difference involved in $R_{n+1}(x)$.

$$\therefore \quad R_{n+1}(x) = \left[(x-a)(x-b) \ldots (x-l) \frac{d^{n+1}}{d\xi^{n+1}} u_\xi \right] \Big/ (n+1)!.$$

When the intervals are all unity, this becomes

$$R_{n+1}(x) = x_{(n+1)} \frac{d^{n+1}}{d\xi^{n+1}} u_\xi,$$

where ξ is some value in the interval including all the arguments involved, i.e. the given arguments $a, b \ldots l$ and also x.

EXAMPLES 3

1. Given terms at unequal intervals, explain how to apply the method of divided differences to find an interpolated value: illustrate your answer by finding u_5 given

$u_{4\cdot50} = 1345$, $u_{4\cdot55} = 1470$, $u_{4\cdot70} = 2010$, $u_{4\cdot90} = 3815$, $u_{5\cdot15} = 10965$.

2. $u_{40} = 43833$, $u_{42} = 46568$, $u_{44} = 49431$, $u_{45} = 50912$. Use divided differences to find u_{43}.

3. Given the following table, find log 656:

No.	654	658	659	661
Log	2·8156	2·8182	2·8189	2·8202

4. $u_{50} = 1\cdot6990$, $u_{52} = 1\cdot7160$, $u_{54} = 1\cdot7324$, $u_{55} = 1\cdot7404$. Find u_{53} by divided differences.

5. $u_{35\cdot0} = 1175$, $u_{35\cdot5} = 1280$, $u_{39\cdot5} = 2180$, $u_{40\cdot5} = 2420$. Obtain a value for u_{40} (i) by advancing differences, (ii) by divided differences.

6. $u_{7\cdot0} = 235$, $u_{7\cdot1} = 256$, $u_{7\cdot9} = 436$, $u_{8\cdot1} = 484$. Find $u_{8\cdot0}$.

7. Find the first three divided differences of the function $y = x^{-2}$ for the arguments $x = l, m, n, p$.

Find by Lagrange's formula the value of

8. u_{48} given $u_{40} = 15\cdot22$, $u_{45} = 13\cdot99$, $u_{50} = 12\cdot62$, $u_{55} = 11\cdot13$.

9. u_8 given $u_0 = 17\cdot378$, $u_5 = 15\cdot894$, $u_{10} = 14\cdot270$, $u_{15} = 12\cdot412$.

10. u_{22} given $u_{10} = 22\cdot40$, $u_{15} = 21\cdot66$, $u_{20} = 20\cdot82$, $u_{25} = 19\cdot85$.

11. u_1 given $u_0 = \cdot400$, $u_2 = \cdot128$, $u_3 = \cdot224$, $u_4 = \cdot376$.

12. Use Lagrange's formula to find the form of the function $y = f(x)$ given

x	0	2	3	6
$f(x)$	659	705	729	804

13. Values of u_x are given for all integral values of x from 0 to $n-1$. Show that u_x is capable of expression in the form

$$\frac{x!}{(x-n)!\,(n-1)!}\left[\frac{u_{n-1}}{x-n+1} - (n-1)_{(1)}\frac{u_{n-2}}{x-n+2}\right.$$
$$\left. + (n-1)_{(2)}\frac{u_{n-3}}{x-n+3} - \ldots \pm (n-1)_{(n-1)}\frac{u_0}{x}\right].$$

Find u_4 given $u_0 = 4$, $u_1 = 7$, $u_2 = 12$, $u_3 = 20$, by using the above formula.

14. By means of Lagrange's formula, prove that, approximately,

(1) $u_1 = u_3 - \cdot 3\,(u_5 - u_{-3}) + \cdot 2\,(u_{-3} - u_{-5})$,

(2) $u_0 = \frac{1}{2}\,[u_1 + u_{-1}] - \frac{1}{8}\,[\frac{1}{2}\,(u_3 - u_1) - \frac{1}{2}\,(u_{-1} - u_{-3})]$.

15. Four equidistant values u_{-1}, u_0, u_1, and u_2 being given, a value is interpolated by Lagrange's formula. Show that it may be written in the form

$$u_x = y u_0 + x u_1 + \frac{y\,(y^2 - 1)}{3!}\,\Delta^2 u_{-1} + \frac{x\,(x^2 - 1)}{3!}\,\Delta^2 u_0,$$

where $x + y = 1$.

16. If $f(a_1, a_0) = \dfrac{f(a_1) - f(a_0)}{a_1 - a_0}$, $f(a_2, a_1) = \dfrac{f(a_2) - f(a_1)}{a_2 - a_1}$, etc. be

divided differences of the first order; $f(a_2, a_1, a_0) = \dfrac{f(a_2, a_1) - f(a_1, a_0)}{a_2 - a_0}$,

etc. divided differences of the second order and so on, find $f(2, 4, 9, 10)$, where $f(x) = $ (i) $x^3 - 2x$, (ii) $x^4 + x^2 + 1$.

17. Prove that if u_x be a polynomial of the nth degree in x, and if values u_a, u_b, u_c, ... of u_x be given, then the expressions for u_x in terms of its divided differences are identically equal whatever the order of arrangement of the u's.

18. Apply Lagrange's formula to find $f(5)$ and $f(6)$, given that

$$f(1) = 2,\ f(2) = 4,\ f(3) = 8,\ f(4) = 16 \text{ and } f(7) = 128;$$

and explain why the results differ from those obtained by completing the series of powers of 2.

19. $u_{-30} = 30$; $u_{-13} = 34$; $u_3 = 38$; $u_{18} = 42$. Find u_0.

20. $u_{70} = 7 \cdot 69$; $u_{72} = 7 \cdot 07$; $u_{73} = 6 \cdot 78$; $u_{75} = 6 \cdot 18$. Interpolate to find u_{71} by divided differences, using the following orders of the argument:

(i) 70, 73, 75, 72;   (ii) 72, 75, 70, 73.

21. By means of divided differences, find the value of u_{19} from the following table:

x	11	17	21	23	31
u_x	14,646	83,526	194,486	279,846	923,526

22. Prove that $\underset{yz}{\Delta^2}\,x^3 = x + y + z$ and that

$$\underset{bc}{\Delta^2}\left(\frac{1}{a}\right) = \frac{1}{abc}.$$

23. If the data are u_0, u_3, u_4, u_7, u_{11}, and the interpolation formula is

$$u_x = u_4 + C_1 \underset{3}{\triangle} u_4 + C_2 \underset{4,7}{\triangle^2} u_3 + C_3 \underset{3,4,7}{\triangle^3} u_0 + C_4 \underset{3,4,7,11}{\triangle^4} u_0,$$

find the values of C_1, C_2, C_3 and C_4.

24. If the data are as in Qu. 23 above, and the formula is

$$u_x = u_3 + (x-3) \triangle u + (x-3)(x-4) \triangle^2 u + (x-3)(x-4)x \triangle^3 u$$
$$+ (x-3)(x-4)x(x-7) \triangle^4 u,$$

find the missing suffixes of the operators and the subscripts of the u's.

CHAPTER IV

CENTRAL DIFFERENCES

1. If a series of values of u_x be given, we can interpolate to find any intermediate value by one of the methods in the preceding chapters. Where the values of the argument x proceed by unit intervals it has been shown that, on certain assumptions, Newton's advancing difference formula can be applied to give satisfactory results. If the value of u_x were required for some value of x between $x = 0$ and $x = 1$, it might be considered that we should obtain a better result if our knowledge of the shape of the curve extended on both sides of the values of x between which we wish to interpolate. That is to say, where we may choose any values of u_x at unit intervals for our data, it might be of advantage if we could use a formula involving values such as u_{-3}, u_{-2}, u_{-1}, u_0, u_1, u_2, u_3, ... rather than u_0, u_1, u_2, u_3, u_4, ... By the advancing difference formula we expand u_x in terms of a given value of u_x and its leading differences and, by giving x a suitable value, such a formula can be made to embrace any values of u that we wish. It is however convenient to use special formulae called *central difference* formulae, based on differences obtained from the values of u_x on either side of the origin; this is found to result in smaller coefficients and a more rapidly converging series of terms.

2. There are various central difference formulae that are of use in actual practice, and the development of the better-known formulae is an exercise in the application of the fundamental principles of finite differences which will be advantageous to the student. These formulae apply whether the values of the function correspond to equidistant values of the argument or to values with unequal intervals. We shall consider first the general case and pass from it to the simpler and more usual case of equal intervals.

3. Gauss's formulae.

Suppose that we are given the values ... u_m, u_l, u_a, u_b, u_c ... and that we wish to deduce a formula for u_x in terms of u_a, the even differences which fall on the line of u_a and the odd differences which fall on the line between u_a and u_b, as shown by the lower of the two series of dotted lines in the following difference table:

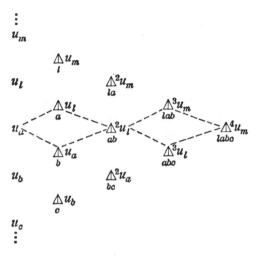

The formula will thus involve in succession

$$u_a, \quad \underset{b}{\triangle} u_a, \quad \underset{ab}{\triangle^2} u_l, \quad \underset{abc}{\triangle^3} u_l, \quad \underset{labc}{\triangle^4} u_m \;....$$

As we pass from each of these to the next, the new arguments brought in, one at a time, are b, l, c, m, ... Hence, applying rule (iii) of Chap. III, paragraph 7, namely, that each new argument gives the new factor for use in the next term, and adopting the abbreviated notation $x - a = A$, $x - b = B$ etc., we can at once write down the required formula.

The formula will be

$$u_x = u_a + A\underset{b}{\triangle} u_a + AB\underset{ab}{\triangle^2} u_l + ABL\underset{abc}{\triangle^3} u_l + ABCL\underset{labc}{\triangle^4} u_m + ...,$$

where the law of formation is evident.

Now let the intervals between the arguments be all equal to unity and let $a = 0$, so that $b = 1$, $c = 2$, ..., $l = -1$, $m = -2$, ...

Then, as in Chap. III, paragraph 10, we have

$$\underset{b}{\triangle} u_a = \Delta u_0;$$

$$\underset{ab}{\triangle^2} u_l = \Delta^2 u_{-1}/2\,!;$$

$$\underset{abc}{\triangle^3} u_l = \Delta^3 u_{-1}/3\,!;$$

$$\underset{labc}{\triangle^4} u_m = \Delta^4 u_{-2}/4\,!.$$

Further,

$$A = x - a = x,$$

$$B = x - b = x - 1,$$

$$L = x - l = x + 1,$$

....

The formula for equal intervals is thus

$$u_x = u_0 + x\Delta u_0 + \frac{x\,(x-1)}{2\,!}\,\Delta^2 u_{-1} + \frac{(x+1)\,x\,(x-1)}{3\,!}\,\Delta^3 u_{-1}$$

$$+ \frac{(x+1)\,x\,(x-1)\,(x-2)}{4\,!}\,\Delta^4 u_{-2} + \dots$$

or

$$u_0 + x_{(1)}\Delta u_0 + x_{(2)}\Delta^2 u_{-1} + (x+1)_{(3)}\Delta^3 u_{-1} + (x+1)_{(4)}\Delta^4 u_{-2} + \dots.$$

This is known as Gauss's "forward" formula for equal intervals.

4. If we take the even differences as above but the odd differences which fall on the line between u_l and u_a (the upper of the two series of dotted lines in the table in the preceding paragraph) we obtain a formula which involves in succession

$$u_a, \ \underset{a}{\triangle} u_l, \ \underset{ab}{\triangle^2} u_l, \ \underset{lab}{\triangle^3} u_m, \ \underset{labc}{\triangle^4} u_m \ \dots.$$

The new arguments brought in are l, b, m, c, ... and, using the rule as before, we evolve the form

$$u_x = u_a + A\underset{a}{\triangle} u_l + AL\underset{ab}{\triangle^2} u_l + ABL\underset{lab}{\triangle^3} u_m + ABLM\underset{labc}{\triangle^4} u_m + \dots.$$

From this we may pass at once to the formula for equal intervals of unity:

$$u_x = u_0 + x_{(1)}\Delta u_{-1} + (x+1)_{(2)}\Delta^2 u_{-1} + (x+1)_{(3)}\Delta^3 u_{-2}$$
$$+ (x+2)_{(4)}\Delta^4 u_{-2} + ...$$

This is Gauss's "backward" formula.

Note. It is useful to remember that, after u_0, as we advance from each term to the next, in the forward form we alternately *deduct* unity from the subscript of u and *add* unity to the number whose factorial is the coefficient; while in the backward form we alternately *add* unity to the number whose factorial is the coefficient and *deduct* unity from the subscript of u.

5. Stirling's formula.

Taking the mean of the two Gauss formulae we arrive at the following expansion:

$$u_x = u_0 + x \cdot \tfrac{1}{2}(\Delta u_0 + \Delta u_{-1}) + \frac{x^2}{2!}\Delta^2 u_{-1}$$
$$+ \frac{x(x^2-1^2)}{3!}\tfrac{1}{2}(\Delta^3 u_{-1} + \Delta^3 u_{-2}) + \frac{x^2(x^2-1^2)}{4!}\Delta^4 u_{-2} + ...,$$

in which we have alternately mean *coefficients* and mean *differences*, falling on the line through u_0 in the difference table.

This is known as Stirling's formula. In using it x should lie in the range $-\tfrac{1}{2}$ to $+\tfrac{1}{2}$, i.e. $\tfrac{1}{2}$ on each side of the line of u_0.

6. Bessel's formula.

Transferring the origin in the Gauss backward formula from 0 to 1, we have

$$u_x = u_1 + (x-1)\Delta u_0 + \frac{x(x-1)}{2!}\Delta^2 u_0 + \frac{x(x-1)(x-2)}{3!}\Delta^3 u_{-1}$$
$$+ \frac{(x+1)x(x-1)(x-2)}{4!}\Delta^4 u_{-1} + ...$$

The mean of this and the forward formula is

$$u_x = \tfrac{1}{2}(u_0+u_1) + (x-\tfrac{1}{2})\Delta u_0$$
$$+ \frac{x(x-1)}{2!}\tfrac{1}{2}(\Delta^2 u_{-1} + \Delta^2 u_0) + \frac{(x-\tfrac{1}{2})x(x-1)}{3!}\Delta^3 u_{-1}$$
$$+ \frac{(x+1)x(x-1)(x-2)}{4!}\tfrac{1}{2}(\Delta^4 u_{-1} + \Delta^4 u_{-2}) + ...,$$

which is Bessel's formula. In using the formula x should lie in the range o to 1, i.e. $\frac{1}{2}$ on each side of the central line.

In this formula we have alternately mean u's or differences, falling on the central line between u_0 and u_1, and mean coefficients.

If we write $y + \frac{1}{2}$ for x in Bessel's formula, we obtain the simpler and more symmetric form:

$$u_x = u_{y+\frac{1}{2}} = \tfrac{1}{2}(u_0 + u_1) + y\Delta u_0 + \frac{y^2 - \frac{1}{4}}{2!}\tfrac{1}{2}(\Delta^2 u_{-1} + \Delta^2 u_0)$$

$$+ \frac{y(y^2 - \frac{1}{4})}{3!}\Delta^3 u_{-1} + \frac{(y^2 - \frac{1}{4})(y^2 - \frac{9}{4})}{4!}\tfrac{1}{2}(\Delta^4 u_{-2} + \Delta^4 u_{-1}) + ...,$$

the most convenient shape of the formula for practical purposes.

7. An alternative method of obtaining Gauss's forward formula for equal intervals is as follows:

The ordinary advancing difference expansion is

$$u_x = u_0 + x_{(1)}\Delta u_0 + x_{(2)}\Delta^2 u_0 + x_{(3)}\Delta^3 u_0 + x_{(4)}\Delta^4 u_0 + ...$$

Now $\Delta^2 u_0 = \Delta^2 u_{-1} + \Delta^3 u_{-1};$

$$\Delta^3 u_0 = \Delta^3 u_{-1} + \Delta^4 u_{-1}; \quad \Delta^4 u_{-1} = \Delta^4 u_{-2} + \Delta^5 u_{-2};$$

....

Therefore we may write

$$u_x = u_0 + x_{(1)}\Delta u_0 + x_{(2)}(\Delta^2 u_{-1} + \Delta^3 u_{-1})$$
$$+ x_{(3)}(\Delta^3 u_{-1} + \Delta^4 u_{-1}) + x_{(4)}(\Delta^4 u_{-1} + \Delta^5 u_{-1}) + ...$$
$$= u_0 + x_{(1)}\Delta u_0 + x_{(2)}\Delta^2 u_{-1} + (x_{(2)} + x_{(3)})\Delta^3 u_{-1}$$
$$+ (x_{(3)} + x_{(4)})\Delta^4 u_{-1} + ...$$
$$= u_0 + x_{(1)}\Delta u_0 + x_{(2)}\Delta^2 u_{-1} + (x + 1)_{(3)}\Delta^3 u_{-1}$$
$$+ (x + 1)_{(4)}(\Delta^4 u_{-2} + \Delta^5 u_{-2}) + ...,$$

since $$x_{(r)} + x_{(r+1)} = (x + 1)_{(r+1)},$$

and so on.

A proof similar to the above, in which the general term is evolved, and which depends upon the method of separation of symbols, will be found in *J.I.A.* vol. L, pp. 31, 32.

The backward form may be obtained similarly by grouping the terms in a slightly different way and using the relations

$$\Delta u_0 = \Delta u_{-1} + \Delta^2 u_{-1},$$
$$\Delta^2 u_0 = \Delta^2 u_{-1} + \Delta^3 u_{-1},$$
$$\Delta^3 u_{-1} = \Delta^3 u_{-2} + \Delta^4 u_{-2},$$
$$\text{etc.}$$

8. Everett's formula.

The Gauss forward formula with interval x and initial term v_1 may be written

$$v_{x+1} = v_1 + x_{(1)}\Delta v_1 + x_{(2)}\Delta^2 v_0 + (x+1)_{(3)}\Delta^3 v_0 + (x+1)_{(4)}\Delta^4 v_{-1}$$
$$+ (x+2)_{(5)}\Delta^5 v_{-1} + \dots$$

The backward formula with interval $(x-1)$ and initial term v_1 gives

$$v_x = v_1 + (x-1)_{(1)}\Delta v_0 + x_{(2)}\Delta^2 v_0 + x_{(3)}\Delta^3 v_{-1} + (x+1)_{(4)}\Delta^4 v_{-1}$$
$$+ (x+1)_{(5)}\Delta^5 v_{-2} + \dots$$

Subtract the second series from the first: then, since

$$v_{x+1} - v_x = \Delta v_x,$$

we have

$$\Delta v_x = x_{(1)}\Delta v_1 + (x+1)_{(3)}\Delta^3 v_0 + (x+2)_{(5)}\Delta^5 v_{-1} + \dots$$
$$- (x-1)_{(1)}\Delta v_0 - x_{(3)}\Delta^3 v_{-1} - (x+1)_{(5)}\Delta^5 v_{-2} - \dots$$

Put u_x, Δu_x, $\Delta^2 u_x$, ... for Δv_x, $\Delta^2 v_x$, $\Delta^3 v_x$, ...
Then

$$u_x = x_{(1)}u_1 + (x+1)_{(3)}\Delta^2 u_0 + (x+2)_{(5)}\Delta^4 u_{-1} + \dots$$
$$- (x-1)_{(1)}u_0 - x_{(3)}\Delta^2 u_{-1} - (x+1)_{(5)}\Delta^4 u_{-2} - \dots \quad \dots\dots(i)$$

When x is less than unity a convenient form of this formula for interpolation between u_0 and u_1 is obtained by putting $\xi = 1 - x$; thus

$$u_x = xu_1 + \frac{x(x^2-1)}{3!}\Delta^2 u_0 + \frac{x(x^2-1)(x^2-4)}{5!}\Delta^4 u_{-1} + \dots$$
$$+ \xi u_0 + \frac{\xi(\xi^2-1)}{3!}\Delta^2 u_{-1} + \frac{\xi(\xi^2-1)(\xi^2-4)}{5!}\Delta^4 u_{-2} + \dots,$$

the most common form of Everett's formula.

The above elegant proof is due to G. J. Lidstone (*J.I.A.* vol. LX, pp. 349–52). In his note on this formula Mr Lidstone shows how to obtain another formula similar to the above for interpolation between $u_{-\frac{1}{2}}$ and $u_{\frac{1}{2}}$.

If we difference formula (i) bearing in mind that

$$\Delta (x+r)_{(t)} = (x+r)_{(t-1)},$$

we have
$$\Delta u_x = u_1 + (x+1)_{(2)} \Delta^2 u_0 + (x+2)_{(4)} \Delta^4 u_{-1} + \dots$$
$$- u_0 - x_{(2)} \Delta^2 u_{-1} - (x+1)_{(4)} \Delta^4 u_{-2} - \dots,$$

or, writing u_x for Δu_x, Δu_x for $\Delta^2 u_x$ and so on,

$$u_x = u_0 + (x+1)_{(2)} \Delta u_0 + (x+2)_{(4)} \Delta^3 u_{-1} + \dots$$
$$- x_{(2)} \Delta u_{-1} - (x+1)_{(4)} \Delta^3 u_{-2} - \dots.$$

The formula then becomes

$$u_{p-\frac{1}{2}} = u_0 + \frac{p^2 - \frac{1}{4}}{2!} \Delta u_0 + \frac{(p^2 - \frac{1}{4})(p^2 - \frac{9}{4})}{4!} \Delta^3 u_{-1} + \dots$$
$$- \frac{q^2 - \frac{1}{4}}{2!} \Delta u_{-1} - \frac{(q^2 - \frac{1}{4})(q^2 - \frac{9}{4})}{4!} \Delta^3 u_{-2} - \dots,$$

where $p = \frac{1}{2} + x$ and $q = \frac{1}{2} - x$.

This form is generally known as Everett's "second" formula. Both formulae, perhaps more particularly the first, are specially adapted for use in statistical work. They can be applied in the case of unequal intervals: see Todhunter, *J.I.A.* vol. L, p. 137, and Lidstone, *Proc. Edin. Math. Soc.* Series 1, vol. XL, pp. 25–6.

9. Everett's formulae can also be obtained from Gauss's formulae by a simple transformation depending upon the properties of the binomial coefficients.

Any pair of terms of the form

$$y_{(r)} \Delta^r u_t + (y+1)_{(r+1)} \Delta^{r+1} u_t$$
$$= (y+1)_{(r+1)} (\Delta^r u_t + \Delta^{r+1} u_t) - \{(y+1)_{(r+1)} - y_{(r)}\} \Delta^r u_t$$
$$= (y+1)_{(r+1)} \Delta^r u_{t+1} - y_{(r+1)} \Delta^r u_t,$$

since
$$(y+1)_{(r+1)} - y_{(r)} = y_{(r+1)}.$$

Taking the pairs

1–2; 3–4; 5–6 … in Gauss's forward formula,

and 2–3; 4–5; 6–7 … in Gauss's backward formula,

the two forms of Everett's formula are at once obtained.

*10. It is of interest to show in a simple manner the relations between Everett's and Bessel's formulae. The formulae are closely related, and the following demonstration indicates clearly the connection between corresponding coefficients in the two expansions.

In Bessel's formula let b_{2n} denote the coefficient of the "mean" difference

$$\tfrac{1}{2}\,(\Delta^{2n}u_{-n}+\Delta^{2n}u_{-n+1})$$

and b_{2n+1} the coefficient of the difference $\Delta^{2n+1}u_{-n}$.

Then, since

$$\Delta^{2n}u_{-n+1}=\Delta^{2n}u_{-n}+\Delta^{2n+1}u_{-n},$$

the sum of the terms

$$b_{2n}\cdot\tfrac{1}{2}\,(\Delta^{2n}u_{-n}+\Delta^{2n}u_{-n+1})+b_{2n+1}\Delta^{2n+1}u_{-n}$$

may be written as

$$b_{2n}\Delta^{2n}u_{-n}+(\tfrac{1}{2}b_{2n}+b_{2n+1})\,\Delta^{2n+1}u_{-n}. \qquad \ldots\ldots(a)$$

Consider the expression

$$e_{2n}\Delta^{2n}u_{-n}+\epsilon_{2n}\Delta^{2n}u_{-n+1}.$$

This is the same as

$$(e_{2n}+\epsilon_{2n})\,\Delta^{2n}u_{-n}+\epsilon_{2n}\Delta^{2n+1}u_{-n}. \qquad \ldots\ldots(b)$$

Again, by reference to Bessel's formula, it will be seen that

$$b_{2n+1}=\frac{x-\tfrac{1}{2}}{2n+1}\,b_{2n}. \qquad \ldots\ldots(c)$$

Equating (a) and (b), and introducing the relation (c), we have

$$e_{2n}+\epsilon_{2n}=b_{2n},$$

and

$$\epsilon_{2n}=\tfrac{1}{2}b_{2n}+b_{2n+1}$$

$$=b_{2n}\{\tfrac{1}{2}+(x-\tfrac{1}{2})/(2n+1)\}$$

$$=\frac{x+n}{2n+1}\,b_{2n};$$

whence

$$e_{2n}=\tfrac{1}{2}b_{2n}-b_{2n+1}$$

$$=b_{2n}\{\tfrac{1}{2}-(x-\tfrac{1}{2})/(2n+1)\}$$

$$=-\frac{x-n-1}{2n+1}\,b_{2n};$$

from which the coefficients already given in Everett's formula can at once be deduced.

The same analysis applies to each pair of terms.

It should be noted that

(i) ϵ_r and e_r are the same functions of x and $1-x$ respectively;

[In fact,
$$\epsilon_{2n} = (x+n)_{(2n+1)},$$
$$e_{2n} = -(x+n-1)_{(2n+1)}$$
$$= (1-x+n)_{(2n+1)}]$$

(ii) the pair of terms in Everett's formula is exactly equivalent to the corresponding pair in Bessel's formula. In Everett's formula, therefore, precise allowance is made for the next odd difference, although this difference does not appear explicitly.

Similarly, by taking the pair of terms

$$s_{2n+1} \cdot \tfrac{1}{2} \left(\Delta^{2n+1} u_{-n} + \Delta^{2n+1} u_{-n-1} \right)$$
and
$$s_{2n+2} \Delta^{2n+2} u_{-n}$$

in Stirling's formula, Everett's second formula may be obtained.

11. It will be instructive to compare the results brought out by applying first, Gauss's forward formula, and, secondly, the ordinary advancing difference formula, to the same set of data.

Example 1.

Interpolate by means of Gauss's forward formula to find the present value of an annuity of 1 p.a. for 27 years at 5 per cent. compound interest, given the following table:

No. of years	15	20	25	30	35	40
Annuity-value	10·3797	12·4622	14·0939	15·3725	16·3742	17·1591

If we take 25 years as the origin and 5 years as the unit, the value required will be $u_{\cdot 4}$.

x	u_x	Δu_x	$\Delta^2 u_x$	$\Delta^3 u_x$	$\Delta^4 u_x$	$\Delta^5 u_x$
-2	10·3797					
		2·0825				
-1	12·4622		$-\cdot4508$			
		1·6317		·0977		
0	14·0939		$-\cdot3531$		$-\cdot0215$	
		1·2786		·0762		·0054
1	15·3725		$-\cdot2769$		$-\cdot0161$	
		1·0017		·0601		
2	16·3742		$-\cdot2168$			
		·7849				
3	17·1591					

The Gauss forward formula is

$$u_x = u_0 + x_{(1)} \Delta u_0 + x_{(2)} \Delta^2 u_{-1} + (x+1)_{(3)} \Delta^3 u_{-1} + (x+1)_{(4)} \Delta^4 u_{-2}$$
$$+ (x+2)_{(5)} \Delta^5 u_{-2}.$$

When $x = \cdot 4$ the successive coefficients are

$$\cdot 4; \quad -\cdot 12; \quad -\cdot 056; \quad \cdot 0224; \quad \cdot 010752$$

and to four decimal places the value of $u_{\cdot 4}$ is $14 \cdot 6430$, which agrees with the tabulated value.

To apply the advancing difference formula we take 15 years as the origin and are required to find u_x when $x = 2 \cdot 4$.

In the formula

$$u_x = u_0 + x_{(1)} \Delta u_0 + x_{(2)} \Delta^2 u_0 + x_{(3)} \Delta^3 u_0 + x_{(4)} \Delta^4 u_0 + x_{(5)} \Delta^5 u_0$$

the coefficients are

$$2 \cdot 4; \quad 1 \cdot 68; \quad \cdot 224; \quad -\cdot 0336; \quad -\cdot 010752.$$

On evaluating the expansion we obtain for $u_{2 \cdot 4}$ the value $14 \cdot 6430$ as above.

It will be seen that the two results are in agreement (as indeed they must be, since the same values of u are used), and it may be asked therefore wherein lies the advantage of using the central difference formula. This question will be discussed in the next paragraph.

12. Consider an approximation to a particular value of u_x based on, say, r values out of n available. The error in the approximation, as measured approximately by the first neglected term, is least when the coefficient of that term is least. It can be shown that this happens when the values of u_x upon which the interpolation is based range round the space in which x falls, so that x is as nearly as possible central. The central difference formulae give a systematic method for building up the table subject to these conditions.

Again, the central difference coefficients are as a general rule smaller and more rapidly convergent than those required for the calculations in the advancing difference formula (as will be seen in the Example) and, by a suitable choice of origin, the arithmetical work may be reduced to a minimum.

It should be noted that, in the phrase "as measured approximately by the first neglected term", this measure is not theoretically complete;

it is however generally sufficient in practice if the first neglected order of differences is constant or is changing but slowly. When this is not so it will not necessarily be true that a central difference formula beginning with u_0 is more accurate than the advancing difference formula beginning with the same term. [See p. 337 of Sheppard's paper, cited on p. 72.]

We may even make the result worse by introducing differences of a higher order (cf. Chap. V, paragraph 15). In general, however, these anomalous cases arise only rarely.

13. It should be noted that the greater accuracy of central difference formulae as compared with the advancing difference form is not due to the formulae but to placing x in the central interval of the range of the given values. Provided that this is done—which is very important—it is immaterial whether we use a central difference formula or the advancing difference formula with the same u's. A disadvantage of the latter form is that the coefficients are larger and are not tabulated as, in practice, are those of the principal central difference formulae.

14. Relative accuracy of the formulae.

The relative accuracy of the various central difference formulae can be investigated in an elementary manner on the following lines.

The Gauss forward formula is

$$u_x = u_0 + x_{(1)}\Delta u_0 + x_{(2)}\Delta^2 u_{-1} + (x+1)_{(3)}\Delta^3 u_{-1} + (x+1)_{(4)}\Delta^4 u_{-2} + \ldots.$$

If we expand u_x by Stirling's formula as far as a certain order of even differences we shall obtain by a simple transformation the above formula to even differences, for the same u's are involved in both. Similarly, Bessel's formula and Gauss's formula are identical to odd differences. Now the Gauss formula involves only ordinary differences while the other two series involve mean differences of the form $\frac{1}{2}(\Delta^n u_r + \Delta^n u_{r+1})$. If instead of proceeding to constant differences the series stop short at, say, rth differences—which are not constant—the use of any of the formulae will involve an error. It remains to examine which of these formulae gives the best result in different circumstances.

The following demonstration is based on that given in greater detail by Mr D. C. Fraser in *J.I.A.* vol. L, p. 25:

Suppose that x is not greater than $\cdot 5$. Then, by calculating the coefficients in Gauss's formula, it will be found that for positive values of x none of the coefficients (except that multiplying Δu_0) differs greatly from $\pm \cdot 5$ times the preceding coefficient. (See Table, *J.I.A.* vol. L, p. 25.) Thus the terms after that involving the third difference are approximately equal to

$$(x+1)_{(4)} \left(\Delta^4 + \tfrac{1}{2}\Delta^5\right) u_{-2},$$

i.e. to $\qquad (x+1)_{(4)} \tfrac{1}{2} \left(\Delta^4 u_{-2} + \Delta^4 u_{-1}\right).$

If therefore we substitute $\tfrac{1}{2}\left(\Delta^4 u_{-2} + \Delta^4 u_{-1}\right)$, the mean difference in line with $u_{\frac{1}{2}}$, for $\Delta^4 u_{-2}$ in Gauss's formula, we make the formula very nearly correct to fifth differences, without having to calculate the actual coefficient of the fifth difference. The substitution therefore greatly improves the accuracy of the formula.

When, however, the substitution is made, it will be found to reproduce Bessel's formula to the fourth mean difference. Therefore Bessel's formula to fourth mean differences is usually more accurate than Stirling's to the fourth difference.

It may be shown similarly that Stirling's formula to odd mean differences is usually more accurate than Bessel's to the same order of differences.

The above demonstration is only approximate: a strict investigation into the relative accuracy of central and advancing difference formulae requires rather more elaborate mathematical discussion. (See Whittaker and Robinson, *Calculus of Observations*, p. 49; Lidstone, *T.F.A.* vol. IX, pp. 246–57; Fraser, *J.I.A.* vol. L, pp. 25–7; Sheppard, *Proceedings of the London Mathematical Society*, Series 2, vol. IV, pp. 320–41 and vol. X, pp. 139–72.)

Mr D. C. Fraser has given the following criteria summarizing the properties of interpolation formulae:

(i) Formulae which proceed to constant differences are exact and are true for all values of n whether integral or fractional.

(ii) Formulae which stop short of constant differences are approximations.

(iii) Formulae which terminate with the same difference are identically equal, for they involve the same u's.

It should be noted that these rules are quite general; they apply to all formulae based on finite differences, not ending with mean differences.

15. Apart from the general superiority of central difference formulae certain of the formulae possess distinct advantages in special circumstances. For example, for the bisection of an interval Bessel's form is convenient, since the alternate terms are zero. We have, at once,

$$u_{\frac{1}{2}}=\tfrac{1}{2}\left(u_{0}+u_{1}\right)-\tfrac{1}{8}\left[\tfrac{1}{2}\left(\Delta^{2}u_{-1}+\Delta^{2}u_{0}\right)\right]+\tfrac{3}{128}\left[\tfrac{1}{2}\left(\Delta^{4}u_{-2}+\Delta^{4}u_{-1}\right)\right]-\ldots.$$

Again, in using Everett's formula for the subdivision of intervals the terms are such that they may be used twice: they occur both in an "x" expansion and in reverse order in the next "ξ" expansion. An example will make this clear.

Example 2.

Given
x	30	35	40	45	50	55	60
u_x	771	862	1001	1224	1572	2123	2983

obtain values for u_x for all integral values of x between $x=40$ and $x=50$.

The difference table is

x	u_x	Δu_x	$\Delta^2 u_x$	$\Delta^3 u_x$	$\Delta^4 u_x$
30	771				
		91			
35	862		48		
		139		36	
40	1001		84		5
		223		41	
45	1224		125		37
		348		78	
50	1572		203		28
		551		106	
55	2123		309		
		860			
60	2983				

Everett's formula gives

$$u_x = x_{(1)}u_1 + (x+1)_{(3)}\,\Delta^2 u_0 + (x+2)_{(5)}\,\Delta^4 u_{-1} + \dots$$
$$+ \xi_{(1)}u_0 + (\xi+1)_{(3)}\,\Delta^2 u_{-1} + (\xi+2)_{(5)}\,\Delta^4 u_{-2} + \dots,$$

also $\quad u_{1+\xi} = \xi_{(1)}u_2 + (\xi+1)_{(3)}\,\Delta^2 u_1 + (\xi+2)_{(5)}\,\Delta^4 u_0 + \dots$
$$+ x_{(1)}u_1 + (x+1)_{(3)}\,\Delta^2 u_0 + (x+2)_{(5)}\,\Delta^4 u_{-1} + \dots,$$

and the second line in $u_{1+\xi}$ is the same as the first line in u_x.

Since the data are given at quinquennial points and we require values at individual points, we may write $x = \cdot2,\ \cdot4,\ \cdot6,\ \dots$ and $\xi = \cdot8,\ \cdot6,\ \cdot4,\ \dots$. The first line of $u_{\cdot2}$ will be the same as the second line for $u_{1\cdot8}$, but in the reverse order, and so on.

The coefficients of the terms in the first line of the formula for u_x are, to fourth differences,

·2	− ·032	·006336
·4	− ·056	·010752
·6	− ·064	·011648
·8	− ·048	·008064

The work is best arranged in tabular form, thus:

x	xu_1	$\dfrac{x(x^2-1)}{3!}\,\Delta^2 u_0$	$\dfrac{x(x^2-1)(x^2-4)}{5!}\,\Delta^4 u_{-1}$	Sum of first three terms (ii)+(iii) +(iv)	Sum of second three terms	Inter- polated result (v)+(vi)
(i)	(ii)	(iii)	(iv)	(v)	(vi)	(vii)
·2	200·2	− 2·7	0·0	197·5		
·4	400·4	− 4·7	0·1	395·8		
·6	600·6	− 5·4	0·1	595·3		
·8	800·8	− 4·0	0·0	796·8		
·2	244·8	− 4·0	0·2	241·0	796·8	1037·8
·4	489·6	− 7·0	0·4	483·0	595·3	1078·3
·6	734·4	− 8·0	0·4	726·8	395·8	1122·6
·8	979·2	− 6·0	0·3	973·5	197·5	1171·0
·2	314·4	− 6·5	0·2	308·1	973·5	1281·6
·4	628·8	− 11·4	0·3	617·7	726·8	1344·5
·6	943·2	− 13·0	0·3	930·5	483·0	1413·5
·8	1257·6	− 9·7	0·2	1248·1	241·0	1489·1

The only column which needs explanation is column (vi). This column represents the second set of three terms of the formula, correct to fourth central differences, and is obtained by writing down *in the reverse order* the values of the previous column applicable to the sum of the first three terms.

It should be mentioned that the values in column (vii) of the table do not quite agree with the tabular values: the tabular values are 1038, 1081, 1122, 1172, 1281, 1345, 1415, 1490. The reason for this is that the function upon which the original values depend is not a rational integral function of the independent variable and that therefore a formula based on finite differences is only an approximate representation of the function. The example is based on the rates of mortality according to the H^M Table, the data being 10^5 times the probability of dying in the year of age x.

16. The following example is instructive:

Example 3.

Use an appropriate formula to obtain successive approximations to $u_{28\cdot3}$ given $u_{26} = \cdot038462$, $u_{27} = \cdot037037$, $u_{28} = \cdot035714$, $u_{29} = \cdot034483$, $u_{30} = \cdot033333$.

It should be noted that, where the data are extensive and it is required to obtain successive approximations to a result by the use of some or all of the data, it is more advantageous to use a central difference formula than advancing differences.

From the data, we obtain

x	$10^6 u_x$	$10^6 \Delta u_x$	$10^6 \Delta^2 u_x$	$10^6 \Delta^3 u_x$	$10^6 \Delta^4 u_x$
26	38462				
		-1425			
27	37037		102		
		-1323		-10	
28	35714		92		-1
		-1231		-11	
29	34483		81		
		-1150			
30	33333				

In its simple form, Stirling's formula is

$$u_x = u_0 + x \cdot \tfrac{1}{2}(\Delta u_0 + \Delta u_{-1}) + \frac{x^2}{2!}\Delta^2 u_{-1}$$
$$+ \frac{x(x^2 - 1^2)}{3!}\tfrac{1}{2}(\Delta^3 u_{-1} + \Delta^3 u_{-2}) + \frac{x^2(x^2 - 1^2)}{4!}\Delta^4 u_{-2}.$$

Taking the origin at 28 and letting $x = \cdot3$ we have, as a first approximation,

$$u_{\cdot3} = 35714 + \cdot3 \left[\tfrac{1}{2}(-1323 - 1231)\right] = 35331.$$

For the next approximation all that we need do is to add

$$\frac{\cdot 09}{2}\, 92 = 4 \cdot 14.$$

$$\therefore \quad u_{\cdot 3} = 35335 \cdot 14 \text{ (say } 35335).$$

Similarly, the next term is $\dfrac{\cdot 3\,(-\cdot 91)}{6} \cdot \tfrac{1}{2} \cdot (-21)$

$$= \cdot 478 \ldots$$

so that $\qquad u_{\cdot 3} = 35335 \cdot 62 \ldots \text{ (say } 35336).$

The addition of the next term will not affect the last figure. The required successive approximations are therefore

$$\cdot 035331, \quad \cdot 035335, \quad \cdot 035336, \quad \cdot 035336.$$

*17. Sheppard's central difference notation.

Just as $\Delta \equiv E - 1$, or $\Delta u_x = u_{x+1} - u_x$, similar symbolic identities may be deduced from the relations existing between u_x, $u_{x+\frac{1}{2}}$ and $u_{x-\frac{1}{2}}$. Dr Sheppard has introduced the following notation, which is widely used by mathematicians:

$$\delta u_x = u_{x+\frac{1}{2}} - u_{x-\frac{1}{2}},$$

and $\qquad \mu u_x = \tfrac{1}{2}\,(u_{x+\frac{1}{2}} + u_{x-\frac{1}{2}}).$

In this notation the difference table takes the following form:

x	u_x				
$\vdots$	$\vdots$				
-2	u_{-2}				
		$\delta u_{-\frac{3}{2}}$			
-1	u_{-1}		$\delta^2 u_{-1}$		
		$\delta u_{-\frac{1}{2}}$		$\delta^3 u_{-\frac{1}{2}}$	
0	u_0		$\delta^2 u_0$		$\delta^4 u_0$
		$\delta u_{\frac{1}{2}}$		$\delta^3 u_{\frac{1}{2}}$	
1	u_1		$\delta^2 u_1$		
		$\delta u_{\frac{3}{2}}$			
2	u_2				

It is specially to be noted that the subscript corresponds to the argument which falls on the same line as the difference.

The relationships between E, δ and μ are quite easy to establish.

$$\delta \equiv E^{\frac{1}{2}} - E^{-\frac{1}{2}} \equiv E^{-\frac{1}{2}}\,[E-\mathrm{I}] \equiv E^{-\frac{1}{2}}\Delta.$$

$$\therefore \quad \delta^{2n} \equiv E^{-n}\Delta^{2n}.$$

Also $\qquad \mu \equiv \tfrac{1}{2}\,(E^{\frac{1}{2}} + E^{-\frac{1}{2}}),$

and $\qquad \mu\delta \equiv \tfrac{1}{2}\,(E - E^{-1}) \equiv \tfrac{1}{2}\,(\Delta E^{-1} + \Delta),$

$$\mu\delta^{2n+1} \equiv \tfrac{1}{2}\,[E^{-(n-1)} - E^{-(n+1)}]\,\Delta^{2n}$$

$$\equiv \tfrac{1}{2}\,(\Delta E^{-1} + \Delta)\,\Delta^{2n}E^{-n} \equiv \tfrac{1}{2}\Delta^{2n+1}\,(E^{-1} + \mathrm{I})\,E^{-n}.$$

Again $\qquad 2\mu \equiv 2E^{\frac{1}{2}} - \delta,$

or $\qquad E^{\frac{1}{2}} \equiv \mu + \tfrac{1}{2}\delta.$

By means of these symbols the central difference formulae can be written down in very convenient form.

For example, Gauss's forward formula is

$$u_x = u_0 + x_{(1)}\delta u_{\frac{1}{2}} + x_{(2)}\delta^2 u_0 + (x+\mathrm{I})_{(3)}\,\delta^3 u_{\frac{1}{2}} + (x+\mathrm{I})_{(4)}\,\delta^4 u_0 + \dots,$$

and Stirling's becomes

$$u_x = u_0 + x\mu\,\delta u_0 + \tfrac{1}{2}x^2\delta^2 u_0 + (x+\mathrm{I})_{(3)}\,\mu\delta^3 u_0 + \dots.$$

EXAMPLES 4

1. Apply a central difference formula to obtain u_{25}, given $u_{20} = 14$, $u_{24} = 32$, $u_{28} = 35$, $u_{32} = 40$.

2. Given $u_2 = 10$, $u_1 = 8$, $u_0 = 5$, $u_{-1} = 10$, find $u_{\frac{1}{2}}$ by Gauss's forward formula.

3. Use Stirling's formula to find u_{28}, given $u_{20} = 49225$, $u_{25} = 48316$, $u_{30} = 47236$, $u_{35} = 45926$, $u_{40} = 44306$.

4. Given $u_{20} = 2854$, $u_{24} = 3162$, $u_{28} = 3544$, $u_{32} = 3992$; find u_{25} by Bessel's formula.

5. $a_{21} = 18\cdot4708$; $\quad a_{25} = 17\cdot8144$; $\quad a_{29} = 17\cdot1070$; $\quad a_{33} = 16\cdot3432$; $a_{37} = 15\cdot5154$. Find a_{30} by Gauss's forward formula.

6. What are the practical advantages arising from the use of central differences in interpolation?

Employ Stirling's formula to obtain successive approximations to $(1·02125)^{50}$, given

$$(1·01)^{50}=1·64463; \quad (1·02)^{50}=2·69159; \quad (1·03)^{50}=4·38391;$$
$$(1·015)^{50}=2·10524; \quad (1·025)^{50}=3·43711.$$

7. Find formulae true to third differences for the bisection of an interval

(i) in terms of the two nearest values of the function and of differences of the functions;

(ii) in terms of values of the function only.

Apply either formula to find P_{35}, given the values of P_x at 20, 30, 40, 50 to be 1313, 1727, 2392, 3493 respectively.

8. Given the table

x	310	320	330	340	350	360
$\log x$	2·4914	2·5052	2·5185	2·5315	2·5441	2·5563

find the value of $\log 3375$ by a central difference formula.

9. Prove that if third differences are assumed to be constant

$$u_x = xu_1 + \frac{x(x^2-1)}{6}\Delta^2 u_0 + yu_0 + \frac{y(y^2-1)}{6}\Delta^2 u_{-1},$$

where $y = 1 - x$.

Apply this formula to find the values of u_{11} to u_{14} and u_{16} to u_{19}, given that $u_0 = 3010$, $u_5 = 2710$, $u_{10} = 2285$, $u_{15} = 1860$, $u_{20} = 1560$, $u_{25} = 1510$ and $u_{30} = 1835$.

10. From the table of annual net premiums given below find the annual net premium at age 25 by means of Bessel's formula:

Age	Annual net premiums
20	·01427
24	·01581
28	·01772
32	·01996

11. Apply a central difference formula to find $f(32)$, given

$$f(25)=·2707, \quad f(30)=·3027, \quad f(35)=·3386, \quad f(40)=·3794.$$

12. Use Gauss's interpolation formula to obtain the value of $f(41)$, given $f(30)=3678·2$, $f(35)=2995·1$, $f(40)=2400·1$, $f(45)=1876·2$, $f(50)=1416·3$.

Verify your result by using Lagrange's formula over the same figures.

13. Prove the following formulae for the general case of unequal intervals:

(i) $u_x = u_a + A \frac{1}{2} (\triangle u_l + \triangle u_a) + \frac{1}{2} A (B+L) \triangle^2 u_l$

$+ ABL \frac{1}{2} (\triangle^3 u_m + \triangle^3 u_l) + \dots$ (Stirling)

(ii) $u_x = \frac{1}{2} (u_a + u_b) + \frac{1}{2} (A+B) \triangle u_a + AB \frac{1}{2} (\triangle^2 u_l + \triangle^2 u_a)$

$+ \frac{1}{2} (ABC + ABL) \triangle^3 u_l + \dots$ (Bessel)

and show how to obtain a general Everett form.

14. Show that any central difference formula can be developed from Lagrange. Apply a central difference formula obtained thus to find $f(3\frac{1}{2})$, given that $f(2) = 2 \cdot 626$; $f(3) = 3 \cdot 454$; $f(4) = 4 \cdot 784$ and $f(5) = 6 \cdot 986$.

15. Given $u_0, u_1, u_2, u_3, u_4, u_5$ (fifth differences constant), prove that

$$u_{2\frac{1}{2}} = \frac{1}{2}c + \frac{25 (c-b) + 3 (a-c)}{256},$$

where $a = u_0 + u_5$; $b = u_1 + u_4$; $c = u_2 + u_3$.

16. A series is formed by the division of the terms of the two series

| u_x | 1 | 2 | 6 | 24 ... $n!$ |
| v_x | 4 | 20 | 120 | 840 ... $\frac{1}{6}(n+3)!$ |

Obtain an interpolated value for $u_{2\frac{1}{2}}/v_{2\frac{1}{2}}$ of the new series by a central difference formula and compare the result with the quotient of $u_{2\frac{1}{2}}$ by $v_{2\frac{1}{2}}$ in the component series.

17. The following is a difference table written down in Woolhouse's notation:

u_{-2}

      a_{-2}

u_{-1} b_{-1}

      a_{-1} c_{-1}

u_0 b_0 d_0

      a_1 c_1

u_1 b_1

      a_2

u_2

If $a_0 = \frac{1}{2}(a_{-1} + a_1)$ and $c_0 = \frac{1}{2}(c_{-1} + c_1)$, show that Stirling's formula (to fourth differences) can be expressed as

$$u_x = u_0 + Ax + Bx^2 + Cx^3 + Dx^4,$$

where A, B, C, D are functions of a_0, b_0, c_0, d_0 only.

18. Prove that in Woolhouse's notation

$$u_x = u_0 + x_{(1)}a_1 + x_{(2)}b_0 + (x+1)_{(3)}c_1 + (x+1)_{(4)}d_0$$

correct to fourth differences.

19. Show that the sum of the terms of the series $u_{-2}, u_{-1}, u_0, u_1, u_2$ can be expressed in the following form

$$Au_0 + B\delta^2 u_0 + C\delta^4 u_0,$$

where $\delta^2 u_0$ and $\delta^4 u_0$ denote the second and fourth central differences of u_0; and find A, B and C.

20. By splitting up the fraction of the form

$$\frac{u_x}{(x^2 - a^2)(x^2 - b^2)(x^2 - c^2)}$$

into partial fractions, show how to arrive at u_x in terms of known values of the function of which x occupies the central position.

21. If $u_x = Au_0 + B\Delta u_0 + C\Delta^2 u_{-1} + \dots$, i.e. a general expression for u_x in terms of central differences, prove by expressing all differences in terms of advancing differences of u_0 that

$$u_x = u_0 + x_{(1)}\Delta u_0 + x_{(2)}\Delta^2 u_{-1} + (x+1)_{(3)}\Delta^3 u_{-1} + \dots,$$

obtaining the general term in the expansion.

22. Show that in the general divided difference interpolation formula any two successive terms can be reduced to a pair in Everett form.

CHAPTER V

INVERSE INTERPOLATION

1. When performing direct interpolation, values of y corresponding to various values of the argument x are given and we are required to find a value of the entry y corresponding to a value of x intermediate between the given values. If it is required to obtain an interpolated value of the *argument* corresponding to an intermediate value of the *entry*, the process adopted is called "inverse interpolation". In other words, for direct interpolation we assume a curve $y = u_x$ passing through the points (x, y) and estimate the value of y corresponding to some intermediate value x': for inverse interpolation we have a similar curve but are required to find a value of x corresponding to a value y'.

For certain functions we may obtain the result easily. If $y = \sin x$, then $x = \sin^{-1} y$; if $y = x^3$, then $x = y^{\frac{1}{3}}$; if $y = a^x$, then $x = \log y / \log a$. The required values of x can be calculated immediately in these examples.

On the other hand, if the data are simply corresponding numerical values of x and y, all that we can write down is a formula such as Newton's or Stirling's: we must then endeavour to obtain a value for x by solving an equation. For example

$$y = u_x = (1 + \Delta)^x u_0 = u_0 + x_{(1)} \Delta u_0 + x_{(2)} \Delta^2 u_0 + x_{(3)} \Delta^3 u_0 + \dots.$$

If second differences may be assumed constant we have a quadratic equation which can be solved at once. Should this assumption be inadmissible, then we are faced with an equation of higher degree than the second and the solution of such an equation may be very laborious. In these circumstances we resort to approximate methods of solution of the equation.

2. Consider the problem of reversion of series. If

$$y = bx + cx^2 + dx^3 + \dots$$

and we wish to obtain an approximate value for x in terms of y, we may write $x = By + Cy^2 + Dy^3 + \ldots + Ky^n + \ldots$. The coefficients $B, C, D \ldots K \ldots$ may then be found by equating the coefficients of the various powers of x in the identity

$$x = B(bx + cx^2 + \ldots) + C(bx + cx^2 + \ldots)^2 + \ldots.$$

If y is numerically less than unity and we use only n terms in the expansion for x in terms of y—i.e. we let

$$x = By + Cy^2 + \ldots + Ky^n$$

—we are neglecting only y^{n+1} and higher powers. Since y is less than unity, the neglected terms will usually be small.

If however $y = u_x = u_0 + x_{(1)}\Delta u_0 + x_{(2)}\Delta^2 u_0 + \ldots + x_{(n)}\Delta^n u_0 + \ldots$ and we wish to find x from this equation, we cannot with equal safety neglect the terms $x_{(n+1)}\Delta^{n+1}u_0 + \ldots$, for these all contain $x, x^2, x^3 \ldots$.

It is thus seen that the problem of inverse interpolation, although analogous to that of reversion of series, involves considerable difficulties. The best method of approach is from a practical point of view.

Given a problem in direct interpolation, the results obtained by the use of an interpolation formula are justified only on certain assumptions. Similarly, in interpolation by differences for an inverse function the results must be judged practically by the progression of the differences. It may be stated however that if interpolation to nth differences is accurate enough for $f(x)$ it does not follow that the same number of differences will suffice or will be required for the inverse function.

3. The problem of inverse interpolation may be viewed in two ways. We may, by graphic or other indication, observe that the value of x which we require corresponding to some given value of u_x lies in a certain narrow interval. Thus, if we are given the following table:

Rate of interest

per cent.	$2\frac{1}{2}$	3	$3\frac{1}{2}$	4	$4\frac{1}{2}$	5
Annuity-value	8·7521	8·5302	8·3166	8·1109	7·9127	7·7217

and we are asked to find the rate of interest for which the annuity-value is 8·000, we may take the interval 4–4½ as the interval (0, 1) or $(-\frac{1}{2}, +\frac{1}{2})$ and write down an interpolation formula, using only a quadratic or cubic function. As the interval and the values of the variable are small and the differences are rapidly decreasing, the solution of such an equation will, in general, give sufficiently satisfactory results. If the equation is a quadratic the solution will present no difficulty; for a cubic various methods are available, some of which are discussed later.

4. Alternatively, we may exchange the dependent and independent variables. That is, given a table of $y = u_x$ we may use the inverse function $x = v_y$.

This method of interchanged variables is subject to very severe restrictions on the function u_x over the range of values used. In the first place, u_x must be strictly monotonic—i.e. uniformly increasing or decreasing—over the range of values given and the unknown value of x, the value of x in all practical cases lying not outside, but within the given range and near the middle of it. If u_x is not strictly monotonic, the inverse function becomes two-valued at least—possibly many-valued—and hence cannot be represented by a polynomial. In these circumstances the ordinary methods of finite difference interpolation are unsafe.

In consequence, before this method of inverse interpolation can be attempted we must have some extraneous knowledge, graphical or otherwise, of the nature of the function u_x. We must usually, in fact, be able to see roughly the position of x. These conditions being premised and being generally satisfied, the necessity for a sufficient number of values of u_x and a small enough interval is naturally seen.

5. The point here made is clearly brought out by a consideration of the following example.

Example 1.

Obtain a value for x when $u_x = 19$, given the following values:

x	0	1	2
u_x	0	1	20

There would seem to be two possible methods at our disposal:

(i) We might write down at once (if we think it safe to assume that second differences are constant)

$$y = u_x = (1 + \Delta)^x\, u_0 = u_0 + x_{(1)}\Delta u_0 + x_{(2)}\Delta^2 u_0;$$

i.e. $$19 = x + 9\,(x^2 - x),$$

so that $$9x^2 - 8x - 19 \doteq 0,$$

from which $$x = 1{\cdot}964 \dots \quad \text{or} \quad -1{\cdot}075 \dots.$$

(ii) Since we have to find an interpolated value of x corresponding to a value of y we might treat y as the argument and x as the entry. Let us write the data in the form

y	0	1	20
$x = v_y$	0	1	2

and apply the Lagrange formula to calculate v_{19} as if for direct interpolation.

We shall have

$$\frac{v_{19}}{19.18.(-1)} = \frac{1}{18.1.(-19)} + \frac{2}{(-1).20.19}$$

or $$v_{19} = 2{\cdot}8.$$

It will be seen therefore that we have obtained two distinct sets of results. By adopting the first method x has the values $1{\cdot}964\dots$ or $-1{\cdot}075\dots$ and by adopting the second method x has the unique value $2{\cdot}8$. It remains to examine the reasons for the difference and to ascertain which result, if any, is more likely to approximate to the true interpolated value or values.

In the first method it will be apparent that we have taken a curve of parabolic form, $y = a + bx + cx^2$, and have obtained values of x corresponding to $y = 19$. This gives two values of x, one on each side of the vertex of the parabola. In applying the Lagrange formula inversely we have assumed that x is a quadratic function of y and have given y a particular value (19) in the equation $x = \alpha + \beta y + \gamma y^2$. If we substitute the value of y corresponding to each value of x from the data, it is easily seen that $\alpha = 0$, $\beta = 398/380$ and $\gamma = -18/380$. The Lagrange equation is therefore $190x = 199y - 9y^2$.

Now if the two curves

$$y = 9x^2 - 8x$$

and
$$x = \frac{199}{190} y - \frac{9}{190} y^2$$

be plotted on the same graph, it will be seen that they take different shapes, thus:

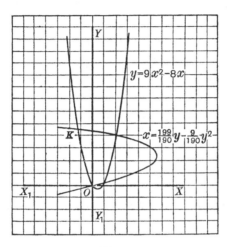

Fig. 1.

On the curve $y = 9x^2 - 8x$ the abscissae of the points whose ordinates are 19 are 1·96... and $-1·07...$, whereas on the other curve there is only one point for which the ordinate is 19, namely the point (2·8, 19). Unless therefore the two curves obtained from the data, (i) by treating x as the argument and (ii) by treating y as the argument, intersect at the required interpolated value, as for example at K in the above figure, the two methods are bound to give different results.

6. Although there would seem to be three different and possible answers to the question above, we must be very careful before we draw any conclusions from the results.

In the first place, we are not told, and have no right to assume, that $\Delta^2 u_x$ is constant, and that consequently second difference interpolation for y is sufficient. On the data as given the only conclusion would be that they are inadequate either for direct or inverse interpolation.

Secondly, even if we may assume that $\Delta^2 u_x$ is constant, we see that

(a) a portion of the curve over the given range, namely from $x = 0$ to $x = 1$, is non-monotonic and one of the essential conditions set out in paragraph 4 is thereby infringed;

(b) notwithstanding the assumption that second differences may be used for direct interpolation, we are not justified in assuming that this order of differences is sufficient for inverse interpolation: we cannot therefore safely use Lagrange's formula.

If we make the assumption that second differences are constant, we cannot properly use the point (0, 0) for inverse interpolation, as the given values do not indicate the form of the curve between $x = 0$ and $x = 1$. By omitting the value (0, 0) and using the values for y when $x = 1, 2, 3$ and 4, a more satisfactory interpolated value can be found. The student should attempt this by one of the methods described below.

7. The formulae of direct interpolation are based on the properties of rational integral functions of the variable, and any formula which proceeds to nth differences gives exact results when applied to a rational integral function of the nth degree. By stopping short of nth differences the formula can, of course, be used to obtain approximate results, and the success of the interpolation depends on the magnitude of the terms omitted. Thus, if we use rth differences for a polynomial of the nth degree in x, the result is the exact value of terms up to and including the term in x^r. The terms beyond x^r are disregarded, and this can only be done legitimately if they are relatively unimportant.

In questions of direct interpolation there is only one value of y, i.e. of u_x, for a given value of x. There may be, however, more than one value of x for a given value of y. In fact, if y is a polynomial in x, x is a polynomial in y only when both functions are of the first degree. In other cases the inverse function may be an infinite series or an irrational function. For example, in the H^M Table of Mortality there is only one value of d_x for a given value of l_x (where l_x represents the number of persons attaining exact age x in any year of time, and d_x is the number of these who die before reaching age $x+1$). In the neighbourhood of the peak of the death curve, however, there will be two values of l_x within a short range of interpolation for a given value in d_x.

For these reasons the subject of inverse interpolation is more troublesome than that of direct interpolation, although it should always be remembered that the conditions attaching to the differences of u_x for direct interpolation are the same as those attaching to the differences of v_y for inverse interpolation. One principal condition is that within the range of interpolation there should be only one value of x corresponding to a given value of y.

Let us consider the equation in Example 1, namely
$$y = -8x + 9x^2,$$
where the range of interpolation is from 0 to 2. The first point to note is that the function is not a good subject for direct interpolation except when the formula is applied to its fullest extent—the second degree. The reason is that the last term is the predominating term throughout the greater part of the range.

In most instances, by altering the interval and reducing the range of interpolation, a function can be reduced to a good form for direct interpolation. Such a question as the following might be put:

Given the function $y = u_x = -8x + 9x^2$, for what intervals of x should u_x be tabulated so that in any interval an interpolated value of y can be obtained by first difference interpolation with an error less than, say, ·001?

Put $\qquad\qquad\qquad x = z/a;$

then $\qquad\qquad u_x = v_z = -\dfrac{8z}{a} + \dfrac{9z^2}{a^2},$

i.e. $\qquad\qquad a^2 v_z = -8az + 9z^2,$

$\qquad\qquad\qquad a^2 \Delta v_z = -8a + 18z + 9,$

and $$a^2 \Delta^2 v_z = 18,$$

so that $$\Delta^2 v_z = 18/a^2.$$

Suppose v_z to be tabulated for values of z at unit intervals. Then, for an interpolated value v_{z+t} between v_z and v_{z+1},

$$v_{z+t} = v_z + t\Delta v_z + \tfrac{1}{2}t\,(t-1)\,\Delta^2 v_z.$$

If we take $v_z + t\Delta v_z$ as the interpolated value, there is an error $\tfrac{1}{2}t\,(t-1)\,\Delta^2 v_z$ and the maximum numerical value of $\tfrac{1}{2}t\,(t-1)$ is $\tfrac{1}{8}$, being the value when t is $\tfrac{1}{2}$.

Therefore, by the conditions,

$$\tfrac{1}{2}t\,(t-1)\,\Delta^2 v_z < \cdot 001,$$

$$\tfrac{1}{8}\Delta^2 v_z < \cdot 001.$$

But $\Delta^2 v_z = 18/a^2,$ $\quad \therefore \quad 18/8a^2 < \cdot 001;$

i.e. $$a^2 > 18000/8,$$

i.e. $$> 2250,$$

or $$a > \sqrt{2250},$$

and the most convenient value for a is 50.

We must therefore tabulate u_x at intervals of $\tfrac{1}{50}$ of unity, i.e. at intervals of $\cdot 02$.

For example, $$y = u_x = -8x + 9x^2.$$

x	z	$u_x = v_z$	Δv_z
1·10	55	2·0900	
			·2396
1·12	56	2·3296	
			·2468
1·14	57	2·5764	
			·2540
1·16	58	2·8304	
			·2612
1·18	59	3·0916	
			·2684
1·20	60	3·3600	

Both for direct and inverse interpolation this table is better than one proceeding by larger intervals. It must not be assumed, however, that a table which is good for direct interpolation is necessarily good for inverse interpolation: in particular, inverse interpolation always presents difficulties if $\Delta u_x / \Delta x$ is small.

8. Practical methods of inverse interpolation.

It is evident that the problem of inverse interpolation is the same as that of direct interpolation for unequal intervals. The methods of Lagrange or of divided differences can therefore be employed to obtain any intermediate value of x corresponding to a value of y, given a table of $y = u_x$, by the use of the inverse relation $x = v_y$. Alternatively, we may treat the problem as one involving the approximate solution of an algebraic equation. Two of the methods often adopted in practice are given below. They are simple to apply and generally lead to satisfactory results. There are, however, certain objections to the methods—for example, it is difficult to ascertain the degree of accuracy which has been reached in the approximate answers—and for many purposes the most convenient and practical plans are probably Aitken's methods of cross-means, to which reference is made in Chapter VIII.

9. Successive approximation.

In the first place we obtain either by inspection or by a rough graph two values of x lying on either side of the required interpolated value. (For example, a value for x when y is zero in the function $y = x^2 - 4x + 2$, i.e. a solution of the equation $x^2 - 4x + 2 = 0$, lies between the values $x = 0$ and $x = 1$.) We then choose a suitable origin and unit of differencing so that if x be the interpolated value and lies between two successive values of the argument, the interval will be small and x will be as near to the origin as possible.

Suppose that the required value lies between 0 and 1.

The method proceeds as follows:

$$u_x = u_0 + x\Delta u_0 + \tfrac{1}{2}x\,(x-1)\,\Delta^2 u_0 + \tfrac{1}{6}x\,(x-1)\,(x-2)\,\Delta^3 u_0 + \ldots.$$

Since x is small, a first approximation (α_1) will be obtained by neglecting terms involving second and higher differences of u_0.

$$\therefore \quad u_x = u_0 + \alpha_1 \Delta u_0 \text{ approximately,}$$

i.e. $\alpha_1 = (u_x - u_0)/\Delta u_0,$ first approximation.

Again, neglecting third and higher differences, we may write

$$u_x = u_0 + \alpha_2 \Delta u_0 + \tfrac{1}{2}\alpha_2 (\alpha_1 - 1)\, \Delta^2 u_0,$$

where α_2 is a second approximation and is therefore not very different from α_1. This gives

$$\alpha_2 = \frac{u_x - u_0}{\Delta u_0 + \tfrac{1}{2}(\alpha_1 - 1)\,\Delta^2 u_0}, \text{ second approximation.}$$

Similarly

$$\alpha_3 = \frac{u_x - u_0}{\Delta u_0 + \tfrac{1}{2}(\alpha_2 - 1)\,\Delta^2 u_0 + \tfrac{1}{6}(\alpha_2 - 1)(\alpha_2 - 2)\,\Delta^3 u_0},$$

and so on.   third approximation,

10. Elimination of third differences.

We have, as far as third differences, by expressing u_x in terms of $u_0, \Delta u_0, \ldots$,

$$u_x = u_0 + x\Delta u_0 + \tfrac{1}{2}x\,(x-1)\,\Delta^2 u_0 + \tfrac{1}{6}x\,(x-1)\,(x-2)\,\Delta^3 u_0.$$

Also, in terms of $u_1, \Delta u_1, \ldots$,

$$u_x = u_1 + (x-1)\,\Delta u_1 + \tfrac{1}{2}(x-1)(x-2)\,\Delta^2 u_1$$
$$+ \tfrac{1}{6}(x-1)(x-2)(x-3)\,\Delta^3 u_1.$$

If now we ignore the terms containing third differences and multiply both sides of the first equation by $3 - \alpha$ and both sides of the second equation by α (where α is an approximation to the required value, found by inspection or otherwise) and add, a new quadratic equation in x will be formed. The error involved in ignoring the third differences will be small, since

$$\tfrac{1}{6}x\,(x-1)(x-2)(3-\alpha)\,\Delta^3 u_0 + \tfrac{1}{6}\alpha\,(x-1)(x-2)(x-3)\,\Delta^3 u_1$$

will be small provided that $\Delta^3 u_0$ and $\Delta^3 u_1$ are not very different.

11. The following question is solved by both these methods:

Example 2.

Find the value of x for which y is 18,600, given

x	52	53	54	55	56
y	19,231	18,868	18,519	18,182	17,855

Changing the origin, the difference table is

x	y	Δy	$\Delta^2 y$	$\Delta^3 y$
0	19,231			
		−363		
1	18,868		14	
		−349		−2
2	18,519		12	
		−337		−2
3	18,182		10	
		−327		
4	17,855			

By the ordinary advancing difference formula

$$18,600 = 19,231 - 363x + \frac{14x\,(x-1)}{2!} - \frac{2x\,(x-1)\,(x-2)}{3!},$$

where the value of x is required corresponding to the value 18,600 of y.

(i) Successive approximation.

Since x is small, a first approximation will be

$$\alpha_1 = \frac{19,231 - 18,600}{363} \quad \text{or} \quad 1\cdot7383\ldots.$$

Including the next term,

$$\alpha_2 = \frac{631}{363 - 7\,(\alpha_1 - 1)} \quad \text{or} \quad 1\cdot7634\ldots.$$

Similarly,

$$\alpha_3 = \frac{631}{363 - 7\,(\alpha_2 - 1) + \frac{1}{3}\,(\alpha_2 - 1)\,(\alpha_2 - 2)} \quad \text{or} \quad 1\cdot7646\ldots.$$

The required result is therefore $52 + 1\cdot7646\ldots = 53\cdot7646\ldots$, where, it should be noted, the last digit is uncertain.

(ii) Elimination of third differences.

We have

$$18,600 = u_x = (1 + \Delta)^x\, u_0 = 19,231 - 363x + 7x\,(x-1) - \tfrac{1}{3}x\,(x-1)\,(x-2)$$

and

$$18,600 = u_x = (1 + \Delta)^{x-1}\, u_1 = 18,868 - 349\,(x-1) + 6\,(x-1)\,(x-2)$$
$$- \tfrac{1}{3}\,(x-1)\,(x-2)\,(x-3).$$

By inspection a rough value of the interpolated value is $1\cdot75$, allowing for the change of origin.

If, therefore, we multiply the two equations by $(3 - 1\cdot75)$ and $1\cdot75$ respectively, and add, we may neglect the fourth term. The factors being $1\cdot25$ and $1\cdot75$ we can use 5 and 7: we thus obtain

$$12 \times 18{,}600 = 5\,[19{,}231 - 363x + 7x\,(x-1)]$$
$$+ 7\,[18{,}868 - 349\,(x-1) + 6\,(x-1)\,(x-2)]$$

or $$223{,}200 = 230{,}758 - 4419x + 77x^2,$$

i.e. $$77x^2 - 4419x + 7558 = 0.$$

Solving the quadratic, the value required is $x = 1\cdot7646...,$ which agrees with the value of α_3 in method (i) to four decimal places.

12. In Example 2 the advancing difference formula has been used; in practice, however, it is more usual for many reasons to employ a central difference formula as the basic equation. Central difference formulae are more convenient because the coefficients are smaller and converge more quickly; this in itself is a decided advantage. Having placed x in the middle interval the first approximation is generally much more accurate (thus, in Example 2, the use of Stirling's formula gives

$$\alpha_1 = 1 + 268/356$$
$$= 1\cdot753).$$

Also, x is smaller, and the maximum number of significant digits which the data will yield may mean an additional place.

Consider the following example.

Example 3.

Find the root of the equation $x^3 - 9x - 14 = 0$ which lies between 3 and 4.

Let $y = x^3 - 9x - 14$. Then we have, by actual calculation,

x	$3\cdot0$	$3\cdot2$	$3\cdot4$	$3\cdot6$	$3\cdot8$	$4\cdot0$
y	$-14\cdot000$	$-10\cdot032$	$-5\cdot296$	$\cdot256$	$6\cdot672$	$14\cdot000$

The difference table is

x	y	Δy	$\Delta^2 y$	$\Delta^3 y$
3·0	−14·000			
		3·968		
3·2	−10·032		·768	
		4·736		·048
3·4	− 5·296		·816	
		5·552		·048
3·6	·256		·864	
		6·416		·048
3·8	6·672		·912	
		7·328		
4·0	14·000			

Taking the origin at 3·6 and using Stirling's formula:

$$u_x = u_0 + x\,\frac{\Delta u_0 + \Delta u_{-1}}{2} + \frac{x^2}{2}\,\Delta^2 u_{-1} + \frac{x\,(x^2 - 1)}{6}\,\frac{\Delta^3 u_{-1} + \Delta^3 u_{-2}}{2},$$

the interval of differencing being 0·2;

i.e. $\qquad 0 = ·256 + 5·984x + ·432x^2 + ·008x\,(x^2 - 1).$

The cubic equation can be solved by successive approximation, or we can repeat Stirling's formula for the next value of u_x and adopt the alternative method outlined above.

If the first of these methods be adopted, it will be found that successive approximations to the value of x are $-·04278$, $-·042913$, $-·042971$. From the last we obtain as the required solution

$$3·6 - (·042971 \times ·2) \quad \text{or} \quad 3·5914058,$$

which is correct to six decimal places, the seventh being nearer to 7.

If we choose our origin at the point (x, y) and the value of the interpolated value is $x + \alpha$, then, when α lies between $-\frac{1}{4}$ and $\frac{1}{4}$, it is advantageous to use Stirling's formula. If α lies between $\frac{1}{4}$ and $\frac{3}{4}$ Bessel's formula should be applied. (Whittaker and Robinson, *Interpolation*, p. 60.)

13. In general, if Δu_x has n significant digits we cannot rely on more than n significant digits in x. Even then the last digit is doubtful and may in fact be misleading. In Example 3 above we have been able to obtain the fifth significant digit in ·042971 from a four-figure value of Δy only because y and Δy happen quite unusually to be exact and not rounded off.

14. The method of successive approximation is a convenient method for ordinary use. If we want a result that can be obtained to the required degree of accuracy by taking out differences as far as $\Delta^3 u$, or if the curve is a cubic, the elimination method will give a satisfactory answer. The disadvantage of this process is that we cannot approach our interpolated value by steps as is done in the method of successive approximation. Moreover when fourth and higher differences are not negligible the elimination method breaks down.

15. The general investigation of the accuracy of finite difference methods of approximation is a problem in direct interpolation, and has been dealt with previously. In dealing with the subject of successive approximation, however, it is of interest to include in the present chapter an elementary illustration of the fact that in certain circumstances a better interpolation can be obtained by neglecting higher differences than by retaining them.

For example, if we have a third difference curve, then

$$u_x = u_0 + x_{(1)}\Delta u_0 + x_{(2)}\Delta^2 u_0 + x_{(3)}\Delta^3 u_0 \text{ exactly.}$$

The error (α) in taking two terms is $x_{(2)}\Delta^2 u_0 + x_{(3)}\Delta^3 u_0$,

and (β) in taking three terms is $x_{(3)}\Delta^3 u_0$.

(α) may be expressed as

$$\frac{x(x-1)(x-2)}{6}\left[\frac{3}{x-2}\frac{\Delta^2 u_0}{\Delta^3 u_0}+1\right]\Delta^3 u_0,$$

and (β) as $\dfrac{x(x-1)(x-2)}{6}\Delta^3 u_0.$

Then, ignoring the sign of $\dfrac{x(x-1)(x-2)}{6}\Delta^3 u_0$, which will be the same for both (α) and (β), (α) will be less than (β) if

$$\frac{3}{x-2}\frac{\Delta^2 u_0}{\Delta^3 u_0}$$

is negative and numerically less than 2.

In these circumstances the error made by retaining first differences only is less than that made in continuing to second differences.

As an illustration consider the function $x^3 + 5x + 50$.

It is easily seen that $u_0 = 50$; $\Delta u_0 = 6$; $\Delta^2 u_0 = 6$; $\Delta^3 u_0 = 6$. If x is $\frac{1}{4}$, for example, $\dfrac{3}{x-2}\dfrac{\Delta^2 u_0}{\Delta^3 u_0} = -3/1\frac{3}{4}$, which is negative and less than 2.

(α) is therefore less than (β).

This can be otherwise shown by finding the values of the errors.

$$u_{\frac{1}{4}} = 51\tfrac{17}{64} \text{ exactly.}$$

Also
$$u_{\frac{1}{4}} = (1+\Delta)^{\frac{1}{4}} u_0$$
$$= u_0 + \tfrac{1}{4}\Delta u_0 - \tfrac{3}{32}\Delta^2 u_0 + \dots,$$
$$u_0 + \tfrac{1}{4}\Delta u_0 = 51\tfrac{1}{2} = 51\tfrac{32}{64},$$
$$u_0 + \tfrac{1}{4}\Delta u_0 - \tfrac{3}{32}\Delta^2 u_0 = 50\tfrac{15}{16} = 50\tfrac{60}{64},$$
$$51\tfrac{32}{64} - 51\tfrac{17}{64} = \tfrac{15}{64}, \qquad \dots\dots(\alpha)$$

and
$$51\tfrac{17}{64} - 50\tfrac{60}{64} = \tfrac{21}{64}. \qquad \dots\dots(\beta)$$

(α) is less than (β), so that the approximation to first differences is better than that to second differences.

16. In conclusion it should be emphasized that the accuracy of the result depends greatly on the fineness of the interval of tabulation. In cases of doubt it may be desirable to halve the interval before applying the process of inverse interpolation. This will reduce first differences by about one-half, second differences in the ratio of about $1:4$, third differences in the ratio of about $1:8$, and so on. The comparative effect of higher differences is therefore much reduced.

EXAMPLES 5

1. Given $u_1 = 0$, $u_2 = 112$, $u_3 = 287$, $u_5 = 612$, find u_4. Using u_1, u_2, u_3 and u_4, find a value for x when $u_x = 270$.

2. The following values of u_x are given: $u_{10} = 544$, $u_{15} = 1227$, $u_{20} = 1775$. Find, correct to one decimal place, the value of x for which $u_x = 1000$.

3. Having given $\log 1 = 0$, $\log 2 = \cdot30103$, $\log 3 = \cdot47712$ and $\log 4 = \cdot60206$, find the number whose logarithm is $\cdot30500$:

(i) by expressing $\log x$ in terms of $\log 1$ and its differences and solving for x;

(ii) by using Lagrange's formula applied inversely.

Explain the nature of the assumptions in each case.

4. Apply Lagrange's formula inversely to find to one decimal place the age for which the annuity-value is $13\cdot6$, given the following table:

Age x	30	35	40	45	50
Annuity-value at $4\frac{1}{2}$ per cent. a_x	15·9	14·9	14·1	13·3	12·5

5. $f(0) = 16\cdot35$, $f(5) = 14\cdot88$, $f(10) = 13\cdot59$, $f(15) = 12\cdot46$. Find x when $f(x) = 14\cdot00$.

6. Given the following table of $f(x)$:

$$f(0) = 217, \quad f(1) = 140, \quad f(2) = 23, \quad f(3) = -6,$$

find approximately the value of x for which the function is zero.

7. The following values of $f(x)$ are given:

$$f(10) = 1754, \quad f(15) = 2648, \quad f(20) = 3564.$$

Find, correct to one decimal place, the value of x for which $f(x) = 3000$.

8. Given four values of a function u_0, u_1, u_2, u_3, show how to calculate an approximate value for x from the equation

$$u_x = u_0 + x\Delta u_0 + \frac{x(x-1)}{2!}\Delta^2 u_0 + \frac{x(x-1)(x-2)}{3!}\Delta^3 u_0$$

by obtaining a quadratic equation in place of a cubic.

Use the method to find x when $u_x = 1\cdot05$, given $u_{1\cdot0} = 1\cdot0000$, $u_{1\cdot1} = 1\cdot0323$, $u_{1\cdot2} = 1\cdot0627$, $u_{1\cdot3} = 1\cdot0914$.

9. Given that $(1\cdot20)^3 = 1\cdot728$, $(1\cdot21)^3 = 1\cdot772$, $(1\cdot22)^3 = 1\cdot816$, $(1\cdot23)^3 = 1\cdot861$, $(1\cdot24)^3 = 1\cdot907$, explain carefully how to find the real root of the equation $x^3 + x - 3 = 0$ by a method of inverse interpolation. What method would you adopt in practice? Obtain a value for the root to four decimal places.

10. The following table is available:

Age x	44	45	46	47
a_x at $4\frac{1}{2}$ per cent.	13·40	13·16	12·93	12·68

Find, to two decimal places, the age corresponding to an annuity of $13\cdot00$.

11. Find, to two decimal places, the real root of the equation
$$x^3 + x - 5 = 0$$
by means of divided differences applied inversely, using the values of the expression when $x = 0$, 1, 2 and 3.

What is the reason for the poor result obtained in this case?

(The true solution is $x = 1.516$ approximately.)

12. The equation $x^3 - 6x - 11 = 0$ has a root between 3 and 4. Obtain it by inverse interpolation correct to three places of decimals.

13. The formula for the value of an annuity-certain for n years at rate per cent. i is given by
$$a_{\overline{n}|} = \frac{1 - v^n}{i}, \text{ where } v = (1 + i)^{-1}.$$

Given the following table, obtain to three decimal places the rate per cent. for which $a_{\overline{20}|}$ is 14:

Rate per cent.	3	$3\frac{1}{2}$	4	$4\frac{1}{2}$
$a_{\overline{20}|}$	14·8775	14·2124	13·5903	13·0079

14. Solve the equation $x = 10 \log_{10} x$, given the following data:

Argument x	1·35	1·36	1·37	1·38
$\log x$ ...	·1303	·1335	·1367	·1399

15. Apply Lagrange's formula (inversely) to find a root of the equation $u_x = 0$, when $u_{30} = -30$, $u_{34} = -13$, $u_{38} = 3$, $u_{42} = 18$.

CHAPTER VI

SUMMATION

1. Certain series whose law is given or of which there are sufficient terms to enable the law to be assumed may be summed by the methods of finite differences.

By definition we have

$$f(a+h)-f(a)=\Delta f(a)=\phi(a), \text{ say,}$$
$$f(a+2h)-f(a+h)=\Delta f(a+h)=\phi(a+h),$$

....

$$f(a+nh)-f(a+\overline{n-1}h)=\Delta f(a+\overline{n-1}h)=\phi(a+\overline{n-1}h);$$

$$\therefore \quad f(a+nh)-f(a)=\phi(a)+\phi(a+h)+\ldots+\phi(a+\overline{n-1}h).$$

If therefore $f(x)$ is the function whose first difference is $\phi(x)$ we can find the sum of any number of terms of the series whose general term is $\phi(x)$ in terms of values of $f(x)$, for any given interval of differencing.

By a suitable change of origin and scale we can make the interval of differencing unity and the first term of the algebraic series under consideration $\phi(1)$. On putting a and h each $=1$, the required relation then becomes

$$\sum_{1}^{n}\phi(x)=f(n+1)-f(1).$$

The expression $f(n+1)-f(1)$ is sometimes written in the form

$$\left[f(x)\right]_{1}^{n+1}.$$

This represents the process of substituting $n+1$ and 1 for x successively in $f(x)$ and deducting the second result from the first.

Note. It should be remembered that $\sum_{a}^{b}\phi(x)$ leads to $\left[f(x)\right]_{a}^{b+1}$ and not to $\left[f(x)\right]_{a}^{b}$.

2. Although any function of x can be differenced, there is only a limited number of functions which are the first differences of other explicit functions. The principal forms of such functions are given below.

(i) It can be easily seen that, since $\Delta a^x = (a-1)\, a^x$,

$$\Delta \left\{ \frac{a^x}{a-1} \right\} = a^x.$$

$\therefore \dfrac{a^x}{a-1}$ is the function whose difference is a^x.

We can therefore find $\sum\limits_{1}^{n} u_x$ by the method above if u_x is of the form ka^x.

(ii) The relations $\Delta x^{(m)} = mx^{(m-1)}$ and $\Delta x_{(m)} = x_{(m-1)}$ enable the sum of any series whose nth term can be expressed in the factorial notation to be summed immediately.

Example 1.

Sum to n terms the series whose xth term is $x\,(x-1)\,(x-2)$.

Now
$$x\,(x-1)\,(x-2) = x^{(3)},$$
and since
$$\Delta x^{(4)} = 4x^{(3)},$$

$$\begin{aligned}
\sum_{1}^{n} x^{(3)} &= \left[\tfrac{1}{4} x^{(4)} \right]_{1}^{n+1} \\
&= \tfrac{1}{4}\left[(n+1)^{(4)} - 1^{(4)} \right] \\
&= \tfrac{1}{4}\,(n+1)\,n\,(n-1)\,(n-2),
\end{aligned}$$

since the product of four successive terms of which 1 is the first includes 0 and is therefore obviously zero.

If the interval of differencing does not happen to be unity the identity $\Delta x^{(m)} = mhx^{(m-1)}$ may be applied, but care must be taken in doing so. Here $x^{(m-1)}$ is the difference of the function $x^{(m)}/mh$, so that in summing a series whose xth term is, for example, $2x\,(2x-2)\,(2x-4)$, we must divide $2x\,(2x-2)\,(2x-4)\,(2x-6)$ by $h=2$ as well as by $m=4$ before taking the limits $n+1$ and 1.

(iii) Any polynomial $P_n\,(x)$ of the nth degree can be expressed by an interpolation formula ending with $\Delta^n u_x$ in which each coefficient is of the form $x_{(m)}$ or $\tfrac{1}{2}\left[x_{(m)} + (x+1)_{(m)} \right]$.

Since $\qquad x_{(r)} = (x+1)_{(r+1)} - x_{(r+1)}$

$$= \Delta x_{(r+1)},$$

it follows that $\qquad \Sigma x_{(r)} = x_{(r+1)}.$

Each term of the formula can therefore be summed at sight. Thus, the advancing difference formula

$$u_{a+x} = u_a + x_{(1)}\Delta u_a + x_{(2)}\Delta^2 u_a + x_{(3)}\Delta^3 u_a + \ldots$$

yields $\quad \Sigma u_{a+x} = x_{(1)}u_a + x_{(2)}\Delta u_a + x_{(3)}\Delta^2 u_a + x_{(4)}\Delta^3 u_a + \ldots.$

The Gauss forward formula in its simple form is

$$u_x = u_0 + x_{(1)}\Delta u_0 + x_{(2)}\Delta^2 u_{-1} + (x+1)_{(3)}\Delta^3 u_{-1} + \ldots$$

and therefore

$$\Sigma u_x = x_{(1)}u_0 + x_{(2)}\Delta u_0 + x_{(3)}\Delta^2 u_{-1} + (x+1)_{(4)}\Delta^3 u_{-1} + \ldots.$$

Stirling's formula may be written in Sheppard's notation as

$$u_x = u_0 + x_{(1)}\mu\delta u_0 + \tfrac{1}{2}\left[(x+1)_{(2)} + x_{(2)}\right]\delta^2 u_0 + (x+1)_{(3)}\mu\delta^3 u_0 + \ldots;$$

whence

$$\Sigma u_x = x_{(1)}u_0 + x_{(2)}\mu\delta u_0 + \tfrac{1}{2}\left[(x+1)_{(3)} + x_{(3)}\right]\delta^2 u_0 + (x+1)_{(4)}\mu\delta^3 u_0 + \ldots.$$

Example 2.

Find the sum of n terms of the series 0, 10, 33, 77, 150, ..., given that third differences are constant.

By taking out the differences it is seen that $\Delta u = 10$, $\Delta^2 u = 13$ and $\Delta^3 u = 8$.

The advancing difference formula gives

$$u_x = 0 + 10x_{(1)} + 13x_{(2)} + 8x_{(3)}.$$

If the series is $u_0, u_1, u_2 \ldots u_x \ldots u_{n-1}$, then we require $\overset{n-1}{\underset{0}{\Sigma}} u_x.$

$$\overset{n-1}{\underset{0}{\Sigma}} u_x = \overset{n-1}{\underset{0}{\Sigma}}\left[10x_{(1)} + 13x_{(2)} + 8x_{(3)}\right]$$

$$= \left[10x_{(2)} + 13x_{(3)} + 8x_{(4)}\right]_0^n$$

$$= 10n_{(2)} + 13n_{(3)} + 8n_{(4)}$$

$$= \tfrac{1}{6}n\,(n-1)\,(2n^2 + 3n + 16)\ \text{on reduction.}$$

Alternatively, we may continue the table backwards to obtain the differences required for the central difference formulae.

Stirling's formula then gives

$$\Sigma u_x = 7 \cdot 5 x_{(2)} + 5 \cdot \tfrac{1}{2} \left[(x+1)_{(3)} + x_{(3)} \right] + 8 \, (x+1)_{(4)}$$

and
$$\sum_{0}^{n-1} u_x = 7 \cdot 5 n_{(2)} + 2 \cdot 5 \left[(n+1)_{(3)} + n_{(3)} \right] + 8 \, (n+1)_{(4)}$$

$$= \tfrac{1}{6} n \, (n-1) \, (2n^2 + 3n + 16) \text{ as before.}$$

Should the series be given in the form $u_1, u_2, u_3 \ldots u_x \ldots u_n$, then

$$u_x = u_1 + (x-1)_{(1)} \Delta u_1 + (x-1)_{(2)} \Delta^2 u_1 + (x-1)_{(3)} \Delta^3 u_1.$$

$$\therefore \ \Sigma u_x = (x-1)_{(1)} u_1 + (x-1)_{(2)} \Delta u_1 + (x-1)_{(3)} \Delta^2 u_1 + (x-1)_{(4)} \Delta^3 u_1$$

and

$$\sum_{1}^{n} u_x = \left[(x-1)_{(1)} u_1 + (x-1)_{(2)} \Delta u_1 + (x-1)_{(3)} \Delta^2 u_1 + (x-1)_{(4)} \Delta^3 u_1 \right]_{1}^{n+1}$$

$$= n_{(1)} u_1 + n_{(2)} \Delta u_1 + n_{(3)} \Delta^2 u_1 + n_{(4)} \Delta^3 u_1,$$

which, on substituting for Δu_1, $\Delta^2 u_1$ and $\Delta^3 u_1$, gives the result obtained above.

3. Since $\Delta x^{(-m)} = -m x^{(-m-1)}$, the series whose xth term is of the form $[(x+1)(x+2) \ldots (x+k)]^{-1}$ can be summed immediately.

Example 3.

Sum to n terms the series whose xth term is $\dfrac{1}{(x+1)(x+2)(x+3)}$.

$$\Delta \left[\frac{1}{(x+1)(x+2)} \right] = -2 \, \frac{1}{(x+1)(x+2)(x+3)}.$$

$$\therefore \ \sum_{1}^{n} \frac{1}{(x+1)(x+2)(x+3)} = -\frac{1}{2} \left[\frac{1}{(x+1)(x+2)} \right]_{1}^{n+1}$$

$$= -\frac{1}{2} \left[\frac{1}{(n+2)(n+3)} - \frac{1}{2 \cdot 3} \right].$$

4. It is worthy of remark that the rules for the summation of series of the types given in paragraphs 2 (ii) and 3, as given in the text-books on algebra, are precisely the same as those stated above, and are based on the same principle. For example, for a series whose nth term is

$$(a+nb)(a+\overline{n+1}b)(a+\overline{n+2}b) \ldots (a+\overline{n+r-1}b),$$

the finite difference method is simply to write this in factorial form, with interval of differencing b, and then to proceed on the lines laid down, thus:

$$\sum_{1}^{n} u_n = \sum_{1}^{n} (a+\overline{n+r-1}b)^{(r)} = \left[\frac{(a+\overline{n+r-1}b)^{(r+1)}}{b(r+1)} \right]_{1}^{n+1}$$

$$= \frac{(a+\overline{n+r}b)^{(r+1)} - (a+rb)^{(r+1)}}{b(r+1)}$$

$$= \frac{(a+\overline{n+r}b)\, u_n}{b(r+1)} + \text{a constant.}$$

This, of course, produces the same result as is given by the algebraic rule: "Write down the nth term, affix the next factor at the end, divide by the number of factors thus increased and by the common difference, and add a constant" (see Hall and Knight, *Higher Algebra*, p. 314).

For the series whose nth term is the reciprocal of the one above the inverse factorial is used, and a similar result is obtained.

5. It sometimes happens that on taking out successive differences of a series a stage is reached where a particular set of differences forms a geometrical progression. In that event the series can be considered as consisting of two separate series, (i) a series whose general term is $a+bx+cx^2+\ldots+kx^{n-1}$ (a rational integral function of x), and (ii) a geometrical progression.

Suppose, for example, that second differences are in geometrical progression with common ratio r. Then

$$u_x = a+bx+cr^x.$$

For
$$\Delta u_x = b+c(r-1)r^x,$$

and
$$\Delta^2 u_x = c(r-1)^2 r^x = kr^x,$$

where
$$k = c(r-1)^2.$$

It follows that for nth differences

$$\Delta^n u_x = c(r-1)^n r^x.$$

Example 4.

Sum to n terms the series $1, 6, 11, 18, 31, 58, 115, \ldots$.

The difference table is

u_x	Δu_x	$\Delta^2 u_x$	$\Delta^3 u_x$
1			
	5		
6		0	
	5		2
11		2	
	7		4
18		6	
	13		8
31		14	
	27		16
58		30	
	57		
115			

Third differences are in G.P. with common ratio 2.

Assume therefore that

$$u_x = a + bx^{(1)} + cx^{(2)} + d2^x,$$
$$\Delta u_x = b + 2cx^{(1)} + d2^x (2-1)$$
$$= b + 2cx^{(1)} + d2^x,$$
$$\Delta^2 u_x = 2c + d2^x,$$
$$\Delta^3 u_x = d2^x.$$

Inserting the differences for the value $x=1$, we have

$$2 = \Delta^3 u_1 = 2d; \quad 0 = \Delta^2 u_1 = 2c + 2d;$$
$$5 = \Delta u_1 = b + 2c + 2d.$$

From these equations we find easily that

$$d = 1; \quad c = -1; \quad b = 5.$$

Putting $x=1$ in $u_x = a + bx^{(1)} + cx^{(2)} + d2^x$, we have

$$1 = u_1 = a + b + 2d,$$

whence

$$a = 1 - b - 2d = -6;$$

$$\therefore \quad u_x = -6 + 5x^{(1)} - x^{(2)} + 2^x;$$

$$\therefore \quad \sum_{1}^{n} u_x = \left[-6x^{(1)} + \frac{5x^{(2)}}{2} - \frac{x^{(3)}}{3} + \frac{2^x}{2-1} \right]_1^{n+1}$$

$$= -6(n+1)^{(1)} + 6 + \frac{5(n+1)^{(2)}}{2} - \frac{(n+1)^{(3)}}{3} + 2^{n+1} - 2,$$

since all the factorials except the first vanish for the lower limit.

This simplifies to

$$2^{n+1} - 2 - \frac{n}{6}(2n^2 - 15n + 19).$$

Alternatively, we may proceed thus:

$$\Delta^3 u_x = d2^x.$$

Deduct $d2^x$ from u_x and difference the function $u_x - d2^x$ in the usual way.

By giving x the values $1, 2, 3, 4$ in succession it is easily seen that $u_x - d2^x$ takes the values $-1, 2, 3, 2$ respectively. On forming a difference table we find that the leading differences are

$$\Delta (u_x - d2^x) = 3, \quad \Delta^2 (u_x - d2^x) = -2.$$

Then $\quad\quad u_x = 2^x - 1 + 3\ (x-1)_{(1)} - 2\ (x-1)_{(2)},$

so that

$$\sum_1^n u_x = \left[2^x - (x-1)_{(1)} + 3\ (x-1)_{(2)} - 2\ (x-1)_{(3)} \right]_1^{n+1}$$

$$= 2^{n+1} - 2 - n_{(1)} + 3n_{(2)} - 2n_{(3)},$$

which, on simplification, gives the same result as that above.

Note. In the methods above we have called the terms $u_1,\ u_2,\ u_3 \dots$ and have used the property $\Delta x^{(t)} = t x^{(t-1)}$. We may shorten the work slightly by beginning with $x = 0$ (so that all the factorials vanish at the lower limit) and using $x_{(t)}$ instead of $x^{(t)}$. Further, the two methods give the same result without transformation. It will be instructive for the student to rework the problem on these lines.

6. The form $u_x v_x$. Summation by parts.

When the general term of the series is the product of two functions of x and the value of each of the summations $\sum_1^n u_x$ and $\sum_1^n v_x$ is known, a method known as "summation by parts" can be adopted.

We have $\quad \Delta (U_x V_x) = U_{x+1} V_{x+1} - U_x V_x$

$$= U_{x+1} (V_{x+1} - V_x) + V_x (U_{x+1} - U_x)$$

$$= U_{x+1} \Delta V_x + V_x \Delta U_x;$$

$$\therefore \quad V_x \Delta U_x = \Delta (U_x V_x) - U_{x+1} \Delta V_x;$$

$$\therefore \quad \sum_1^n [V_x \Delta U_x] = \left[U_x V_x \right]_1^{n+1} - \sum_1^n [U_{x+1} \Delta V_x].$$

It follows that when the function $u_x v_x$ can be put in the form $V_x \Delta U_x$ the summation can be performed at once if $\sum_1^n [U_{x+1} \Delta V_x]$ can be evaluated (but not otherwise).

Note. For extensions of the formulae for summation by parts see Chapter VII.

Example 5.

Find the sum of the series $a+2a^2+3a^3+4a^4+\dots$ to n terms. The terms are successive values of the function $y=xa^x$, and since

$$\Delta\left(\frac{a^x}{a-1}\right)=a^x,$$

we may write x for V_x and $\dfrac{a^x}{a-1}$ for U_x in the relation above.

$$\therefore \ \sum_{1}^{n}[xa^x]=\sum_{1}^{n}\left[x\Delta\left(\frac{a^x}{a-1}\right)\right]$$

$$=\left[\frac{a^x}{a-1}x\right]_{1}^{n+1}-\sum_{1}^{n}\left[\frac{a^{x+1}}{a-1}\Delta x\right]$$

$$=\left[\frac{a^x}{a-1}x\right]_{1}^{n+1}-\sum_{1}^{n}\left[\frac{a^{x+1}}{a-1}\right],\quad\text{since }\Delta x=1,$$

$$=\left[\frac{a^x}{a-1}x\right]_{1}^{n+1}-\left[\frac{a^{x+1}}{(a-1)^2}\right]_{1}^{n+1}$$

$$=(n+1)\frac{a^{n+1}}{a-1}-\frac{a}{a-1}-\frac{a^{n+2}}{(a-1)^2}+\frac{a^2}{(a-1)^2}.$$

7. The result in paragraph 1, namely, that $\overset{n}{\underset{1}{\sum}}\phi(x)=f(n+1)-f(1)$, where $\Delta f(x)=\phi(x)$, can be obtained by the use of the operator E.

We have $$\sum_{1}^{n}\phi(x)=\phi(1)+\phi(2)+\dots+\phi(n)$$

$$=(1+E+E^2+\dots+E^{n-1})\phi(1)$$

$$=\frac{E^n-1}{E-1}\phi(1)$$

$$=\frac{E^n-1}{E-1}(E-1)f(1),$$

since $$\phi(1)=\Delta f(1)=(E-1)f(1).$$

$$\therefore \ \sum_{1}^{n}\phi(x)=(E^n-1)f(1)$$

$$=f(n+1)-f(1).$$

Thus the operator $\overset{n}{\underset{1}{\Sigma}}$ is equivalent to the operator $\dfrac{E^n-1}{E-1}$, and we may safely substitute $\dfrac{E^n-1}{E-1}$ for $\overset{n}{\underset{1}{\Sigma}}$ in any series of operations.

Again, since $E^n u_x = u_{x+n}$, the identity $\overset{n}{\underset{1}{\Sigma}} u_x = \dfrac{E^n-1}{E-1} u_1$ can be expressed as

$$\overset{n}{\underset{1}{\Sigma}} u_x = \frac{1}{E-1}(u_{n+1}-u_1)$$

$$= \frac{1}{\Delta}(u_{n+1}-u_1)$$

$$= \Delta^{-1}(u_{n+1}-u_1).$$

8. The relation between the operators Σ and Δ.

It has been seen that if

$$\Delta f(x) = \phi(x)$$

then $\qquad\qquad f(x) = \Sigma\phi(x),$

where the summation is performed between certain limits.

If therefore we omit the limits we may say that with certain reservations summation is the inverse process to differencing.

Consequently $\qquad \phi(x) = \Delta f(x) = \Delta\Sigma\phi(x),$

so that $\qquad\qquad\qquad \Delta\Sigma \equiv 1,$

i.e. $\qquad\qquad\qquad\qquad \Sigma \equiv \dfrac{1}{\Delta} \equiv \Delta^{-1}.$

Now although $\Delta\Sigma \equiv 1$ it does not follow that $\Sigma\Delta \equiv 1$, for we shall obtain the same result by differencing $f(x)+c$, where c is a constant, as by differencing $f(x)$ alone.

Thus $\qquad\qquad \Delta[f(x)+c] = \phi(x);$

$\qquad \therefore\ f(x)+c = \Delta^{-1}\phi(x) = \Sigma\phi(x) = \Sigma\Delta f(x),$

so that $\qquad\qquad\qquad \Sigma\Delta \not\equiv 1.$

The symbol Σ may be and often is used in place of the inverse symbol Δ^{-1} provided that it be remembered that Σ (or Δ^{-1}) and

Δ are not commutative, and that in the indefinite finite integral we must include, or imagine, an arbitrary constant which disappears in the definite integral.

Thus, the process of summation in finite differences is similar to the corresponding process in the integral calculus and the relations between the symbols are analogous to those existing between the symbols of differentiation and integration. As a result, finite difference summation is often referred to as finite integration. Σu_x is said to be the indefinite finite integral of u_x; $\overset{n}{\underset{1}{\Sigma}} u_x$ the definite finite integral; and a function that can be integrated, such as a^x, to be "immediately integrable".

9. Other uses of the symbol Σ.

One of the commonest functions in the theory of life contingencies is the expression obtained by multiplying l_x (the number attaining age x) by the interest factor v^x. This product is denoted by D_x, and the connection between certain functions dependent on D_x is indicated thus:

$$N_x = \Sigma D_x; \quad S_x = \Sigma N_x.$$

Here Σ denotes summation from age x to the end of the mortality table, it being understood that values beyond the end of the table are zero.

In point of fact, the correct way of showing the relation between the functions D and N, etc., is

$$N_x = \sum_{t=0}^{t=\infty} D_{x+t},$$

where x is fixed and t is the variable.

In modern mathematical works it is now usual to use the notations $\overset{\infty}{\underset{t=0}{\Sigma}}$, $\overset{n}{\underset{t=a}{\Sigma}}$ etc., where the variable t is specified for the lower limit only. The still shorter form $\overset{b}{\underset{a}{\Sigma}}$ is often used where there is no doubt about the variable.

(i) When Σ is used in the special sense

$$\Sigma u_x = u_x + u_{x+1} + u_{x+2} + \dots \text{ to the end of the table;}$$
$$\Delta \Sigma u_x = (u_{x+1} + u_{x+2} + u_{x+3} + \dots) - (u_x + u_{x+1} + u_{x+2} + \dots)$$
$$= -u_x,$$

so that here $\qquad\qquad \Delta\Sigma \equiv -1.$

(ii) If, however, Σ is specially defined so that Σu_x indicates a summation beginning with u_1 and ending with the last term preceding u_x, then

$$\Sigma u_x = u_1 + u_2 + u_3 + \dots + u_{x-1};$$
$$\therefore \;\; \Delta\Sigma u_x = (u_1 + u_2 + u_3 + \dots + u_x) - (u_1 + u_2 + u_3 + \dots + u_{x-1})$$
$$= u_x.$$

In these circumstances therefore $\Delta\Sigma \equiv 1$.

(iii) Again, in algebraic series, Σ is often used loosely to indicate the sum of the first x terms of a series, thus:

$$\Sigma u_x = u_1 + u_2 + \dots + u_x;$$
$$\therefore \;\; \Delta\Sigma u_x = (u_1 + u_2 + \dots + u_{x+1}) - (u_1 + u_2 + \dots + u_x)$$
$$= u_{x+1}$$
$$= Eu_x,$$

whence $\qquad \Delta\Sigma \equiv E$.

These illustrations serve to show that great care must be exercised in introducing Σ into any formula. The sense in which it is to be used should be clearly defined in every instance: the safest course is always to state the limits where possible.

10. Application of the relation between Σ and Δ.

By treating the operator Σ as equivalent to Δ^{-1}, the method of separation of symbols can be employed for the solution of problems. For example, a convenient formula for the evaluation of $\Sigma a^x u_x$ can be evolved by which the necessity for the continued application of summation by parts can be obviated.

Example 6.

Prove that

$$\Sigma a^x u_x = \frac{a^x}{a-1}\left\{1 - \frac{a\Delta}{a-1} + \frac{a^2\Delta^2}{(a-1)^2} - \frac{a^3\Delta^3}{(a-1)^3} + \dots\right\} u_x.$$

Now $\qquad E^p a^x u_x = a^{x+p} u_{x+p} = a^x (aE)^p u_x$

and $\qquad \Sigma a^x u_x = \Delta^{-1} a^x u_x$, omitting the arbitrary constant
$$= (E-1)^{-1} a^x u_x.$$

Let $\qquad \phi(E) \equiv A_0 + A_1 E + A_2 E^2 + \ldots + A_r E^r + \ldots$

Then the $(r+1)$th term in $\phi(E) a^x u_x$ is $A_r E^r a^x u_x$.

I.e. $\qquad A_r a^{x+r} u_{x+r} = a^x A_r a^r u_{x+r}$
$$= a^x A_r a^r E^r u_x$$
$$= a^x A_r (aE)^r u_x;$$
$$\therefore \quad \phi(E) a^x u_x = a^x \phi(aE) u_x,$$

so that if $\phi(E)$ is the operation $(E-1)^{-1}$

$$(E-1)^{-1} a^x u_x = a^x (aE-1)^{-1} u_x;$$
$$\therefore \quad \Sigma a^x u_x = a^x (aE-1)^{-1} u_x$$
$$= a^x (a+a\Delta-1)^{-1} u_x$$
$$= a^x (a-1)^{-1} \left[1 + \frac{a\Delta}{a-1} \right]^{-1} u_x$$
$$= \frac{a^x}{a-1} \left[1 - \frac{a\Delta}{a-1} + \frac{a^2 \Delta^2}{(a-1)^2} - \ldots \right] u_x,$$

omitting the arbitrary constant.

Note. An alternative (and simpler) proof of this formula can be obtained by the use of the expansion of $\Sigma u_x v_x$ in a series. See Chap. VII, paragraph 12.

Example 7.

Apply the above formula to evaluate $\Sigma 3^x (x^3 + x^2 + x + 1)$.
$$\Delta u_x = \Delta (x^3 + x^2 + x + 1) = 3x^2 + 5x + 3,$$
$$\Delta^2 u_x = \Delta^2 (x^3 + x^2 + x + 1) = 6x + 8,$$

and $\qquad \Delta^3 u_x = \Delta^3 (x^3 + x^2 + x + 1) = 6;$

$\therefore \quad \Sigma 3^x (x^3 + x^2 + x + 1)$
$$= \frac{3^x}{3-1} \left\{ u_x - \frac{3}{(3-1)} \Delta u_x + \frac{3^2}{(3-1)^2} \Delta^2 u_x - \frac{3^3}{(3-1)^3} \Delta^3 u_x \right\} + c$$
$$= \frac{3^x}{2} \left[x^3 + x^2 + x + 1 - \tfrac{3}{2} (3x^2 + 5x + 3) + \tfrac{9}{4} (6x + 8) - \tfrac{27}{8}.6 \right] + c$$
$$= \frac{3^x}{8} (4x^3 - 14x^2 + 28x - 23) + c.$$

It is often of advantage to set out the rational integral function in factorial or binomial notation; the successive differences can then be obtained with little difficulty.

Thus, by the method given in Chap. I, paragraph 22,

$$x^3 + x^2 + x + 1 = x^{(3)} + 4x^{(2)} + 3x^{(1)} + 1,$$

so that

$$\Delta u_x = 3x^{(2)} + 8x^{(1)} + 3,$$

$$\Delta^2 u_x = 6x^{(1)} + 8,$$

$$\Delta^3 u_x = 6,$$

and, by adopting the formula for $\Sigma a^x u_x$, we have easily that

$$\Sigma 3^x (x^3 + x^2 + x + 1) = \frac{3^x}{8} (4x^{(3)} - 2x^{(2)} + 18x^{(1)} - 23) + c.$$

To express $4x^{(3)} - 2x^{(2)} + 18x^{(1)} - 23$ in the form

$$ax^3 + bx^2 + cx + d,$$

we use the method of detached coefficients applied inversely:

2	4	−2	18	−23
	0	8	−10	
1	4	−10	28	
	0	4		
0	4	−14		
	0			
	4			

Hence

$$\Sigma 3^x (x^3 + x^2 + x + 1) = \frac{3^x}{8} (4x^3 - 14x^2 + 28x - 23) + c,$$

as before.

11. The following examples are instructive.

Example 8.

Evaluate

$$\sum_{1}^{n} \frac{2x+3}{x(x+1)} 3^{-x}.$$

$$u_x = \frac{2x+3}{x(x+1)} \frac{1}{3^x} = \left\{\frac{3}{x} - \frac{1}{x+1}\right\} \frac{1}{3^x}$$

$$= \frac{3}{x} \frac{1}{3^x} - \frac{3}{x+1} \frac{1}{3^{x+1}}$$

$$= -3\Delta \left[\frac{1}{x} \frac{1}{3^x}\right];$$

$$\therefore \sum_1^n u_x = 3 \left[-\frac{1}{x} \frac{1}{3^x}\right]_1^{n+1}$$

$$= 1 - \frac{1}{n+1} \frac{1}{3^n}.$$

Example 9.

Show that the general term of the recurring series

$$u_0 + u_1 x + u_2 x^2 + \ldots + u_r x^r + \ldots,$$

for which the scale of relation is $1 - px - qx^2$, is $Aa^n + Bb^n$, where a, b are functions of p, q and A, B are constants.

Since $1 - px - qx^2$ is the scale of relation,

$$u_n - pu_{n-1} - qu_{n-2} = 0;$$

i.e. $$u_n - pE^{-1}u_n - qE^{-2}u_n = 0,$$

or $$(1 - pE^{-1} - qE^{-2}) u_n = 0.$$

Therefore $$(1 - aE^{-1})(1 - bE^{-1}) u_n = 0$$

if $$a + b = p \quad \text{and} \quad ab = -q.$$

This will be true if either

$$(1 - aE^{-1}) u_n \quad \text{or} \quad (1 - bE^{-1}) u_n = 0,$$

i.e. if $$u_n - au_{n-1} \quad \text{or} \quad u_n - bu_{n-1} = 0.$$

Now if $$u_n - au_{n-1} = 0,$$

then $$u_n = au_{n-1},$$

and the series is a geometrical progression with common ratio a. The general term of the "a" series is therefore Aa^n.

Similarly the general term of the "b" series is Bb^n, where A and B are constants. But if a new series be formed by the addition of these two progressions the relationship will hold good for this new series. In other words the most general solution is

$$u_n = Aa^n + Bb^n,$$

where we may give A and B any values, but a and b must satisfy the equations

$$a + b = p \quad \text{and} \quad ab = -q.$$

Example 10.

If fourth and higher differences are ignored, prove that the sum of n successive terms of a function, of which u_0 is the central term, is

$$nu_0 + \tfrac{1}{24}(n^3 - n)\,\Delta^2 u_{-1},$$

where n is odd.

Since u_0 is the central term, it will be convenient to use a central difference formula.

Gauss's forward formula gives

$$u_x = u_0 + x\Delta u_0 + \tfrac{1}{2}x(x-1)\,\Delta^2 u_{-1} + \tfrac{1}{6}(x+1)\,x\,(x-1)\,\Delta^3 u_{-1}$$

$$= u_0 + x^{(1)}\Delta u_0 + \tfrac{1}{2}x^{(2)}\Delta^2 u_{-1} + \tfrac{1}{6}(x+1)^{(3)}\,\Delta^3 u_{-1};$$

$$\therefore \quad \Sigma u_x = C + xu_0 + \tfrac{1}{2}x^{(2)}\,\Delta u_0 + \tfrac{1}{6}x^{(3)}\,\Delta^2 u_{-1} + \tfrac{1}{24}(x+1)^{(4)}\,\Delta^3 u_{-1}.$$

On summation between the limits $-\tfrac{1}{2}(n-1)$ and $\tfrac{1}{2}(n-1)$ the coefficients of Δu_0 and $\Delta^3 u_{-1}$ will cancel, and we shall have

$$\overset{\frac{1}{2}(n-1)}{\underset{-\frac{1}{2}(n-1)}{\Sigma}} u_x = \left[C + xu_0 + \tfrac{1}{2}x^{(2)}\,\Delta u_0 + \tfrac{1}{6}x^{(3)}\,\Delta^2 u_{-1} + \tfrac{1}{24}(x+1)^{(4)}\,\Delta^3 u_{-1} \right]_{-\frac{1}{2}(n-1)}^{\frac{1}{2}(n+1)}$$

$$= \left[\frac{n+1}{2} - \left(-\frac{n-1}{2} \right) \right] u_0$$

$$+ \frac{1}{6}\left[\frac{n+1}{2} \cdot \frac{n-1}{2} \cdot \frac{n-3}{2} - \left(-\frac{n-1}{2} \cdot \frac{n+1}{2} \cdot \frac{n+3}{2} \right) \right] \Delta^2 u_{-1}$$

$$= nu_0 + \tfrac{1}{24}(n^3 - n)\,\Delta^2 u_{-1}.$$

12. The use of symbols of operation in the summation of algebraic series.

Many forms of algebraic series which at first sight do not seem to lend themselves to summation by the method of separation of symbols can in fact be summed very simply by that method.

For example, if c_r be the coefficient of x^r in the expansion of $(1+x)^n$, where n is a positive integer, the sum of the series whose rth term is $(-1)^{r-1} c_{r-1}[a-(r-1)]$ may be written down almost at sight. The series is

$$c_0 a - c_1(a-1) + c_2(a-2) - \ldots$$

i.e.
$$c_0 a - c_1 E^{-1} a + c_2 E^{-2} a - \ldots = (1 - E^{-1})^n\, a$$

$$= \Delta^n E^{-n} a$$

$$= \Delta^n (a-n)$$

$$= 0, \text{ for all values of } a.$$

Again, consider the well-known series

$$\frac{c_0}{x} - \frac{c_1}{x+1} + \frac{c_2}{x+2} - \dots$$

This may be written as

$$(c_0 - c_1 E + c_2 E^2 - \dots)\, x^{-1}$$
$$= (1 - E)^n\, x^{-1}$$
$$= (-1)^n\, \Delta^n x^{-1}$$
$$= \frac{n!}{x\,(x+1)\,(x+2)\,\dots\,(x+n)}.$$

The following examples are illustrative of the method.

Example 11.

Evaluate

$$\frac{1}{x+1} - \frac{n}{(x+1)\,(x+2)} + \frac{n\,(n-1)}{(x+1)\,(x+2)\,(x+3)} - \dots + \frac{(-1)^n\,n!}{(x+1)\,\dots\,(x+n+1)}.$$

This series is $x^{(-1)} - n x^{(-2)} + n\,(n-1)\,x^{(-3)} \dots + (-1)^n\,n!\,x^{(-n-1)}$

$$= x^{(-1)} + \frac{n}{1!} \Delta x^{(-1)} + \frac{n\,(n-1)}{2!}\Delta^2 x^{(-1)} + \dots + \frac{n!}{n!}\Delta^n x^{(-1)}$$
$$= (1 + \Delta)^n\, x^{(-1)}$$
$$= E^n x^{(-1)}$$
$$= (x+n)^{(-1)}$$
$$= \frac{1}{(x+n+1)}.$$

Example 12.

Find the value of

$$a^{n+1} - n\,(a+b)^{n+1} + \frac{n\,(n-1)}{2!}\,(a+2b)^{n+1}$$
$$- \frac{n\,(n-1)\,(n-2)}{3!}\,(a+3b)^{n+1} - \dots.$$

Taking the interval of differencing to be b, the series may be written as

$$(1 - n_{(1)} E + n_{(2)} E^2 - \dots)\, a^{n+1}$$
$$= (1 - E)^n\, a^{n+1}$$
$$= (-1)^n\, \Delta^n a^{n+1}.$$

Now
$$a^{n+1} = a^{(n+1)} + \tfrac{1}{2}n\,(n+1)\,a^{(n)}\,b + \text{terms in } a^{(r)}\,b^{n+1-r} \quad (r<n).$$

$\therefore \quad \Delta^n a^{n+1} = (n+1)!\,b^n a^{(1)} + \tfrac{1}{2}n\,(n+1)\,b^{n+1}n!$

$$= \tfrac{1}{2}b^n\,(n+1)!\,(2a+nb),$$

and the sum of the series

$$= \tfrac{1}{2}\,(-b)^n\,(n+1)!\,(2a+nb).$$

Example 13.

Sum the series

$$x^3 + (x+1)^3 + (x+2)^3 + \ldots + (x+n-1)^3.$$

The series may be written in the form

$$S = (1 + E + E^2 + \ldots + E^{n-1})\,x^3$$

$$= \frac{E^n - 1}{E-1}\,x^3$$

$$= (E^n - 1)\,\Delta^{-1} x^3$$

$$= \Delta^{-1}\,(x+n)^3 - \Delta^{-1} x^3$$

$$= \Delta^{-1}\,[(x+n)_{(1)} + 6\,(x+n)_{(2)} + 6\,(x+n)_{(3)}]$$

$$\qquad - \Delta^{-1}\,[x_{(1)} + 6x_{(2)} + 6x_{(3)}]$$

$$= \tfrac{1}{4}\,[(x+n)^2\,(x+n-1)^2 - x^2\,(x-1)^2], \text{ on reduction.}$$

Note. It is unnecessary to introduce any constant of integration: for if we put

$$\Delta^{-1} x^3 = u_x + c,$$

the constant disappears on operation by $E^n - 1$.

13. "Summation n", or $[n]$.

An interesting example of the development of a series of operations by the method of separation of symbols occurs in the theory of graduation. One of the objects of graduation is to obtain a smooth series of numbers instead of the rough series given by the actual data. A step to the solution of the problem consists in replacing each term of the series by the arithmetic mean of the **n** successive terms of which the given term is the central term. The operation of summing these successive terms is generally denoted by $[n]$ ("summation n"). For the present we will assume that n is odd.

For example $\quad [5]\, u_0 = u_{-2} + u_{-1} + u_0 + u_1 + u_2,$

$$[n]\, u_0 = u_{-\frac{n-1}{2}} + u_{-\frac{n-3}{2}} + \ldots + u_{\frac{n-3}{2}} + u_{\frac{n-1}{2}}.$$

Consider a simple summation: $[3]\, u_0$

By definition $\quad [3]\, u_0 = u_{-1} + u_0 + u_1,$

and if we write v_0 for $[3]\, u_0$ we may operate again on v_0 to obtain $[3]\, v_0$.

In that event we shall have

$$\begin{aligned}
[3]\, v_0 &= [3]\, u_{-1} + [3]\, u_0 + [3]\, u_1 \\
&= u_{-2} + 2u_{-1} + 3u_0 + 2u_1 + u_2 \\
&= u_0 + (u_{-1} + u_0 + u_1) + (u_{-2} + u_{-1} + u_0 + u_1 + u_2) \\
&= [1]\, u_0 + [3]\, u_0 + [5]\, u_0.
\end{aligned}$$

If therefore we denote the double operation $[3]\,[3]\, u_0$ by $[3]^2\, u_0$, we have the symbolic identity

$$[3]^2 \equiv [1] + [3] + [5].$$

Similarly $\quad [5]^2 \equiv [1] + [3] + [5] + [7] + [9],$

and $\qquad [n]^2 \equiv [1] + [3] + [5] + [7] + \ldots + [2n-1],$

where n is odd.

The identity between $[3]^2$ and $[1] + [3] + [5]$ can be seen at once by writing down the terms in diagrammatic form:

$$[3]^2\, u_0 = [3]\, u_{-1} + [3]\, u_0 + [3]\, u_1$$

$$= [5]\, u_0 + [3]\, u_0 + [1]\, u_0. \qquad \text{(Fraser.)}$$

These results are general. The sum of n consecutive odd operations is $[n] [r]$, where $[r]$ is the middle operator. E.g.

$$[5]+[7]+[9]+[11]+[13]\equiv[5] [9]\equiv[9] [5].$$

14. We can express $[n]$ in terms of the ordinary finite difference symbols thus:

For a simple value of n, say 3,

$$[3] u_0 = u_{-1}+u_0+u_1 = 3u_0+u_{-1}-2u_0+u_1$$
$$= 3u_0+\Delta^2 u_{-1}$$
$$= (3+\delta^2) u_0,$$

where δ^2 is the symbol denoting the second central difference.

Generally $[n] \equiv n+\dfrac{n^3-n}{24}\delta^2+$ terms in δ^4 and higher differences if these exist. (Cf. Ex. 10.)

The relations above are on the assumption that n is odd. If n be even we must find a meaning for the summation symbol.

By analogy $[2] u_0$ is the sum of two values of u whose suffixes are such that their sum is zero and their difference unity.

I.e.
$$[2] u_0 = u_{-\frac{1}{2}}+u_{\frac{1}{2}}.$$

Hence
$$[2]^2 u_0 = \{[1]+[3]\} u_0$$
$$= (4+\delta^2) u_0,$$

so that
$$[2] \equiv 2 (1+\tfrac{1}{4}\delta^2)^{\frac{1}{2}}$$
$$\equiv 2 (1+\tfrac{1}{8}\delta^2-\tfrac{1}{128}\delta^4+...),$$

which is otherwise obtained by expressing $u_{-\frac{1}{2}}+u_{\frac{1}{2}}$ in terms of central differences. This agrees with

$$[n] \equiv n+\frac{n^3-n}{24}\delta^2$$

as far as third differences.

The meaning of $[n]$ when n is even is now evident, and we need no longer restrict the values of n to odd integers. Thus the formula

$$[n] u_0 = u_{-\frac{n-1}{2}}+u_{-\frac{n-3}{2}}+...+u_{\frac{n-3}{2}}+u_{\frac{n-1}{2}}$$

applies for any integral value of n whether odd or even.

*15. The following alternative form for exhibiting relations between the operators, whether odd or even, is due to Mr G. J. Lidstone:

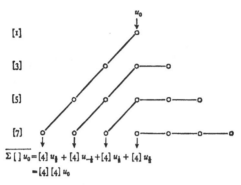

$$\overline{\Sigma\,[\,]\,u_0} = [4]\,u_{\frac{3}{2}} + [4]\,u_{-\frac{1}{2}} + [4]\,u_{\frac{1}{2}} + [4]\,u_{\frac{3}{2}}$$
$$= [4]\,[4]\,u_0$$

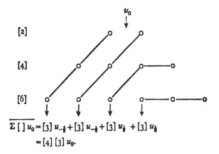

$$\overline{\Sigma\,[\,]\,u_0} = [3]\,u_{-\frac{1}{2}} + [3]\,u_{-\frac{1}{2}} + [3]\,u_{\frac{1}{2}} + [3]\,u_{\frac{3}{2}}$$
$$= [4]\,[3]\,u_0.$$

The tracks marked —— show the re-grouping. The diagram is of virtually the same form if we begin later:

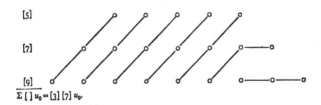

$$\overline{\Sigma\,[\,]\,u_0} = [3]\,[7]\,u_0.$$

16. By means of the relations already proved we may develop an unlimited number of formulae involving $[n]$, $[m]$, etc.

Example 14.

Prove that $10\,[1] - 3\,[3] \equiv 2\,[3] - [5]$ as far as third differences.

$$\{10\,[1] - 3\,[3]\}\,u_0 = 10u_0 - 3\left(3u_0 + \tfrac{24}{24}\delta^2 u_0\right)$$

$$= u_0 - 3\delta^2 u_0.$$

Also $\qquad \{2\,[3] - [5]\}\,u_0 = 2\left(3u_0 + \tfrac{24}{24}\delta^2 u_0\right) - \left(5u_0 + \tfrac{120}{24}\delta^2 u_0\right)$

$$= u_0 - 3\delta^2 u_0.$$

Example 15.

Given $[5]\,u_{-5}$, $[5]\,u_0$, $[5]\,u_5$, find u_0, fourth and higher differences being neglected.

By Stirling's formula,

$$u_x = u_0 + x\,\frac{\Delta u_{-1} + \Delta u_0}{2} + \frac{x^2}{2}\,\Delta^2 u_{-1} + \frac{x\,(x^2 - 1)}{6}\,\frac{\Delta^3 u_{-1} + \Delta^3 u_{-2}}{2} + \ldots,$$

$$u_{-x} = u_0 - x\,\frac{\Delta u_{-1} + \Delta u_0}{2} + \frac{x^2}{2}\,\Delta^2 u_{-1} - \frac{x\,(x^2 - 1)}{6}\,\frac{\Delta^3 u_{-1} + \Delta^3 u_{-2}}{2} + \ldots.$$

$$\therefore \quad u_x + u_{-x} = 2u_0 + x^2 \Delta^2 u_{-1}.$$

$$\therefore \quad [5]\,u_0 = u_{-2} + u_{-1} + u_0 + u_1 + u_2 = (u_2 + u_{-2}) + (u_1 + u_{-1}) + u_0$$

$$= 5u_0 + 5\Delta^2 u_{-1}.$$

Similarly $\qquad [5]\,u_{-5} + [5]\,u_5 = 10u_0 + 135\Delta^2 u_{-1}.$

Eliminating $\Delta^2 u_{-1}$, we have

$$125u_0 = 27\,[5]\,u_0 - [5]\,u_{-5} - [5]\,u_5.$$

An interesting note by Mr D. C. Fraser on the properties of the operator $[n]$ occurs in the *Actuarial Students' Magazine*, No. 3 (Edinburgh, 1930). Here the general form for $[n]\,u_0$ is given by Mr Fraser as

$$\frac{E^{\frac{n}{2}} - E^{-\frac{n}{2}}}{E^{\frac{1}{2}} - E^{-\frac{1}{2}}}\,u_0,$$

which defines the operation whether n is odd or even; and the proof of the identity $[3]^2 \equiv [1] + [3] + [5]$ is made to depend on the development of the operator E. Thus:

$$[3]^2 u_0 = \frac{E^{\frac{3}{2}} - E^{-\frac{3}{2}}}{E^{\frac{1}{2}} - E^{-\frac{1}{2}}} [3] u_0$$

$$= \frac{E^{\frac{3}{2}} - E^{-\frac{3}{2}}}{E^{\frac{1}{2}} - E^{-\frac{1}{2}}} (u_{-1} + u_0 + u_1)$$

$$= \frac{(E^{\frac{3}{2}} - E^{-\frac{3}{2}})(E^{-1} + E^0 + E^1)}{E^{\frac{1}{2}} - E^{-\frac{1}{2}}} u_0$$

$$= \frac{(E^{\frac{1}{2}} - E^{-\frac{1}{2}}) + (E^{\frac{3}{2}} - E^{-\frac{3}{2}}) + (E^{\frac{5}{2}} - E^{-\frac{5}{2}})}{E^{\frac{1}{2}} - E^{-\frac{1}{2}}} u_0$$

$$= [1] u_0 + [3] u_0 + [5] u_0.$$

The general formula for $[n]^2 u$ can be proved in the same manner.

Many further examples of the use of $[n]$ will be found in various papers in the *Journal of the Institute of Actuaries*. For simple extensions of the method see particularly Hardy, *J.I.A.* vol. XXXII, p. 371, and Todhunter, *J.I.A.* vol. XXXII, p. 378, and for generalizations, Lidstone, *J.I.A.* vol. LV, p. 177, and Aitken, *J.I.A.* vol. LX, p. 339.

EXAMPLES 6

Sum the following series:

1. 7, 14, 19, 22, 23, 22, ... to n terms.

2. 2, 12, 36, 80, 150, 252, ... to n terms.

3. 10, 9, 7, 4, 0, -5, ... to 30 terms.

4. 5, 10, 17, 28, 47, 82, ... to 20 terms.

5. 10, 23, 60, 169, 494, ... to n terms.

6. 1, 2, 4, 8, 17, 40, 104, ... to n terms.

7. 1, 0, -1, 0, 7, 28, 79, ... to $2k$ terms.

8. 10, 14, 10, 6, ... to n terms.

9. 125, 343, 729, 1331, 2197, ... to n terms.

10. 1, 0, 1, 8, 29, 80, 193, ... to 17 terms.

Use the methods of finite differences to sum to n terms the series whose xth terms are

11. $(x+3)(x+4)(x+5)$.   12. $x(x+2)(x+4)$.

13. $(3x-2)(3x+1)(3x+4)$.   14. $x(x+1)(x+3)$.

15. $x(x+1)(x+3)(x+4)$.   16. $(2x+3)(2x+5)(2x+7)(2x+9)$.

17. $\dfrac{1}{(x+3)(x+4)}$.   18. $\dfrac{1}{(x+1)(x+3)}$.

19. $\dfrac{x}{(x+2)(x+3)(x+4)}$.   20. $\dfrac{1}{(3x-2)(3x+1)(3x+4)}$.

21. $\dfrac{x+3}{x(x+1)(x+2)}$.

22. Sum to n terms $2.4.8.14+4.6.10.16+6.8.12.18+\ldots$.

23. Obtain the general term of the series

$$\frac{3}{1.4.10}+\frac{5}{4.7.13}+\frac{7}{7.10.16}+\ldots$$

and find the sum to n terms and to infinity.

24. Find $\overset{n}{\underset{1}{\Sigma}}\, u_x$, where $u_x=x(x+2)(x+5)$.

25. The two series 6, 24, 60, 120, ... and 0, 0, 0, 6, 24, 60, 120, ... are given. Find the sum of n terms of each of the two series. Compare the results and explain the difference.

26. Sum the series 1, 5, 17, 53, 161, ... to n terms.

27. Evaluate $\Delta^{-1}(x^2 a^x)$.

28. Show that $\Delta(x!)=x(x!)$ and hence sum to n terms the series

$$1+3.2!+7.3!+13.4!+21.5!+\ldots$$

29. Find $\overset{n}{\underset{1}{\Sigma}}\, u_x$, where $u_x=(3x-1)(3x+2)(3x+5)(3x+8)$.

30. Sum to n terms $1.3^2+3.5^2+5.7^2+7.9^2+\ldots$.

31. Obtain the formula

$$\overset{a+n-1}{\underset{a}{\Sigma}}\, u_x=n_{(1)}u_a+n_{(2)}\Delta u_a+n_{(3)}\Delta^2 u_a+\ldots$$

and use the formula to find the sum of n terms of the series

$$-8,\ -5,\ 0,\ 14,\ 44,\ \ldots.$$

32. Prove that $\overset{n}{\underset{1}{\Sigma}}\,(x^2+1).x!=n.(n+1)!$.

33. Sum to n terms the series whose xth terms are (i) $x^2(3x+2)$, (ii) $2^x(x^3+x)$ by finite integration.

34. Evaluate $\sum\limits_1^n\left\{\dfrac{x^2 4^x}{(x+1)(x+2)}\right\}$.

35. Sum to infinity $\dfrac{1}{2.6.10}+\dfrac{1}{4.8.12}+\dfrac{1}{6.10.14}+\ldots$

36. Find the sum of n terms of the series

$$1^2+\frac{3^2}{2}+\frac{5^2}{2^2}+\frac{7^2}{2^3}+\ldots$$

37. Obtain the indefinite integral of $(2x-1)3^x$.

38. Show that the series 10, 24, 61, 163, 452, 1290, 3759, ... can be split up into two other series. Find the two series and hence sum the original series to n terms.

39. Prove that $\Delta^{-1}[u_x v_x]=u_x\Delta^{-1}v_x-\Delta^{-1}[\Delta u_x\Delta^{-1}v_{x+1}]$ and apply this formula to find the sum of the first n terms of the series whose rth term is $(r+1)x^{r-1}$.

40. Evaluate $\quad \Delta^{-1}\left\{\dfrac{(x+1)^2}{x(x+2)(x+3)(x+4)}\right\}$.

41. Find the sum of the squares of the first n natural numbers by the method of finite integration.

42. Sum to n terms $\dfrac{3}{2.5.8}+\dfrac{5}{5.8.11}+\dfrac{7}{8.11.14}+\ldots$

43. Find the sum of the infinite series $\dfrac{1.3}{2}+\dfrac{3.5}{2^2}+\dfrac{5.7}{2^3}+\ldots$

44. Find the sum of n terms of the series

$$2.2+7.4+14.8+23.16+34.32+\ldots$$

45. Prove that $\sum\limits_0^{n-1} u_r x^r=\dfrac{u_0-x^n u_n}{1-x}+\dfrac{x}{(1-x)^2}(\Delta u_0-x^n\Delta u_n)$

$$+\frac{x^2}{(1-x)^3}(\Delta^2 u_0-x^n\Delta^2 u_n)+\ldots$$

Apply this formula to find the sum of the first n terms of the series whose rth term is $r(r+1)x^{r-1}$.

46. Evaluate $\Delta^{-1}\left[2^x.x.\dfrac{x!}{(2x+1)!}\right]$.

47. Use the method of finite integration to obtain the sum of n terms of the series $1.3^3 + 3.5^3 + 5.7^3 + \ldots$.

48. Find the function whose first difference is $ax^3 + bx^2 + cx + d$.

49. Prove that $1^r + 2^r x + 3^r x^2 + \ldots$ is a recurring series, and find its scale of relation.

50. If u_n is the nth term of the series $1, 2, 3, 5, 8, 13, \ldots$ in which each term after the second is the sum of the two preceding terms, prove by the process of mathematical induction or otherwise that

$$u_n{}^2 - u_{n-1}u_{n+1} = (-1)^n.$$

51. Show how the methods of finite differences can be employed to find the sum of a series of the form

$$(a+k)^r + (a+2k)^r + \ldots + (a+xk)^r + \ldots.$$

52. Sum the series

$$\frac{1!}{a+1} + \frac{2!}{(a+1)(a+2)} + \ldots + \frac{n!}{(a+1)(a+2)\ldots(a+n)}.$$

53. Find the value of $\sum\limits_{r=1}^{r=n} n_{(r)} r^4$.

54. Prove that $\quad \{2\,[3] - [5]\}\, u_0 = u_0 - 3\Delta^2 u_{-1}$ approximately.

55. Obtain the approximate formula

$$125u_0 = [5]^3 \{u_0 + \Delta u_{-2} - \Delta u_1\}. \qquad \text{(Woolhouse.)}$$

56. Prove that $\quad [n]^2 - [m]^2 \equiv \{[n] - [m]\}\, \{[n] + [m]\}$.

57. One of Hardy's graduation formulae is

$$\frac{[4]\,[5]\,[6]}{120} \{u_0 + \Delta u_{-2} - \Delta u_1\} = u_0.$$

Prove that this is approximately true.

58. Express $\{[3] + [5] - [7]\}\, u_0$ in terms of u_{-3}, u_{-1}, u_0, u_1, u_3, and hence prove that

$$\frac{[5]\,[13]}{65} \{[3] + [5] - [7]\}\, u_0 \text{ reproduces } u_0 \text{ to third differences.}$$

59. If $w_n = [5]\, u_n$, prove King's formula:

$$u_0 = \cdot 2w_0 - \cdot 008\Delta^2 w_{-5},$$

fourth and higher differences being neglected.

CHAPTER VII

MISCELLANEOUS THEOREMS

1. In this chapter it is proposed to treat of certain propositions and applications of finite difference methods which are not essential to a first reading of the subject and which may conveniently be dealt with at a later stage. Some of the theorems are developments of familiar processes: others are alternative methods of approach for the solution of problems involving the principles of finite differences.

DIFFERENCES OF ZERO

2. If in the identical relation

$$\Delta^n x^m = (E-1)^n x^m$$
$$= (x+n)^m - n_{(1)}(x+n-1)^m + n_{(2)}(x+n-2)^m - \ldots$$

we put $x=0$, we obtain

$$[\Delta^n x^m]_{x=0} = n^m - n_{(1)}(n-1)^m + n_{(2)}(n-2)^m - \ldots.$$

By continued application of this formula we can obtain values of $\Delta^n x^m$ when $x=0$ for all integral values of n and m.

For example, if $m=3$,

$$[\Delta x^3]_{x=0} = 1^3 = 1,$$
$$[\Delta^2 x^3]_{x=0} = 2^3 - 2 \cdot 1^3 = 6,$$
$$[\Delta^3 x^3]_{x=0} = 3^3 - 3 \cdot 2^3 + 3 \cdot 1^3 = 6.$$

The values of $[\Delta^n x^m]_{x=0}$ are known as "differences of zero", and in accordance with this definition the expression is often written as $\Delta^n 0^m$.

It is evident that a table of values of differences of zero can be constructed if we can obtain a relation between corresponding values of $\Delta^n 0^m$.

We have from the above

$$\Delta^n o^m = n^m - n_{(1)}\,(n-1)^m + n_{(2)}\,(n-2)^m - \dots$$

$$= n\left[n^{m-1} - (n-1)_{(1)}\,(n-1)^{m-1} + (n-1)_{(2)}\,(n-2)^{m-1} - \dots\right]$$

$$= n\left[(1+n-1)^{m-1} - (n-1)_{(1)}\,(1+n-2)^{m-1}\right.$$
$$\left. + (n-1)_{(2)}\,(1+n-3)^{m-1} - \dots\right]$$

$$= n\left[(E-1)^{n-1}\,x^{m-1}\right]_{x=1}$$

$$= n\Delta^{n-1}\,1^{m-1}$$

$$= n\Delta^{n-1}\,E o^{m-1}$$

$$= n\Delta^{n-1}\,(1+\Delta)\,o^{m-1}$$

$$= n\left(\Delta^{n-1}o^{m-1} + \Delta^n o^{m-1}\right).$$

Alternatively,

$$\Delta^n o^m = n^m - n_{(1)}\,(n-1)^m + n_{(2)}\,(n-2)^m - \dots. \qquad (a)$$

But, since

$$\Delta^n x^m = (x+n)^m - n_{(1)}\,(x+n-1)^m + n_{(2)}\,(x+n-2)^m - \dots$$

we may put $n-1$ for n, $m-1$ for m and 1 for x, and obtain

$$\Delta^{n-1}1^{m-1} = n^{m-1} - (n-1)_{(1)}\,(n-1)^{m-1} + (n-1)_{(2)}\,(n-2)^{m-1} - \dots$$

$$= \frac{1}{n}\,(a)$$

$$= \frac{1}{n}\,\Delta^n o^m;$$

$$\therefore \quad \Delta^n o^m = n\Delta^{n-1}1^{m-1} = n\left(\Delta^{n-1}o^{m-1} + \Delta^n o^{m-1}\right).$$

This proof is given by de Morgan.

Another method for obtaining this relation, depending upon the formula for the nth difference of the compound function $u_x v_x$, is given below (paragraph 11).

3. Since $\Delta^n x^n = n!$ for interval of differencing unity

$$\Delta^n o^n = n!.$$

Similarly, since

$$\Delta^{n+r}x^n = 0, \quad \Delta^{n+r}o^n = 0.$$

i.e. $$\Delta^n o^m = 0, \quad \text{when } n > m.$$

We can now build up a table of differences of zero by continued application of the relation given in paragraph 1 above.

The table is

m	$\Delta 0^m$	$\Delta^2 0^m$	$\Delta^3 0^m$	$\Delta^4 0^m$	$\Delta^5 0^m$	$\Delta^6 0^m$
1	1	0				
2	1	2	0			
3	1	6	6	0		
4	1	14	36	24	0	
5	1	30	150	240	120	0
6	1	62	540	1560	1800	720

and so on.

4. An interesting application of the use of the differences of zero for the calculation of the coefficients in an expansion is as follows.

The fundamental formula

$$u_x = u_0 + x_{(1)}\Delta u_0 + x_{(2)}\Delta^2 u_0 + x_{(3)}\Delta^3 u_0 + \dots$$

can be written as

$$u_x = u_0 + x^{(1)}\Delta u_0 + \frac{x^{(2)}}{2!}\Delta^2 u_0 + \frac{x^{(3)}}{3!}\Delta^3 u_0 + \dots.$$

$$\therefore \quad x^m = 0^m + x^{(1)}\Delta 0^m + \frac{x^{(2)}}{2!}\Delta^2 0^m + \frac{x^{(3)}}{3!}\Delta^3 0^m + \dots.$$

By use of the relation

$$\Delta^n 0^m = n\left(\Delta^n 0^{m-1} + \Delta^{n-1} 0^{m-1}\right), \quad \text{i.e.} \quad \frac{\Delta^n 0^m}{n!} = \frac{n\Delta^n 0^{m-1}}{n!} + \frac{\Delta^{n-1} 0^{m-1}}{(n-1)!},$$

a table of the coefficients in the expansion of x^m in terms of successive values of the factorial $x^{(k)}$ can be written down in a similar manner to that given above.

5. The differences of zero have many special properties, and they are used in higher work in the theory of series. A simple example involving their use is given below.

Example 1.

If $(1+x)^n = c_0 + c_1 x + \dots + c_n x^n$, n being a positive integer, find the value of

$$(n-1)^2 c_1 + (n-3)^2 c_3 + (n-5)^2 c_5 + \dots.$$

Now $(x-1)^2 c_1 + (x-3)^2 c_3 + (x-5)^2 c_5 + \ldots$

$$= (E^{-1}c_1 + E^{-3}c_3 + E^{-5}c_5 + \ldots) x^2$$

$$= \tfrac{1}{2} \left[(1 + E^{-1})^n - (1 - E^{-1})^n \right] x^2$$

$$= \tfrac{1}{2} \left[(\Delta + 2)^n - \Delta^n \right] E^{-n} x^2$$

$$= \tfrac{1}{2} \left[(\Delta + 2)^n - \Delta^n \right] (x - n)^2$$

$$= \tfrac{1}{2} \left[(\Delta + 2)^n - \Delta^n \right] 0^2 \quad \text{when } x = n$$

$$= \tfrac{1}{2} \left[2^n 0^2 + n 2^{n-1} \Delta 0^2 + \tfrac{1}{2} n (n-1) 2^{n-2} \Delta^2 0^2 + \ldots \right]$$

$$= \tfrac{1}{2} \left[n 2^{n-1} + n (n-1) 2^{n-2} \right]$$

$$= 2^{n-3} n (n+1) \text{ on simplification.}$$

RELATIONS BETWEEN THE OPERATORS D AND Δ

6. It is shown in Part I (p. 65, paragraph 5) that

$$f(x) + hf'(x) + \frac{h^2}{2!} f''(x) + \ldots + \frac{h^{n-1}}{(n-1)!} f^{(n-1)}(x) + \ldots$$

converges to the limit $f(x+h)$, provided that $\underset{n \to \infty}{\text{Lt}} R_n(x)$ is zero, where

$$R_n(x) \equiv \frac{h^n}{n!} f^{(n)}(x + \theta h).$$

This is Taylor's theorem for a convergent series, and we may write it in the following form:

$$u_{x+rh} = u_x + rhDu_x + \frac{(rh)^2}{2!} D^2 u_x + \frac{(rh)^3}{3!} D^3 u_x + \ldots$$

$$= \left\{ 1 + rhD + \frac{(rh)^2}{2!} D^2 + \frac{(rh)^3}{3!} D^3 + \ldots \right\} u_x$$

$$= e^{rhD} u_x.$$

But, for interval of differencing h,

$$u_{x+rh} = E^r u_x.$$

$$\therefore \quad E^r \equiv e^{rhD},$$

so that $\qquad hD \equiv \log E \equiv \log (1 + \Delta)$

$$\equiv \Delta - \frac{\Delta^2}{2} + \frac{\Delta^3}{3} - \frac{\Delta^4}{4} + \dots$$

and $\qquad Du_x = \frac{1}{h}\left[\Delta u_x - \frac{\Delta^2}{2} u_x + \frac{\Delta^3}{3} u_x - \frac{\Delta^4}{4} u_x + \dots \right].$

If $h = 1$, then $\qquad (1 + \Delta)^r \equiv e^{rD}$

and we have a result analogous to the important relation in the theory of Compound Interest, namely $(1 + i)^n = e^{n\delta}$, where δ is the force of interest corresponding to a rate of interest i.

7. Since $\qquad D \equiv \frac{1}{h}\left[\Delta - \frac{\Delta^2}{2} + \frac{\Delta^3}{3} - \frac{\Delta^4}{4} + \dots \right],$

$$D^2 \equiv \frac{1}{h^2}\left[\Delta - \frac{\Delta^2}{2} + \frac{\Delta^3}{3} - \frac{\Delta^4}{4} + \dots \right]^2$$

$$\equiv \frac{1}{h^2}[\Delta^2 - \Delta^3 + \tfrac{11}{12}\Delta^4 - \tfrac{5}{6}\Delta^5 + \dots].$$

Similarly, $\qquad D^3 \equiv \frac{1}{h^3}[\Delta^3 - \tfrac{3}{2}\Delta^4 + \tfrac{7}{4}\Delta^5 - \dots].$

We have therefore a convenient method for expressing the differential coefficients of a function of x in terms of the differences of the function.

Example 2.

μ_x (the force of mortality) $= -\frac{1}{l_x}\frac{dl_x}{dx}$, where l_x is the number of persons at exact age x in any year of time. Given the following table, find a value for μ_{50}.

Age x ...	50	51	52	53
l_x	73,499	72,724	71,753	70,599

The difference table is

x	l_x	Δl_x	$\Delta^2 l_x$	$\Delta^3 l_x$
50	73,499			
		-775		
51	72,724		-196	
		-971		13
52	71,753		-183	
		-1154		
53	70,599			

$$\therefore \quad \frac{dl_x}{dx} = \left(\Delta - \frac{\Delta^2}{2} + \frac{\Delta^3}{3} \right) l_x,$$

since the interval of differencing is unity

$$= -775 + 98 + 4 \cdot 333 \cdots, \quad \text{when } x = 50,$$

$$= -672 \cdot 667.$$

$$\therefore \quad \mu_{50} = \left[-\frac{1}{l_x} \frac{dl_x}{dx} \right]_{x=50} = \frac{672 \cdot 667}{73,499} = \cdot 00915 \cdots.$$

Note. If $h \neq 1$, care must be taken to divide by the appropriate power of h in applying the formula. Thus, if u_x is given for quinquennial intervals of x, $\dfrac{d^3 u_x}{dx}$ will be $\dfrac{1}{5^3} (\Delta^3 u_x - \frac{3}{2}\Delta^4 u_x + \ldots)$ and not simply

$$\Delta^3 u_x - \tfrac{3}{2}\Delta^4 u_x + \ldots.$$

8. The result

$$\frac{du_x}{dx} = \frac{1}{h} \left[\Delta u_x - \frac{\Delta^2}{2} u_x + \frac{\Delta^3}{3} u_x - \cdots \right]$$

can easily be obtained by the differentiation of the advancing difference formula for u_x.

Taking the simple case when $h = 1$,

$$u_x = u_0 + x\Delta u_0 + \frac{x(x-1)}{2} \Delta^2 u_0 + \frac{x(x-1)(x-2)}{6} \Delta^3 u_0 + \cdots$$

$$\therefore \quad \frac{du_x}{dx} = \Delta u_0 + \frac{2x-1}{2} \Delta^2 u_0 + \frac{3x^2 - 6x + 2}{6} \Delta^3 u_0 + \cdots$$

or

$$\left(\frac{du_x}{dx} \right)_{x=0} = \Delta u_0 - \frac{\Delta^2 u_0}{2} + \frac{\Delta^3 u_0}{3} - \cdots$$

which becomes, on changing the origin to x,

$$\frac{du_x}{dx} = \Delta u_x - \frac{\Delta^2 u_x}{2} + \frac{\Delta^3 u_x}{3} - \cdots.$$

Similarly, we can express $\dfrac{du_x}{dx}$ in terms of central differences. For example, Stirling's formula is

$$u_x = u_0 + x \frac{\Delta u_0 + \Delta u_{-1}}{2} + \frac{x^2}{2!} \Delta^2 u_{-1} + \frac{x(x^2-1)}{3!} \frac{\Delta^3 u_{-1} + \Delta^3 u_{-2}}{2} + \cdots.$$

Differentiating with respect to x:

$$\frac{du_x}{dx} = \frac{\Delta u_0 + \Delta u_{-1}}{2} + x\Delta^2 u_{-1} + \frac{3x^2 - 1}{6}\frac{\Delta^3 u_{-1} + \Delta^3 u_{-2}}{2} + \ldots.$$

$$\therefore \ \left(\frac{du_x}{dx}\right)_{x=0} = \frac{\Delta u_0 + \Delta u_{-1}}{2} - \frac{1}{12}\left[\Delta^3 u_{-1} + \Delta^3 u_{-2}\right]$$

as far as third differences

$$= \frac{u_1 - u_{-1}}{2} - \frac{1}{12}\left[u_2 - 3u_1 + 3u_0 - u_{-1} + u_1 - 3u_0 + 3u_{-1} - u_{-2}\right]$$

$$= \frac{2}{3}(u_1 - u_{-1}) - \frac{1}{12}(u_2 - u_{-2}) \quad \text{on simplifying.}$$

Changing the origin, we have

$$\frac{du_x}{dx} = \frac{2}{3}(u_{x+1} - u_{x-1}) - \frac{1}{12}(u_{x+2} - u_{x-2}).$$

A first approximation will evidently be

$$\frac{du_x}{dx} = \frac{u_{x+1} - u_{x-1}}{2}.$$

or, if the unit of differencing be h,

$$= \frac{u_{x+h} - u_{x-h}}{2h}.$$

This simple approximation can be seen quite easily from a consideration of the geometry of the figure.

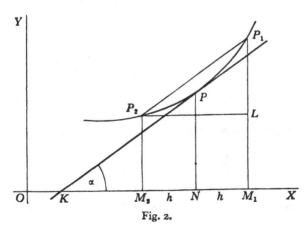

Fig. 2.

Let P be the point whose coordinates are (x, u_x) and let P_1, P_2 be the two points whose coordinates are $(x+h, u_{x+h})$ and $(x-h, u_{x-h})$ respectively.

Then if PK be the tangent at P

$$\frac{du_x}{dx} = \tan \alpha$$

$$= \frac{P_1 L}{P_2 L} \text{ nearly}$$

$$= \frac{P_1 M_1 - LM_1}{M_2 M_1}$$

$$= \frac{u_{x+h} - u_{x-h}}{2h}.$$

9. Another formula, giving the differential coefficient in terms of central differences, can be obtained from Bessel's formula.

$$u_x = \frac{u_0 + u_1}{2} + (x - \tfrac{1}{2}) \Delta u_0 + \frac{x(x-1)}{2!} \frac{\Delta^2 u_{-1} + \Delta^2 u_0}{2}$$

$$+ \frac{(x - \tfrac{1}{2}) x (x-1)}{3!} \Delta^3 u_{-1} + \dots$$

Changing x to $x + \tfrac{1}{2}$,

$$u_{x+\frac{1}{2}} = \frac{u_0 + u_1}{2} + x\Delta u_0 + \frac{(x + \tfrac{1}{2})(x - \tfrac{1}{2})}{2!} \frac{\Delta^2 u_{-1} + \Delta^2 u_0}{2}$$

$$+ \frac{x (x + \tfrac{1}{2})(x - \tfrac{1}{2})}{3!} \Delta^3 u_{-1} + \dots$$

Differentiating:

$$\frac{d}{dx} u_{x+\frac{1}{2}} = \Delta u_0 + x \frac{\Delta^2 u_{-1} + \Delta^2 u_0}{2} + \left(\frac{x^2}{2} - \frac{1}{24}\right) \Delta^3 u_{-1} + \dots$$

If $x = 0$, $\qquad \dfrac{d}{dx} u_{\frac{1}{2}} = \Delta u_0 - \dfrac{\Delta^3 u_{-1}}{24} + \dots$

Changing the origin to $x - \tfrac{1}{2}$ we have the approximation

$$\frac{d}{dx} u_x = \Delta u_{x-\frac{1}{2}} - \frac{\Delta^3 u_{x-\frac{3}{2}}}{24} + \dots$$

An interesting discussion on the calculation of the values of differential coefficients of a function by means of selected values of the variable will be found in *T.F.A.* vol. IX, pp. 238 *et seq.* (G. J. Lidstone). By means of tables of coefficients prepared for convenience of practical working Mr Lidstone evolves formulae for the values of the successive differential coefficients, both for advancing differences and central differences. In addition, alternative processes are given for the values of the derivatives when the intervals are unequal.

*10. It should be borne in mind that, in choosing a formula for the expression of the differential coefficient of a function in terms of its differences, central difference formulae are to be preferred to advancing differences. These formulae possess smaller coefficients and have the additional advantage that alternate coefficients vanish. Further, a greater degree of accuracy may be obtained by the use of a suitable central difference formula.

Mr G. J. Lidstone has pointed out that if for any reason it is decided to use the relation

$$D \equiv \Delta - \tfrac{1}{2}\Delta^2 + \tfrac{1}{3}\Delta^3 - \dots$$

considerable increase of accuracy can be secured by the simple and easily remembered device of ending with $\dfrac{1}{n}\Delta^n u_{x-1}$ instead of $\dfrac{1}{n}\Delta^n u_x$. We bring in u_{-1} for the purpose of obtaining $\Delta^n u_{x-1}$, omit u_{x+n+1} and otherwise use the formula as before, beginning with Δu_x. This reverses the sign of the error and reduces it numerically in the ratio $1:(n+1)$. Thus, $\dfrac{1}{n}\Delta^n - \dfrac{1}{n+1}\Delta^{n+1}$ is replaced by

$$\frac{1}{n}\Delta^n - \frac{1}{n}\Delta^{n+1}.$$

It is assumed that $\Delta^{n+1}u$, though not negligible, is not varying greatly. The proportionate improvement increases with n, and if n is at all considerable, we attain approximately the accuracy of a further order of differences with no additional work.

The same process may be employed for the second and third differential coefficients, after which the improvement, though present, is not proportionately so marked.

THE COMPOUND FUNCTION $u_x v_x$

11. We can adapt the principle of separation of symbols to the evaluation of such expressions as $\Delta^n u_x v_x$ by a simple extension of the process of differencing.

Let $\Delta_1, E_1, \Sigma_1, \ldots$ denote operations on u_x alone and $\Delta_2, E_2, \Sigma_2, \ldots$ operations on v_x alone.

Then
$$\Delta u_x v_x = u_{x+1} v_{x+1} - u_x v_x$$
$$= E_1 u_x . E_2 v_x - u_x v_x$$
$$= (E_1 E_2 - 1) u_x v_x.$$
$$\therefore \quad \Delta^n u_x v_x = (E_1 E_2 - 1)^n u_x v_x.$$

By expressing $E_1 E_2$ in terms of Δ_1 and Δ_2 we are enabled to obtain expressions for the expansion of $\Delta^n u_x v_x$.

First, if $n = 1$, we have
$$\Delta u_x v_x = [(1 + \Delta_1)(1 + \Delta_2) - 1] u_x v_x$$
$$= (\Delta_1 + \Delta_2 + \Delta_1 \Delta_2) u_x v_x$$
$$= (\Delta_1 + \Delta_2 E_1) u_x v_x$$
$$= \Delta_1 u_x v_x + \Delta_2 E_1 u_x v_x$$
$$= v_x \Delta_1 u_x + E_1 u_x . \Delta_2 v_x$$
$$= v_x \Delta_1 u_x + u_{x+1} \Delta_2 v_x,$$

or, dropping the suffixes,
$$= v_x \Delta u_x + u_{x+1} \Delta v_x,$$

which is otherwise evident.

Again,
$$\Delta^n u_x v_x = (\Delta_1 + E_1 \Delta_2)^n u_x v_x$$
$$= (\Delta_1^n + n_{(1)} \Delta_1^{n-1} E_1 \Delta_2 + n_{(2)} \Delta_1^{n-2} E_1^2 \Delta_2^2 + \ldots) u_x v_x,$$

which is easily seen to be

$$v_x \Delta^n u_x + n_{(1)} \Delta v_x \Delta^{n-1} u_{x+1} + n_{(2)} \Delta^2 v_x \Delta^{n-2} u_{x+2} + \ldots + u_{x+n} \Delta^n v_x.$$

If in the above expression we put $u_x = x^{m-1}$ and $v_x = x$, we have

$$\Delta^n (x^{m-1} . x) = x \Delta^n x^{m-1} + n \Delta^{n-1} (x+1)^{m-1}.$$

Let $x = 0$; then

$$\Delta^n o^m = n\Delta^{n-1} 1^{m-1} = n\Delta^{n-1} E o^{m-1} = n\left(\Delta^{n-1} o^{m-1} + \Delta^n o^{m-1}\right),$$

which is the relation proved in paragraph 2.

12. The ordinary formula for finite integration by parts is

$$\Sigma u_x v_x = u_x \Sigma v_x - \Sigma\left[\Delta u_x \Sigma v_{x+1}\right] + \text{an arbitrary constant.}$$

In cases where the formula has to be applied more than once we may use the series found below.

$$\begin{aligned}
\Sigma \equiv \Delta^{-1} &\equiv (\Delta_1 + \Delta_2 + \Delta_1 \Delta_2)^{-1}\\
&\equiv [\Delta_2 + \Delta_1(1+\Delta_2)]^{-1}\\
&\equiv \Delta_2^{-1}[1+\Delta_1\Delta_2^{-1}(1+\Delta_2)]^{-1}\\
&\equiv \Delta_2^{-1}[1-\Delta_1\Delta_2^{-1}(1+\Delta_2)+\Delta_1^2\Delta_2^{-2}(1+\Delta_2)^2-\ldots]\\
&\equiv \Delta_2^{-1}-\Delta_1\Delta_2^{-2}(1+\Delta_2)+\Delta_1^2\Delta_2^{-3}(1+\Delta_2)^2-\ldots\\
&\equiv \Delta_2^{-1}-\Delta_1\Delta_2^{-2}E_2+\Delta_1^2\Delta_2^{-3}E_2^2-\ldots.
\end{aligned}$$

On dropping the suffixes and inserting the appropriate functions, we have

$$\Sigma u_x v_x = u_x \Sigma v_x - \Delta u_x \Sigma^2 v_{x+1} + \Delta^2 u_x \Sigma^3 v_{x+2} - \ldots. \qquad (a)$$

By an alternative treatment another formula is obtained:

$$\Sigma u_x v_x = u_{x-1} \Sigma v_x - \Delta u_{x-2} \Sigma^2 v_x + \Delta^2 u_{x-3} \Sigma^3 v_x - \ldots. \qquad (b)$$

As an example of the use of a series for $\Sigma u_x v_x$ we may prove the formula for $\Sigma a^x u_x$ given in Chap. VI, paragraph 10.

Example 3.

Prove that

$$\Sigma a^x u_x = \frac{a^x}{a-1}\left\{1-\frac{a\Delta}{a-1}+\frac{a^2\Delta^2}{(a-1)^2}-\frac{a^3\Delta^3}{(a-1)^3}+\ldots\right\}u_x$$

$$\Sigma a^x = \frac{a^x}{a-1}, \quad \Sigma^2 a^{x+1} = \frac{a^{x+1}}{(a-1)^2}, \quad \Sigma^3 a^{x+2} = \frac{a^{x+2}}{(a-1)^3}, \quad \Sigma^4 a^{x+3} = \frac{a^{x+3}}{(a-1)^4},$$

and so on.

Let $a^x = v_x$ in series (a).

Then

$$\Sigma u_x a^x = u_x \Sigma a^x - \Delta u_x \Sigma^2 a^{x+1} + \Delta^2 u_x \Sigma^3 a^{x+2} - \Delta^3 u_x \Sigma^4 a^{x+3} + \dots$$

$$= u_x \frac{a^x}{a-1} - \Delta u_x \frac{a^{x+1}}{(a-1)^2} + \Delta^2 u_x \frac{a^{x+2}}{(a-1)^3} - \Delta^3 u_x \frac{a^{x+3}}{(a-1)^4} + \dots$$

$$= \frac{a^x}{a-1} \left\{ 1 - \frac{a\Delta}{a-1} + \frac{a^2 \Delta^2}{(a-1)^2} - \frac{a^3 \Delta^3}{(a-1)^3} + \dots \right\} u_x.$$

13. The following is a further illustration of the application of the above method.

Example 4.

Prove that

$$\Sigma^n (u_x v_x) = u_x \Sigma^n v_x - n_{(1)} \Delta u_x \Sigma^{n+1} v_{x+1} + (n+1)_{(2)} \Delta^2 u_x \Sigma^{n+2} v_{x+2}$$
$$- (n+2)_{(3)} \Delta^3 u_x \Sigma^{n+3} v_{x+3} + \dots.$$

Now $\Delta u_x v_x = [\Delta_2 + \Delta_1 (1 + \Delta_2)] u_x v_x.$

$$\therefore \quad \Sigma^n \equiv \Delta^{-n} \equiv [\Delta_2 + \Delta_1 (1 + \Delta_2)]^{-n} \equiv \Delta_2^{-n} (1 + \Delta_1 \Delta_2^{-1} E_2)^{-n}.$$

$$\therefore \quad \Sigma^n u_x v_x = \Delta_2^{-n} [1 - n_{(1)} \Delta_1 \Delta_2^{-1} E_2 + (n+1)_{(2)} \Delta_1^2 \Delta_2^{-2} E_2^2$$
$$- (n+2)_{(3)} \Delta_1^3 \Delta_2^{-3} E_2^3 + \dots] u_x v_x$$
$$= u_x \Sigma^n v_x - n_{(1)} \Delta u_x \Sigma^{n+1} v_{x+1} + (n+1)_{(2)} \Delta^2 u_x \Sigma^{n+2} v_{x+2}$$
$$- (n+2)_{(3)} \Delta^3 u_x \Sigma^{n+3} v_{x+3} + \dots$$

If $n = 1$ we have

$$\Sigma u_x v_x = \Delta_2^{-1} (1 + \Delta_1 \Delta_2^{-1} E_2)^{-1} u_x v_x$$

$$= \Delta_2^{-1} \left(1 - \frac{\Delta_1 \Delta_2^{-1} E_2}{1 + \Delta_1 \Delta_2^{-1} E_2} \right) u_x v_x$$

$$= \left(\Delta_2^{-1} - \frac{\Delta_1 \Delta_2^{-1} E_2}{\Delta_2 + \Delta_1 E_2} \right) u_x v_x$$

$$= \left(\Delta_2^{-1} - \frac{\Delta_1 \Delta_2^{-1} E_2}{E_1 E_2 - 1} \right) u_x v_x$$

$$= u_x \Sigma v_x - \Delta^{-1} (\Delta u_x \Sigma v_{x+1})$$

$$= u_x \Sigma v_x - \Sigma (\Delta u_x \Sigma v_{x+1}),$$

the ordinary formula for summation by parts.

The subject of finite integration by parts is treated more fully in Chapter VIII.

FUNCTIONS OF TWO VARIABLES

14. When x and y are independent variables, u_{xy}, $f(x, y)$, ... represent functions which assume different values according to the values of x and y. An alternative notation is $u_{x:y}$ or $f(x:y)$. For example, the function

$$x^2 + 2xy + y^2 + x + 3y,$$

in which x and y both vary, may be written shortly as either u_{xy} or $u_{x:y}$. If y is a function of x, we may reduce u_{xy} to the form v_x and thus obtain a function depending on x alone.

Now suppose that x is changed to $x+h$ and that y is changed to $y+k$ while x remains constant. Then the new value of the function is dependent on $x+h$ and $y+k$. It is not necessary for both x and y to vary: x may become $x+h$ while y remains constant or vice versa.

If the values of the function proceed by equidistant intervals, we have the following scheme:

$u_{x:y}$	$u_{x+h:y}$	$u_{x+2h:y}$	$u_{x+3h:y}$	...
$u_{x:y+k}$	$u_{x+h:y+k}$	$u_{x+2h.y+k}$	$u_{x+3h:y+k}$	...
$u_{x:y+2k}$	$u_{x+h:y+2k}$	$u_{x+2h:y+2k}$	$u_{x+3h:y+2k}$	...
$u_{x:y+3k}$	$u_{x+h:y+3k}$	$u_{x+2h:y+3k}$	$u_{x+3h:y+3k}$	...
$\vdots$	$\vdots$	$\vdots$	$\vdots$	

or, if our origin be (0, 0) and $h = k = 1$,

$u_{0:0}$	$u_{1:0}$	$u_{2:0}$	$u_{3:0}$	...
$u_{0:1}$	$u_{1:1}$	$u_{2:1}$	$u_{3:1}$	...
$u_{0:2}$	$u_{1:2}$	$u_{2:2}$	$u_{3:2}$	...
$\vdots$	$\vdots$	$\vdots$	$\vdots$	

15. If we are to apply the processes of finite differences as hitherto defined we must distinguish between an increase in the value of x and an increase in the value of y. We therefore write E_x to denote the operation of increasing the value of x by a unit difference while y remains constant, and E_y similarly for y while x remains constant.

That is, $E_x u_{0:0} = u_{1:0}$ and $E_y u_{0:0} = u_{0:1}$,

so that $\Delta_x u_{0:0} = u_{1:0} - u_{0:0}$ and $\Delta_y u_{0:0} = u_{0:1} - u_{0:0}$.

Again,
$$\begin{aligned}
\Delta_x \Delta_y u_{0:0} &= \Delta_x \left(\Delta_y u_{0:0} \right) \\
&= \Delta_x \left(u_{0:1} - u_{0:0} \right) \\
&= \Delta_x u_{0:1} - \Delta_x u_{0:0} \\
&= u_{1:1} - u_{0:1} - u_{1:0} + u_{0:0},
\end{aligned}$$

and
$$\begin{aligned}
\Delta_x^2 \Delta_y u_{0:0} &= \Delta_x^2 \left(u_{0:1} - u_{0:0} \right) \\
&= \Delta_x^2 u_{0:1} - \Delta_x^2 u_{0:0} \\
&= \left(u_{2:1} - 2u_{1:1} + u_{0:1} \right) - \left(u_{2:0} - 2u_{1:0} + u_{0:0} \right).
\end{aligned}$$

The general formula corresponding to the advancing difference formula for one independent variable is

$$\begin{aligned}
u_{m:n} &= \left(1 + \Delta_x \right)^m \left(1 + \Delta_y \right)^n u_{0:0} \\
&= \left(1 + m_{(1)} \Delta_x + m_{(2)} \Delta_x^2 + \ldots \right) \left(1 + n_{(1)} \Delta_y + n_{(2)} \Delta_y^2 + \ldots \right) u_{0:0} \\
&= \left(1 + m_{(1)} \Delta_x + m_{(2)} \Delta_x^2 + m_{(3)} \Delta_x^3 + \ldots \right. \\
&\qquad + n_{(1)} \Delta_y + m_{(1)} n_{(1)} \Delta_x \Delta_y + m_{(2)} n_{(1)} \Delta_x^2 \Delta_y + \ldots \\
&\qquad + n_{(2)} \Delta_y^2 + m_{(1)} n_{(2)} \Delta_x \Delta_y^2 + \ldots \\
&\qquad \left. + n_{(3)} \Delta_y^3 + \ldots \right) u_{0:0} \\[4pt]
&= u_{0:0} + \left(m_{(1)} \Delta_x + n_{(1)} \Delta_y \right) u_{0:0} \\
&\quad + \left(m_{(2)} \Delta_x^2 + m_{(1)} n_{(1)} \Delta_x \Delta_y + n_{(2)} \Delta_y^2 \right) u_{0:0} \\
&\quad + \left(m_{(3)} \Delta_x^3 + m_{(2)} n_{(1)} \Delta_x^2 \Delta_y + m_{(1)} n_{(2)} \Delta_x \Delta_y^2 + n_{(3)} \Delta_y^3 \right) u_{0:0} + \ldots
\end{aligned}$$

It often happens that a certain order of differences, say the rth, is sufficient for interpolation along the x-line, while a higher order is necessary for the y-line. This is especially so when x is a young age and y an older age (see p. 137, Ex. 5). In this case, the formula can be simplified by omitting all terms involving $\Delta_x^{r+1} u$ whether standing alone or combined with values of $\Delta_y u$. For the same reason it may be desirable in tabulating to use smaller intervals for y than for x, according to the nature of the function.

16. Application of the formula.

Example 5.

Given the following table of values of $u_{x:y}$, estimate the value of $u_{23:17}$.

x	$y=15$	$y=20$	$y=25$
20	5·947	4·418	3·547
25	6·046	4·530	
30	6·144		

Here the interval of differencing is 5. Changing the origin to the point (0, 0) and the unit to 1, the data are given for the points (0, 0), (1, 0), (2, 0); (0, 1), (0, 2); (1, 1). The value required is $u_{.6:.4}$. Differencing downwards for values of $\Delta_x u_{0:0}$, etc., we have

$$\Delta_x u_{0:0} = \cdot099; \quad \Delta_x^2 u_{0:0} = -\cdot001.$$

Differencing across for values of $\Delta_y u_{0:0}$, etc.,

$$\Delta_y u_{0:0} = -1\cdot529; \quad \Delta_y^2 u_{0:0} = \cdot658.$$

Also $\quad \Delta_x \Delta_y u_{0:0} = u_{1:1} - u_{0:1} - u_{1:0} + u_{0:0} = \cdot013.$

$$\therefore \quad u_{.6:.4} = (1 + \cdot6\Delta_x - \cdot12\Delta_x^2 \ldots)(1 + \cdot4\Delta_y - \cdot12\Delta_y^2 \ldots) u_{0:0}$$
$$= (1 + \cdot6\Delta_x + \cdot4\Delta_y - \cdot12\Delta_x^2 + \cdot24\Delta_x\Delta_y - \cdot12\Delta_y^2) u_{0:0}$$
$$= 5\cdot319.$$

Note. Here it is not really necessary to use $\Delta_x^2 u_{0:0}$: see end of paragraph 15.

17. While for most purposes the formula given above is convenient, special circumstances may arise in which other methods may be more suitable. Where the intervals are not equidistant we may apply either a method of divided differences or one of various adaptations of Lagrange's formula depending upon the number of points given. If, for example, four values of $u_{x:y}$ are given, namely $u_{\alpha:a}$; $u_{\alpha:b}$; $u_{\beta:b}$, $u_{\beta:a}$; then it is quite easy to show that

$$u_{x:y} = u_{\alpha:a} \frac{(x-\beta)(y-b)}{(\alpha-\beta)(a-b)} + u_{\alpha.b} \frac{(x-\beta)(y-a)}{(\alpha-\beta)(b-a)}$$
$$+ u_{\beta:b} \frac{(x-\alpha)(y-a)}{(\beta-\alpha)(b-a)} + u_{\beta:a} \frac{(x-\alpha)(y-b)}{(\beta-\alpha)(a-b)}.$$

If more than four values are given the formula becomes unwieldy. It is seldom necessary to interpolate except between equidistant values of the function, and in that event a form of advancing or central difference series is generally preferable.

Two-variable functions are of great frequency in actuarial work. Tables of annuity-values $(a_{x:y})$ depending upon joint lives are often available for quinquennial values of x and y, and when values at ages other than those tabulated are required recourse must be had to methods of interpolation. Although the formulae given above are of general application special methods can be found to meet the requirements of the problem to be solved.

For example, if quinquennial values of $a_{x:y}$ are available, and if the two ages concerned are such that their sum is a multiple of 5, we may choose our origin and interval of differencing so that $x+y=1$. We have then, from the general formula for $u_{x.y}$,

$$u_{x:1-x}=u_{0:0}+[x\Delta_x+(1-x)\Delta_y+\tfrac{1}{2}x(x-1)(\Delta_x^2-2\Delta_x\Delta_y+\Delta_y^2)]u_{0:0};$$

i.e.

$$u_{x:1-x}=u_{0:1}+x(u_{1:0}-u_{0:1})+\tfrac{1}{2}x(x-1)(u_{2:0}-2u_{1:1}+u_{0:2}).$$

Again, if $x+y=2$, this formula becomes

$$u_{x:2-x}=\tfrac{1}{2}x(x-1)u_{2:0}-x(x-2)u_{1:1}+\tfrac{1}{2}(x-1)(x-2)u_{0:2},$$

or, on changing the origin,

$$u_{x:-x}=\tfrac{1}{2}(x-1)(x-2)u_{0:0}-x(x-2)u_{1:-1}+\tfrac{1}{2}x(x-1)u_{2:-2},$$

for which the data required are $u_{0:0}$, $u_{1:-1}$ and $u_{2:-2}$. The problem is thus reduced to a single variable interpolation.

This second formula is very useful in practice. As a rule we can choose our data within wide limits, and it has been found that with certain functions the three-term formula gives as good approximations to the true results as do formulae involving higher orders of differences (see Spencer, *J.I.A.* vol. XL, pp. 293–301).

The general second difference formula of which the above is a particular example is

$$u_{x:rx}=mu_{0:0}+nu_{1:r}+pu_{2:2r},$$

and in the note referred to above, Spencer gives a table showing the application of this formula according as r takes the values 0, 1, −1 or 2.

Another form of the formula for an interpolated value of $u_{x:y}$ when four values are given is $u_{x:y} = \xi\,(\eta u_{0:0} + yu_{0:1}) + x\,(\eta u_{1:0} + yu_{1:1})$, where x and y are both less than unity and $x + \xi = y + \eta = 1$. The second difference formula can be written as

$$u_{x:y} = [1 - (k_1\delta_x{}^2 + k_2\delta_y{}^2)]\,[\xi\,(\eta u_{0:0} + yu_{0:1}) + x\,(\eta u_{1:0} + yu_{1:1})],$$

where $\delta_x{}^2u$ and $\delta_y{}^2u$ are second central differences with respect to x and y respectively and k_1 and k_2 are factors depending upon the values of x and y (Buchanan, *T.F.A.* vol. x, pp. 329, 330).

Example 6.

Values of the joint-life annuity $a_{x:y}$ for quinquennial ages being available, find a value for $a_{44:51}$.

(i) Take the origin at $(40:50)$; then if the interval of differencing be 5 years, $(44:51)$ will be represented by $(\cdot8:\cdot2)$ and $x + y = 1$.

$$u_{x:1-x} = u_{0:1} + x\,(u_{1:0} - u_{0:1}) + \tfrac{1}{2}x\,(x-1)\,(u_{2:0} - 2u_{1:1} + u_{0:2}).$$

The data required are

$$a_{40:55} = 10\cdot135 \qquad a_{40:60} = 8\cdot926 \qquad a_{45:50} = 10\cdot763$$
$$a_{50:50} = 10\cdot202 \qquad a_{45:55} = 9\cdot854$$

Then
$$u_{\cdot8:\cdot2} = 10\cdot135 + \cdot8\,(10\cdot763 - 10\cdot135)$$
$$\qquad + \tfrac{1}{2}\cdot8\,(-\cdot2)\,(10\cdot202 - 19\cdot708 + 8\cdot926)$$
$$= 10\cdot135 + \cdot5024 + \cdot0464$$
$$= 10\cdot684.$$

(ii) Take the origin at $(40:45)$ so that $(44:51)$ will be $(\cdot8:1\cdot2)$ and $x + y = 2$.

$$u_{x:2-x} = \tfrac{1}{2}\,(x-1)\,(x-2)\,u_{0:2} - x\,(x-2)\,u_{1:1} + \tfrac{1}{2}x\,(x-1)\,u_{2:0}.$$

The three values required are

$$a_{40:55} = 10\cdot135,$$
$$a_{45:50} = 10\cdot763,$$
$$a_{50:45} = 10\cdot763.$$

$$u_{\cdot8:1\cdot2} = \tfrac{1}{2}\,(-\cdot2)\,(-1\cdot2)\,10\cdot135 - \cdot8\,(-1\cdot2)\,10\cdot763 + \tfrac{1}{2}\,(\cdot8)\,(-\cdot2)\,10\cdot763$$
$$= 10\cdot688.$$

If nine values surrounding the point $(44:51)$ be taken and a Lagrange formula for these nine values be used, the value for $a_{44:51}$ becomes $10\cdot684$.

This nine-point formula is a safe formula for occasional interpolation, and by its use the risk and labour attaching to the calculation of differences may be avoided. The formula is used centrally, the area of interpolation being as shown in the diagram below. The ordinary single-variable Lagrange interpolation formula is used to interpolate for x in each column, and the formula is used again to interpolate for y from the three calculated values.

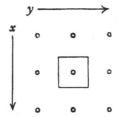

This process is very simple with the aid of a machine, especially for quinquennial intervals, when the coefficients are as follows:

Interval	u_{-1}	u_0	u_1
$-\cdot4$	$-\cdot12$	$+\cdot84$	$+\cdot28$
$-\cdot2$	$-\cdot08$	$+\cdot96$	$+\cdot12$
$+\cdot2$	$+\cdot12$	$+\cdot96$	$-\cdot08$
$+\cdot4$	$+\cdot28$	$+\cdot84$	$-\cdot12$

18. The above example shows that different degrees of accuracy may be obtained by choosing different sets of data on which to work. The general theory follows the same lines as that for single-variable interpolation. It will be remembered that the ordinary advancing difference formula may be applied to the expansion of u_x in terms of the differences of u_x on the assumption that $y = u_x$ is a rational integral function of x. In these circumstances we may represent the function graphically, and the successive values of x and y will be points on the plane curve $y = u_x$. When we are considering a function of two variables x and y we assume similarly that we may represent $z = u_{x:y}$ as a surface. Now in Chapter V (paragraph 15) it was proved that the effect of including higher differences in the expansion for u_x does not necessarily give better results than if they are neglected. In the same way it may be shown that by choosing more points on which to work we may exceptionally produce a result farther from the true value z on the surface $z = u_{x:y}$ than we should obtain by relying on fewer data.

With regular data the formulae with x, y in the central area of the given points are usually preferable. In the space for which x, y are both positive and less than $\frac{1}{2}$, which includes all cases if the origin and direction of the axes are suitably chosen, a simple central difference formula is

$$u_{x:y} = u_{0:0} + \tfrac{1}{2}x\,(u_{1:0} - u_{-1:0}) + \tfrac{1}{2}y\,(u_{0:1} - u_{0:-1}).$$

This is based on five points.

This formula and the six-point formula consisting of the same terms with the addition of

$$\tfrac{1}{2}x^2\,(u_{-1:0} - 2u_{0:0} + u_{1:0}) + \tfrac{1}{2}y^2\,(u_{0:1} - 2u_{0:0} + u_{0:-1})$$
$$+ xy\,(u_{1:1} + u_{0:0} - u_{1:0} - u_{0:1})$$

are probably the most useful interpolation formulae for ordinary actuarial purposes (Todhunter, *J.I.A.* vol. LIII, p. 89). In some cases either the first or the second additional terms may be omitted (see end of paragraph 15).

*19. Taylor's theorem for a function of a single variable,

$$f(x+h) = f(x) + hf'(x) + \frac{h^2}{2!}f''(x) + \dots,$$

may be written symbolically as

$$f(x+h) = e^{hD}f(x) \quad \text{(see paragraph 6 above)}.$$

Denoting as usual partial differentiation by $\dfrac{\partial}{\partial x}$, $\dfrac{\partial}{\partial y}$, we have

$$f(x+h,\, y+k) = e^{h\frac{\partial}{\partial x}}f(x,\, y+k)$$
$$= e^{h\frac{\partial}{\partial x}} e^{k\frac{\partial}{\partial v}}f(x,\, y)$$
$$= e^{h\frac{\partial}{\partial x} + k\frac{\partial}{\partial v}}f(x,\, y)$$
$$= f(x,\, y) + \left(h\frac{\partial}{\partial x} + k\frac{\partial}{\partial y}\right)f(x,\, y) + \frac{1}{2!}\left(h\frac{\partial}{\partial x} + k\frac{\partial}{\partial y}\right)^2 f(x,\, y) + \dots.$$

This formula is of theoretical interest. For use with tables the partial differential coefficients must be replaced by differences, so that in effect the formula repeats the difference formula already given.

Thus, for quinquennial intervals,

$$(1 + \Delta_x)^{\frac{h}{5}}\,(1 + \Delta_y)^{\frac{k}{5}} \equiv e^{h\frac{\partial}{\partial x} + k\frac{\partial}{\partial v}}$$

so that $\quad \dfrac{h}{5}\log\left(1+\Delta_x\right)+\dfrac{k}{5}\log\left(1+\Delta_y\right)\equiv h\dfrac{\partial}{\partial x}+k\dfrac{\partial}{\partial y};$

$$\therefore\quad h\dfrac{\partial}{\partial x}+k\dfrac{\partial}{\partial y}\equiv\dfrac{1}{5}\left[h\left(\Delta_x-\dfrac{\Delta_x{}^2}{2}+\ldots\right)+k\left(\Delta_y-\dfrac{\Delta_y{}^2}{2}+\ldots\right)\right]$$

and $\quad\left(h\dfrac{\partial}{\partial x}+k\dfrac{\partial}{\partial y}\right)^2\equiv\dfrac{1}{25}\left[h^2\Delta_x{}^2+2hk\Delta_x\Delta_y+k^2\Delta_y{}^2\right]+\ldots.$

INTERPOLATION FORMULAE: FRASER'S HEXAGON DIAGRAMS

20. No demonstration of interpolation formulae would be complete without reference to Fraser's graphic method. In this method the ordinary differences of a function of x are combined with the relation $(x+1)_{(r)}=x_{(r)}+x_{(r-1)}$ in diagrammatic form so that by adopting certain conventions any finite difference formula can be written down immediately (Fraser, *J.I.A.* vol. XLIII, pp. 235 *et seq.*).

We have $\quad(x+t+1)_{(r)}=(x+t)_{(r)}+(x+t)_{(r-1)},$

or $\quad(x+t+1)_{(r)}-(x+t)_{(r)}=(x+t)_{(r-1)}.$

A relation similar to the fundamental finite difference identity $u_{x+h}-u_x=\Delta u_x$ exists therefore between these coefficients. If we carry the analogy still further we can construct a table of values of $(x+t)_{(r)}$ corresponding to a difference table.

The tables are set down in reverse order thus:

					$(x+3)_{(3)}$
u_{-2}				$(x+2)_{(2)}$	
Δu_{-2}			$(x+1)_{(1)}$		$(x+2)_{(3)}$
u_{-1}	$\Delta^2 u_{-2}$			$(x+1)_{(2)}$	
Δu_{-1}	$\Delta^3 u_{-2}$	$x_{(0)}$		$(x+1)_{(3)}$	
u_0	$\Delta^2 u_{-1}$	$\Delta^4 u_{-2}$	$x_{(1)}$		
Δu_0	$\Delta^3 u_{-1}$	$(x-1)_{(0)}$	$x_{(2)}$		
u_1	$\Delta^2 u_0$		$(x-1)_{(1)}$	$x_{(3)}$	
Δu_1			$(x-1)_{(2)}$		
u_2				$(x-1)_{(3)}$	

If now these two tables be combined, we have the following scheme, where, by convention, $x_{(0)}$, $(x-1)_{(0)} \ldots = 1$:

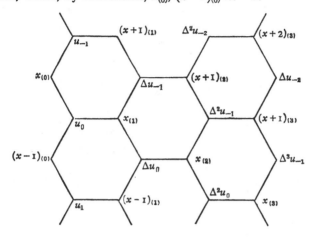

where for any one of the hexagons we may write in general

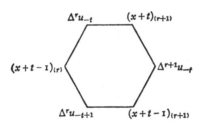

Now

$$(x+t-1)_{(r)}\, \Delta^r u_{-t} + (x+t)_{(r+1)}\, \Delta^{r+1} u_{-t} - (x+t-1)_{(r+1)}\, \Delta^{r+1} u_{-t}$$
$$- (x+t-1)_{(r)}\, \Delta^r u_{-t+1}$$
$$= (x+t-1)_{(r)}\, [\Delta^r u_{-t} - \Delta^r u_{-t+1}] + \Delta^{r+1} u_{-t}\, [(x+t)_{(r+1)}$$
$$- (x+t-1)_{(r+1)}]$$
$$= (x+t-1)_{(r)}\, [-\Delta^{r+1} u_{-t}] + \Delta^{r+1} u_{-t}\, (x+t-1)_{(r)}$$
$$= 0.$$

A relation is therefore established between the constituents of the various hexagons. If we make the following assumptions:

(i) the oblique lines denote multiplication and the horizontal lines addition; (ii) a line taken in a right-hand direction gives the product a positive sign, and in the opposite direction a negative sign, we can say that the sum of the operations performed in travelling round any hexagon is zero. It follows easily that the sum of the operations in travelling round any closed circuit is also zero.

It is evident from a consideration of the diagram that if we travel from any value of $(x+t)_{(k)}$ to any difference $\Delta^m u_n$ the result will be the same whatever route be taken. For example, from $(x-1)_{(0)}$ through u_0, $x_{(1)}$, Δu_0, $x_{(2)}$ to $\Delta^2 u_0$ and (by completing the hexagons) back along $(x-1)_{(2)}$, Δu_1, $(x-2)_{(1)}$, u_2, $(x-2)_{(0)}$, u_1 to $(x-1)_{(0)}$ again enables the following identity to be established:

$$(x-1)_{(0)}u_0 + x_{(1)}\Delta u_0 + x_{(2)}\Delta^2 u_0 - (x-1)_{(2)}\Delta^2 u_0 - (x-2)_{(1)}\Delta u_1$$
$$-(x-2)_{(0)}u_2 + (x-2)_{(0)}u_1 - (x-1)_{(0)}u_1 = 0.$$

Re-writing this, we have

$$u_0 + x\Delta u_0 + \tfrac{1}{2}x(x-1)\Delta^2 u_0 - \tfrac{1}{2}(x-1)(x-2)\Delta^2 u_0$$
$$-(x-2)\Delta u_1 - u_2 + u_1 - u_1 = 0,$$

or

$$u_0 + x\Delta u_0 + \tfrac{1}{2}x(x-1)\Delta^2 u_0 = u_2 + (x-2)\Delta u_1 + \tfrac{1}{2}(x-2)(x-1)\Delta^2 u_0.$$

Exactly the same result will be obtained by proceeding along an alternative route

$$(x-1)_{(0)}, u_0, x_{(1)}, \Delta u_0, x_{(2)}, \Delta^2 u_0$$

and back through

$$(x-1)_{(2)}, \Delta u_1, (x-1)_{(1)}, u_1, (x-1)_{(0)}.$$

The identity will be

$$(x-1)_{(0)}u_0 + x_{(1)}\Delta u_0 + x_{(2)}\Delta^2 u_0 - (x-1)_{(2)}\Delta^2 u_0 - (x-1)_{(1)}\Delta u_1$$
$$-(x-1)_{(0)}u_1 = 0,$$

or $\quad u_0 + x\Delta u_0 + \tfrac{1}{2}x(x-1)\Delta^2 u_0 = \tfrac{1}{2}(x-1)(x-2)\Delta^2 u_0$
$$+(x-1)\Delta u_1 + u_1;$$

i.e. $\qquad\qquad = \tfrac{1}{2}(x-1)(x-2)\Delta^2 u_0 + (x-2)\Delta u_1 + u_2,$

the same result as before.

21. Application of the hexagon diagram.

The above example gives a formula for u_2 in terms of u_0, Δu_0, $\Delta^2 u_0$ and Δu_1, and if we put $x=2$ we have a well-known identity. A similar process will give a formula for u_n, and since we may take various routes a number of different expansions of u_n will arise, all giving exact expressions for u_n. It should be further observed that when an nth difference has been reached by travelling along the upper route the terms other than u_n in the lower route will be zero, and it follows that by travelling round any circuit we obtain expressions involving an initial term u_n and terms of lower degree than n. This is seen to be so by considering $\Delta^n u_0$: all the coefficients along the lower route will contain $(x-n)$ as a factor and will therefore vanish when $x=n$.

We have therefore from the diagram the following expansions:

(i) $u_n = u_0 + n_{(1)}\Delta u_0 + n_{(2)}\Delta^2 u_0 + n_{(3)}\Delta^3 u_0 + \ldots$ (Newton's formula).

(ii) $u_n = u_0 + n_{(1)}\Delta u_0 + n_{(2)}\Delta^2 u_{-1} + (n+1)_{(3)}\Delta^3 u_{-1}$
$\qquad\qquad + (n+1)_{(4)}\Delta^4 u_{-2} + \ldots$ (Gauss's forward formula).

(iii) $u_n = u_0 + n_{(1)}\Delta u_{-1} + (n+1)_{(2)}\Delta^2 u_{-1} + (n+1)_{(3)}\Delta^3 u_{-2} + \ldots$
$\qquad\qquad\qquad\qquad$ (Gauss's backward formula).

(iv) $u_n = u_1 + (n-1)_{(1)}\Delta u_0 + n_{(2)}\Delta^2 u_0 + n_{(3)}\Delta^3 u_{-1}$
$\qquad\qquad + (n+1)_{(4)}\Delta^4 u_{-2} + \ldots$.

The mean of (ii) and (iii) gives Stirling's formula, and the mean of (iii) and (iv) can be arranged to give either Bessel's or Everett's form.

22. Mr Fraser has shown that the hexagon diagram can be used for divided differences in a similar manner to that given above for differences at equal intervals. (D. C. Fraser, *Newton and Interpolation*—a Memorial volume issued by the Mathematical Association, 1927.)

A typical hexagon involving divided differences is

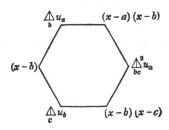

and the construction of the system follows closely the lines of that for ordinary differences.

The Δ diagram is a special case of the $\triangle$ diagram, since ordinary differences are themselves divided differences when the given values correspond to successive integral values of the argument. The results in the preceding paragraph could therefore be obtained by a consideration of the hexagon diagram for $\triangle$, the modifications necessary to produce the simpler forms of the central difference formulae being introduced at the last stage.

OTHER SYMBOLS OF OPERATION

*23. It has already been shown when considering the common operations of finite differences, Δu, Eu, Σu, that the symbols denoting the operations can, within limits, be treated as obeying the ordinary algebraic laws. By omitting the function u the various processes can be applied to the operators alone, with a resultant simplification of procedure. For example, the method can be adapted to the needs of the infinitesimal calculus, and Dr Aitken's introduction of his θ operator has produced an interpolation formula of extreme generality (see Chap. VIII). Other operators have been devised for special purposes connected with finite differences, and an interesting example is given below.

*24. The operator ∇.

In Chapter IV attention was drawn to certain symbols of operation which may be considered as supplementary to the Δ and E which are the basic operators in finite differences. These symbols —namely δ and μ—may also be assumed to follow the normal algebraic laws (with the usual limitations), and the method of separation of symbols may be applied to them equally with Δ, E and Σ. A further symbol has been introduced connecting u_x with the next lower value u_{x-1} instead of with the more usual value u_{x+1}. This symbol is ∇, and ∇u_x is defined as $u_x - u_{x-1}$.

Corresponding to $\qquad \Delta u_x = (E-1)\,u_x,$

we have therefore $\qquad \nabla u_x = (1 - E^{-1})\,u_x.$

Thus, for example,

$$\nabla^n u_x = (1 - E^{-1})^n u_x$$

$$= u_x - n_{(1)} u_{x-1} + n_{(2)} u_{x-2} - n_{(3)} u_{x-3} + \dots.$$

In addition to the familiar

$$\Delta x^{(m)} = m x^{(m-1)},$$

there is a similar relation

$$\nabla x^{(-m)} = m x^{(-m+1)},$$

where $x^{(-m)} \equiv (-1)^m (-x)^{(m)}$ and not the inverse factorial defined on p. 19; and if we denote the product

$$x (x + \tfrac{1}{2}n - 1)(x + \tfrac{1}{2}n - 2) \dots (x - \tfrac{1}{2}n + 1)$$

by $x^{[n]}$ it is easy to show that

$$\delta x^{[m]} = m x^{[m-1]}$$

(Steffensen, *Interpolation*, pp. 8, 9).

No new principle is involved in dealing with these further symbols of operation; their introduction simply enables us to develop expansions and to write down formulae for interpolation with a minimum of labour.

OSCULATORY INTERPOLATION

*25. It may happen that we know the values of u_x at intervals of a unit, and that we wish to calculate a complete table of values with smaller intervals. For example it is a common practice to calculate every fifth value in a life-table, and to complete the table by interpolation: here the unit interval for the preliminary calculations is five years.

If we decide to use a third difference formula then every interpolation involves four of the given values. For the interval 0 to 1 the best course is to base the formula on the four values u_{-1}, u_0, u_1, u_2, thus giving equal weight to values on either side of the interval. An appropriate formula is Bessel's formula, namely,

$$u_x = \tfrac{1}{2}(u_0 + u_1) + (x - \tfrac{1}{2}) \Delta u_0 + \frac{x(x-1)}{2!} \frac{\Delta^2 u_0 + \Delta^2 u_{-1}}{2}$$

$$+ \frac{(x - \tfrac{1}{2}) x (x-1)}{3!} \Delta^3 u_{-1}. \quad \dots\dots(i)$$

This is the formula for the interval o to 1. For the interval 1 to 2 we should use the corresponding formula based on the four given values u_0, u_1, u_2, u_3.

Thus for the two intervals o to 1 and 1 to 2, the two interpolation curves have a common ordinate when $x = 1$; they may not necessarily have a common tangent. Two neighbouring interpolation curves will usually cut one another at the point of junction, and while there will be a smooth run of values within each unit interval the values will not run smoothly with those in the next interval.

We are led therefore to enquire whether we can find a series of curves of interpolation which shall have common tangents as well as common ordinates at the points of junction. Such curves are said to have *contact of the first order* at the points where they join, and the necessary condition for this contact is evidently that u_x and $\dfrac{du_x}{dx}$ must have the same values at these points on the one curve as on the other.

The interpolation curve given by Bessel's formula (i) for the interval o to 1 was based on the conditions that it should have u_{-1}, u_0, u_1, u_2 as ordinates. We retain the condition that u_0 and u_1 should be ordinates and abandon the condition that u_{-1} and u_2 should be ordinates. Instead, we shall stipulate that the differential coefficients of u_x when $x = 0$ and when $x = 1$ have known values. To fix these values we shall proceed as follows:

The interpolation curves for the two intervals -1 to o and o to 1 are to have the same tangent when $x = 0$ as the curve of second degree which has u_{-1}, u_0 and u_1 for ordinates. The equation to this curve may be written

$$F_x(-1, 0, 1) = \tfrac{1}{2}(u_0 + u_1) + (x - \tfrac{1}{2})\Delta u_0 + \tfrac{1}{2}x(x-1)\Delta^2 u_{-1}. \quad \text{...(ii)}$$

The interpolation curves for the two intervals o to 1 and 1 to 2 are to have the same tangent when $x = 1$ as the curve of the second degree which has u_0, u_1 and u_2 for ordinates. In a similar manner to the above the equation to this curve may be written

$$F_x(0, 1, 2) = \tfrac{1}{2}(u_0 + u_1) + (x - \tfrac{1}{2})\Delta u_0 + \tfrac{1}{2}x(x-1)\Delta^2 u_0. \quad \text{...(iii)}$$

It will be noticed that the forms which we have chosen for the equations (ii) and (iii) differ only in the last term.

Differentiating (ii),

$$F_x' (-1, 0, 1) = \Delta u_0 + (x - \tfrac{1}{2}) \Delta^2 u_{-1},$$

so that $\qquad F_0' (-1, 0, 1) = \Delta u_0 - \tfrac{1}{2}\Delta^2 u_{-1}.$ ......(iv)

Differentiating (iii),

$$F_x' (0, 1, 2) = \Delta u_0 + (x - \tfrac{1}{2}) \Delta^2 u_0,$$

and $\qquad F_1' (0, 1, 2) = \Delta u_0 + \tfrac{1}{2}\Delta^2 u_0.$ ......(v)

The values of $F_0' (-1, 0, 1)$ and $F_1' (0, 1, 2)$ in (iv) and (v) are to be values of the differential coefficients of the required interpolation curve for the interval 0 to 1.

Let v_x be that curve, so that its ordinates when $x = -1, 0, 1, 2$ form the basis for an ordinary interpolation formula of the third degree:

$$v_x = \tfrac{1}{2} (v_0 + v_1) + (x - \tfrac{1}{2}) \Delta v_0 + \frac{x (x-1)}{2!} \frac{\Delta^2 v_0 + \Delta^2 v_{-1}}{2}$$

$$+ \frac{(x - \tfrac{1}{2}) x (x-1)}{3!} \Delta^3 v_{-1}. \quad ......(vi)$$

The tangents to this curve are given by the equation

$$v_x' = \Delta v_0 + (x - \tfrac{1}{2}) \frac{\Delta^2 v_0 + \Delta^2 v_{-1}}{2} + \frac{3x^2 - 3x + \tfrac{1}{2}}{6} \Delta^3 v_{-1}. \quad ...(vii)$$

The conditions to be satisfied are:

$$v_0 = u_0,$$

$$v_1 = u_1,$$

$$v_0' = F_0' (-1, 0, 1) = \Delta u_0 - \tfrac{1}{2}\Delta^2 u_{-1},$$

$$v_1' = F_1' (0, 1, 2) = \Delta u_0 + \tfrac{1}{2}\Delta^2 u_0. \qquad ......(viii)$$

We have at once $\tfrac{1}{2} (v_0 + v_1) = \tfrac{1}{2} (u_0 + u_1)$, and $\Delta v_0 = \Delta u_0$; these determine the first and second terms in (vi).

From (vii), $\quad v_0' = \Delta v_0 - \frac{1}{2} \frac{\Delta^2 v_0 + \Delta^2 v_{-1}}{2} + \frac{1}{12} \Delta^3 v_{-1},$

$$v_1' = \Delta v_0 + \frac{1}{2} \frac{\Delta^2 v_0 + \Delta^2 v_{-1}}{2} + \frac{1}{12} \Delta^3 v_{-1},$$

and therefore $\qquad v_0' + v_1' = 2\Delta v_0 + \frac{1}{6}\Delta^3 v_{-1},$

$$v_1' - v_0' = \frac{1}{2}\left(\Delta^2 v_0 + \Delta^2 v_{-1}\right).$$

But, from (viii),

$$v_0' + v_1' = 2\Delta u_0 + \frac{1}{2}\Delta^3 u_{-1},$$

$$v_1' - v_0' = \frac{1}{2}\left(\Delta^2 u_0 + \Delta^2 u_{-1}\right).$$

Comparing the two expressions for $v_0' + v_1'$ we have at once

$$\Delta^3 v_{-1} = 3\Delta^3 u_{-1} \text{ (since } \Delta v_0 = \Delta u_0),$$

and from the two expressions for $v_1' - v_0'$

$$\frac{1}{2}\left(\Delta^2 v_0 + \Delta^2 v_{-1}\right) = \frac{1}{2}\left(\Delta^2 u_0 + \Delta^2 u_{-1}\right).$$

We have now found the values of all four terms of the formula (vi), and we can write the formula in terms of u's as follows:

$$v_x = \frac{1}{2}\left(u_0 + u_1\right) + \left(x - \frac{1}{2}\right)\Delta u_0 + \frac{x\left(x-1\right)}{2}\frac{\Delta^2 u_0 + \Delta^2 u_{-1}}{2}$$

$$+ \frac{x\left(x-1\right)\left(x-\frac{1}{2}\right)}{2}\Delta^3 u_{-1}. \quad\ldots\ldots(\text{ix})$$

This result is a formula of *osculatory interpolation,* and differs from the ordinary central difference formula (i) only in the last term.

The difference is

$$v_x - u_x = \frac{x\left(x-1\right)\left(x-\frac{1}{2}\right)}{3}\Delta^3 u_{-1} = \frac{x\left(x-1\right)\left(2x-1\right)}{6}\Delta^3 u_{-1}.$$

26. The problem of osculatory interpolation has been a fruitful source of discussion by eminent actuarial authorities. The method was devised by Dr Sprague (see *J.I.A.* vol. XXII, p. 270) and was subsequently developed by Prof. Karup, Mr George King and Dr Buchanan. An elementary demonstration of the method, depending upon advancing differences, is given by Mr King in the Supplement to the 75th *Annual Report of the Registrar-General.*

The following modification of Sprague's method, using King's approach, has been suggested by Mr P. G. Neal.

Consider the four values of u_x: u_{-1}, u_0, u_1 and u_2.

The second degree curve through u_{-1}, u_0 and u_1 is

$$u_x = u_{-1} + (1+x)\,\Delta u_{-1} + \frac{(1+x)\,x}{2}\,\Delta^2 u_{-1}$$

$$= u_0 + x\Delta u_0 + \frac{x(x-1)}{2}\,\Delta^2 u_{-1};$$

$$\therefore u_x' = \Delta u_0 + x\Delta^2 u_{-1} - \tfrac{1}{2}\Delta^2 u_{-1}$$

so that
$$[u_x']_{x=0} = \Delta u_0 - \tfrac{1}{2}\Delta^2 u_{-1}. \qquad \ldots\ldots(1)$$

The second degree curve through u_0, u_1 and u_2 is

$$u_x = u_0 + x\Delta u_0 + \frac{x(x-1)}{2}\,\Delta^2 u_0;$$

$$\therefore u_x' = \Delta u_0 + x\Delta^2 u_0 - \tfrac{1}{2}\Delta^2 u_0$$

$$[u_x']_{x=0} = \Delta u_0 + \tfrac{1}{2}\Delta^2 u_0. \qquad \ldots\ldots(2)$$

Let the third degree curve through u_{-1}, u_0, u_1 and u_2 be

$$u_x = u_0 + ax + bx^2 + cx^3.$$

Then
$$u_x' = a + 2bx + 3cx^2,$$

$$a + b + c = u_1 - u_0 = \Delta u_0. \qquad \ldots\ldots(3)$$

From (1)
$$a = \Delta u_0 - \tfrac{1}{2}\Delta^2 u_{-1}. \qquad \ldots\ldots(4)$$

From (2)
$$a + 2b + 3c = \Delta u_0 + \tfrac{1}{2}\Delta^2 u_0. \qquad \ldots\ldots(5)$$

Whence, solving equations (3), (4) and (5),

$$a = \Delta u_0 - \tfrac{1}{2}\Delta^2 u_0 + \tfrac{1}{2}\Delta^3 u_{-1},$$

$$b = \tfrac{1}{2}\Delta^2 u_0 - \Delta^3 u_{-1},$$

$$c = \tfrac{1}{2}\Delta^3 u_{-1}.$$

$$\therefore u_x = u_0 + x\left(\Delta u_0 - \tfrac{1}{2}\Delta^2 u_0 + \tfrac{1}{2}\Delta^3 u_{-1}\right) + x^2\left(\tfrac{1}{2}\Delta^2 u_0 - \Delta^3 u_{-1}\right) + x^3\tfrac{1}{2}\Delta^3 u_{-1}$$

$$= u_0 + x\Delta u_0 + \tfrac{1}{2}x(x-1)\Delta^2 u_0 + \tfrac{1}{2}x(x-1)(x-1)\Delta^3 u_{-1}$$

(where, it should be noted, the last term replaces

$$\frac{x(x-1)(x-2)}{6}\,\Delta^3 u_0$$

in the ordinary advancing difference formula).

Putting $\Delta u_0 = \Delta u_{-1} + \Delta^2 u_{-1}$ and $\Delta^2 u_0 = \Delta^2 u_{-1} + \Delta^3 u_{-1}$ we obtain easily

$$u_x = u_0 + x\Delta u_{-1} + \tfrac{1}{2}\left(x^2 + x\right)\Delta^2 u_{-1} - \tfrac{1}{2}\left(x^2 - x^3\right)\Delta^3 u_{-1}$$

or

$$u_{1+x} = u_1 + x\Delta u_0 + \tfrac{1}{2}\left(x^2 + x\right)\Delta^2 u_0 - \tfrac{1}{2}\left(x^2 - x^3\right)\Delta^3 u_0,$$

which is the form given by King.

*27. The proof in paragraph 25 above is due to Mr D. C. Fraser, and depends on Bessel's formula. The ordinary interpolation formula ending with the term $\Delta^3 u_{-1}$ can be written in many different forms, all giving identical results, and the addition of the expression $\dfrac{x\left(x-1\right)\left(2x-1\right)}{6}\Delta^3 u_{-1}$ produces an osculatory formula.

Suppose, for example, that we take the descending difference formula

$$u_x = u_{-1} + \left(x+1\right)\Delta u_{-1} + \frac{x\left(x+1\right)}{2}\Delta^2 u_{-1} + \frac{x\left(x^2-1\right)}{6}\Delta^3 u_{-1}.$$

Adding the term $\dfrac{x\left(x-1\right)\left(2x-1\right)}{6}\Delta^3 u_{-1}$ we have

$$v_x = u_{-1} + \left(x+1\right)\Delta u_{-1} + x\left(x+1\right)\Delta^2 u_{-1}$$
$$+ \left\{\frac{x\left(x^2-1\right)}{2} + \frac{x\left(x-1\right)\left(2x-1\right)}{6}\right\}\Delta^3 u_{-1}$$

$$= u_0 + x\Delta u_{-1} + \frac{x\left(x+1\right)}{2}\Delta^2 u_{-1} + \frac{x^2\left(x-1\right)}{2}\Delta^3 u_{-1},$$

which is the form obtained in Lidstone's proof appended to Dr Buchanan's paper, *J.I.A.* vol. XLII, p. 394.

An interesting Note on the application of a graphic scheme to formulae of osculatory interpolation appears in the *Actuarial Students' Magazine*, No. 3 (Edinburgh, 1930). By treating osculatory interpolation as a particular case of divided differences, Mr Fraser shows that a diagram similar to the hexagon diagram for ordinary differences can be employed to obtain the various forms of osculatory interpolation formulae.

*28. Modern writers, notably American and Scandinavian actuaries, have of recent years turned their attention to the construction of formulae of osculatory interpolation. In a paper read by Dr Buchanan before the Faculty of Actuaries in 1929 there is an extremely interesting account of the development of the subject up to that date (*T.F.A.* vol. XII, pp. 117–56 and 277–82). Of the numerous formulae given in that paper those of Mr R. Henderson and Mr W. A. Jenkins are of particular interest.

Henderson's formula is

$$u_x = \xi u_0 + \tfrac{1}{6}\xi \, (\xi^2 - 1) \, (\delta^2 u_0 - \tfrac{1}{8}\delta^4 u_0)$$
$$+ x u_1 + \tfrac{1}{6}x \, (x^2 - 1) \, (\delta^2 u_1 - \tfrac{1}{8}\delta^4 u_1),$$

where $\xi = 1 - x$ and the δ's are central difference operators in Sheppard's notation.

It will be seen that this is Everett's formula with fourth difference adjustments.

Jenkins's formulae are also based on Everett's formula. His earlier one is

$$u_x = \xi u_0 + \tfrac{1}{6}\xi \, (\xi^2 - 1) \, \delta^2 u_0 - \tfrac{1}{12}\xi^3 \, (\xi - 1) \, \delta^4 u_0$$
$$+ x u_1 + \tfrac{1}{6}x \, (x^2 - 1) \, \delta^2 u_1 - \tfrac{1}{12}x^3 \, (x - 1) \, \delta^4 u_1,$$

where, as above, $\xi = 1 - x$; while his "modified" osculatory interpolation formula (which, in many respects, possesses advantages over existing formulae) is

$$u_x = \xi u_0 + \tfrac{1}{6}\xi \, (\xi^2 - 1) \, \delta^2 u_0 - \tfrac{1}{36}\xi^3 \delta^4 u_0$$
$$+ x u_1 + \tfrac{1}{6}x \, (x^2 - 1) \, \delta^2 u_1 - \tfrac{1}{36}x^3 \delta^4 u_1.$$

It should be noted that, in general, Henderson's and Jenkins's curves do not, as do Sprague's and King's, pass through the given points. They thus involve an element of adjustment as well as interpolation.

The student who wishes to pursue the subject further would be well advised to read this paper, with special reference to Buchanan's demonstration of Jenkins's modified formula and the derivation of the formula from first principles given by Mr D. C. Fraser in the discussion which followed the paper.

A comprehensive study of the methods adopted by the latest writers on osculatory interpolation will be found in an illuminating article by Mr J. E. Kerrich in *J.I.A.* vol. LXVI (pp. 88–124). The methods of

American and English actuaries differ from those of the Scandinavian authorities, and in his paper Mr Kerrich discusses the differences between these methods and gives a general procedure for the derivation of the various formulae that have been evolved.

EXAMPLES 7

1. Show that $\Delta^m x^n = 0$ or $n!$ according as $m >$ or $= n$.

Hence prove that if n and r are positive integers

$$n^r - n_{(1)} (n-1)^r + n_{(2)} (n-2)^r - n_{(3)} (n-3)^r + \ldots = 0 \text{ or } n!$$

according as $r <$ or $= n$.

2. Use differences of zero to find $(2 \cdot 75)^3$ and $(-\tfrac{1}{4})^3$.

3. Prove that $\Delta^n 0^{n+1} = \tfrac{1}{2} n (n+1) \Delta^n 0^n$.

4. Prove the identity

$$\Delta^m 0^n + n_{(1)} \Delta^m 0^{n-1} + n_{(2)} \Delta^m 0^{n-2} + \ldots + \frac{n!}{(n-m)!} = \frac{\Delta^{m+1} 0^{n+1}}{m+1}.$$

5. Show that $\quad (n+1) \Delta^n 0^n = 2 \left[\Delta^{n-1} 0^n + \Delta^n 0^n \right]$.

6. If $\delta u, \delta^2 u, \delta^3 u, \ldots$ represent differences for intervals of $1/m$ and $\Delta u, \Delta^2 u, \Delta^3 u, \ldots$ differences for unit intervals, then if fifth differences are constant, prove that

$$\delta^4 u_0 = \frac{\Delta^4 0^4}{4!} \cdot \frac{\Delta^4 u_0}{m^4} - \frac{10 m \Delta^4 0^4 - \Delta^4 0^5}{5!} \cdot \frac{\Delta^5 u_0}{m^5}.$$

7. Show that $f(E^n) 0^m = n^m f(E) 0^m$.

8. If x be any quantity less than unity, prove that the limit of the series $1^n + 2^n x + 3^n x^2 + \ldots$ to infinity

$$= \frac{1}{(1-x)^2} \left\{ \Delta 0^n + \frac{x}{1-x} \Delta^2 0^n + \left(\frac{x}{1-x} \right)^2 \Delta^3 0^n + \ldots \right\}.$$

9. Prove that the differential coefficient of $f(n)$ with respect to n is approximately equal to

$$\tfrac{2}{3} \{ f(n+1) - f(n-1) \} - \tfrac{1}{12} \{ f(n+2) - f(n-2) \}.$$

10. Find the first three differential coefficients of $\sqrt[3]{x}$, when $x = 50$, given the following cube roots:

$$\sqrt[3]{50} = 3 \cdot 6840; \quad \sqrt[3]{51} = 3 \cdot 7084; \quad \sqrt[3]{52} = 3 \cdot 7325; \quad \sqrt[3]{53} = 3 \cdot 7563;$$
$$\sqrt[3]{54} = 3 \cdot 7798; \quad \sqrt[3]{55} = 3 \cdot 8030; \quad \sqrt[3]{56} = 3 \cdot 8259.$$

11. $u_6 = 1{\cdot}556, \quad u_7 = 1{\cdot}690, \quad u_9 = 1{\cdot}908, \quad u_{12} = 2{\cdot}158.$

Find the value of $\dfrac{du_x}{dx}$, when $x = 8$, by using divided differences.

12. Prove that

$$\frac{du_x}{dx} = \frac{1}{h}\left(u_{x+h} - u_{x-h}\right) - \frac{1}{2h}\left(u_{x+2h} - u_{x-2h}\right) + \frac{1}{3h}\left(u_{x+3h} - u_{x-3h}\right) - \ldots.$$

13. The first differences of the first differential coefficient of $\log u_x$ are in geometrical progression. Determine the form of u_x.

14. Show that $\dfrac{d^3 f(x)}{dx^3} = \Delta^3 f(x - \tfrac{3}{2})$ approximately.

By considering the function $f(x) = a + bx + c^x$ and using the above relation, prove that $\log c = c^{\frac{1}{2}} - c^{-\frac{1}{2}}$ approximately, where c is a small quantity.

15. Given that $u_0 = 5$, $u_1 = 15$ and $u_2 = 57$, and that the value of $\dfrac{du_x}{dx}$ is 4 when $x = 0$ and 72 when $x = 2$, find the values of $\Delta^3 u_0$ and $\Delta^4 u_0$.

16. Show that $(1 + \log E)^r \, o^m = \dfrac{r!}{(r-m)!}$, when $r > m$.

17. If $\delta u_x = u_{x+\frac{1}{2}} - u_{x-\frac{1}{2}}$, prove that

$$\frac{du_x}{dx} = \delta u_x - \frac{1}{24}\,\delta^3 u_x + \frac{3}{640}\,\delta^5 u_x - \ldots.$$

18. Prove that

$$\Sigma u_x v_x = u_{x-1}\Sigma v_x - \Delta u_{x-2}\Sigma^2 v_x + \Delta^2 u_{x-3}\Sigma^3 v_x - \ldots.$$

19. Given

$$u_{20:15} = 6{\cdot}004 \qquad u_{20:20} = 4{\cdot}304 \qquad u_{20:25} = 3{\cdot}325$$
$$u_{25:15} = 6{\cdot}029 \qquad u_{25:20} = 4{\cdot}346$$
$$u_{30:15} = 6{\cdot}075$$

find $u_{23:17}$ as accurately as possible.

20. Obtain a Lagrange formula for $u_{x:y}$, given $u_{0:0}, u_{1:0}, u_{0:1}, u_{1:1}$.

21. Show that if $u_{0:1} = u_{1:0}$ and $u_{0:2} = u_{2:0}$, then

$$u_{x:y} = u_{0:0} + (x+y)\left[\Delta_x + \frac{x+y-1}{2}\,\Delta_x^2\right]u_{0:0} + xy\,[u_{1:1} - u_{2:0}].$$

22. $a_{40:45} = 13{\cdot}133 \qquad a_{40:50} = 12{\cdot}450 \qquad a_{45:40} = 12{\cdot}880$
$a_{50:40} = 11{\cdot}898 \qquad a_{45:45} = 12{\cdot}432$

Find $a_{42:43}$.

23. Given the following premiums for endowment assurances, obtain as accurately as possible the premium for age 23, term 17 years:

Premiums

Age	Term 15 years	Term 20 years	Term 25 years
20	5·947	4·418	3·547
25	6·046	4·530	
30	6·144		

24. Find $u_{27:34}$, given

$$u_{20:20} = 3·1000 \qquad u_{25:30} = 3·6875$$

$$u_{20:25} = 3·2625 \qquad u_{25:35} = 3·9542$$

$$u_{20:30} = 3·5042 \qquad u_{30:30} = 3·9333$$

$$u_{20:35} = 3·8458 \qquad u_{30:35} = 4·1417$$

$$u_{25:25} = 3·5000 \qquad u_{35:35} = 4·5500$$

25. The following values of $f(x, y)$ are given:

$$f(35, 55) = 10·020, \quad f(35, 50) = 11·196, \quad f(35, 45) = 12·019,$$

$$f(40, 55) = 9·796, \quad f(40, 50) = 10·894, \quad f(40, 45) = 11·641,$$

$$f(45, 55) = 9·583, \quad f(45, 50) = 10·591, \quad f(45, 45) = 11·243.$$

(i) Using only six of the above values, find $f(42, 52)$.

(ii) Making use of all the data, calculate $f(44, 51)$.

26. Prove that $\Delta(u_x v_x w_x)$ can be expressed in either of the two following forms:

(a) $u_{x+1} v_{x+1} \Delta w_x + u_{x+1} w_x \Delta v_x + v_x w_x \Delta u_x.$

(b) $\Delta u_x \Delta v_x \Delta w_x + u_x v_x \Delta w_x + \text{two similar terms}$
$\qquad\qquad + u_x \Delta v_x \Delta w_x + \text{two similar terms}.$

*27. If $\qquad\qquad \nabla f(x) = f(x) - f(x-1),$

prove that

$$\nabla^n f(x) = f(x) - n_{(1)} f(x-1) + n_{(2)} f(x-2) - \dots + (-1)^n f(x-n).$$

*28. Prove that

$$E^x u_0 = [1 + x_{(1)} \nabla + (x+1)_{(2)} \nabla^2 + (x+2)_{(3)} \nabla^3 + \dots$$
$$+ (x+n)_{(n+1)} \nabla^{n+1} + \dots] u_0.$$

29. If
$$x^{[n]} = x \left(x + \tfrac{1}{2}n - 1\right)^{(n-1)},$$

prove that
$$x^{[2n]} = x^2 \left(x^2 - 1^2\right)\left(x^2 - 2^2\right) \ldots \left(x^2 - \overline{n-1}^2\right)$$

and
$$x^{[2n+1]} = x \left(x^2 - \tfrac{1}{4}\right)\left(x^2 - \tfrac{9}{4}\right) \ldots \left[x^2 - \tfrac{1}{4}\left(2n-1\right)^2\right].$$

30. Show that
$$f(x) = f(0) + \frac{x^{[1]}}{1!}\,\delta f(0) + \frac{x^{[2]}}{2!}\,\delta^2 f(0) + \ldots + \frac{x^{[n]}}{n!}\,\delta^n f(0) + \ldots,$$

where $x^{[n]}$ has the same meaning as in Qu. 29, and
$$\delta f(x) = f\left(x + \tfrac{1}{2}\right) - f\left(x - \tfrac{1}{2}\right).$$

CHAPTER VIII

MODERN EXTENSIONS AND SPECIAL DEVICES

*1. In this chapter we shall deal briefly with certain modern methods of interpolation and summation. The proofs and applications are not intended to be exhaustive, and for further information on any of the theorems or methods a study of the original papers or notes is recommended.

AITKEN'S THEOREM FOR POLYNOMIAL INTERPOLATION

*2. Dr A. C. Aitken has devised a remarkable general theorem for polynomial interpolation which covers a very wide field, embracing all the ordinary formulae as particular cases. The basis of the theorem is that when a difference operator is applied to a given polynomial u_x of the nth degree in x, the result is a polynomial of the $(n-1)$th degree, and when performed on a constant the result is zero. This obviously holds when the operator is Δ. Similarly, when u_x is differentiated with respect to x, a polynomial of one degree less in x is produced; and if A is a constant, then dA/dx is o. In this case the operator is D.

The general operators are θ and Θ. Θ denotes that form of inverse operation θ^{-1} which produces a polynomial divisible by x, so that constants (of integration, etc.) do not enter into the inverse processes, which are therefore perfectly definite.

It is evident, in the first place, that whatever operation is represented by θ, Θ i is x, and the effect of operating with Θ, or a succession of Θ's, gives a multiple of x.

From the definition, since u_0 is the constant part of u_x, which is removed by the operation θ,

$$\Theta\theta u_x = u_x - u_0$$

so that

$$u_x = u_0 + \Theta\theta u_x.$$

If for example $\theta \equiv \Delta$ and the interval of differencing is unity, then

$$\Theta \, \mathbf{1} = x_{(1)}, \quad \Theta x_{(1)} = x_{(2)}, \quad \Theta x_{(2)} = x_{(3)} \ldots$$

and generally $\qquad \Theta x_{(n-1)} = x_{(n)}.$

Again, since $\qquad \Delta \, (x - \mathbf{1})_{(n)} = (x - \mathbf{1})_{(n-1)}$

$$\Theta \, (x - \mathbf{1})_{(n-1)} = \Theta \theta \, (x - \mathbf{1})_{(n)} = (x - \mathbf{1})_{(n)} \pm \mathbf{1},$$

according as n is odd or even.

Similarly, if $\theta \equiv D$, it can easily be shown that

$$\Theta \, \frac{(x - \mathbf{1})^{n-1}}{(n-1)!} = \Theta \theta \, \frac{(x - \mathbf{1})^n}{n!} = \frac{(x - \mathbf{1})^n - (-\mathbf{1})^n}{n!}.$$

*3. The general formula for determining the polynomial $P_n(x)$, being given values when $x = 0$ of u_x and of all such results as $\ldots \theta_r \ldots \theta_2 \theta_1 u_x$, is

$$u_x = u_0 + (\theta_1 u_0) \, \Theta_1 \mathbf{1} + (\theta_2 \theta_1 u_0) \, \Theta_1 \Theta_2 \mathbf{1} + \ldots$$
$$+ (\theta_n \ldots \theta_2 \theta_1 u_0) \, \Theta_1 \Theta_2 \ldots \Theta_n \mathbf{1},$$

where the expressions in brackets are numerical values, and the expressions following them, such as $\Theta_1 \mathbf{1}$, $\Theta_1 \Theta_2 \mathbf{1}$, $\ldots$, are functions of x. It will be understood that, in each term, the first operator is the one that stands next to the operand u or $\mathbf{1}$, and that the remaining operators are taken in their order from right to left; in this order the subscripts of θ increase and those of Θ decrease.

It should be noted also that the θ's are not necessarily all the same operation, nor need they be commutative. The following proof is due substantially to Mr G. J. Lidstone.

First, let u_x be a cubic in x and $= ax^3 + bx^2 + cx + d$.

Then since u_x is of the third degree, $\theta_1 u_x$ is of the second degree, $\theta_2 \theta_1 u_x$ is of the first degree, and $\theta_3 \theta_2 \theta_1 u_x$ is a constant.

Now $\qquad u_x = u_0 + \Theta_1 \theta_1 u_x.$

Hence, putting $\theta_1 u_x$ for u_x, $\Theta_2 \theta_2$ for $\Theta_1 \theta_1$ and similarly,

$$\theta_1 u_x = \theta_1 u_0 + \Theta_2 \theta_2 \theta_1 u_x,$$
$$\theta_2 \theta_1 u_x = \theta_2 \theta_1 u_0 + \Theta_3 \theta_3 \theta_2 \theta_1 u_x,$$
$$\theta_3 \theta_2 \theta_1 u_x = \theta_3 \theta_2 \theta_1 u_0 = \text{a constant}.$$

There is no term in Θ in the last identity because the process has been continued until x disappears.

From the last line above, operating with Θ_3,

$$\Theta_3\theta_3\theta_2\theta_1 u_x = \Theta_3\theta_3\theta_2\theta_1 u_0$$

and since $\theta_3\theta_2\theta_1 u_0$ is constant we may write this line as

$$\Theta_3\theta_3\theta_2\theta_1 u_x = (\theta_3\theta_2\theta_1 u_0)\,\Theta_3 1.$$

Substitute this result in the third line:

$$\theta_2\theta_1 u_x = \theta_2\theta_1 u_0 + (\theta_3\theta_2\theta_1 u_0)\,\Theta_3 1.$$

Operate on this with Θ_2 and substitute in the second line:

$$\theta_1 u_x = \theta_1 u_0 + (\theta_2\theta_1 u_0)\,\Theta_2 1 + (\theta_3\theta_2\theta_1 u_0)\,\Theta_2\Theta_3 1.$$

Finally, operate on this with Θ_1 and substitute in the first line:

$$u_x = u_0 + (\theta_1 u_0)\,\Theta_1 1 + (\theta_2\theta_1 u_0)\,\Theta_1\Theta_2 1 + (\theta_3\theta_2\theta_1 u_0)\,\Theta_1\Theta_2\Theta_3 1.$$

This process can evidently be extended to the general case, so that we arrive at the general formula:

$$u_x = u_0 + (\theta_1 u_0)\,\Theta_1 1 + (\theta_2\theta_1 u_0)\,\Theta_1\Theta_2 1 + \ldots$$
$$+ (\theta_n\ldots\theta_2\theta_1 u_0)\,\Theta_1\Theta_2\ldots\Theta_n 1,$$

which is Aitken's formula.

It will be observed that the proof is exactly analogous to that of the divided difference formula (Chap. III, p. 44).

*4. By replacing the θ's by more familiar operators various well-known formulae can easily be obtained:

(i) If $\theta_1 \equiv \theta_2 \equiv \theta_3 \equiv \ldots \equiv \Delta$, then as shown above, $\Theta_1 1 = x_{(1)}$, $\Theta_1\Theta_2 1 = x_{(2)} \ldots$, and the formula in paragraph 3 becomes

$$u_x = u_0 + \Delta u_0 x_{(1)} + \Delta^2 u_0 x_{(2)} + \Delta^3 u_0 x_{(3)} + \ldots$$

which is the ordinary advancing difference formula.

(ii) If the θ's are all equivalent to the operator D, we have

$$u_x = u_0 + Du_0 x + D^2 u_0 \frac{x^2}{2!} + D^3 u_0 \frac{x^3}{3!} + \ldots$$

which is Maclaurin's series.

(iii) Let $\theta_1 u_x = (u_x - u_a)/(x - a)$ so that $\theta_1 \equiv \underset{a}{\triangle}$, $\theta_1\theta_2 \equiv \underset{ba}{\triangle^2}$, and so on; then it can easily be shown that the formula reproduces

$$u_x = u_a + (x-a) \underset{b}{\triangle} u_a + (x-a)(x-b) \underset{bc}{\triangle^2} u_a + \ldots,$$

Newton's divided difference formula.

*5. These paragraphs are based on the note by Dr Aitken in *J.I.A.* vol. LXI, pp. 107 *et seq.* In the same volume appears a note on Lidstone's extension of the theorem to interpolation in Everett's form. In thus extending Aitken's theorem, Mr Lidstone has introduced an operator, λ, which reduces the degree of a polynomial by 2, and not by 1, as in the general form, and the corresponding inverse operator $\Lambda \equiv \lambda^{-1}$. This ingenious modification results in some very interesting identities and renders the development of Everett's series a comparatively simple matter. (*Ibid.* pp. 113–16 and the original paper cited therein.)

The student who desires further information on the subject of Aitken's formula is advised to read Dr Aitken's original paper, *Proc. Edin. Math. Soc.*, Series II, vol. I (1929), pp. 203 *et seq.*

FINITE INTEGRATION BY PARTS

*6. A formula for the finite integration of a function which is the product of two other functions is

$$\Sigma u_x v_x = u_x \Sigma v_x - \Sigma (\Delta u_x \Sigma v_{x+1}).$$

An extension of the formula (Chap. VII, paragraph 12) is

$$\Sigma u_x v_x = u_x \Sigma v_x - \Delta u_x \Sigma^2 v_{x+1} + \Delta^2 u_x \Sigma^3 v_{x+2} - \ldots \quad \ldots\ldots(a)$$

If u_x is a polynomial of the nth degree in x, differences of a higher order than n will vanish, and the last term in the series above will be

$$(-1)^n \Delta^n u_x \Sigma^{n+1} v_{x+n}.$$

The series can however be terminated at any stage with a remainder term.

For example,

$$\Delta\,(u_x \Sigma v_x) = u_x v_x + \Delta u_x \Sigma v_{x+1}$$

so that $$u_x v_x = \Delta\,(u_x \Sigma v_x) - \Delta u_x \Sigma v_{x+1}$$

or $$\Sigma u_x v_x = u_x \Sigma v_x - \Sigma\,(\Delta u_x \Sigma v_{x+1}). \qquad \ldots\ldots(b)$$

If in place of u_x and v_x we write $-\Delta u_x$ and Σv_{x+1} respectively, we have

$$-\Sigma\,(\Delta u_x \Sigma v_{x+1}) = -\Delta u_x \Sigma^2 v_{x+1} + \Sigma\,(\Delta^2 u_x \Sigma^2 v_{x+2}).$$

Identity (b) then becomes

$$\Sigma u_x v_x = u_x \Sigma v_x - \Delta u_x \Sigma^2 v_{x+1} + \Sigma\,(\Delta^2 u_x \Sigma^2 v_{x+2}). \qquad \ldots\ldots(c)$$

By substituting $\Delta^2 u_x$ and $\Sigma^2 v_{x+2}$ for u_x and v_x respectively in (c) it can easily be seen that the remainder term after $(-1)^n\,\Delta^n u_x \Sigma^{n+1} v_{x+n}$ will be

$$(-1)^{n+1}\,\Sigma\,(\Delta^{n+1} u_x \Sigma^{n+1} v_{x+n+1}).$$

(See G. J. Lidstone, *J.I.A.* vol. LXIV, pp. 160 *et seq.*)

*7. If in formula (a) we replace u_x by Δu_x and v_x by 1, and insert the limits x and 0, we have

$$\sum_0^x (\Delta u_x \,.\, 1) = \Delta u_x x_{(1)} - \Delta^2 u_x\,(x+1)_{(2)} + \Delta^3 u_x\,(x+2)_{(3)} - \ldots.$$

But $\Sigma\,(\Delta u_x) = u_x - C$, where C is a constant

$$= u_x - u_0, \text{ say};$$

$$\therefore\quad u_x - u_0 = x_{(1)}\,\Delta u_x - (x+1)_{(2)}\,\Delta^2 u_x + (x+2)_{(3)}\,\Delta^3 u_x - \ldots$$

or $$u_0 = u_x - x_{(1)}\,\Delta u_x + (x+1)_{(2)}\,\Delta^2 u_x - (x+2)_{(3)}\,\Delta^3 u_x + \ldots$$

which is the ordinary advancing formula for u_0 in terms of u_x and its differences. An alternative form for $\Sigma u_x v_x$ is

$$\Sigma u_x v_x = u_{x-1} \Sigma v_x - \Delta u_{x-2} \Sigma^2 v_x + \Delta^2 u_{x-3} \Sigma^3 v_x - \ldots. \qquad \ldots\ldots(d)$$

(See Examples VII, No. 18.) If we make the same substitutions as above, we shall have

$$u_x - u_0 = x_{(1)}\,\Delta u_{x-1} - x_{(2)}\,\Delta^2 u_{x-2} + x_{(3)}\,\Delta^3 u_{x-3} - \ldots$$

or $$u_0 = u_x - x_{(1)}\,\Delta u_{x-1} + x_{(2)}\,\Delta^2 u_{x-2} - x_{(3)}\,\Delta^3 u_{x-3} + \ldots.$$

an interpolation formula involving backward differences.

To distinguish between the two expansions for $\Sigma u_x v_x$ we shall therefore refer to formula (*a*) as the "forward difference" summation formula and formula (*d*) as the "backward difference" summation formula.

*8. These formulae can be adapted to the problem of calculation of $\Sigma u_x v_x$ when numerical values of u_x and v_x are available. Mr G. J. Lidstone has shown that by making some simple substitutions the arithmetical work is reduced to a minimum.

The proof below follows Lidstone's proof in *J.I.A.* vol. LXX.

Let S_x denote the *indefinite* finite integral of $u_x v_x$. Then S_x can be expressed in either the forward or backward form as given above. If we wish to find the sum of *n* terms we must calculate $S_n - S_0$, and if in the formula we make either S_n or S_0 vanish by so arranging the summations as to give zero values to the particular values of the sums Σv, Σv^2, Σv^3, ..., we reduce the definite sum to a single expression, S_n or $-S_0$. Further, from the zero values we can build up the whole table of sums by using the fundamental relation $\Delta \Sigma^n \equiv \Sigma^{n-1}$.

Since in either the forward difference or backward difference summation formula we may choose our values so that S_n or S_0 is zero, there will be four forms of tabulation. For the purposes of illustrating the process it will be sufficient to use one of these forms: they are all illustrated in Lidstone's paper, *loc. cit.*

*9. Consider the simple case in which the following values are given:

x	0		2	3
u_x	27	64	125	216
v_x	1	3	7	5

Here *n* is 4. By simple arithmetic

$$\Sigma u_x v_x = 27 + 192 + 875 + 1080 = 2174.$$

(In this example u_x has been taken as $(x+3)^3$ so that third differences will be constant: the values of v_x are quite arbitrary.)

The difference table is

x	u_x	Δu_x	$\Delta^2 u_x$	$\Delta^3 u_x$
0	27			
		37		
1	64		24	
		61		6
2	125		30	
		91		
3	216			

We will use the backward form, making $S_0 = 0$.

Thus, to use u_{n-1} (the last term—in this case u_3) and its backward differences, we make $0 = \Sigma v_x = \Sigma^2 v_x = \ldots$ for $x = 0$; and in that case

$$\sum_0^{n-1} u_x v_x = S_n = u_{n-1} \Sigma v_n - \Delta u_{n-2} \Sigma^2 v_n + \ldots.$$

Construct the following table, where the sums of v_x are taken downwards and stepped down one line at a time:

	x	v_x	Σv_x	$\Sigma^2 v_x$	$\Sigma^3 v_x$	$\Sigma^4 v_x$
	0	1	0	0	0	0
	1	3	1	0	0	0
	2	7	4	1	0	0
$(n-1)$	3	5	11	5	1	0
(n)	4	—	16	16	6	1

Then, substituting in the formula for $\overset{n-1}{\underset{0}{\Sigma}} u_x v_x$, the required sum is

$$
\begin{array}{rcl}
+\,216 \times 16 &=& +\,3456 \\
-\,91 \times 16 &=& -\,1456 \\
+\,30 \times 6 &=& +\,180 \\
-\,6 \times 1 &=& -\,6 \\
\hline
&& +\,2174
\end{array}
$$

which agrees with the result found by direct calculation.

*10. The methods adopted in taking any of the other forms are similar, and the student will find it instructive to use these other forms in further examples of the same type.

It should be noted that, by combining two forms, we may take the sums from some convenient central point and so reduce the figures involved in the summations.

These formulae and methods are of great use in forming statistical "moments" of the form $\Sigma x^m u_{a+x}$.

INTERPOLATION BY CROSS-MEANS

*11. The divided difference formula is

$$u_x = u_a + (x-a) \underset{b}{\triangle} u_a + (x-a)(x-b) \underset{bc}{\triangle^2} u_a + \dots.$$

If we are given only two values of u_x, namely u_a and u_b, then

$$u_x = u_a + (x-a) \underset{b}{\triangle} u_a$$

$$= u_a + (x-a)(u_b - u_a)/(b-a)$$

$$= \frac{b-x}{b-a} u_a + \frac{x-a}{b-a} u_b$$

$$= \begin{vmatrix} u_a & a-x \\ u_b & b-x \end{vmatrix} \div b - a.$$

This is a blend of u_a and u_b in the proportions $(b-x)/(b-a)$ and $(x-a)/(b-a)$ and, from the determinant form, we may note that a first difference approximation to u_x is in fact a cross-product divided by the difference between the two given arguments. This is called a *linear cross-mean*.

*12. Dr A. C. Aitken has evolved a method of interpolation by cross-means which enables simple arithmetical processes to be used without the need for either a formula or differences.

The following is an elementary description of the method.

If in the general divided difference formula we substitute successively $a, b, c, \dots$ for x giving one, two, three ... terms, we may write down the following table:

No. of terms		Parts
One	$u_a = u_a$	$a-x$
Two	$u_b = u_a + (b-a)\underset{b}{\triangle}u_a$	$b-x$
Three	$u_c = u_a + (c-a)\underset{b}{\triangle}u_a + (c-a)(c-b)\underset{bc}{\triangle^2}u_a$	$c-x$
Four	$u_d = u_a + (d-a)\underset{b}{\triangle}u_a + (d-a)(d-b)\underset{bc}{\triangle^2}u_a$	
	$\quad + (d-a)(d-b)(d-c)\underset{bcd}{\triangle^3}u_a$	$d-x$

where the column headed "parts" represents the factors to be used later.

The first step in the process is to find first difference approximations based on u_a and u_b, u_a and u_c, u_a and u_d … as in paragraph 11. These may be denoted by $u_x(a, b)$, $u_x(a, c)$, $u_x(a, d)$ …. In order to obtain these approximations we use the parts in the last column above, and it is evident that the first two terms of the general formula (i.e. $u_a + (x-a)\underset{b}{\triangle}u_a$) appear in all the approximations.

Thus
$$u_x(a, d) = \begin{vmatrix} u_a & a-x \\ u_d & d-x \end{vmatrix} \div (d-a).$$

The first difference results are therefore of the form
$$u_a + (x-a)\underset{b}{\triangle}u_a + (x-a)\,k_1,$$

where k_1 represents the multipliers of the common factor $(x-a)$ in $u_x(a, b)$, $u_x(a, c)$, $u_x(a, d)$ ….

We may construct a table similar to that above, the expressions in the middle columns giving the various values of k_1:

$u_x(a, b)$	$0 \cdot \underset{bc}{\triangle^2}u_a$	$b-x$
$u_x(a, c)$	$(c-b)\underset{bc}{\triangle^2}u_a$	$c-x$
$u_x(a, d)$	$(d-b)\underset{bc}{\triangle^2}u_a + (d-b)(d-c)\underset{bcd}{\triangle^3}u_a$	$d-x$
$u_x(a, e)$	$(e-b)\underset{bc}{\triangle^2}u_a + (e-b)(e-c)\underset{bcd}{\triangle^3}u_a$	
	$\quad + (e-b)(e-c)(e-d)\underset{bcde}{\triangle^4}u_a$	$e-x$

The second difference approximations are found in the same way by the use of the parts as stated, and the results are of the form

$$u_x = \{u_a + (x-a) \underset{b}{\triangle} u_a + (x-a)(x-b) \underset{bc}{\triangle^2 u_a}\} + (x-a)(x-b) k_2,$$

the first three terms being common to all the values, and the respective values of k_2 being those in the middle column below:

$u_x(a, b, c)$	$0 \cdot \underset{bcd}{\triangle^3 u_a}$	$c-x$
$u_x(a, b, d)$	$(d-c) \underset{bcd}{\triangle^3 u_a}$	$d-x$
$u_x(a, b, e)$	$(e-c) \underset{bcd}{\triangle^3 u_a} + (e-c)(e-d) \underset{bcde}{\triangle^4 u_a}$	$e-x$
	....	

and so on.

*13. An example will make the method clear. In order to simplify the arithmetic equidistant intervals have been used, but the processes are, of course, perfectly general.

Example 1.

Find u_x when $x = \cdot 7352$ from the following data:

x	-2	-1	0	1	2
u_x	15849	16218	16596	16982	17378

We require the following table:

a	u_a			
b	u_b	$u_x(a, b)$		
c	u_c	$u_x(a, c)$	$u_x(a, b, c)$	
d	u_d	$u_x(a, d)$	$u_x(a, b, d)$	$u_x(a, b, c, d)$
e	u_e	$u_x(a, e)$	$u_x(a, b, e)$	$u_x(a, b, c, e)$ ...

where the parts are $-2 \cdot 7352$, $-1 \cdot 7352$, $- \cdot 7352$, $\cdot 2648$, $1 \cdot 2648$.

Now
$$u_x(a, b) = \frac{b-x}{b-a} u_a + \frac{x-a}{b-a} u_b,$$

where
$$b - x = -1 \cdot 7352,$$
$$a - x = -2 \cdot 7352,$$
$$u_a = 15849,$$
$$u_b = 16218,$$

and
$$b - a = 1.$$

$$\therefore \quad u_x(a, b) = 15849 \times -1.7352 - (16218 \times -2.7352)$$
$$= 16858.3.$$

The calculation is performed very quickly by the aid of an arithmometer.

Similarly,

$$u_x(a, c) = \tfrac{1}{2}\left[(15849 \times -.7352) - (16596 \times -2.7352)\right],$$

since $\qquad c - a = 2,$

$$= 16870.6$$

and so on.

Again, $\qquad u_x(a, b, c) = \dfrac{c-x}{b-a} u_x(a, b) + \dfrac{x-b}{b-a} u_x(a, c),$

where $\qquad\qquad\qquad\qquad c - x = -.7352,$

$$b - x = -1.7352,$$
$$u_x(a, b) = 16858.3,$$
$$u_x(a, c) = 16870.6,$$

and $\qquad\qquad\qquad\qquad b - a = 1;$

$$\therefore \quad u_x(a, b, c) = 16879.6.$$

The completed table is as under.

x	u_x						
-2	15849						
-1	16218	16	858.3				
0	16596		870.6	87	9.6		
1	16982		882.0		8.9	9	.1
2	17378		894.3		9.1		.4

In practice, work is saved by omitting common figures in the columns, as in the calculations of the cross-means these figures will merely be repeated.

The final result is 16879.

The gradual closing-up of the approximation is clearly seen. It is best to arrange the u's in the order in which they come into Gauss's formula, namely, $u_0, u_1, u_{-1}, u_2 \ldots$. In this way quicker convergence is secured.

*14. A further adaptation of this method is by the use of *quadratic cross-means*. Here the values of u_x are taken in the order $u_{-a}, u_a,$

u_{-b}, u_b ... and the divided difference formula becomes

$$u_x = u_{-a} + (x+a) \underset{a}{\triangle} u_{-a} + (x^2 - a^2) \underset{a,-b}{\triangle^2} u_{-a}$$
$$+ (x^2 - a^2)(x+b) \underset{a,-b,b}{\triangle^3} u_{-a} + ...$$

The first stage in the calculations is interpolation to first differences by linear cross-means as before; at each subsequent stage, by an arithmetically similar process, two further differences are allowed for simultaneously.

Dr Aitken's method of application is as follows:

$$u_x(a, -a) = [(a+x) u_a + (a-x) u_{-a}]/2a.$$

Since this expression is unaltered by substituting $-a$ for a, it is an even polynomial in a, say $v_x(a^2)$.

By letting $a = x$ in $u_x(a, -a)$, we have $u_x(x, -x)$, which is $v_x(x^2)$.

The problem is therefore reduced to interpolating for $v_x(x^2)$, given $v_x(a^2)$, $v_x(b^2)$, $v_x(c^2)$ .... The repeated cross-means are therefore available, beginning with

$$v_x(a^2, b^2) = [(b^2 - x^2) v_x(a^2) - (a^2 - x^2) v_x(b^2)]/(b^2 - a^2)$$

and similarly for $v_x(a^2, c^2)$ ....

Again,

$$v_x(a^2, b^2, c^2) = \frac{(c^2 - x^2) v_x(a^2, b^2) - (b^2 - x^2) v_x(a^2, c^2)}{c^2 - b^2}$$

and so on.

It is evident now that by interpolating on variables of the form r^2 we are moving by two orders of differences at a time, which improves the convergence to a marked degree. Further, with a central origin a, b, c ... are ·5, 1·5, 2·5 ... and the factors $a^2 - x^2$, $b^2 - x^2$, $c^2 - x^2$ ... all have the same decimal part. Also, the divisors $b^2 - a^2$, $c^2 - a^2$, $c^2 - b^2$ ... are all even integers, which enables *halved* cross-multipliers and divisors to be used. Where the arguments are ·5, 1·5, 2·5 ... these halved divisors become 1, 3, 6, 10 ..., the coefficients in the ordinary binomial expansion.

Finally, for these arguments the first multiplier is $\frac{1}{2}(\frac{1}{4} - x^2)$ of $\frac{1}{2}(\frac{1}{2} - x)(\frac{1}{2} + x)$, which is one-half the product of the multipliers used in the first linear cross-mean for $v(\frac{1}{4})$.

An example will help to explain the method.

Example 2.

Using the data in Example 1, together with $u_3 = 17773$, interpolate to find $u_{.7352}$.

The extra value is required, as in the quadratic method we need an even number of terms.

The working is as follows:

The decimal part of the multiplier is

$$\tfrac{1}{2}(\cdot 7352 \times \cdot 2648) = \cdot 0973405.$$

The v's are

$$\cdot 7352 \times 16982 + \cdot 2648 \times 16596 = 16879 \cdot 8$$

$$1 \cdot 7352 \times 17378 + 1 \cdot 2648 \times 16218 = 16888 \cdot 9$$

$$2 \cdot 7352 \times 17773 + 2 \cdot 2648 \times 15849 = 16901 \cdot 5$$

The next steps are

$$879 \cdot 8 \times 1 \cdot 0973405 - 888 \cdot 9 \times \cdot 0973405 = 878 \cdot 9$$

$$879 \cdot 8 \times 3 \cdot 0973405 - 901 \cdot 5 \times \cdot 0973405 = 879 \cdot 1$$

Further values of v are unnecessary, and the table, similar to that for linear cross-means interpolations, is

16	879·8			·0973405
	888·9	87	8·9	1·0973405
	901·5		9·1	3·0973405

Hence $u_{.7352} = 16879$, as before.

*15. The cross-means methods possess particular advantages. No interpolation formula and no differences are required and we may stop the calculation at any point, so that any required degree of accuracy may be attained. For equidistant intervals the quadratic method is much to be preferred. When the intervals are unequal the linear process has considerable practical value; it is, in fact, one of the most direct and effective methods for inverse interpolation.

Generally, the quadratic method is very advantageous for direct interpolation. It can also be readily adapted to inverse interpolation. When the arguments are equally spaced and the calculations can be effected by the aid of an arithmometer this device enables interpolated results to be obtained much more rapidly than by any other method. For instance, in Example 2, after the multiplier has been calculated, the successive values of v can be obtained on an arithmometer without clearing the machine after each operation. After the method has been mastered simple interpolations can be obtained in a very few minutes.

*16. This part of the chapter is based largely on the note by Mr G. J. Lidstone, "Aitken's new processes for direct and inverse interpolation" in *J.I.A.* vol. LXVIII, pp. 272–86. In this note there is a full and lucid description of the methods of interpolation by cross-means with a number of fully-worked examples, and the student will find it instructive to compare the advantages and disadvantages of interpolation by difference formulae and the methods of cross-means, by working out actual numerical questions.

COMRIE'S "THROW-BACK" DEVICE

*17. In the same paper (*loc. cit.* pp. 286–93), Mr Lidstone gives a comprehensive account (with references) of the *throw-back* device of Dr L. J. Comrie, based on Bessel's or Everett's formula. This process is of great advantage when the interpolation is to be taken beyond third differences, as it shortens the work and reduces the number of differences to be recorded in the Tables. The nature of the process is indicated in the next paragraph; for a fuller account reference may be made to the paper mentioned above and to Comrie's papers cited therein.

*18. In Bessel's formula (Chap. IV, paragraph 6), let the coefficients of the odd differences be called $B^{\mathrm{I}}u$, $B^{\mathrm{III}}u$, $B^{\mathrm{v}}u$ ..., and the coefficients of the mean even differences $B^{\mathrm{II}}u$, $B^{\mathrm{IV}}u$, $B^{\mathrm{VI}}u$ .... Then for the practical range of interpolation $x = 0$ to $x = 1$, it is found that the ratios

$$\frac{B^{\mathrm{III}}u}{B^{\mathrm{I}}u}, \quad \frac{B^{\mathrm{v}}u}{B^{\mathrm{I}}u}, \cdots$$

and

$$\frac{B^{\mathrm{IV}}u}{B^{\mathrm{II}}u}, \quad \frac{B^{\mathrm{VI}}u}{B^{\mathrm{II}}u}, \cdots$$

change so slightly with x that they may, with sufficient accuracy, be assigned constant mean values provided that higher differences are not too large.

Adopting these values the formula takes the convenient form

$$u_x = u_0 + x\Delta u_0 + \frac{x\,(x-1)}{2!}\,[\bar{\Delta}^2 - \cdot184\bar{\Delta}^4 + \cdot038\bar{\Delta}^6 \ldots]\,u_0$$

$$+ \frac{x\,(x-1)\,(x-\tfrac{1}{2})}{3!}\,[\Delta^3 - \cdot108\Delta^5 + \cdot016\Delta^7 \ldots]\,u_0,$$

where Δu, $\Delta^3 u$, $\Delta^5 u$ ... represent the odd central differences and $\bar{\Delta}^2 u$, $\bar{\Delta}^4 u$, $\bar{\Delta}^6 u$ ... the mean even central differences.

The quantities in the square brackets are evidently independent of x and may therefore be tabulated.

The throw-back device may be used with great advantage in double-entry tables (i.e. functions of x and y). Its use curtails very considerably the complicated interpolation formulae otherwise required when even moderately high orders of differences are involved.

The device is also very useful for inverse interpolation, since it enables differences beyond the third to be included by a direct process without increasing the degree of the equation to be solved. Further, the last coefficient, $B^{\mathrm{iii}}u$, is very small and changes slowly, so that allowance is easily made for the last term in the formula given above.

CHAPTER IX

APPROXIMATE INTEGRATION

1. In order to obtain the area of a curve by the methods of the integral calculus two conditions must necessarily hold. These conditions are

(i) the equation of the curve must be known; and in that event

(ii) the function $y = u_x$ representing the equation of the curve must be integrable.

In the theory of life contingencies these conditions are rarely satisfied. Rates of mortality, marriage, etc. are generally obtained from actual observations and the functions derived from these rates are seldom capable of expression in the form of a mathematical expansion. For example, if l_x be the number of persons attaining exact age x in any year of time, the number living between ages x and $x+1$ is given by

$$L_x = \int_0^1 l_{x+t}\, dt,$$

where x and t are independent.

Unless l_{x+t} follows some definite mathematical law, we cannot evaluate the integral by the methods hitherto employed. By making certain assumptions, however, we can obtain approximations to the value of the integral which are accurate enough for practical purposes.

Thus, if we expand l_{x+t} in terms of l_x and differences of l_x, we have

$$l_{x+t} = (1 + \Delta)^t l_x$$

$$= l_x + t\Delta l_x \qquad \text{to first differences.}$$

But $\qquad \Delta l_x = l_{x+1} - l_x,$

and $l_x - l_{x+1}$ is d_x, the number out of the l_x persons who die before reaching age $x+1$.

$$\therefore \quad L_x = \int_0^1 l_{x+t}\, dt$$

$$= \int_0^1 (l_x - t d_x)\, dt \quad \text{as far as first differences}$$

$$= \left[t l_x - \tfrac{1}{2} t^2 d_x \right]_0^1$$

$$= l_x - \tfrac{1}{2} d_x$$

$$= l_x - \tfrac{1}{2} (l_x - l_{x+1})$$

$$= \tfrac{1}{2} (l_x + l_{x+1}).$$

This is an approximate value of L_x on the assumption that l_{x+t} is a first difference function of l_x.

It is evident that a simple approximation to first differences will not be justifiable except in a limited number of instances: the construction of formulae for approximate integration will necessarily depend on the data available and on the degree of accuracy required.

2. Simpson's rule.

Suppose that we are given two values of u_x only and that we represent these two values by means of the points H and K whose co-ordinates are (a, u_a) and (b, u_b) respectively. Suppose also that we have sufficient information to justify our representing the function $y = u_x$ by a curve of small changes of slope, not affected by periodic changes. An infinite number of such mathematical curves can be drawn to pass through H and K. The simplest curve passing through the points is a straight line, and for the purpose of interpolation it is often sufficient to adopt a first difference formula, as was done for example in obtaining the approximation to L_x in the preceding paragraph. If the straight line be drawn, the area

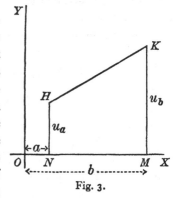

Fig. 3.

cut off by the curve, the x-axis and the ordinates $x=a$ and $x=b$ will be that of the trapezium $HNMK$. The area of the trapezium is $\frac{1}{2}(u_a+u_b)(b-a)$.

Accurately, this area is $\int_a^b u_x dx$.

A first approximation to the integral is therefore $\frac{1}{2}(u_a+u_b)(b-a)$. If $y=u_x=l_{x+t}$ and the limits b and a are 1 and 0 respectively, we have the approximation to $\int_0^1 l_{x+t}\,dt$ given above, namely

$$\frac{1}{2}(l_x+l_{x+1}).$$

Let us now improve the approximation by introducing a third known value of u_x. In other words, suppose our data to be u_a, u_b, u_c. Then there is still an unlimited number of curves which can be drawn to pass through the three points H, K, L. The simplest of these curves will now no longer be a straight line, but a second difference curve. The form of this curve will be $y=A+Bx+Cx^2$, and since three points on the curve are given we are in possession of sufficient data to determine the coefficients A, B, C.

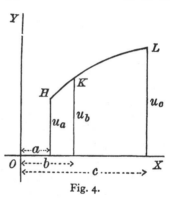

Fig. 4.

In practice the data will generally be available at equidistant intervals, and since we may choose our origin where we please, the problem is therefore reduced to one of finding the second difference curve which passes through the points $(0, u_0)$, $(1, u_1)$, $(2, u_2)$.

Having found the equation of the curve we can then find the area enclosed by the curve, the extreme ordinates and the x-axis, by integrating the function thus obtained between the limits 0 and 2.

Assume therefore that $y=u_x=a+bx+cx^2$ is the required equation.

Then, by substitution,

$$u_0 = a,$$
$$u_1 = a + b + c,$$
$$u_2 = a + 2b + 4c,$$

whence
$$a = u_0,$$
$$b = \tfrac{1}{2}(-u_2 + 4u_1 - 3u_0) = \Delta u_0 - \tfrac{1}{2}\Delta^2 u_0,$$
$$c = \tfrac{1}{2}(u_2 - 2u_1 + u_0) = \tfrac{1}{2}\Delta^2 u_0.$$

Also
$$\int_0^2 u_x\,dx = \int_0^2 (a + bx + cx^2)\,dx$$
$$= \left[ax + \tfrac{1}{2}bx^2 + \tfrac{1}{3}cx^3 \right]_0^2$$
$$= 2a + 2b + \tfrac{8}{3}c$$
$$= \tfrac{1}{3}(u_0 + 4u_1 + u_2),$$

on substituting for a, b and c.

This is *Simpson's rule* for approximate integration.
We can obtain this formula by alternative methods.
For example, let

$$u_x = (1 + \Delta)^x\, u_0 = u_0 + x\Delta u_0 + \tfrac{1}{2}x\,(x-1)\,\Delta^2 u_0$$

as far as second differences.

Then
$$\int_0^2 u_x\,dx = \int_0^2 \{u_0 + x\Delta u_0 + \tfrac{1}{2}x\,(x-1)\,\Delta^2 u_0\}\,dx$$
$$= \int_0^2 \{u_0 + x\,(\Delta u_0 - \tfrac{1}{2}\Delta^2 u_0) + \tfrac{1}{2}x^2\Delta^2 u_0\}\,dx$$
$$= \left[xu_0 + \tfrac{1}{2}x^2\,(\Delta u_0 - \tfrac{1}{2}\Delta^2 u_0) + \tfrac{1}{6}x^3\Delta^2 u_0 \right]_0^2$$
$$= 2u_0 + 2\,(\Delta u_0 - \tfrac{1}{2}\Delta^2 u_0) + \tfrac{4}{3}\Delta^2 u_0$$
$$= 2u_0 + 2\Delta u_0 + \tfrac{1}{3}\Delta^2 u_0,$$

and since
$$u_0 = u_0,$$
$$u_1 = u_0 + \Delta u_0,$$
$$u_2 = u_0 + 2\Delta u_0 + \Delta^2 u_0,$$

this reduces to $\tfrac{1}{3}(u_0 + 4u_1 + u_2)$ as before.

A third method is to assume that the integral can be expressed in the form

$$mu_0 + nu_1 + pu_2.$$

Then if $y = a + bx + cx^2$ we have eventually that

$$\int_0^2 u_x dx = 2a + 2b + \tfrac{8}{3}c,$$

as in the first method.

Substituting in the assumed expression for the integral:

$$ma + n(a + b + c) + p(a + 2b + 4c) = 2a + 2b + \tfrac{8}{3}c.$$

Whence, by equating coefficients of a, b, c and solving the resulting equations,

$$m = \tfrac{1}{3}; \quad n = \tfrac{4}{3}; \quad p = \tfrac{1}{3}.$$

3. Change of unit.

The formula $\int_0^2 u_x dx = \tfrac{1}{3}(u_0 + 4u_1 + u_2)$ is an approximate formula obtained by considering unit intervals. If we wish to transform the formula to a form in which the interval is changed to, say, n, then the given values of u_x will be u_0; u_n; u_{2n}. Our new variable is z, where $z = nx$.

$$\therefore \quad dz = n\,dx.$$

The new limits are evidently o and $2n$.

The formula is

$$\int_0^{2n} \frac{1}{n} u_z dz = \tfrac{1}{3}(u_0 + 4u_n + u_{2n}),$$

i.e.

$$\int_0^{2n} u_z dz = \tfrac{1}{3}n(u_0 + 4u_n + u_{2n}),$$

or, on changing the variable to x,

$$\int_0^{2n} u_x dx = \tfrac{1}{3}n(u_0 + 4u_n + u_{2n}).$$

This principle is of universal application and any formula of approximate integration can immediately be transferred from unit intervals to $n$thly intervals and vice versa.

For example, the approximate formula

$$\int_0^{10} u_x\,dx = \tfrac{5}{2}\,(u_1 + u_4 + u_6 + u_9)$$

becomes

$$\int_0^{20} u_x\,dx = 5\,(u_2 + u_8 + u_{12} + u_{18})$$

on doubling the interval;

and

$$\int_0^{10n} u_x\,dx = \frac{5n}{2}\,(u_n + u_{4n} + u_{6n} + u_{9n})$$

when the interval is n.

4. Change of origin.

Consider again Simpson's rule:

$$\int_0^2 u_x\,dx = \tfrac{1}{3}\,(u_0 + 4u_1 + u_2).$$

We have obtained a formula which gives in terms of u_0, u_1 and u_2 the area of the curve cut off by the ordinates $x=0$ and $x=2$. If we change the origin so that the point $(1, u_1)$ becomes the point $(0, v_0)$, as in Fig. 5, we shall have a formula of integration between the limits -1 and 1 in terms of v_{-1}, v_0 and v_1. The formula will be otherwise unaltered and we shall have found an approximation to the same area with reference to a new y-axis $O_1 Y_1$.

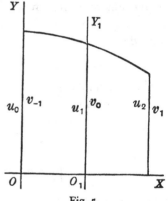

Fig. 5.

In its new form the formula becomes

$$\int_{-1}^1 v_x\,dx = \tfrac{1}{3}\,(v_{-1} + 4v_0 + v_1),$$

or, changing back to u's,

$$\int_{-1}^1 u_x\,dx = \tfrac{1}{3}\,(u_{-1} + 4u_0 + u_1).$$

Now when it is desired to obtain an approximate integration formula it is evident that integration between -1 and 1 (or between $-n$ and n) involves much simpler algebra than integration between 0 and 2 (or between 0 and $2n$). Thus, if

$$u_x = a + bx + cx^2,$$

then

$$u_0 = a,$$

$$u_{-1} = a - b + c,$$

$$u_1 = a + b + c,$$

and

$$\tfrac{1}{3}(u_{-1} + 4u_0 + u_1) = \tfrac{1}{3}\{4u_0 + (u_{-1} + u_1)\}$$
$$= \tfrac{1}{3}(4a + 2a + 2c)$$
$$= \tfrac{1}{3}(6a + 2c).$$

Also

$$\int_{-1}^{1}(a + bx + cx^2)\,dx = \left[ax + \tfrac{1}{2}bx^2 + \tfrac{1}{3}cx^3\right]_{-1}^{1}$$
$$= 2a + \tfrac{2}{3}c,$$

which proves the approximation.

Again, since in this form the coefficients of odd powers of x disappear in the definite integral and also in the paired terms u_t and u_{-t}, we could equally well employ as our assumed expansion for u_x the third difference function $a + bx + cx^2 + dx^3$.

We should have

$$4u_0 + (u_{-1} + u_1) = 4a + a - b + c - d + a + b + c + d = 6a + 2c$$

as before, and

$$\left[ax + \tfrac{1}{2}bx^2 + \tfrac{1}{3}cx^3 + \tfrac{1}{4}dx^4\right]_{-1}^{1} = 2a + \tfrac{2}{3}c.$$

This leads to the important fact that Simpson's rule is true to one more order of differences than was originally assumed, i.e. to third differences.

Generally, formulae involving $2r + 1$ terms, placed symmetrically with reference to the centre of the range, are correct to $(2r+1)$th differences.

For the above reasons, namely

    (i) for simplicity in working;

(ii) to enable us to find the true order of differences to which the approximation is correct;

it is advisable to integrate between $-n$ and n in preference to any other limits.

This can always be done by a suitable change of limits; for example, integration between $\frac{1}{2}$ and 1 can be simplified to integration between, say, 2 and 4 by increasing the interval from $\frac{1}{2}$ to 2. Then, by changing the origin, a formula can be obtained for integration between -1 and 1. To express the formula in the required form the process can then be reversed.

Example 1.

Show that $\displaystyle\int_{1\cdot5}^{2\cdot5} v_x\,dx = \frac{1}{24}\,(v_1 + 22v_2 + v_3)$ approximately.

$$\int_{1\cdot5}^{2\cdot5} v_x\,dx = \frac{1}{2}\int_{3}^{5} u_x\,dx \text{ (if we double the interval).}$$

This will produce a formula in u_2; u_4; u_6.

In the first place we will obtain a formula for $\displaystyle\int_{-1}^{1} u_x\,dx$.

This formula will have to be of the form $mu_{-2} + nu_0 + pu_2$, since we have moved our origin to the point where x was originally 4.

Let $u_x = a + bx + cx^2 + dx^3$.

Then $u_0 = a$,

$u_{-2} = a - 2b + 4c - 8d$,

and $u_2 = a + 2b + 4c + 8d$,

so that $\frac{1}{24}\,(u_{-2} + 22u_0 + u_2) = \frac{1}{24}\,(22a + 2a + 8c) = a + \frac{1}{3}c.$

$$\int_{-1}^{1} u_x\,dx = \left[ax + \tfrac{1}{2}bx^2 + \tfrac{1}{3}cx^3 + \tfrac{1}{4}dx^4 \right]_{-1}^{1} = 2a + \tfrac{2}{3}c.$$

$$\therefore\quad \frac{1}{24}\,(u_{-2} + 22u_0 + u_2) = \frac{1}{2}\int_{-1}^{1} u_x\,dx.$$

Reverting to the first origin:

$$\frac{1}{24}\,(u_2 + 22u_4 + u_6) = \frac{1}{2}\int_{3}^{5} u_x\,dx.$$

$$\therefore\quad \frac{1}{24}\,(v_1 + 22v_2 + v_3) = \int_{1\cdot5}^{2\cdot5} v_x\,dx.$$

Moreover, although only three values of v_x have been given (so that only second differences are known), the formula is true to third differences, for it is symmetrical about the middle point.

5. Some well-known approximate integration formulae.

(1) *Extension of Simpson's rule.*

We have
$$\int_0^2 u_x \, dx = \tfrac{1}{3} \, (u_0 + 4u_1 + u_2).$$

Therefore by changing the origin
$$\int_2^4 u_x \, dx = \tfrac{1}{3} \, (u_2 + 4u_3 + u_4).$$

Similarly
$$\int_4^6 u_x \, dx = \tfrac{1}{3} \, (u_4 + 4u_5 + u_6).$$

....

In general, by addition,
$$\int_0^{2n} u_x \, dx = \tfrac{1}{3} \, (u_0 + 4u_1 + 2u_2 + 4u_3 + 2u_4 + \ldots + u_{2n}).$$

This is a formula for approximate integration used extensively in practical mathematics. In engineering problems, where the curve to be integrated has actually been sketched as the result of experiments, a small unit may be chosen and a large number of ordinates drawn. In that event the extended formula can be applied. This will in general give better results than the single formula
$$\int_0^{2n} u_x \, dx = \frac{n}{3} \, (u_0 + 4u_n + u_{2n}).$$

It should be noted that Simpson's rule, applied in sections (as above), does not assume that a smooth curve can be drawn between all the points u_0, u_1, ... u_{2n}. The method of obtaining the formula has in fact been to draw a number of disjointed curves between u_0, u_1, u_2; u_2, u_3, u_4; ... u_{2n-2}, u_{2n-1}, u_{2n}, and the curve passing through three points such as u_0, u_1, u_2 will not as a rule pass through the next series u_3 and u_4.

(2) *The "three-eighths" rule.*

The following symmetrical formula can be derived by working on the above lines, when four consecutive points are given.

If the four points were u_0, u_1, u_2, u_3 we should commonly integrate between 0 and 3. Change the unit and origin so that we pass firstly to the limits 0 and 6 and secondly to the limits -3 and 3.

We require $\int_{-3}^{3} u_x dx$, given u_{-3}, u_{-1}, u_1, u_3.

Let $$u_x = a + bx + cx^2 + dx^3,$$

so that $$u_{-1} + u_1 = 2(a+c)$$

and $$u_{-3} + u_3 = 2(a + 9c).$$

If $$\int_{-3}^{3} u_x dx = m(u_{-1} + u_1) + n(u_{-3} + u_3),$$

we have

$$\left[ax + \tfrac{1}{2}bx^2 + \tfrac{1}{3}cx^3 + \tfrac{1}{4}dx^4\right]_{-3}^{3} = m(u_{-1} + u_1) + n(u_{-3} + u_3);$$

i.e. $$6a + 18c = m(u_{-1} + u_1) + n(u_{-3} + u_3)$$
$$= m(2a + 2c) + n(2a + 18c)$$
$$= a(2m + 2n) + c(2m + 18n),$$

from which, easily, $m = 18/8$ and $n = 6/8$.

$$\therefore \int_{-3}^{3} u_x dx = \tfrac{3}{8}\{6(u_{-1} + u_1) + 2(u_{-3} + u_3)\},$$

i.e. $$\int_{0}^{6} u_x dx = \tfrac{3}{8}\{6(u_2 + u_4) + 2(u_0 + u_6)\},$$

or $$\int_{0}^{3} u_x dx = \tfrac{3}{8}\{3(u_1 + u_2) + (u_0 + u_3)\}$$
$$= \tfrac{3}{8}(u_0 + 3u_1 + 3u_2 + u_3)$$
$$= \tfrac{3}{8}(1 + E)^3 u_0.$$

This formula, like Simpson's rule, is correct to third differences.

(3) *Weddle's rule.*

Suppose that seven equidistant ordinates are given. In order to reduce the algebra to a minimum, we integrate between limits -3 and $+3$, and write the assumed formula for u_x thus:

$$u_x = a + bx + \frac{cx^2}{2} + \frac{dx(x^2 - 1)}{6} + \frac{ex^2(x^2 - 1)}{24} + \frac{fx(x^2 - 1)(x^2 - 4)}{120}$$
$$+ \frac{gx^2(x^2 - 1)(x^2 - 4)}{720}.$$

This is Stirling's formula with the constants a, b, c, ... g replacing the differences of u_x.

Then

$$\int_{-3}^{3} u_x\,dx = \left[ax + \frac{bx^2}{2} + \frac{cx^3}{6} + \frac{d}{6}\left(\frac{x^4}{4} - \frac{x^2}{2}\right) + \frac{e}{24}\left(\frac{x^5}{5} - \frac{x^3}{3}\right) \right.$$

$$\left. + \frac{f}{120}\left(\frac{x^6}{6} - \frac{5x^4}{4} + \frac{4x^2}{2}\right) + \frac{g}{720}\left(\frac{x^7}{7} - \frac{5x^5}{5} + \frac{4x^3}{3}\right) \right]_{-3}^{3}$$

$$= 6a + 54\left(\frac{c}{6} - \frac{e}{72} + \frac{g}{540}\right) + 486\left(\frac{e}{120} - \frac{g}{720}\right) + \frac{243}{280}g$$

$$= 6a + 9c + \tfrac{33}{10}e + \tfrac{41}{140}g.$$

Replacing a, c, e, g by the differences of u_x in Stirling's formula, we have

$$\int_{-3}^{3} u_x\,dx = 6a + 9c + \tfrac{33}{10}e + \tfrac{41}{140}g$$

$$= 6u_0 + 9\Delta^2 u_{-1} + \tfrac{33}{10}\Delta^4 u_{-2} + \tfrac{41}{140}\Delta^6 u_{-3}.$$

If now $\Delta^2 u_{-1}$, $\Delta^4 u_{-2}$ and $\Delta^6 u_{-3}$ are expressed in terms of u_{-3}, u_{-2}, ... u_2, u_3, we shall obtain a formula correct to seventh differences. It will be found, however, that the coefficients of the terms are large. This is due to the awkward fraction $\tfrac{41}{140}$ multiplying $\Delta^6 u_{-3}$. As sixth differences are usually small, the error involved in replacing $\tfrac{41}{140}\Delta^6 u_{-3}$ by $\tfrac{42}{140}\Delta^6 u_{-3}$, i.e. by $\tfrac{3}{10}\Delta^6 u_{-3}$, will, in general, be negligible. By this substitution the coefficients in the final formula will be much simplified. The modified formula will involve an error of $\tfrac{1}{140}\Delta^6 u_{-3}$ and will therefore be strictly correct to fifth differences only but virtually correct to seventh differences.

The terms in the expression thus adjusted, namely,

$$6u_0 + 9\Delta^2 u_{-1} + \tfrac{33}{10}\Delta^4 u_{-2} + \tfrac{3}{10}\Delta^6 u_{-3},$$

may be expressed in terms of the u's and collected as shown in the following table:

	u_{-3}	u_{-2}	u_{-1}	u_0	u_1	u_2	u_3
$6u_0$				6·0			
$9\Delta^2 u_{-1}$			9·0	−18·0	9·0		
$3·3\Delta^4 u_{-2}$		3·3	−13·2	19·8	−13·2	3·3	
$·3\Delta^6 u_{-3}$	·3	−1·8	4·5	− 6·0	4·5	−1·8	·3
Total ...	·3	1·5	·3	1·8	·3	1·5	·3

Therefore $\int_{-3}^{3} u_x dx$ is approximately equal to

$$\cdot 3u_{-3} + 1\cdot 5u_{-2} + \cdot 3u_{-1} + 1\cdot 8u_0 + \cdot 3u_1 + 1\cdot 5u_2 + 0\cdot 3u_3$$
$$= \tfrac{3}{10}\left[(u_{-3} + u_3) + 5(u_{-2} + u_2) + (u_{-1} + u_1) + 6u_0\right]$$

or $\quad \int_{0}^{6} u_x dx = \tfrac{3}{10}\left[(u_0 + u_6) + 5(u_1 + u_5) + (u_2 + u_4) + 6u_3\right].$

This is Weddle's rule.

An alternative method of obtaining Weddle's rule is by combining a 7-ordinate Simpson's formula with a 7-ordinate three-eighths formula in the ratio $9:-4$. This method proceeds by eliminating the principal error terms in each of the two formulae involved.

(4) Hardy's formulae.

Certain approximate formulae due to G. F. Hardy are used extensively in actuarial work.

Let $\quad u_x = a + bx + cx^2 + dx^3 + ex^4 + fx^5$

so that $\quad \int_{-3}^{3} u_x dx = 6a + 18c + \tfrac{486}{5}e;$

$u_0 = a; \quad u_{-2} + u_2 = 2a + 8c + 32e; \quad u_{-3} + u_3 = 2a + 18c + 162e.$

Solving for a, c and e, and substituting:

$$\int_{-3}^{3} u_x dx = 2\cdot 2u_0 + 1\cdot 62(u_{-2} + u_2) + \cdot 28(u_{-3} + u_3)$$

or $\quad \int_{0}^{6} u_x dx = 2\cdot 2u_3 + 1\cdot 62(u_1 + u_5) + \cdot 28(u_0 + u_6)$
$$= \cdot 28(u_0 + u_6) + 1\cdot 62(u_1 + u_5) + 2\cdot 2u_3,$$

which is Hardy's "formula (37)".

If the interval of differencing be n, this becomes

$$\int_{0}^{6n} u_x dx = n\left\{\cdot 28(u_0 + u_{6n}) + 1\cdot 62(u_n + u_{5n}) + 2\cdot 2u_{3n}\right\}.$$

Similarly

$$\int_{6n}^{12n} u_x dx = n\left\{\cdot 28(u_{6n} + u_{12n}) + 1\cdot 62(u_{7n} + u_{11n}) + 2\cdot 2u_{9n}\right\},$$

and so on.

Since

$$\int_0^\infty u_x \, dx = \int_0^{6n} u_x \, dx + \int_{6n}^{12n} u_x \, dx + \int_{12n}^{18n} u_x \, dx + \dots,$$

$$\int_0^\infty u_x \, dx = n \, \{ \cdot 28 \, (u_0 + 2u_{6n} + 2u_{12n} + \dots)$$
$$+ 1 \cdot 62 \, (u_n + u_{5n} + u_{7n} + \dots) + 2 \cdot 2 \, (u_{3n} + u_{9n} + \dots) \}.$$

This is Hardy's "formula (38)".

If we are dealing with functions derived from a mortality table, and we choose n so that $7n$ falls just within or just without the limits of the table—so that $7n$ is in fact about 100—we can write the above formula thus:

$$\int_0^\infty u_x \, dx = n \, (\cdot 28 u_0 + 1 \cdot 62 u_n + 2 \cdot 2 u_{3n} + 1 \cdot 62 u_{5n} + \cdot 56 u_{6n} + 1 \cdot 62 u_{7n}).$$

In this form the formula is known as Hardy's "formula (39 a)". (See G. King, *Life Contingencies*, p. 488.)

6. (i) Since all these approximations give in effect the area of the curve bounded by u_x, the limiting ordinates and the x-axis, they are often termed "quadrature formulae", the word "quadrature" being defined as the exact or approximate calculation of the area of the square equal in area to that of the given figure.

(ii) In any of the foregoing formulae the sum of the coefficients must equal the range of integration, where this is finite. This may easily be seen by making all the u's involved equal to the same constant.

7. Practical applications of the formulae.

Integration formulae of the above type may be used to advantage in obtaining approximations to the values of certain complicated forms of integral which occur in the theory of life contingencies. Where the functions involved are such that the summation extends to the end of the life table, it is customary to calculate the values of the functions by Hardy's formula (39 a). If, on the other hand, the upper limit is at an age-point short of the limiting age of the life table, any of the simpler integration formulae can be employed to advantage. (See, for example, Spurgeon, *Life Contingencies*, pp. 262, 263.)

It is evident that we can neither integrate the function u_x nor interpolate between given values of u_x if we are absolutely without information regarding the value of the function between the ordinates. For example, in a mortality table we may integrate between, say, l_{30} and l_{31}, assuming first differences constant, for we know that in general the decrements between ages 30 and 31 are small and may be fairly considered as being evenly distributed over the interval. We could not reasonably adopt the same assumption for interpolation between l_0 and l_1, since the deaths of infants in the first year of age are not evenly distributed over the year. Again, a reliable estimate of the population of a seaside resort in June of any calendar year would not be obtained by a first difference interpolation between the population figures for January and December of the same year. In the two latter illustrations further information would be necessary before we could proceed to interpolation or integration.

In applying the formulae of approximate integration to the solution of a problem it is therefore essential that we have sufficient knowledge of the function to justify our assumptions regarding the nature of the curve passing through the given points.

When the function to be integrated is one in which the neglected differential coefficients of the curve are small between the limits of the integration, almost any of the above formulae will give satisfactory results. If these differential coefficients are not small, i.e. those of lower order are changing rapidly between the limits, there may be considerable differences between the approximate results.

Example 2.

The formula for a continuous annuity-certain is

$$\bar{a}_{\overline{m}|} = \int_0^m e^{-\delta t}\, dt,$$

where δ is the force of interest corresponding to the rate of interest i at which the annuity is valued.

By means of an approximate integration formula find the value of $\bar{a}_{\overline{6}|}$ at 4 per cent.

Since we have to evaluate $\bar{a}_{\overline{6}|}$ we shall require some or all of the values of u_t from $t=0$ to $t=6$, where $u_t=e^{-\delta t}$.

By a well-known formula in the theory of interest,

$$e^{-\delta t}=v^t, \text{ where } v=(1+i)^{-1}.$$

Values of v^t at 4 per cent. are available from any tables of interest. We have, therefore:

$$u_0=e^0 \quad\quad = 1,$$
$$u_1=e^{-\delta} =v = \cdot96154,$$
$$u_2=e^{-2\delta}=v^2= \cdot92456,$$
$$u_3=e^{-3\delta}=v^3= \cdot88900,$$
$$u_4=e^{-4\delta}=v^4= \cdot85480,$$
$$u_5=e^{-5\delta}=v^5= \cdot82193,$$
$$u_6=e^{-6\delta}=v^6= \cdot79031.$$

The following results will be obtained:

(i) Simpson's rule applied three times:

$$\tfrac{1}{3}\left(u_0+4u_1+2u_2+4u_3+2u_4+4u_5+u_6\right)$$
$$=5\cdot34630.$$

(ii) The three-eighths rule (with interval of differencing 2):

$$\tfrac{3}{8}\{2\left(u_0+3u_2+3u_4+u_6\right)\}$$
$$=5\cdot34629$$

(iii) Weddle's rule:

$$\cdot3\left(u_0+5u_1+u_2+6u_3+u_4+5u_5+u_6\right)$$
$$=5\cdot34631.$$

The result obtained by integrating $\displaystyle\int_0^6 e^{-\delta t}\,dt$ will be $\left[-\dfrac{1}{\delta}e^{-\delta t}\right]_0^6$ or $\dfrac{v^0-v^6}{\delta}$, and since the value of δ at 4 per cent. as given by an interest table is $\cdot039220713...$, the integral becomes

$$\frac{1-\cdot7903145257...}{\cdot039220713...}=5\cdot34629....$$

The three approximate formulae all give results which differ very little from this. The excellence of the approximations is due to the fact that between the limits $t=0$ and $t=6$ the higher differential coefficients of $y=u_t=e^{-\delta t}$ are very small and the range is short.

8. The Euler-Maclaurin expansion.

We have considered quadrature formulae in which the integral is expressed in terms of a number of particular ordinates. All formulae of this type can be deduced in a straightforward manner by means of Lagrange's interpolation formula, as shown at the end of this chapter. We will now proceed to investigate the problem of approximate integration more generally.

The basic formula for expressing a definite integral in terms of given ordinates, with adjustments, is the *Euler-Maclaurin expansion*. This expansion is in effect of similar form to the expressions already obtained, a greater degree of accuracy being ensured by the addition of functions, not of the ordinates themselves, but of derivatives of certain of the ordinates.

The formula may be derived by the expansion of operators, thus:

$$\sum_{x=0}^{x=n-1} f(x) = f(0) + f(1) + \ldots + f(n-1)$$

$$= F(n) - F(0), \text{ where } f(x) \text{ is } \Delta F(x).$$

Since $f(x) = \Delta F(x)$,

$$F(x) = \Delta^{-1} f(x)$$

$$= (e^D - 1)^{-1} f(x) \text{ (since } 1 + \Delta \equiv e^D. \text{ Chap. VII, para. 6)}$$

$$= \left[\left(1 + D + \frac{D^2}{2!} + \frac{D^3}{3!} + \ldots \right) - 1 \right]^{-1} f(x)$$

$$= D^{-1} \left[1 + \frac{D}{2!} + \frac{D^2}{3!} + \ldots \right]^{-1} f(x)$$

$$= D^{-1} \left[1 - \frac{D}{2} + \frac{D^2}{12} - \frac{D^4}{720} \ldots \right] f(x)$$

$$= \left[D^{-1} - \tfrac{1}{2} + \frac{D}{12} - \frac{D^3}{720} \ldots \right] f(x)$$

$$= D^{-1} f(x) - \tfrac{1}{2} f(x) + \frac{D}{12} f(x) - \frac{D^3}{720} f(x) \ldots$$

$$= \int f(x) \, dx - \tfrac{1}{2} f(x) + \frac{1}{12} \frac{df(x)}{dx} - \frac{1}{720} \frac{d^3 f(x)}{dx^3} \ldots$$

Between limits o and n, we have therefore

$$F(n) - F(o) = \int_0^n f(x)\, dx - \tfrac{1}{2}\{f(n) - f(o)\} + \tfrac{1}{12}\{f'(n) - f'(o)\}$$
$$- \tfrac{1}{720}\{f'''(n) - f'''(o)\} \ldots .$$

For $F(n) - F(o)$ we may write

$$\overset{x=n-1}{\underset{x=0}{\Sigma}} f(x) \quad \text{or} \quad f(o) + f(1) + f(2) + \ldots + f(n-1).$$

$$\therefore \int_0^n f(x)\, dx = f(o) + f(1) + f(2) + \ldots + f(n-1) + \tfrac{1}{2}\{f(n) - f(o)\}$$
$$- \tfrac{1}{12}\{f'(n) - f'(o)\} + \tfrac{1}{720}\{f'''(n) - f'''(o)\} \ldots$$
$$= \tfrac{1}{2}f(o) + f(1) + f(2) + \ldots + f(n-1) + \tfrac{1}{2}f(n)$$
$$- \tfrac{1}{12}\{f'(n) - f'(o)\} + \tfrac{1}{720}\{f'''(n) - f'''(o)\} \ldots .$$

This is a simple form of the Euler-Maclaurin expansion.

A more general form can be obtained by changing the origin to the point a and the unit of measurement to r, thus:

$$\frac{1}{r}\int_a^{a+nr} f(x)\, dx = \tfrac{1}{2}f(a) + f(a+r) + f(a+2r) + \ldots$$

$$+ f(a + \overline{n-1}r) + \tfrac{1}{2}f(a+nr) - \frac{r}{12}\{f'(a+nr) - f'(a)\}$$

$$+ \frac{r^3}{720}\{f'''(a+nr) - f'''(a)\} \ldots .$$

It will be noted that, since

$$\frac{x}{e^x - 1} = 1 - \tfrac{1}{2}x + B_1\frac{x^2}{2!} - B_2\frac{x^4}{4!} + B_3\frac{x^6}{6!} - \ldots$$

we can express the coefficients in $(e^D - 1)^{-1}$ in terms of Bernouilli's numbers. As, however, the resulting approximation formula is to be used for numerical computation, it is of advantage to give the coefficients their actual numerical values.

9. The following examples are illustrative of the use of the formula.

Example 3.

Evaluate $\displaystyle\int_0^1 \frac{dx}{1+x}$ to five places of decimals.

Choose a convenient unit, say o·1. Then in the Euler-Maclaurin expansion we have

$$a = 0, \quad n = 10, \quad r = 0·1, \quad \text{and} \quad u_x = \frac{1}{1+x}.$$

$$\frac{du_x}{dx} = -\frac{1}{(1+x)^2}; \quad \frac{d^3u}{dx^3} = -\frac{6}{(1+x)^4}.$$

$$\therefore \quad \frac{1}{0·1} \int_0^1 \frac{dx}{1+x} = \frac{1}{2} \cdot \frac{1}{1} + \frac{1}{1·1} + \frac{1}{1·2} + \frac{1}{1·3} + \dots + \frac{1}{1·9} + \frac{1}{2} \cdot \frac{1}{2}$$

$$- \frac{0·1}{12} \left[-\frac{1}{2^2} + \frac{1}{1^2} \right] + \frac{0·001}{720} \left[-\frac{6}{2^4} + \frac{6}{1^4} \right] \dots$$

$$= ·50000 - \frac{1}{120} \cdot \frac{3}{4} + \frac{1}{720000} \cdot 6 \cdot \frac{15}{16}$$

$$\begin{aligned}
&·90909 \\
&·83333 \\
&·76923 \\
&·71429 \\
&·66667 \\
&·62500 \\
&·58824 \\
&·55556 \\
&·52632 \\
&·25000 \\
\hline
&6·93773
\end{aligned}$$

$$= 6·93773 - ·00625 + ·00001$$
$$= 6·93149.$$

$$\therefore \quad \int_0^1 \frac{dx}{1+x} = ·69315 \text{ to five places of decimals.}$$

This agrees with the true result ($\log_e 2$) to the required degree of accuracy.

Example 4.

Find the sum of the fourth powers of the first n natural numbers by means of the Euler-Maclaurin formula.

In the formula

$$\frac{1}{r} \int_a^{a+nr} u_x \, dx = \tfrac{1}{2} u_a + u_{a+r} + u_{a+2r} + \dots$$

$$+ \tfrac{1}{2} u_{a+nr} - \frac{r}{12} (u'_{a+nr} - u'_a) + \frac{r^3}{720} (u'''_{a+nr} - u'''_a) \dots,$$

put $a = 0$, $r = 1$, $u_x = x^4$; then

$$\int_0^n x^4 dx = 1^4 + 2^4 + 3^4 + \dots$$

$$+ (n-1)^4 + \frac{1}{2} n^4 - \frac{1}{12} [4x^3]_{x=n} + \frac{1}{720} [4 \cdot 3 \cdot 2x]_{x=n},$$

since higher differential coefficients of u_x than the fourth will be zero.

I.e.

$$\left[\frac{x^5}{5} \right]_0^n = \sum_{r=1}^{r=n} r^4 - \frac{1}{2} n^4 - \frac{1}{12} 4n^3 + \frac{1}{720} 24n.$$

$$\therefore \sum_{r=1}^{r=n} r^4 = \frac{1}{5} n^5 + \frac{1}{2} n^4 + \frac{1}{3} n^3 - \frac{1}{30} n.$$

By proceeding on the above lines it can easily be proved that the general formula for the sum of the pth powers of the first n natural numbers is

$$\sum_{r=1}^{r=n} r^p = \frac{1}{p+1} n^{p+1} + \frac{1}{2} n^p + \frac{1}{12} p n^{p-1} - \frac{1}{720} p (p-1) (p-2) n^{p-3}$$

$$+ \frac{p (p-1) (p-2) (p-3) (p-4)}{30,240} n^{p-5} \dots$$

10. Lubbock's formula.

The previous formulae have been developed for the purpose of relating a definite integral to the sum of a number of weighted ordinates at finite distances apart. We have, in effect, obtained approximate formulae for the value of

$$\operatorname*{Lt}_{h \to 0} h (u_a + u_{a+h} + u_{a+2h} + \dots + u_b).$$

In addition to formulae of this type we can find expressions which enable us to find the value of the sum of a number of ordinates at finite distances apart in terms of the ordinates at greater or less finite intervals apart. Thus, if for the curve $y = u_x$ there are m unit intervals, so that we have Σu_x from $x = 0$ to $x = m - 1$, we may develop a relationship between this sum and the sum when the intervals are, say, h, where $nh = 1$.

In place of the sum $h (u_a + u_{a+h} + u_{a+2h} + \dots + u_b)$, we may consider, without loss of generality, the simpler form when the series commences with u_0.

Let there be m ordinates at unit distances apart, and let each of these unit distances be divided into n equal parts, so that the new ordinates are

$$u_0, u_{1/n}, u_{2/n}, \ldots u_{r/n}, \ldots u_{m-1/n}.$$

We have
$$S \equiv u_0 + u_{1/n} + u_{2/n} + \ldots + u_{m-1/n}$$

$$= \frac{E^m - 1}{E^{1/n} - 1} u_0 = \frac{\Delta}{E^{1/n} - 1} \cdot \frac{E^m - 1}{\Delta} u_0.$$

By ordinary algebra, putting h for $1/n$,

$$\frac{\Delta}{E^{1/n} - 1} \equiv \frac{\Delta}{(1 + \Delta)^h - 1} \equiv \frac{\Delta}{h\Delta + h_{(2)}\Delta^2 + \ldots}$$

$$\equiv \frac{1}{h} - \frac{h-1}{2h} \Delta + \frac{h^2 - 1}{12h} \Delta^2 - \frac{h^2 - 1}{24h} \Delta^3 \ldots,$$

so that the operator is

$$n + \frac{n-1}{2} \Delta - \frac{n^2 - 1}{12n} \Delta^2 + \frac{n^2 - 1}{24n} \Delta^3 \ldots.$$

To obtain S we apply this operator to

$$\frac{E^m - 1}{\Delta} u_0 = u_0 + u_1 + \ldots + u_{m-1}.$$

We note the first difference of this is

$$(E^m - 1) u_0 = u_m - u_0,$$

the second difference is $\Delta u_m - \Delta u_0$ and so on.

Thus, applying the operator,

$$S \equiv u_0 + u_{1/n} + u_{2/n} + \ldots + u_{m-1/n}$$

$$= n (u_0 + u_1 + \ldots + u_{m-1}) + \frac{n-1}{2} (u_m - u_0) - \frac{n^2 - 1}{12n} (\Delta u_m - \Delta u_0)$$

$$+ \frac{n^2 - 1}{24n} (\Delta^2 u_m - \Delta^2 u_0) \ldots.$$

This is Lubbock's formula.

The coefficients of higher differences than the second were not given by Lubbock and are cumbersome. The terms in $\Delta^3 u$ and $\Delta^4 u$ are respectively

$$- \frac{(n^2 - 1)(19n^2 - 1)}{720n^3} (\Delta^3 u_m - \Delta^3 u_0)$$

and
$$\frac{(n^2-1)(9n^2-1)}{480n^3}(\Delta^4 u_m - \Delta^4 u_0).$$

If the interval of differencing be originally n instead of unity, Lubbock's formula becomes, on changing the unit,

$$u_0 + u_1 + u_2 + \ldots + u_{mn-1}$$
$$= n\left(u_0 + u_n + u_{2n} + \ldots + u_{(m-1)n}\right) + \frac{n-1}{2}\left(u_{mn} - u_0\right)$$
$$- \frac{n^2-1}{12n}(\Delta u_{mn} - \Delta u_0) + \frac{n^2-1}{24n}(\Delta^2 u_{mn} - \Delta^2 u_0) \ldots$$

*11. Lubbock's original formula involves Δu_m, $\Delta^2 u_m$, ... and these involve u_{m+1}, u_{m+2}, ..., i.e. values of u beyond the range of summation; these u's may have to be specially calculated or may even be completely unavailable. De Morgan (*Differential and Integral Calculus*, pp. 317–18) and T. B. Sprague (*J.I.A.* vol. XVIII, pp. 309–10) transformed the formula so as to involve only $u_0 \ldots u_m$. If the numerical values (without sign) of the coefficients of the differences in Lubbock's formula be represented by C_1, C_2, ..., the transformed formula is

$$n(u_0 + u_1 + \ldots + u_{m-1}) + \frac{n-1}{2}(u_m - u_0) - C_1(\Delta u_{m-1} - \Delta u_0)$$
$$- C_2(\Delta^2 u_{m-2} + \Delta^2 u_0) - C_3(\Delta^3 u_{m-3} - \Delta^3 u_0) - C_4(\Delta^4 u_{m-4} + \Delta^4 u_0)\ldots,$$

where all C coefficients are negative and the terms involve alternately the *difference* between the terminal *odd* differences and the *sum* of the terminal *even* differences. The differences Δu_{m-1}, $\Delta^2 u_{m-2}$, $\Delta^3 u_{m-3}$, ... are the concluding differences of the scheme based on $u_0 \ldots u_m$, and lie on a diagonal sloping upwards (Sprague, *loc. cit.* p. 310).

12. Woolhouse's formula.

Although Lubbock's formula has the advantage that it may be used when the function is not capable of expression as a mathematical expansion—as for example when the data are based on a mortality table—there are disadvantages in adopting the formula. In the first place, if it is necessary to proceed further than second differences the calculations are heavy, and secondly it may happen that the differences converge slowly, so that if we stop at second or third differences we are likely to obtain a result differing considerably from the true value of the function. In the case of a mathematical function whose differential coefficients are easily evaluated an alternative summation formula can be adopted in which differential coefficients of odd order replace the finite differences in Lubbock's formula.

The formula involving differential coefficients is due to Woolhouse, and may be developed directly from the Euler-Maclaurin expansion.

The Euler-Maclaurin expansion is

$$\int_0^m u_x dx = \tfrac{1}{2}u_0 + u_1 + u_2 + \ldots + u_{m-1} + \tfrac{1}{2}u_m - \frac{1}{12}(u_m{}' - u_0{}')$$
$$+ \frac{1}{720}(u_m{}''' - u_0{}''') \ldots.$$

If the interval of differencing be $1/n$, the formula becomes

$$n \int_0^m u_x dx = (\tfrac{1}{2}u_0 + u_{1/n} + u_{2/n} + \ldots + \tfrac{1}{2}u_m) - \frac{1}{12n}(u_m{}' - u_0{}')$$
$$+ \frac{1}{720n^3}(u_m{}''' - u_0{}''') \ldots.$$

If, however, we multiply both sides of the first expression by n we have

$$n \int_0^m u_x dx = n(\tfrac{1}{2}u_0 + u_1 + u_2 + \ldots + \tfrac{1}{2}u_m) - \frac{n}{12}(u_m{}' - u_0{}')$$
$$+ \frac{n}{720}(u_m{}''' - u_0{}''') \ldots.$$

Equating the two values of $n \int_0^m u_x dx$:

$$\tfrac{1}{2}u_0 + u_{1/n} + u_{2/n} + \ldots + \tfrac{1}{2}u_m - \frac{1}{12n}(u_m{}' - u_0{}') + \frac{1}{720n^3}(u_m{}''' - u_0{}''') \ldots$$

$$= n(\tfrac{1}{2}u_0 + u_1 + u_2 + \ldots + \tfrac{1}{2}u_m) - \frac{n}{12}(u_m{}' - u_0{}') + \frac{n}{720}(u_m{}''' - u_0{}''') \ldots$$

or

$$u_0 + u_{1/n} + u_{2/n} + \ldots + u_m - \tfrac{1}{2} (u_0 + u_m) - \frac{1}{12n} (u_m' - u_0')$$

$$+ \frac{1}{720n^3} (u_m''' - u_0''') \ldots$$

$$= n (u_0 + u_1 + u_2 + \ldots + u_m) - \frac{n}{2} (u_0 + u_m) - \frac{n}{12} (u_m' - u_0')$$

$$+ \frac{n}{720} (u_m''' - u_0''') \ldots.$$

Re-arranging:

$$u_0 + u_{1/n} + u_{2/n} + \ldots + u_m = n (u_0 + u_1 + u_2 + \ldots + u_m)$$

$$- \frac{n-1}{2} (u_0 + u_m) - \frac{n^2-1}{12n} (u_m' - u_0') + \frac{n^4-1}{720n^3} (u_m''' - u_0''') \ldots.$$

If the unit of measurement be changed to n, we have

$$u_0 + u_1 + u_2 + \ldots + u_{mn} = n (u_0 + u_n + u_{2n} + \ldots + u_{mn})$$

$$- \frac{n-1}{2} (u_0 + u_{mn}) - \frac{n^2-1}{12} (u_{mn}' - u_0') + \frac{n^4-1}{720} (u_{mn}''' - u_0''') \ldots,$$

the usual form of Woolhouse's formula.

It should be noted that, by replacing the derivatives of u by their values in finite differences, Lubbock's formula can be obtained directly from the formula above.

In applying these formulae to certain actuarial functions the values of u, $\frac{du}{dx}$, $\frac{d^3u}{dx^3}$, ... at the end of the mortality table will disappear. Woolhouse's formula may then be written as

$$\frac{1}{n} (u_0 + u_{1/n} + u_{2/n} + \ldots)$$

$$= (u_0 + u_1 + \ldots) - \frac{n-1}{2n} u_0 + \frac{n^2-1}{12n^2} u_0' - \frac{n^4-1}{720n^4} u_0''' \ldots.$$

This is a convenient form for expressing the value of a benefit paid at $n$thly intervals in terms of the values at intervals of a year.

13. Other formulae for approximate integration.

It will have been observed that in the formulae of the type of Simpson's, Weddle's, etc., the function of the u's is symmetrical about the central value. If, however, a number of fixed ordinates be given and it is desired to obtain an approximation to the area of a curve in terms of these ordinates, the resulting form will not necessarily be symmetrical. Again, the formula for the area of the curve may be related not only to ordinates falling within the area to be measured, but to ordinates outside the area. It may be noted therefore that although standard formulae are available, it is not difficult to devise approximations to fit the particular problems under investigation. (See paragraph 15.)

Example 5.

If u_x is of the form $a + bx + cx^2$, find a formula for $\int_0^1 u_x \, dx$ in terms of u_0, u_1 and u_2.

The interpolation formula which involves the terms u_0, u_1 and u_2 is

$$u_x = u_0 + x\Delta u_0 + \tfrac{1}{2}x\,(x-1)\,\Delta^2 u_0.$$

$$\therefore \int_0^1 u_x \, dx = \left[xu_0 + \tfrac{1}{2}x^2\Delta u_0 + (\tfrac{1}{6}x^3 - \tfrac{1}{4}x^2)\,\Delta^2 u_0 \right]_0^1$$

$$= u_0 + \tfrac{1}{2}\Delta u_0 - \tfrac{1}{12}\Delta^2 u_0$$

$$= u_0 + \tfrac{1}{2}\,(u_1 - u_0) - \tfrac{1}{12}\,(u_2 - 2u_1 + u_0)$$

$$= \tfrac{5}{12}u_0 + \tfrac{8}{12}u_1 - \tfrac{1}{12}u_2.$$

The required formula is therefore

$$\int_0^1 u_x \, dx = \tfrac{1}{12}\,(5u_0 + 8u_1 - u_2).$$

It should be noted that (i) the expression is unsymmetrical in the u's, and (ii) the ordinate u_2 falls without the area to be integrated.

Example 6.

If u_x is of the same form as in the example above, derive a formula for $\int_0^1 u_x \, dx$ in terms of u_{-1}, u_1 and u_2.

Let u_x be expressed in the divided difference formula, thus:

$$u_x = u_{-1} + (x+1)\,\underset{1}{\triangle} u_{-1} + (x+1)\,(x-1)\,\underset{1,\,2}{\triangle^2} u_{-1}.$$

Then
$$\int_0^1 u_x = \left[x u_{-1} + \left(\frac{x^2}{2} + x \right) \underset{1}{\triangle} u_{-1} + \left(\frac{x^3}{3} - x \right) \underset{1,2}{\triangle^2} u_{-1} \right]_0^1$$

$$= u_{-1} + \tfrac{3}{2} \underset{1}{\triangle} u_{-1} - \tfrac{2}{3} \underset{1,2}{\triangle^2} u_{-1};$$

$$\underset{1}{\triangle} u_{-1} = \frac{u_1 - u_{-1}}{2},$$

$$\underset{1,2}{\triangle^2} u_{-1} = \left\{ \frac{u_2 - u_1}{1} - \frac{u_1 - u_{-1}}{2} \right\} \Big/ \{2 - (-1)\}.$$

On reduction, the integral is easily found to be

$$\tfrac{1}{36} (5u_{-1} + 39u_1 - 8u_2).$$

It is obviously impossible to quote all the formulae that are in current use. Further examples and illustrations of various approximation integration formulae will be found in the following sources: Whittaker and Robinson's *Calculus of Observations*, Chap. VII; C. H. Wickens, *J.I.A.* vol. LIV, pp. 209–13; A. E. King, *T.F.A.* vol. IX, pp. 218–31; Elderton's *Frequency Curves and Correlation*, 3rd ed., pp. 26–8; J. Buchanan, *J.I.A.* vol. XXXVII, p. 384.

14. Alternative methods of proof of the formulae.

It has been stated above that the Euler-Maclaurin expansion can be used as the basic quadrature formula. It will be instructive to develop Simpson's formula from this expansion.

$$\int_0^{2mn} u_x dx = n \left(\tfrac{1}{2} u_0 + u_n + u_{2n} + \ldots + u_{(2m-1)n} + \tfrac{1}{2} u_{2mn} \right) - \frac{n^2}{12} \left(u'_{2mn} - u_0' \right)$$

approximately.

Writing $2n$ for n, but preserving the same range 0 to $2mn$,

$$\int_0^{2mn} u_x dx = 2n \left(\tfrac{1}{2} u_0 + u_{2n} + u_{4n} + \ldots + u_{(2m-2)n} + \tfrac{1}{2} u_{2mn} \right)$$
$$- \frac{4n^2}{12} \left(u'_{2mn} - u_0' \right).$$

Subtracting this from four times the first:

$$3 \int_0^{2mn} u_x dx = 2n \left(\tfrac{1}{2} u_0 + 2u_n + u_{2n} + 2u_{3n} + \ldots + u_{(2m-2)n} \right.$$
$$\left. + 2u_{(2m-1)n} + \tfrac{1}{2} u_{2mn} \right);$$

i.e.

$$\int_0^{2mn} u_x dx = \frac{n}{3} (u_0 + 4u_n + 2u_{2n} + 4u_{3n} + \ldots + 2u_{(2m-2)n} \\ + 4u_{(2m-1)n} + u_{2mn}),$$

which is the extended Simpson's formula.

15. Proofs by Lagrange's formula.

We have shown in paragraph 2 (p. 176) that we may adopt the expression for u_x in terms of u_0 and differences of u_0 as the assumed form of function. Since Lagrange's formula is based on the same assumption it is evident that, given selected ordinates, at either equal or unequal intervals, we can obtain any approximate formula by the use of the Lagrange formula.

For example, given u_0, u_1, u_2,

$$u_x = u_0 \frac{(x-1)(x-2)}{(-1)(-2)} + u_1 \frac{x(x-2)}{1 \cdot (-1)} + u_2 \frac{x(x-1)}{2 \cdot 1}$$
$$= \tfrac{1}{2}u_0 (x^2 - 3x + 2) + u_1 (2x - x^2) + \tfrac{1}{2}u_2 (x^2 - x),$$

so that

$$\int_0^2 u_x dx = \left[u_0 \left(\frac{x^3}{6} - \frac{3x^2}{4} + x \right) + u_1 \left(x^2 - \frac{x^3}{3} \right) + u_2 \left(\frac{x^3}{6} - \frac{x^2}{4} \right) \right]_0^2$$
$$= \tfrac{1}{3} (u_0 + 4u_1 + u_2), \text{ which is Simpson's rule.}$$

If we integrate between 0 and 1 we shall obtain

$$\int_0^1 u_x dx = \tfrac{1}{12} (5u_0 + 8u_1 - u_2),$$

the formula given in Example 5.

By this method it is easy and straightforward to deduce special formulae for particular cases.

*16. Remainder terms.

It is known (Chap. III, paragraph 17) that if an interpolation formula is used to find u_x from n values $u_a, u_b, \ldots u_k$, the error involved, or remainder term, is of the form

$$(x-a)(x-b) \ldots (x-k) \frac{d^n}{dx^n} u_\xi,$$

where ξ is an unknown number falling in the range which includes $x, a, b \ldots k$. By means of this result, expressions in similar form have been found for the errors or remainder terms of the principal quadrature formulae.

For example, if the range of integration is a to b, the remainder term in Simpson's formula is

$$-\cdot 00035 \, (b-a)^5 \frac{d^4}{dx^4} u_\xi$$

and that of the three-eighths rule is

$$-\cdot 00016 \, (b-a)^5 \frac{d^4}{dx^4} u_\xi.$$

We cannot usually find ξ, but if the maximum value of the differential coefficient can be found the expression gives an upper limit for the error.

For further information on this point the student is referred to Steffensen, *Interpolation*, Sections 12–16, and Milne-Thomson, *Calculus of Finite Differences*, Chap. VII.

EXAMPLES 9

1. Prove that

$$\int_0^{2a} u_x \, dx = \int_0^a (u_x + u_{2a-x}) \, dx,$$

and illustrate the result geometrically.

2. If $u_x = a + bx + cx^2$, prove that

$$\int_1^3 u_x \, dx = 2u_2 + \tfrac{1}{12} (u_0 - 2u_2 + u_4),$$

and hence find an approximate value for

$$\int_{-\frac{1}{2}}^{\frac{1}{2}} e^{-\frac{x^2}{10}} \, dx.$$

3. Show that $\int_0^1 u_x \, dx = \tfrac{1}{12} (5u_1 + 8u_0 - u_{-1})$ approximately.

Find the approximate mileage travelled between 12.0 and 12.30 by use of the above formula, from the following:

Time	Speed (m.p.h.)
11.50	24·2
12.0	35·0
12.10	41·3
12.20	42·8
12.30	39·2

4. Prove that, if u_x is a rational integral function of x, then

$$\int e^{\frac{x}{a}} u_x\, dx = a e^{\frac{x}{a}} \left(1 - aD + a^2 D^2 - a^3 D^3 + \ldots\right) u_x,$$

where $D \equiv \dfrac{d}{dx}$.

5. Show that the area of a curve, divided into n parts by $n+1$ equidistant ordinates $u_0, u_1, \ldots u_n$, is given approximately by the series

$$n u_0 + \frac{n^2}{2}\Delta u_0 + \left\{\frac{n^3}{3} - \frac{n^2}{2}\right\}\frac{\Delta^2 u_0}{1.2} + \left\{\frac{n^4}{4} - n^3 + n^2\right\}\frac{\Delta^3 u_0}{1.2.3}\ldots$$

to $n+1$ terms.

6. Between the limits $x=0$ and $x=n$ the functions u_x and du_x/dx are continuously increasing.

Show that $\displaystyle\int_0^n u_x\, dx$ is less than $\frac{1}{2}u_0 + \sum_1^{n-1} u_x + \frac{1}{2}u_n$.

7. Obtain the approximate formula

$$\int_{-1}^{1} u_x\, dx = \frac{13\,(u_1 + u_{-1}) - (u_3 + u_{-3})}{12},$$

showing up to what order of differences it holds.

8. Assuming u_x to be of the fourth degree in x, express $\displaystyle\int_0^5 u_x\, dx$ in terms of u_0, u_1, u_2, u_3 and u_4.

9. A plane area is bounded by a curve, the axis of x, and two ordinates. The area is divided into five figures by equidistant ordinates 2 inches apart, the lengths of the ordinates being 21·65, 21·04, 20·35, 19·61, 18·75 and 17·80 inches respectively. Apply the method of integration to obtain an approximate value of the area.

10. Prove the approximate formula

$$\int_0^{10} u_x\, dx = 2\cdot5\,(u_1 + u_4 + u_6 + u_9),$$

and show that the formula involves a small second difference error.

---

11. Find the value of $\int_0^6 (1+x)^{-2}\,dx$.

Obtain approximations to the value by applying

(i) Weddle's rule:

$$\int_0^6 u_x\,dx = 0\cdot3\,(u_0 + 5u_1 + u_2 + 6u_3 + u_4 + 5u_5 + u_6),$$

(ii) Simpson's rule:

$$\int_0^2 u_x\,dx = \tfrac{1}{3}\,(u_0 + 4u_1 + u_2),\text{ applied three times.}$$

12. Which of the two following formulae would you expect to give the better approximation for $\int_0^4 u_x\,dx$?

$$(a)\ \tfrac{1}{9}\{5\,(u_0 + u_4) + 4\,(u_1 + u_3) + 18u_2\},$$
$$(b)\ \tfrac{2}{15}\{2\,(u_0 + u_2 + u_4) + 12\,(u_1 + u_3)\}.$$

13. Prove the approximate integration formula:

$$\int_0^n u_x\,dx = n\,\{\tfrac{3}{8}u_0 + \tfrac{1}{24}\,(19u_n - 5u_{2n} + u_{3n})\},$$

and hence find $\int_0^1 u_x\,dx$ given the following table:

x	0	1	2	3
u_x	27,650	31,252	35,154	39,368

14. Prove that

$$\int_{-\frac{1}{2}}^{\frac{1}{2}} f(x)\,dx = \tfrac{1}{2}\{f(-\tfrac{1}{2}) + f(\tfrac{1}{2})\} + \tfrac{1}{24}\{\Delta f(-\tfrac{3}{2}) - \Delta f(\tfrac{1}{2})\}\text{ approximately.}$$

Hence find $\int_1^3 f(x)\,dx$, when $f(0)=105$, $f(1)=212$, $f(2)=421$, $f(3)=749$ and $f(4)=1050$.

15. If u_x either increases continually or decreases continually as x increases, prove that $\int_1^n u_x\,dx$ differs from $\overset{n-1}{\underset{1}{\Sigma}}\, u_x$ by less than the difference between u_1 and u_n.

Prove that the difference between $\log n$ and

$$1 + \tfrac{1}{2} + \tfrac{1}{3} + \ldots + 1/(n-1) < 1,$$

however great n may be.

16. If third differences are constant, prove that

$$\int_0^2 u_x\,dx = \tfrac{1}{24}\left(u_{-\frac{1}{2}}+23u_{\frac{1}{2}}+23u_{\frac{3}{2}}+u_{\frac{5}{2}}\right).$$

Adapt this formula to find the approximate value of $\log_e 2$ from the integral $\int_a^{2a}\dfrac{dx}{x}$.

17. Prove that, approximately,

$$\int_{-3}^3 u_x\,dx = 0\cdot3\left(1\cdot1u_{-3}+4\cdot4u_{-2}+2\cdot5u_{-1}+4u_0+2\cdot5u_1+4\cdot4u_2+1\cdot1u_3\right).$$

18. $f(x)$ is a rational integral function of the fifth degree in x. Prove that

$$\int_{-1}^1 f(x)\,dx = \tfrac{8}{9}f(0)+\tfrac{5}{9}\left\{f(\sqrt{0\cdot6})+f(-\sqrt{0\cdot6})\right\}.$$

19. Use Simpson's rule to prove that $\log_e 7$ is approximately $1\cdot95$.

20. Apply the Euler-Maclaurin formula to find a formula for the sum of the fifth powers of the first n natural numbers.

21. Obtain Shovelton's integration formula:

$$\int_0^{10} u_x\,dx = \tfrac{5}{126}\left\{8\left(u_0+u_{10}\right)+35\left(u_1+u_3+u_7+u_9\right)\right.$$
$$\left.+15\left(u_2+u_4+u_6+u_8\right)+36u_5\right\}.$$

22. By means of Hardy's formula

$$\int_0^6 u_x\,dx = \cdot28u_0+1\cdot62u_1+2\cdot2u_3+1\cdot62u_5+\cdot28u_6,$$

calculate the value of

$$\int_0^{\frac{1}{2}}(1-x^2)^{-\frac{1}{2}}\,dx$$

correct to four places of decimals.

23. If $f(x)$ be a function of the third degree in x, and if

$$u_{-1}=\int_{-3t}^{-t}f(x)\,dx,\quad u_0=\int_{-t}^{t}f(x)\,dx,\quad u_1=\int_t^{3t}f(x)\,dx,$$

show that

$$f(0)=\frac{1}{2t}\left\{u_0-\frac{\Delta^2 u_{-1}}{24}\right\}.$$

24. AB is the base of a semicircle, centre O and radius unity. The points P and Q bisect OA and OB respectively. The area between the

semicircle, the base PQ and the ordinates at P and Q is $\dfrac{\pi}{6}+\dfrac{\sqrt{3}}{4}$. Use Weddle's rule that

$$\int_0^6 f(x)\,dx = 0.3\,\{f(0)+5f(1)+f(2)+6f(3)+f(4)+5f(5)+f(6)\}$$

to find an approximate value of π to three places of decimals.

25. The following values of u_x are given:

x	0	1	2	3	4	5	6
u_x	·146	·161	·176	·190	·204	·217	·230

Use an approximate integration formula to find the value of $\displaystyle\int_0^6 u_x\,dx$.

It is found that, for the values given, $y=\log_{10}(\cdot 05x+1\cdot 4)$ fits the data. Verify that this is so by integrating $\log_{10}(\cdot 05x+1\cdot 4)$ between the limits 0 and 6. ($\log_{10} e = \cdot 4343$; $\log_{10} 1\cdot 7 = \cdot 2304$; $\log_{10} 1\cdot 4 = \cdot 1461$.)

26. If u_x is a function whose fifth differences are constant, $\displaystyle\int_{-1}^1 u_x\,dx$ can be expressed in the form

$$pu_{-\alpha}+qu_0+pu_{\alpha}.$$

Find the values of p, q and α.

Use this formula, after making the necessary changes in the origin and scale, to find the value of $\log_e 2$ to four places of decimals from the equation

$$\int_0^1 \frac{1}{1+x}\,dx = \log_e 2.$$

27. Prove that, if $a=0$,

$$\int_a^{a+r} u_x\,dx = \tfrac{1}{2}u_0+u_1+u_2+\ldots+u_{r-1}+\tfrac{1}{2}u_r-\tfrac{1}{12}(\Delta u_{r-1}-\Delta u_0)$$
$$-\tfrac{1}{24}(\Delta^2 u_{r-2}+\Delta^2 u_0)-\tfrac{19}{720}(\Delta^3 u_{r-3}-\Delta^3 u_0)$$
$$-\tfrac{3}{160}(\Delta^4 u_{r-4}+\Delta^4 u_0)\ldots.$$

If u_x be the function $(1+x^2)^{-1}$ find an approximate value for π.

28. Obtain an approximate formula for $\displaystyle\int_{-3}^3 u_x\,dx$ in the form

$$a\,(u_{-2}+u_2)+b\,(u_{-3}+u_3)$$

and find the values of a and b.

29. Use Lagrange's formula to show that

$$\int_{-\frac{1}{2}}^{\frac{1}{2}} y_x\,dx = \tfrac{1}{5760}\,[5178y_0+308\,(y_{-1}+y_1)-17\,(y_{-2}+y_2)].$$

PROBABILITY AND ELEMENTARY STATISTICS

CHAPTER X

PROBABILITY

1. Suppose that a bag contains a hundred balls of exactly the same size and shape, of which one is coloured and the remaining ninety-nine white. If one of these balls be drawn at random it is safe to say that there is a greater probability of drawing a white ball than of drawing the coloured ball. Again, of a number of men in a community, all subject to the same conditions, the probability that one aged 20 will survive 10 years is obviously greater than the probability that one aged 90 will survive the same period. These examples serve to illustrate what is understood by the term "probability". Many more such simple examples could be given, from which we could say that the probability that event A would happen is greater or less than that event B would happen. A difficulty arises, however, when we attempt to assign a measure to the probability that one of the events A or B might happen.

In the first of the above examples it is not unreasonable to argue that since there is one coloured ball among a hundred balls, the probability that this coloured ball would be drawn is one in a hundred. Whether this be so or not, we have used the data at our command and have given a measure to the probability. In the second example, however, we have no data immediately available to enable us to assign a numerical value to the probability in question. It would be necessary to collect statistics of the mortality of the men in the community, and to supplement the collection of these statistics by more or less elaborate calculations. In the application of the theory of probability to most actuarial problems the aggregation of statistics is necessary before the data are available, and it is not often that we are immediately in possession of such simple facts as are given in the first type of question. A complete answer to a problem in actuarial work would involve the collection and interpretation of the relevant statistics, and in many of the questions on probability that are dealt with later it will be assumed that sufficient data are available to enable us to proceed to the required conclusions.

2. In the study of probability we are concerned with the number of times that an event occurs on the average out of a very large number of occasions on which it is in question. The proportion of such favourable cases to the total number of cases may then be said to be the "probability" of the happening of the event. For example, consider the following extract from a mortality table:

Age x	Number of persons who are alive at exact age x
0	1000
10	812
20	793
30	762

This table may be interpreted thus. Out of 1000 births, 812 children survive to age 10; of these 793 survive to age 20; of these 762 survive to age 30; and so on. Since "living to age 10" is an event, and we start with 1000 births, this event is in question on 1000 occasions; the proportion of times that this event happens is 812/1000 or ·812.

·812 is therefore the "probability" that, according to the particular mortality table given above, a child just born will survive to age 10. Similarly, the probability that the child will survive to age 20 is ·793 and that it will survive to age 30 is ·762.

These probabilities are all averages, and being averages require adequate data for their calculation. In ordinary circumstances little can be argued from an event which happens on one occasion only; in probability nothing of value can be deduced from solitary instances. In fact, probability as applied to a solitary occasion rarely has any meaning; not only can few deductions be made from solitary instances, but in general they cannot be applied to future solitary occasions even if they have been drawn from sufficient data.

The collection and interpretation of the data necessary for the calculation of averages and probabilities is the work of the statistician, but it is the mathematician who is concerned with the laws followed by these averages and probabilities. It is worthy of note that although probability and statistics are in effect inseparable, the theory of probability was evolved from a very different source—namely, a consideration of gambling and games of chance. The association between the two sciences came at a much later date.

3. It will be observed that the term "probability" has been employed in two senses. It has been used as the name of the subject itself, and also as the name of a ratio—the proportion of the number of favourable events to the total number of cases when the happening of an event is in question. There is yet a third sense in which the word is frequently employed, namely in the sense of "credibility". Such terms as "credibility" and "likelihood" in their ordinary colloquial meaning are incapable of exact mathematical measurement and with probability in this sense mathematicians are not concerned.

In this and the following chapters the term "probability" will be used in the sense of an average, but in so doing it must be repeated that the study of the subject will be of no assistance in forecasting the results of solitary events.

4. When the cases which constitute the totality of possibilities for any event are counted, care must be taken that all the cases are strictly comparable. If we are considering the probability of living a number of years we must be careful to state whether we are dealing with male lives only or with female lives only or with an aggregation of both sexes; for the longevity of males is different from that of females. Similarly, if it be required to find the probability that a coin of particular value is drawn from a bag containing a number of coins it must be stated at the outset whether or not all coins are equally likely to be drawn. If one of the coins were a half-crown and the others were all sixpences, it could hardly be said that it would be equally likely that any one particular coin would be drawn; the cases would not be homogeneous.

This important question of homogeneity arose quite early in the history of the subject. Errors were often made in the solution of what are now recognized as quite simple problems through the neglect of this principle. D'Alembert's solution to the following problem is classic:

What is the chance that heads will turn up at least once in two tossings of a coin?

The solution given was as follows:

"Only three different events are possible, namely,

(i) heads the first time—which makes it unnecessary to toss again;

(ii) tails the first time and heads the second;

(iii) tails both times.

There are thus two favourable cases out of three, and the required probability is therefore $\frac{2}{3}$."

The three cases of d'Alembert are not equally probable. The classification is wrong. This should be

	First toss	Second toss
(a)	Head	Head
(b)	Head	Tail
(c)	Tail	Head
(d)	Tail	Tail

Of these four cases (a), (b) and (c) are favourable to the event in question, namely, "heads at least once", and the required chance is therefore $\frac{3}{4}$.

5. At first sight it would seem that the examples above have been drawn from different sorts of experience. In paragraph 2 a result has been obtained from a consideration of a mortality table—which is a matter of records—while in D'Alembert's problem we used an illustration based on the tossing of a coin—a matter of presumption and not of records. The difference between these two kinds of phenomena is real, but it does not render them incompatible in the study of probability, nor does it destroy the general idea of the average value. When we speak of tossing a coin we do not mean the ordinary coin of commerce, but an ideal coin, which is a perfectly uniform circular disc with its centre of gravity at the centre of the coin. The same ideal conditions will be assumed to be present in all subsequent experiments with dice and cards. Thus a die will be a perfect cube and in a pack of cards each card will be assumed to be drawn as often as any other card in a large number of drawings. On these assumptions it is unnecessary to refer to records; we base our arguments on the definitions of the objects themselves. The illustrative examples that can be drawn from a consideration of the ideal objects are most suitable for demonstrations of the principles of probability; examples obtained from statistical records generally involve large and unwieldy figures.

6. Definitions of the probability of an event.

(a) The "unitary" or "a priori" definition.

If an event can happen in a ways and fail to happen in b ways, all these ways being equally likely and such that not more than one of them can occur, then the probability of the event happening is $a/(a+b)$.

If the probability that an event E will happen be denoted by p, then $p = a/(a+b)$; this is called the "a priori" definition of probability because we have reasoned from general considerations and not from statistical observations. Since, however, we have inserted the proviso that all the ways of happening are equally likely—or, to put it in another way, if the experiment were continued a very large number of times the different cases would occur with equal frequency—then we may say that $p = a/(a+b)$ is the proportion or average of the number of times that the event E will happen.

(b) The "statistical" definition.

If on taking any very large number N out of a series of cases in which an event E is in question, E happens on pN occasions, the probability of the event E is said to be p.

This definition is of greater generality than the "a priori" definition; it gives the practical interpretation that the probability of an event is a relative frequency. Further, it suggests that the probability arises from statistical investigation.

The meaning of the statistical definition has already been exemplified by the probabilities of survival in paragraph 2. Further illustrations will be given later by reference to a correlation table.

7. From the definitions above we may immediately deduce the following facts:

(1) The probability of an event is a ratio.

(2) The ratio can never exceed unity.

> The measure of certainty is unity. If an event is certain to happen the probability of its happening is 1; if it is certain not to happen the probability is 0.

(3) The sum of the probabilities of the happening and of the failing of an event is unity.

(4) If the probability that an event will happen is known, the probability of its failing is also known.

Instead of using the fraction $a/(a+b)$ for the probability of an event, we may use an alternative form: if $p = a/(a+b)$ and, therefore, $1 - p = b/(a+b)$, then the odds in favour of the event are said to be $a : b$.

8. The simplest problems in probability are those in which both the number of favourable ways and the total number of ways in which the event may happen can be counted, either arithmetically or by the aid of elementary rules. The enumeration is often best performed by the application of the theorems of permutations and combinations, and a thorough knowledge of this branch of algebra is essential for the speedy solution of many of these questions.

Example 1.

An ordinary pack of cards contains 13 cards of each of four suits: spades, hearts, diamonds and clubs. Ten cards of each suit are numbered 1 (the ace), 2, 3 ... 10, the remaining three being "court cards", namely, knave, queen, king.

Find the chance that if a card be drawn at random from an ordinary pack it will be a heart.

Since there are 52 cards in a pack, the number of ways in which a card can be drawn (i.e. the total number of ways in which the event can happen) is 52.

The number of ways favourable to the event is 13, since there are 13 hearts in the pack.

The required probability is therefore $\frac{13}{52}$ or $\frac{1}{4}$.

Notes. (i) The above result means that over a long series of trials the proportion of favourable draws would approximate to one-fourth of the whole number of trials. It is convenient, however, to think in terms of a single trial, although the results of our calculations merely epitomize the experience of a long series of trials.

(ii) The word "chance" may be taken to be the same as the word "probability". There is a shade of difference between the two ideas, "probability" referring to past, present and future events, and "chance" to future events only. This distinction can be ignored.

Example 2.

Three cards are drawn at random from an ordinary pack. Find the chance that they are a king, a queen and a knave.

The total number of different ways in which three cards can be drawn is $^{52}C_3$ and all these ways are equally likely.

The number of ways in which a king, a queen and a knave can be drawn together is 4^3.

The required chance is therefore $\dfrac{4^3 \cdot 3\,!}{52 \cdot 51 \cdot 50}$ or $\dfrac{16}{5525}$.

Example 3.

Out of $2n + 1$ tickets consecutively numbered, three are drawn at random. Find the chance that the numbers on them are in arithmetical progression.

This problem can be solved by virtually writing down the sets of numbers that can be in A.P. Consider, for example, the sets of three numbers in A.P. beginning with 4: they will be

$$4\,;\,5\,;\,6 \qquad 4\,;\,6\,;\,8 \qquad 4\,;\,7\,;\,10 \ldots 4\,;\,n+1\,;\,2n-2 \qquad 4\,;\,n+2\,;\,2n$$

where the highest number that can enter into any set is $2n$. There will evidently be $n - 2$ such sets of numbers (being the number of numbers from 5 to $n + 2$, both numbers inclusive). We can therefore write down the following schedule:

Lowest number of the three	Number of favourable ways
1	n
2	$n-1$
3	$n-1$
4	$n-2$
5	$n-2$
6	$n-3$
.	.
.	.
.	.
$2n-2$	1
$2n-1$	1

The total number of favourable ways is $\left\{\dfrac{2n\,(n+1)}{2}-n\right\}$ or n^2, and since

the total number of ways of drawing three tickets is $\dfrac{(2n+1)\,2n\,(2n-1)}{6}$,

it is easily seen that the required probability is $\dfrac{3n}{4n^2-1}$.

Example 4.

If the letters of the word REGULATIONS be arranged at random, what is the chance that there will be exactly four letters between the R and the E?

The conditions are satisfied if

the R is in the first place and the E in the sixth,

		R		second		E		seventh,
or	„	R	„	second	„	E	„	seventh,
„	„	R	„	third	„	E	„	eighth,
„	„	R	„	fourth	„	E	„	ninth,
„	„	R	„	fifth	„	E	„	tenth,
„	„	R	„	sixth	„	E	„	eleventh,

or if the R and the E are transposed in any of the above.

Now there are 11 letters in the word; therefore the letters R and E can jointly occupy 11 × 10 positions. Since there are 6 × 2 favourable positions (as above) the chance that the R and the E are in the favourable position is $\frac{12}{110}$ or $\frac{6}{55}$.

Example 5.

Find the probability that the number 8 will be thrown in a single throw with two dice.

The total number of numbers that can be thrown with two dice is 36, since each of the 6 ways of throwing the first die can be associated with each of the 6 ways of throwing the second.

The number of ways favourable to the event can be found by simple enumeration, thus:

First die	Second die
2	6
3	5
4	4
5	3
6	2

Total: 5 ways.

The required probability is therefore $\frac{5}{36}$.

9. Let us consider the simple question: if a die be thrown, what is the chance that an ace appears?

There are 6 equally likely cases, one of which is favourable to the event. Therefore, by the unitary definition, the required chance is $\frac{1}{6}$.

Again, by the statistical definition, we may say that since each face is as likely to appear as any other, in a very large number of throws (N) the ace will appear $N/6$ times; the required chance is therefore $\frac{1}{6}$, as before.

Whichever definition is employed it must be borne in mind that the probability $\frac{1}{6}$ denotes the proportion of times that the ace would appear out of a very large number of throws, and that we are quite unable to predict on which occasions in a series of trials the ace will be presented. This leads us to examine more fully the meaning of the word "single" in such a question as "what is the probability of throwing an ace in a single throw with an ordinary die?" This point can best be explained by reference to an illustration similar to the first illustration in paragraph 1.

If there be five exactly similar balls in a bag, two coloured and three white, then by the unitary definition the probability that a coloured ball will be drawn (supposing one ball be drawn at random) is $\frac{2}{5}$. This does not mean that if a ball were drawn five times, being replaced each time, two of the draws would necessarily give coloured balls. The true interpretation of the fraction $\frac{2}{5}$ is that if the experiment were repeated a large number of times a coloured ball would be drawn on the average twice in five times.

The meaning to be attached to the word "single" in the original question is that the records are to be per sets of one throw.

In a similar manner, we may define the words "the next throw". Suppose that it is required to find the chance that in two consecutive throws of a single die the numbers 2 and 3 will appear. The word "next" refers to a specific order, and what we set out to find is the proportion of times that the order 2, 3 appears in a very large number of trials.

10. It has been remarked that illustrative examples in probability can most easily be given from a consideration of ideal objects, such as coins, dice, cards, etc. Examples from statistical records involve the collection and tabulation of statistics, and, moreover, often necessitate lengthy calculations. It is instructive, however, to consider the results that can be obtained from certain statistical records, and the following examples, based on what is known as a *correlation table*, are of interest. A correlation table may be regarded as a table giving the values of $f(x, y)$, where x and y are two variables which it is known or suspected follow some kind of law of variation. In the table on p. 214 the x variable is the age of husband, while the y variable is the age of his wife. The data are taken from the Census of 1921 and give to the nearest thousand the numbers of husbands in the various age-groups shown down the side with wives of the ages in the groups shown along the top. Thus, the figure 86 along the line (45–) and in column (50–) means that there were, to the nearest thousand, 86,000 husbands aged between 45 and 50 at the time when the Census was taken who had wives aged between 50 and 55. It should be noted that quinquennial age-groups have been taken in constructing the table, although more accurate results would be obtained by the use of individual ages. Apart from other considerations, it would, however, be impracticable to give for the present purpose a table at individual ages, and the results obtained below may be taken as sufficiently accurate. We may make the convenient assumption that each husband has the age represented by the mid-interval value, and similarly for each wife. In other words,

the number 86 may be read as indicating that there are 86,000 couples of exact age 47½ for the husband and 52½ for the wife.

1921 CENSUS

Number of married couples for quinquennial age-groups of husband and wife (1000's)

Ages of Husbands	\ Ages of Wives → 15-	20-	25-	30-	35-	40-	45-	50-	55-	60-	65-	70-	75-	80-	85-	Total
15-	2	3														5
20-	17	161	47	5	1											231
25-	5	177	393	88	11	2										676
30-	1	46	282	458	101	14	3	1								906
35-		12	77	294	470	104	16	3	1							977
40-		4	22	84	291	445	99	15	3	1						964
45-		2	9	28	91	278	404	86	14	3	1					916
50-		1	3	10	27	81	230	315	67	11	2	1				748
55-			2	4	10	25	69	177	234	51	9	2	1			583
60-			1	2	4	10	21	53	126	163	35	6	4	1		422
65-				1	2	4	8	17	38	84	103	23	11	1		285
70-					1	1	3	6	10	22	49	50	20	4		154
75-								2	3	6	12	23	7	4	1	72
80-								1	1	2	3	5	1	5	1	25
85-											1	1		1		5
Total	25	406	836	974	1009	965	854	676	497	343	215	111	44	12	2	6969

It should be noted that the values in the table are termed *frequencies*, since they show how often that particular conjunction of ages occurred in the tabulation of the data. (See Chap. XI, paragraph 2.)

We will now apply the figures from the table to answer some typical questions involving probabilities and averages.

Note. The results will not be affected if the figures are read as they stand. In effect the values are all divided by 1000.

Example 6.

Find the probability that a husband aged 40–45 will have a wife

    (i) under 40 years of age,

    (ii) over 45 years of age,

    (iii) between 40 and 45 years of age.

(i) We have to find p such that

pN = number of husbands aged 40–45 having wives under age 40,

  N = total number of husbands aged 40–45.

$$\therefore \ p = pN/N = \frac{4+22+84+291}{964} = \frac{401}{964} = \cdot 416.$$

(ii) As above,

pN = number of husbands aged 40–45 having wives over age 45,

  N = total number of husbands aged 40–45.

$$\therefore \ p = pN/N = \frac{99+15+3+1}{964} = \frac{118}{964} = \cdot 122.$$

(iii)

pN = number of husbands aged 40–45 having wives aged 40–45,

  N = total number of husbands aged 40–45.

$$\therefore \ p = pN/N = \frac{445}{964} = \cdot 462.$$

Note. The sum of the three probabilities obtained $= \dfrac{401+118+445}{964} = 1.$
This is as it should be, for the three cases exhaust all those in which the husband is in the age-group 40–45.

Example 7.

Find the probability that a wife aged over 50 will have a husband aged less than 50.

If p is the required probability, then

pN = number of wives over age 50 having husbands less than age 50,

N = total number of wives over age 50.

$$\therefore \ p = pN/N = \frac{1+4+18+105}{676+497+343+215+111+44+12+2} = \frac{128}{1900}$$

$$= \cdot 067.$$

Example 8.

In a sample of 10,000 husbands between ages 30 and 50, how many might be expected to have wives less than 40 years old?

We require 10,000p,

where N = number of husbands in the table between ages 30 and 50,

pN = number of husbands between 30 and 50 having wives less than 40 years old.

$$\therefore \ 10,000p = 10,000pN/N$$

$$= \frac{1+64+390+864+953}{906+977+964+916} \times 10,000$$

$$= \frac{22,720,000}{3763}$$

$$= 6038.$$

11. Mutually exclusive events.

If an event can happen in more than one way, all ways being mutually exclusive, the probability of its happening at all is the sum of the probabilities of its happening in the several ways.

This proposition is sometimes known as the *addition rule*, and is fundamental in the application of the theory of probability. The rule may otherwise be stated thus:

If p_1, p_2, p_3, ... p_n are the probabilities of n mutually exclusive events, the probability that one of these events happens on any occasion in which the n events are in question is

$$p_1 + p_2 + p_3 + \ ... \ + p_n.$$

The words "mutually exclusive" in this proposition are of the utmost importance. A proof of the rule depending on the statistical definition of probability will show that unless the events are mutually exclusive we cannot add the simple probabilities. Thus, if there be a large number N out of a series in which the n events are in question, the first will happen on p_1N occasions, the second on p_2N occasions, the third on p_3N occasions, and so on. Since the events are mutually exclusive, one and only one of the events can occur on any one occasion. Therefore, out of N occasions, one or other of the events will happen on $p_1N+p_2N+p_3N+ \dots +p_nN$ occasions. The probability that one of the events happens is therefore $(p_1N+p_2N+p_3N+ \dots +p_nN)/N$ or $p_1+p_2+p_3+ \dots +p_n$.

It will be seen that this proof breaks down and the proposition is not true if any one event happens on any one of the occasions that any other happens, i.e. if the events are not mutually exclusive.

It follows easily that if instead of keeping in view separate events we consider the various ways in which a single event may happen, the probability of the happening of the event is the sum of the probabilities of the mutually exclusive ways in which the event may happen. For, if there be n different ways in which the event may happen and p_r is the probability that the event happens in the rth out of the n different ways, then if the event must happen, $\sum_{r=1}^{r=n} p_r N$ is the total number of occasions on which it happens in N trials. Since the event always happens, $\Sigma p_r N = N$, so that $\Sigma p_r = 1$.

The whole number of ways in which an event may happen is sometimes called the *universe* of the event. If an event may fail, the failing of the event is also included in the universe.

The following example illustrates the principle outlined above.

Example 9.

What is the chance of throwing a total of 3 or 5 or 11 with two dice?

The three events, i.e. throwing 3, throwing 5 and throwing 11, are mutually exclusive, since the occurrence of any one of them precludes the occurrence of any other.

We require the proportion of times out of a large number of trials in which one or other of the three events will happen.

Let there be a large number of trials N. Then since the chances of throwing 3, 5, 11 are $\frac{2}{36}$, $\frac{4}{36}$, $\frac{2}{36}$ respectively, totals of 3, 5, 11 will be obtained on $\frac{2}{36}N$, $\frac{4}{36}N$, $\frac{2}{36}N$ occasions respectively. The total number of times on which one or other of the events will happen is therefore

$$\frac{2}{36}N + \frac{4}{36}N + \frac{2}{36}N \text{ or } \frac{2}{9}N.$$

Hence, by definition, the probability of throwing a total of 3 or 5 or 11 is $\frac{2}{9}$, which is the sum of the separate probabilities of the three mutually exclusive events.

In practice it is sufficient to apply the addition rule at once and to write the solution as $\frac{2}{36} + \frac{4}{36} + \frac{2}{36} = \frac{2}{9}$.

12. Compound probability: independent events.

If there be a series of events such that the happening of any one of them in no way affects the happening of any other of them, the events are said to be *independent*.

The probability that two independent events happen on any one occasion on which they are both in question is the product of the chances of their happening severally.

For consider two independent events E and E', the probabilities of which are p and p' respectively. Out of a large number N in which the events are in question E will happen on pN occasions, and out of these pN occasions E' will happen on $p'(pN)$ or $pp'N$ occasions. The probability that they both happen is therefore pp'.

Similarly, it may be shown that if there are n independent events the respective probabilities of which are $p_1, p_2, p_3, \ldots p_n$, the probability of the joint happening of them all is $p_1 p_2 p_3 \ldots p_n$.

We may use the *a priori* or unitary definition of probability to prove this proposition.

Let there be two independent events the probabilities of which are p and p' and let $p = a/(a+b)$, $p' = a'/(a'+b')$, where a and b are respectively the numbers of favourable and unfavourable equally likely ways in which the first event can happen; and similarly for a' and b' with regard to the second event.

Then there are $(a+b)(a'+b')$ equally likely ways in which the two events are jointly in question. Of this number there are aa' equally likely ways favourable to the joint happenings of the two events.

Hence, by the unitary definition the probability of the joint event is

$$\frac{aa'}{(a+b)\,(a'+b')}=\frac{a}{a+b}\cdot\frac{a'}{a'+b'}=pp'=P,$$

where P is the required probability of the joint event.

In a similar manner we may prove the proposition for n independent events.

This rule is known as the *multiplication rule*, and its application to the probabilities of happening or otherwise of two independent events may be seen from a consideration of the following schedule.

Let the probabilities of happening of two independent events be p and p' respectively. Then

(i) the chance that they both happen $=pp'$;

(ii) the chance that the first happens and the second fails
$=p\,(1-p')$;

(iii) the chance that the second happens and the first fails
$=p'\,(1-p)$;

(iv) the chance that they both fail $=(1-p)\,(1-p')$.

The total of these chances

$$=pp'+p\,(1-p')+p'\,(1-p)+(1-p)\,(1-p')$$
$$=pp'+p-pp'+p'-pp'+1-p-p'+pp'$$
$$=1,$$

which is obviously true, since we have exhausted all the possibilities.

13. The application of the principles enunciated above can best be appreciated by reference to actual examples.

Example 10.

Find the chance that (i) three heads, (ii) two heads and one tail will turn up in three successive spins of a coin.

(i) The chance of a head at the first   spin $=\tfrac{1}{2}$

    ,,   ,,   second ,, $=\tfrac{1}{2}$

    ,,   ,,   third   ,, $=\tfrac{1}{2}$

        Combined chance $=(\tfrac{1}{2})^3=\tfrac{1}{8}$.

(ii) The chance of a tail is the same as that of a head, so that the total chance might appear to be $(\frac{1}{2})^3$ as before. This is in fact the chance that 2 heads and 1 tail occur in a specified order, say, HTH. The conditions of the question would, however, be satisfied if the order were HHT or THH. These three favourable events are mutually exclusive. The chance that the two heads and tail are obtained in one of the three orders is found by adding the three probabilities. The required chance is therefore $3 \times (\frac{1}{2})^3 = \frac{3}{8}$.

Example 11.

Q is the probability that a man aged x will die in a year. Find the probability that out of 5 men, A, B, C, D, E, each aged x, A will die in the year and be the first to die.

The chance that a given man dies in the year $= Q$.

The chance that a given man does not die in the year $= 1 - Q$.

The chance that none of the five dies in the year $= (1 - Q)^5$.

The chance that at least one man dies in the year $= 1 - (1 - Q)^5$.

Since the chance that A is the first to die is obviously $\frac{1}{5}$, and since this is independent of the chance that at least one man dies in the year, the required chance $= \frac{1}{5} \{1 - (1 - Q)^5\}$.

Example 12.

A throws 3 coins and B throws 2 coins. Find the chance that A will throw a greater number of heads than B.

- (a) The chance that A throws 3 heads is $(\frac{1}{2})^3$. The chance in this case is $(\frac{1}{2})^3 \times 1$, since B must obviously throw less than A.

- (b) The chance that A throws 2 heads and 1 tail is $3(\frac{1}{2})^2(\frac{1}{2})$, for he may throw HHT, HTH or THH. For B to throw less he must not throw 2 heads; the chance of this is $1 - (\frac{1}{2})^2$.
  The chance in this case is $3(\frac{1}{2})^3[1 - (\frac{1}{2})^2]$.

- (c) The chance that A throws 1 head and 2 tails is $3(\frac{1}{2})(\frac{1}{2})^2$. In order that B may throw less he must throw 2 tails, the chance of which is $(\frac{1}{2})^2$.
  The chance in this case is $3(\frac{1}{2})^5$.

The three contingencies (a), (b) and (c) exhaust all the cases for the required event and they are mutually exclusive.

The result is therefore $(\frac{1}{2})^3 + 3(\frac{1}{2})^3[1 - (\frac{1}{2})^2] + 3(\frac{1}{2})^5$ or, on simplification, $\frac{1}{2}$.

14. Compound probability: dependent events.

If two or more events are not independent we may still apply the multiplication rule. Thus, if p be the chance of happening of an event, and p' the chance of happening of a second when the first has happened, then the chance that they both should happen is pp'.

We may prove the proposition in the following manner.

Let there be two events E and E' which are to happen in that order. Let the probability of E be p and the probability of E' after E has happened be p'.

Then if the double event is in question on a very large number of occasions N, the number of times that E happens is pN—which may also be assumed to be large. Out of these pN occasions E' happens on $p'(pN)$ occasions. Therefore out of the total occasions, N, there are $pp'N$ occasions on which the event E' follows the event E. It follows that the probability of the double event is pp'.

By similar reasoning we may show that if there be n events $E_1, E_2, \ldots E_n$ such that the probability of the $(r+1)$th event after the previous specified r consecutive events have happened is p_{r+1}, then the probability of the happening of the n events is given by the product $p_1 p_2 \ldots p_r \ldots p_n$.

Care must be taken to distinguish between independent and dependent events. In considering independent events the happening of either event does not affect the happening of the other, and to find the probability that they both happen we multiply the simple probabilities of each event. Where the events are not independent, we must find the chance p_2 that the second happens when the first has happened before we can apply the multiplication rule. For example, if there be two urns, one containing one white and two coloured balls, and the other one white and three coloured balls, the probability that the combined result of two drawings, one from each urn, will give the two white balls is $\frac{1}{3} \times \frac{1}{4}$, since the drawing from the first urn in no way affects the drawing from the second. If, however, we were required to find the chance that in two successive drawings from an urn containing two white and five coloured balls the two white balls would be drawn (a ball drawn not being replaced) we should reason thus. The chance that a white ball is drawn at the first drawing is $\frac{2}{7}$; *after this has happened* there will be left one white and five coloured balls, and the chance of drawing the other white ball at the second drawing will be $\frac{1}{6}$. The combined chance is therefore $\frac{2}{7} \times \frac{1}{6}$.

15. It has been shown in paragraph 12 that the multiplication rule can be applied to the probability of happening of any number of independent events, so that if $p, p', p'', \ldots$ be the chances of the events happening severally, the chance that they all happen is $pp'p'' \ldots$.

Again, if the chance that an event happens in a single trial be p, the chance that it will happen in each of r trials is p^r, and the chance that it will fail in each of, say, $(n-r)$ trials is $(1-p)^{n-r}$.

Suppose that it is desired to find the chance that an event will happen *exactly* r times in n trials.

Let the chance that in any one trial the event does not happen be $q\ (=1-p)$. Then if the event happen in r trials and fail in $n-r$, the combined chance is $p^r q^{n-r}$. But of the n trials we can select the r trials in which the event happens in $n_{(r)}$ ways. The chance that the event happens in exactly r trials out of the n is the chance that it happens in these r trials and fails in the remaining $n-r$ trials. The required chance is therefore $n_{(r)}p^r q^{n-r}$.

Now it will be noted that $n_{(r)}p^r q^{n-r}$ is the term containing p^r in the expansion of $(p+q)^n$. The successive terms of this expansion will therefore give the probabilities of the event happening $n, n-1, n-2, \ldots n-r, \ldots$ times exactly in n trials.

16. The following examples are illustrative of the principles outlined above.

Example 13.

Find the chance of drawing a king, a queen and a knave in that order from an ordinary pack in three consecutive draws, the cards drawn not being replaced.

This is an example of the application of the multiplication rule to dependent probabilities.

If p_1 be the chance of drawing a king;

| p_2 | ,, | ,, | ,, | a queen, a king having been drawn; |

| p_3 | ,, | ,, | ,, | a knave, a king and a queen having been drawn; |

then the chance of drawing a king, a queen and a knave in succession is $p_1 p_2 p_3$.

Now there are 4 kings in the pack, so that the chance of drawing a king is $\frac{4}{52}$. When the king has been drawn there are 51 cards left of which 4 are queens. The chance of drawing a queen is therefore $\frac{4}{51}$. Similarly, the chance of drawing a knave from the remaining 50 cards is $\frac{4}{50}$.

$$p_1 = \tfrac{4}{52}; \quad p_2 = \tfrac{4}{51}; \quad p_3 = \tfrac{4}{50}.$$

The required chance $= p_1 p_2 p_3 = \dfrac{4^3}{52.51.50}$.

[Compare Example 2, where the three cards are drawn *at random* (not in a specified order) and the problem is treated as one in simple probability.]

Example 14.

A bag contains three balls, one red, one white and one blue. X and Y draw a ball at random alternately. If X draws the red ball or Y the white ball it is retained. Otherwise the ball drawn is immediately replaced. Find the chance that just before the fifth draw is made the blue ball only is in the bag.

Let R, W, B denote the red, white and blue ball respectively. Now the blue ball is the only one in the bag just before the fifth draw if any of the following have happened:

	X first draw	Y first draw	X second draw	Y second draw
(i)	R	B	B	W
(ii)	R	B	W	W
(iii)	B	W	R	B
(iv)	W	W	R	B
(v)	R	W	B	B
(vi)	B	R	R	W
(vii)	B	B	R	W
(viii)	W	R	R	W
(ix)	W	B	R	W

The chances of these events happening are:

					Product
(i)	$\frac{1}{3}$	$\frac{1}{4}$	$\frac{1}{2}$	$\frac{1}{2}$	$\frac{1}{24}$
(ii)	$\frac{1}{3}$	$\frac{1}{2}$	$\frac{1}{2}$	$\frac{1}{2}$	$\frac{1}{24}$
(iii)	$\frac{1}{3}$	$\frac{1}{3}$	$\frac{1}{2}$	1	$\frac{1}{18}$
(iv)	$\frac{1}{3}$	$\frac{1}{3}$	$\frac{1}{2}$	1	$\frac{1}{18}$
(v)	$\frac{1}{3}$	$\frac{1}{2}$	1	1	$\frac{1}{6}$
(vi)	$\frac{1}{3}$	$\frac{1}{3}$	$\frac{1}{3}$	$\frac{1}{2}$	$\frac{1}{54}$
(vii)	$\frac{1}{3}$	$\frac{1}{3}$	$\frac{1}{3}$	$\frac{1}{2}$	$\frac{1}{54}$
(viii)	$\frac{1}{3}$	$\frac{1}{3}$	$\frac{1}{3}$	$\frac{1}{2}$	$\frac{1}{54}$
(ix)	$\frac{1}{3}$	$\frac{1}{3}$	$\frac{1}{3}$	$\frac{1}{2}$	$\frac{1}{54}$

The total chance is therefore $\frac{2}{24}+\frac{2}{18}+\frac{1}{6}+\frac{4}{54}=\frac{47}{108}$.

Note. A systematic enumeration of possibilities is of great importance, and although in the above example the work may be shortened by alternative methods, for illustrative purposes the eventualities have been set out in full.

Example 15.

A bag contains three red and three green balls and a person draws out three at random. He then drops three blue balls into the bag and again draws out three at random. Show that he may just lay 8 to 3 with advantage to himself against the latter three balls all being of different colours.

After the insertion of the three blue balls the bag may contain:

	Red	Green	Blue
(*a*)	3	–	3
(*b*)	2	1	3
(*c*)	1	2	3
(*d*)	–	3	3

The probability that the bag contains (*a*) is $\frac{3}{6}\cdot\frac{2}{5}\cdot\frac{1}{4}$ or $\frac{1}{20}$, for the chance that a green ball is drawn is obviously $\frac{3}{6}$, the chance that a second green ball is drawn is $\frac{2}{5}$ and the chance of a third green ball is then $\frac{1}{4}$. Similarly, the chances under (*b*), (*c*), (*d*) are $\frac{9}{20}$, $\frac{9}{20}$, $\frac{1}{20}$ respectively.

Now three different colours on the second draw can be obtained only if the six balls come under headings (*b*) and (*c*).

Under (*b*) the probability at the second draw of drawing three different coloured balls is $\frac{6}{20}$, and therefore the compound probability that this will happen is $\frac{6}{20}\cdot\frac{9}{20}$. Under (*c*) the probability is the same.

The chance required is the sum of the chances under (*b*) and (*c*) and amounts to $\frac{27}{100}$. Therefore, since the odds against the favourable happening are 73 to 27, the person drawing the balls may lay 8 to 3 against his drawing three balls of different colours and obtain a slight advantage.

17. The methods for the solution of the above examples depend largely on the simple application of the formulae for permutations and combinations. It is safer as a general rule to use permutations rather than combinations. If repetitions are not allowed this is not very material, as each combination of *r* things forms *r*! permutations. If, however, repetitions are allowed then in most instances it is *essential* to use arrangements.

Other algebraic devices are often useful. For example, in dealing with questions involving the sum of the numbers that can be thrown with dice and kindred problems dealing with homogeneous products, it is of advantage to employ the binomial theorem.

The following examples illustrate the use of this method.

Example 16.

Four dice are thrown. Find the chance that the sum of the numbers appearing will be 18.

Regard being had to the different ways of making up the same total, the number of numbers that can be thrown with four dice is the sum of the coefficients in the expansion

$$(x + x^2 + x^3 + x^4 + x^5 + x^6)^4.$$

The sum of the coefficients will be found by putting $x = 1$. The total number of possible numbers is therefore 6^4.

The number of ways of throwing 18 is the coefficient of x^{18} in the above expansion.

The coefficient of x^{18} in $(x + x^2 + x^3 + x^4 + x^5 + x^6)^4$

$=$,, x^{18} in $x^4 (1 + x + x^2 + x^3 + x^4 + x^5)^4$

$=$,, x^{14} in $(1 + x + x^2 + x^3 + x^4 + x^5)^4$

$=$,, x^{14} in $\dfrac{(1 - x^6)^4}{(1 - x)^4}$

$=$,, x^{14} in $(1 - x^6)^4 (1 - x)^{-4}$

$=$ The coefficient of x^{14} in $(1 - 4x^6 + 6x^{12} \ldots)\Big(1 + 4x + 10x^2 + \ldots$

$$+ \frac{9.10.11}{6} x^8 + \ldots + \frac{15.16.17}{6} x^{14} + \ldots\Big)$$

$$= \frac{15.16.17}{6} - \frac{4.9.10.11}{6} + 6.10 = 80.$$

The required chance is therefore $\dfrac{80}{6^4}$.

Note. We are here dealing with arrangements which would be distinguishable if one die were red, one blue, one yellow and one green. Selections in an example of this type would give quite wrong results.

Example 17.

Nine cards are drawn at random from a set of cards. Each card is marked with one of the numbers 1, 0 or -1, and it is equally likely that any of the three numbers will be drawn. Find the chance that the sum of the numbers on the cards thus drawn is zero.

The number of favourable drawings will be the coefficient of x^0 in the expansion of $(x^{-1} + x^0 + x^1)^9$; the total number of possible drawings will be the sum of all the coefficients in the same expansion.

The coefficient of x^0 in $(x^{-1} + x^0 + x^1)^9$

$=$	,,	x^0 in $x^{-9}(1 + x + x^2)^9$
$=$	,,	x^9 in $(1 + x + x^2)^9$
$=$	,,	x^9 in $(1 - x^3)^9 (1 - x)^{-9}$.

Proceeding on the same lines as in Example 16, the required probability is found to be $\dfrac{3139}{3^9}$.

18. The theory of probability was evolved from a consideration of games of chance, and many problems dealing with these games can be solved by the elementary methods outlined above. No new principles are involved; all that is required in attacking these problems is a clear understanding of the particular happenings that may arise. The following examples are illustrative of the methods: the first of these examples is analysed fully, and the student should be able to solve problems of the same type by the application of similar reasoning.

Example 18.

A and B throw alternately with a pair of ordinary dice. A wins if he throws six before B throws seven, and B if he throws seven before A throws six. If A begins, show that his chance of winning is $\frac{30}{61}$. (Huyghens's Problem.)

First, let us consider the chances of throwing six or seven with two dice. We can find the number of ways of throwing these numbers either by actually counting the number of ways (as in Example 5) or by finding the coefficients of x^6 and x^7 in the expansion of $(x + x^2 + x^3 + x^4 + x^5 + x^6)^2$ (as in Example 16). Since the figures are small, the first way is simpler, and it is easily seen that six can be thrown in 5 ways, and seven in 6 ways. The chance of throwing six in one throw with the two dice is therefore $\frac{5}{36}$, and of throwing seven $\frac{6}{36}$.

A can win if he throws six the first time. His chance of throwing this number is $\frac{5}{36}$.

He may fail to throw six the first time. He can then win if B fails to throw seven at his first throw and A throws six with his second throw. The chance that A fails to throw six is $1 - \frac{5}{36} = \frac{31}{36}$.

The chance that B throws seven is $\frac{6}{36}$ and the chance that he fails to throw this number is $1 - \frac{6}{36} = \frac{30}{36}$.

Therefore the chance that A wins at the second throw is $\frac{31}{36} \cdot \frac{30}{36} \cdot \frac{5}{36}$.

If A fails to win at the second throw, he can win at the third throw if B has not thrown seven at his second throw. The chance of this is

$$\frac{31}{36} \cdot \frac{30}{36} \cdot \frac{31}{36} \cdot \frac{30}{36} \cdot \frac{5}{36} \qquad \text{and so on.}$$

A's chance of winning in the long run, i.e. after a very large number of trials, is therefore

$$\frac{5}{36} + \frac{31}{36} \cdot \frac{30}{36} \cdot \frac{5}{36} + \frac{31}{36} \cdot \frac{30}{36} \cdot \frac{31}{36} \cdot \frac{30}{36} \cdot \frac{5}{36} + \dots$$
$$= \frac{5}{36} (1 + r + r^2 + r^3 + \dots),$$

where $r = \frac{31}{36} \cdot \frac{30}{36}$.

If we sum this geometrical progression to infinity, we find that A's chance

$$= \frac{5}{36} \frac{1}{1 - r} = \frac{5}{36} \cdot \frac{1296}{366} = \frac{30}{61}.$$

Example 19.

A and B play a match to be decided as soon as either has won two games. The chance of either winning a game is $\frac{1}{20}$ and of its being drawn $\frac{9}{10}$. What is the chance that the match is finished in 10 or less games?

If the match is *not* finished in 10 games, the following must occur:

   (i) All the games must be drawn; or

   (ii) A or B must win one game and the remaining 9 must be drawn; or

   (iii) A and B must each win one game and the remaining 8 must be drawn.

The chances of these mutually exclusive events are:

$$\text{(i)} \quad \left(\frac{9}{10}\right)^{10},$$

$$\text{(ii)} \quad \left(\frac{9}{10}\right)^{9} . \frac{1}{20} . 2 . 10,$$

since this result may occur in 10 different ways and either A or B may win;

$$\text{(iii)} \quad \left(\frac{9}{10}\right)^{8} . \left(\frac{1}{20}\right)^{2} . 10 . 9,$$

since the number of orders in which this may occur is $^{10}P_{2}$.

The chance that the match is not finished in 10 games is, by the addition rule,

$$\left(\frac{9}{10}\right)^{10} + \left(\frac{9}{10}\right)^{9} . \frac{1}{20} . 2 . 10 + \left(\frac{9}{10}\right)^{8} . \left(\frac{1}{20}\right)^{2} . 10 . 9$$

$$= \frac{9^{8} . 387}{2 . 10^{10}},$$

i.e. the chance that the match is finished in 10 games or less

$$= 1 - \frac{9^{8} . 387}{2 . 10^{10}} = \cdot 17 \text{ approximately.}$$

Example 20.

A, B, C, D each throw two dice for a prize. The highest throw wins, but if equal highest throws are made by two or more players, those players continue. A throws 9, B throws 7. Find C's chance of winning the prize.

Consider the following scheme, showing the total number of possible ways in which C may win:

C may win if		Probability
C throws 12, D less than 12		$\frac{1}{6^2} \cdot \frac{35}{36}$
C throws 12, D 12, and C wins later ...		$\frac{1}{6^2} \cdot \frac{1}{6^2} \cdot \frac{1}{2}^*$
C throws 11, D less than 11		$\frac{2}{6^2} \cdot \frac{33}{36}$
C throws 11, D 11, and C wins later ...		$\frac{2}{6^2} \cdot \frac{2}{6^2} \cdot \frac{1}{2}^*$
C throws 10, D less than 10		$\frac{3}{6^2} \cdot \frac{30}{36}$
C throws 10, D 10, and C wins later ...		$\frac{3}{6^2} \cdot \frac{3}{6^2} \cdot \frac{1}{2}^*$
C throws 9, D less than 9 and C wins later (since A has thrown 9)		$\frac{4}{6^2} \cdot \frac{26}{36} \cdot \frac{1}{2}^*$
C throws 9, D 9, and C wins later ...		$\frac{4}{6^2} \cdot \frac{4}{6^2} \cdot \frac{1}{3}^*$.

The total of these chances is $\frac{383}{1944}$.

19. Examples based on mortality tables.

A mortality table is a table of the successive values of l_x for integral values of x, where l_x is the number of persons out of l_0 born who attain precise age x. We are not here concerned with the construction of a mortality table from the original data. For the present purpose we may, however, note that

(i) the table is constructed from data sufficient for us to use the N of the statistical definition of probability;

(ii) the successive values of l_x are not absolute, but relative, referring to a common "radix" chosen for convenience of tabulation.

In explanation of this second point it may be stated that the radix may be any number and may be taken anywhere in the table.

---

* The final factor in each of these terms expresses the chance that C will win after having equalled the number thrown by D and/or A.

For example, the radix may be 1000 at age 50, so that $l_{50} = 1000$; it may be 10,000 at age 20 or even 1,000,000 at age 0. The purpose for which the table is constructed determines the position and magnitude of the radix.

In the following table the radix is 1,000,000 at age 0; for the purposes of illustration only that portion of the table from age 90 to the end of the table has been taken.

ENGLISH LIFE TABLE No. 10 (1930–32). MALES

Age x	Number living at age x l_x	Number dying between ages x and $x+1$ $d_x = l_x - l_{x+1}$
90	16090	4600
91	11490	3478
92	8012	2564
93	5448	1841
94	3607	1287
95	2320	873
96	1447	574
97	873	364
98	509	223
99	286	132
100	154	74
101	80	41
102	39	21
103	18	10
104	8	8

In the l_x column we have the number 16090 at age 90, while in the same column we have the number 873 at age 97. This does not mean that precisely 16090 persons aged 90 were observed and that seven years later there survived exactly 873 of these persons. The numbers of persons actually observed at ages 90 and 97 were quite different. We may, however, use the two numbers given at these ages to obtain the probability that a person aged 90 shall survive to age 97, thus:

If p is the required probability, then $pN = 873$, where $N = 16090$.

p is therefore $pN/N = 873/16090 = \cdot05426$.

It should be noted that each value in the mortality table is the radix at its own age for all subsequent values in the table. For example, if l_{97}/l_{90} gives the probability at age 90 of living 7 years at least, so also does l_{95}/l_{91} give the probability at age 91 of living 4 years at least. Generally l_{x+n}/l_x gives the probability at age x of living n years at least.

The following example is based on the mortality table given above.

Example 21.

The ages of three men, A, B and C, are 90, 91 and 92 respectively. Find the following probabilities:

(i) that A, B and C will be alive in two years' time;

(ii) that one at least of the three will be alive in two years' time;

(iii) that exactly one of the three will be alive in two years' time;

(iv) that exactly two of the three will be alive in two years' time;

(v) that all will be dead in two years' time.

The required probabilities are

(i) $\dfrac{l_{92}}{l_{90}} \cdot \dfrac{l_{93}}{l_{91}} \cdot \dfrac{l_{94}}{l_{92}} = \dfrac{8012}{16090} \times \dfrac{5448}{11490} \times \dfrac{3607}{8012} = \cdot 106.$

(ii) $1 - \left(1 - \dfrac{l_{92}}{l_{90}}\right)\left(1 - \dfrac{l_{93}}{l_{91}}\right)\left(1 - \dfrac{l_{94}}{l_{92}}\right)$

$\quad = 1 - (1 - 8012/16090)(1 - 5448/11490)(1 - 3607/8012) = \cdot 855.$

(iii) $\dfrac{l_{92}}{l_{90}}\left(1 - \dfrac{l_{93}}{l_{91}}\right)\left(1 - \dfrac{l_{94}}{l_{92}}\right) + \dfrac{l_{93}}{l_{91}}\left(1 - \dfrac{l_{94}}{l_{92}}\right)\left(1 - \dfrac{l_{92}}{l_{90}}\right) + \dfrac{l_{94}}{l_{92}}\left(1 - \dfrac{l_{92}}{l_{90}}\right)\left(1 - \dfrac{l_{93}}{l_{91}}\right)$

$\quad = \cdot 394$ on substituting and simplifying.

(iv) $\dfrac{l_{92}}{l_{90}} \cdot \dfrac{l_{93}}{l_{91}}\left(1 - \dfrac{l_{94}}{l_{92}}\right) + \dfrac{l_{92}}{l_{90}}\left(1 - \dfrac{l_{93}}{l_{91}}\right)\dfrac{l_{94}}{l_{92}} + \left(1 - \dfrac{l_{92}}{l_{90}}\right)\dfrac{l_{93}}{l_{91}} \cdot \dfrac{l_{94}}{l_{92}}$

$\quad = \cdot 355.$

(v) $\left(1 - \dfrac{l_{92}}{l_{90}}\right)\left(1 - \dfrac{l_{93}}{l_{91}}\right)\left(1 - \dfrac{l_{94}}{l_{92}}\right)$

$\quad = \cdot 145.$

Note. If we add the results under (i), (iii), (iv) and (v) we obtain unity. These exhaust all the possibilities. The result under (ii), however, is not included, and it is instructive for the student to discover why this is so.

The following are further examples involving the probabilities of living and dying, not based on the figures in the table on p. 230. The same principles are involved in the solutions of these questions.

Example 22.

Three men were known to be alive five years ago when their ages were 31, 48, 69. Assuming that of 98 males born together one dies annually until there are no survivors, find the chances that

(1) all are alive now;

(2) none are alive now;

(3) one, and only one, is alive now;

(4) two are alive and one dead.

The chance that a man aged x dies in five years is clearly $\dfrac{5}{98-x}$.

The required probabilities are

(1) $\dfrac{62}{67} \cdot \dfrac{45}{50} \cdot \dfrac{24}{29}$;

(2) $\dfrac{5}{67} \cdot \dfrac{5}{50} \cdot \dfrac{5}{29}$;

(3) $\dfrac{62}{67} \cdot \dfrac{5}{50} \cdot \dfrac{5}{29}$ + two similar expressions;

(4) $\dfrac{62}{67} \cdot \dfrac{45}{50} \cdot \dfrac{5}{29}$ + two similar expressions.

As the above are the only possible events that can happen, the total of the chances is unity and the reader should verify this.

Example 23.

Three men, P, Q and R, are each of exact age 96. Find the chance that they will all die at different ages last birthday in the order P, Q, R given that

Exact age	Chance of dying before next exact age
96	$\frac{1}{2}$
97	$\frac{2}{3}$
98	$\frac{3}{4}$
99	1

We have to find the chance of their dying in a given order. There will be no need therefore to take into consideration the different orders in which the men may die.

(i) P may die at age 96   Chance $=\frac{1}{2}$.

Q may die at age 97, i.e. may survive
a year and die in the following year   ,, $=(1-\frac{1}{2})\frac{2}{3}$.

R may die at age 98 or later; i.e. may
survive 2 years and die in the
following year   ,, $=(1-\frac{1}{2})(1-\frac{2}{3})\,1$

The total chance under this heading is therefore

$$\tfrac{1}{2}\times(1-\tfrac{1}{2})\tfrac{2}{3}\times(1-\tfrac{1}{2})(1-\tfrac{2}{3})\,1=\tfrac{1}{36}.$$

(ii) P may die at age 96   Chance $=\frac{1}{2}$.

Q ,,   98   ,, $=(1-\frac{1}{2})(1-\frac{2}{3})\frac{3}{4}$.

R ,,   99   ,, $=(1-\frac{1}{2})(1-\frac{2}{3})(1-\frac{3}{4})\,1$.

Total chance under heading (ii)

$$=\tfrac{1}{2}\times(1-\tfrac{1}{2})(1-\tfrac{2}{3})\tfrac{3}{4}\times(1-\tfrac{1}{2})(1-\tfrac{2}{3})(1-\tfrac{3}{4})\,1=\tfrac{1}{384}.$$

(iii) P may die at age 97   Chance $=(1-\frac{1}{2})\frac{2}{3}$.

Q ,,   98   ,, $=(1-\frac{1}{2})(1-\frac{2}{3})\frac{3}{4}$.

R ,,   99   ,, $=(1-\frac{1}{2})(1-\frac{2}{3})(1-\frac{3}{4})\,1$.

Total chance under heading (iii)

$$=(1-\tfrac{1}{2})\tfrac{2}{3}\times(1-\tfrac{1}{2})(1-\tfrac{2}{3})\tfrac{3}{4}\times(1-\tfrac{1}{2})(1-\tfrac{2}{3})(1-\tfrac{3}{4})\,1=\tfrac{1}{576}.$$

$$\text{Required chance}=\tfrac{1}{36}+\tfrac{1}{384}+\tfrac{1}{576}=\tfrac{37}{1152}.$$

20. A simple problem in probability may sometimes be capable of more than one reading. When giving the solution to a question which may be construed in more than one way it is essential that the assumptions on which the solution is based should be stated at the outset.

The two examples given below illustrate this point.

Example 24.

What is the chance that a hand of five cards contains a pair of two like cards of different suits?

If the problem is to find the chance that of five cards two are to be like cards and the other three unlike, a result is obtained which is quite different from the chance that there are to be two like cards, it being immaterial what the other cards are. Moreover, this second reading is capable of two alternatives: there may be two like cards and two other like cards (e.g. two kings and two fours) in the five cards; or there may be three or more like cards—this is not expressly excluded by the question.

It will be instructive before setting down all the chances that are possible to examine what would seem to be the obvious solution.

Let N denote the number of ways of selecting five cards from 52.

Then
$$N = \frac{52 \cdot 51 \cdot 50 \cdot 49 \cdot 48}{5!}.$$

The probability of drawing exactly two like cards of given denomination (aces, say) will be

$$\frac{\frac{4 \cdot 3}{2!} \times \frac{48 \cdot 47 \cdot 46}{3!}}{N} \quad \text{or} \quad \frac{2162}{54145},$$

and since there are 13 different cards in each suit it might be thought that to multiply the above fraction by 13 would give the result. This answer is, however, incorrect, in that there is "overlapping", for the remaining three cards out of the five may be a pair of like cards which have already been counted.

The possible arrangements, with their respective chances, are

Arrangement	Chance	
(a) 4 like cards and 1 different	$\dfrac{48 \times 13}{N}$	or $\dfrac{1}{4165}$,
(b) 3 like cards and 2 like cards	$\dfrac{13 \times \frac{4 \cdot 3 \cdot 2}{3!} \times 12 \times \frac{4 \cdot 3}{2!}}{N}$	or $\dfrac{6}{4165}$,
(c) 3 like cards and 2 different	$\dfrac{13 \times \frac{4 \cdot 3 \cdot 2}{3!} \times 4^2 \times \frac{12 \cdot 11}{2!}}{N}$	or $\dfrac{88}{4165}$,
(d) 2 sets of 2 like cards, 1 different	$\dfrac{\frac{13 \cdot 12}{2!} \times \frac{4 \cdot 3}{2!} \times \frac{4 \cdot 3}{2!} \times 44^*}{N}$	or $\dfrac{198}{4165}$,
(e) 2 like cards and 3 different	$\dfrac{13 \times \frac{4 \cdot 3}{2!} \times 4^3 \times \frac{12 \cdot 11 \cdot 10}{3!}}{N}$	or $\dfrac{1760}{4165}$.

The reasoning to obtain these chances is straightforward, and it will be necessary to examine one only: the others are on the same lines. Consider the arrangement in which there are to be exactly two like

---

* 44 because 8 cards are unallowable, being 4 of each of the previous numbers chosen. This avoids duplication with (b).

cards and consequently three different ones. Having settled on the denomination of the like cards—which can be done in 13 ways—there remain 12 denominations from which to choose 3. This can be done in $\dfrac{12 \cdot 11 \cdot 10}{3!}$ ways. The two like cards can be selected from the four (one of each suit) in $\dfrac{4 \cdot 3}{2}$ ways. This does not quite complete the selection, for the three different cards may be selected from any of the four suits, and this can be done in $4 \times 4 \times 4$ ways.

Returning now to the analysis above. If the problem is confined to the chance where exactly two like cards are to be chosen, the result will be (e); if there are not to be more than two like cards, two sets of two like cards being permitted, the chance will be $(d)+(e)$; if there are no restrictions, and we are given that two like cards at least are to be among the five, we shall require the total of the chances (a) to (e).

These results are respectively $\frac{1760}{4165}$, $\frac{1958}{4165}$, and $\frac{2053}{4165}$.

The above method of solution is designed to show, in full, the several probabilities of the various arrangements that may occur. If, however, it is known that there are no restrictions other than that there shall be at least two like cards, a simpler method of solving this problem obviously presents itself. It is sufficient to calculate the probability that there shall not be any like cards among the five; this probability is evidently the complement of that required. The probability that there are no like cards is

$$\dfrac{\dfrac{13 \cdot 12 \cdot 11 \cdot 10 \cdot 9}{5!}}{N} \times 4^5 \text{ or } \dfrac{2112}{4165},$$

the complement of which agrees with the third answer given above.

Example 25.

A network of wires forms n^2 squares like a chess-board. Two spiders, starting at the same time from opposite ends of a diagonal, crawl to the end opposite them at the same speed and by one of the shortest routes. What is the chance that they meet?

Let the square $AQBR$ be the boundary of the network. Since the spiders start from A and B at the same time and crawl at the same pace, after having crawled for the same length of time they must arrive at points on the diagonal QR. They will meet if the points on QR are identical, but not otherwise. Also, any point on the diagonal relevant to the problem must be an angular point of one of the n^2 squares of which $AQBR$ is the boundary. The number of squares which have diagonals lying along QR is n.

Let P be such a point with coordinates (x, y) reckoned from A as origin and AR and AQ as axes. Then $x+y=n$, and x and y are integers.

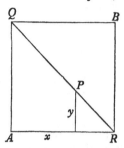

The number of routes from A to B is $^{2n}C_n$, for any route consists of n steps in the direction A to R and n steps in the direction A to Q. These steps may be arranged in any of $(2n)\,!/(n\,!)\,(n\,!)$ ways. As all these routes are equally likely, the chance that any one route is taken is $1/^{2n}C_n$.

But the number of ways of arriving at P will vary according to the position of P. The number of ways of arriving at P from A is $n\,!/(x\,!)\,(y\,!)$ or ^nC_x (since $x+y=n$), and this is also the number of ways from P to B. Therefore, of the $^{2n}C_n$ routes from A to B, $(^nC_x)^2$ pass through P, and the probability that a route passes through P is thus $(^nC_x)^2/^{2n}C_n$.

The chance that the spiders meet at P is therefore $\dfrac{(^nC_x)^2 \cdot (^nC_x)^2}{^{2n}C_n \cdot {}^{2n}C_n}$, and the chance that they meet at all is $\dfrac{\overset{x=n}{\underset{x=0}{\Sigma}} (^nC_x)^4}{(^{2n}C_n)^2}$.

Now this result is based on the supposition that *all routes from A to B are equally likely*. It may, however, be argued that once the diagonal QR is reached, the event has or has not happened, so that it is unnecessary to consider routes beyond the diagonal. On this assumption *all routes to the diagonal* are supposed equally likely.

Thus, to reach P from A, the first spider may take one of ^nC_x different routes. To reach the diagonal, the number of possible routes, each of which is, under the present assumption, equally likely, is $\overset{x=n}{\underset{x=0}{\Sigma}} {}^nC_x$.

The probability that each spider reaches P is therefore $^nC_x/\Sigma^nC_x$, and that they both do so is the square of this expression.

Therefore the probability that they meet at all is

$$\frac{\overset{x=n}{\underset{x=0}{\Sigma}} (^nC_x)^2}{2^{2n}},$$

since
$$\Sigma^nC_x = {}^nC_0 + {}^nC_1 + {}^nC_2 + \ldots + {}^nC_n = 2^n.$$

It should be noted that, while the numerator of the fraction denoting the probability under the first assumption—namely $\sum\limits_{x=0}^{x=n} ({}^{n}C_{x})^{4}$—cannot be evaluated in the general case, the numerator of the corresponding fraction under the second assumption can easily be shown to be ${}^{2n}C_{n}$.

The two results are not the same. While a general proof is difficult, it is a straightforward matter to show that in a special case the numerical values are different. Thus, if $n=8$, the probability in the first case is about ·208 and that in the second about ·196.

21. The method of induction.

There is a certain type of problem in probability for which it is not possible to obtain a solution by the direct methods outlined in the preceding paragraphs. In these problems it is necessary to find a relation connecting the chance at any stage with that at succeeding stages and then to calculate the required probability by adopting an inductive process. The difficulty in these questions is to ascertain the fundamental relation: when this has been established the problem can be solved by the application of algebraic methods.

Since we have to obtain a relation connecting the probability of an event of the nth stage with those at succeeding stages, it is often of advantage to investigate the relation for simple numerical values of n and then to deduce the general result. The following is an excellent example of this method of solution.

Example 26.

Five green balls and sixteen red balls are placed in a bag. A ball is drawn at random n times in succession and replaced after each drawing. Find the chance that no two successive drawings shall have given green balls.

To satisfy the required conditions the events must have taken place as follows:

At the first draw either a red or a green ball must be drawn:

$$R$$
$$G$$

At the second draw one of the following draws must have taken place:

$$R \mid R \qquad R\ G$$
$$G \mid R$$

i.e. first drawing associated with R; or $R\ G$.

At the third draw:

$$\begin{array}{cc|c} R & R & R \\ G & R & R \\ R & G & R \end{array} \qquad \begin{array}{c|cc} R & R & G \\ G & R & G \end{array}$$

i.e. second drawing associated with R; or first drawing associated with $R\,G$.

At the fourth draw:

$$\begin{array}{ccc|c} R & R & R & R \\ G & R & R & R \\ R & G & R & R \\ R & R & G & R \\ G & R & G & R \end{array} \qquad \begin{array}{cc|cc} R & R & R & G \\ G & R & R & G \\ R & G & R & G \end{array}$$

i.e. third drawing associated with R; or second drawing associated with $R\,G$.

It is evident therefore that if we have attained success at the $(n-1)$th stage, i.e. if no two successive green balls have been drawn, we shall attain success at the nth stage provided that, either

(i) the nth draw gives a red ball;

or (ii) if the nth draw gives a green ball the drawing at the $(n-1)$th stage gave a red ball.

The chance of drawing a red ball $=\frac{16}{21}$, and the chance of drawing a green ball $=\frac{5}{21}$.

If therefore u_n be the required chance after n drawings, we shall have

$$u_n = \tfrac{16}{21}u_{n-1} + \tfrac{5}{21}\cdot\tfrac{16}{21}u_{n-2}.$$

This is a relation connecting three successive coefficients of the series

$$u_0 + u_1 x + u_2 x^2 + \ldots + u_{n-2}x^{n-2} + u_{n-1}x^{n-1} + u_n x^n + \ldots.$$

The series is therefore a recurring series with scale of relation

$$1 - \tfrac{16}{21}x - \tfrac{5}{21}\cdot\tfrac{16}{21}x^2.$$

Also $u_0 = 1$ and $u_1 = 1$, since the conditions are satisfied if no ball or one ball is drawn.

Proceeding in the usual way, we find that the generating function is

$$\frac{u_0 + x\,(u_1 - 16u_0/21)}{(1+4x/21)\,(1-20x/21)} \text{ or } \frac{1+5x/21}{(1+4x/21)\,(1-20x/21)}$$

$$= \frac{25}{24}\cdot\frac{1}{1-20x/21} - \frac{1}{24}\cdot\frac{1}{1+4x/21}$$

$$= \frac{25}{24}\left(1-\frac{20x}{21}\right)^{-1} - \frac{1}{24}\left(1+\frac{4x}{21}\right)^{-1}.$$

The required chance, u_n, is the coefficient of x^n in these two expansions. This is easily seen to be

$$\tfrac{1}{24}\left[25\left(\tfrac{20}{21}\right)^n-(-1)^n\left(\tfrac{4}{21}\right)^n\right].$$

Note. As an alternative method of obtaining the coefficients of $\left(\tfrac{20}{21}\right)^n$ and $\left(-\tfrac{4}{21}\right)^n$ we may say that $u_n=a\left(\tfrac{20}{21}\right)^n+b\left(-\tfrac{4}{21}\right)^n$. a and b can then be found from the conditions $u_0=1$ and $u_1=1$.

The following examples are illustrative of the same method of attack.

Example 27.

A player tosses a coin and is to score one point for every head turned up and two for every tail. He is to play on until his score reaches or passes n. If p_n is his chance of attaining exactly n, show that

$$p_n=\tfrac{1}{2}\left(p_{n-1}+p_{n-2}\right)$$

and hence find the value of p_n.

There are two ways of reaching n exactly, namely, by throwing

(i) a tail when the score is $n-2$; or

(ii) a head when the score is $n-1$.

The respective chances are $\tfrac{1}{2}p_{n-2}$ and $\tfrac{1}{2}p_{n-1}$. Since these are mutually exclusive, we have

$$p_n=\tfrac{1}{2}\left(p_{n-1}+p_{n-2}\right).$$

The value of p_n may be found in either of two ways:

(a) $\qquad\qquad p_n=\tfrac{1}{2}\left(p_{n-1}+p_{n-2}\right),$

or $\qquad\qquad p_n+\tfrac{1}{2}p_{n-1}=p_{n-1}+\tfrac{1}{2}p_{n-2}.$ $\qquad$ ......(1)

Also $\qquad\qquad p_1=\tfrac{1}{2}$

and $\qquad\qquad p_2=\tfrac{3}{4}$ obviously. $\qquad$ ......(2)

By repetition of (1) and use of the facts in (2) we find that

$$p_n=1-\tfrac{1}{2}+\tfrac{1}{4}-\tfrac{1}{8}+\ldots+(-1)^{n-2}\frac{1}{2^{n-2}}+\frac{1}{2}(-1)^{n-1}\frac{1}{2^{n-1}},$$

which simplifies easily to

$$\frac{1}{3}\left\{2+(-1)^n\frac{1}{2^n}\right\}.$$

(b) We may treat $1-\tfrac{1}{2}x-\tfrac{1}{2}x^2$ as the scale of relation of a recurring series and proceed as in Example 26.

If the series is

$$p_0 + p_1 x + p_2 x^2 + p_3 x^3 + \ldots + p_{n-2} x^{n-2} + p_{n-1} x^{n-1} + p_n x^n + \ldots,$$

$$p_1 = \tfrac{1}{2}, \; p_2 = \tfrac{3}{4} \text{ and } p_0 = 1.$$

The generating function of the series is

$$\frac{1}{1 - \tfrac{1}{2}x - \tfrac{1}{4}x^2} = \frac{1}{(1-x)(1+\tfrac{1}{2}x)}.$$

By partial fractions this becomes

$$\frac{2}{3(1-x)} + \frac{1}{3(1+\tfrac{1}{2}x)}.$$

Expanding by the binomial theorem, we obtain for the value of p_n (the coefficient of x^n) the same result as is found by the first method.

Example 28.

A has 10 counters and B has 5; their chances of winning a single game are in the ratio 2 : 1. The loser in each game is to give a counter to his opponent. The game stops when one or the other has lost all his counters. Find A's chance of winning all B's counters.

Let u_n be A's chance of winning all B's counters when A has n counters. In the next game A must either win or lose a counter. His chances of these contingencies are $\tfrac{2}{3}$ and $\tfrac{1}{3}$ respectively. When he has lost the next game his chance of winning all B's counters is u_{n-1} and when he has won the next game it is u_{n+1}.

Hence
$$u_n = \tfrac{2}{3} u_{n+1} + \tfrac{1}{3} u_{n-1}.$$

It is required to find u_{10} from the above relation, given that $u_{15} = 1$ (since A will then have won) and $u_0 = 0$ (since he will have lost).

The required relation for the recurring series is therefore

$$\tfrac{2}{3} - x + \tfrac{1}{3} x^2.$$

Since we may write this relation as

$$\tfrac{2}{3}(1 - \tfrac{3}{2}x + \tfrac{1}{2}x^2) = \tfrac{2}{3}(1 - \tfrac{1}{2}x)(1 - x),$$

we may put $u_n = a \left(\tfrac{1}{2}\right)^n + b$, and then obtain a and b from the values of u_0 and u_{15}.

This is a particular example of the problem of "duration of play". The problem in its general form gives m counters to A and n counters to B, and states that A's chances of winning, drawing and losing a single game are p, q, r respectively, where $p + q + r = 1$. The method of solution is precisely similar to that above.

The inductive method can be adapted to other types of question in probability. An excellent example will be found in *J.I.A.* vol. LVI, pp. 102–104, where a problem in direct probability is solved very simply by the inductive process.

22. We will conclude this chapter with some miscellaneous examples. These problems require only a careful application of the ordinary methods, and no special comment is necessary.

Example 29.

The sum of two positive quantities is constant and equal to $2n$. Find the chance that the product of the two quantities is not less than $\frac{3}{4}$ their greatest product.

The product of two positive quantities whose sum is constant is greatest when the quantities are equal. The greatest product is therefore

$$\frac{2n}{2} \cdot \frac{2n}{2} = n^2.$$

If the two quantities are x and $2n - x$ we must have

$$x(2n - x) \geqslant \frac{3n^2}{4},$$

i.e. $$4x^2 - 8nx + 3n^2 \leqslant 0,$$

i.e. $$(2x - 3n)(2x - n) \leqslant 0.$$

Therefore x must lie between $\frac{3n}{2}$ and $\frac{n}{2}$.

The possible values of x range from 0 to $2n$, and the chance required is therefore

$$\frac{1}{2n}\left\{\frac{3n}{2} - \frac{n}{2}\right\} = \tfrac{1}{2}.$$

Example 30.

Ten clubs compete annually for a cup which is to become the absolute property of the club which wins it for three years in succession. Assuming that all the clubs are of equal skill, find the chance that last year's winners, not having won the previous year, will ultimately win the cup.

Let $\frac{x}{10}$ be A's chance of winning outright, A having won the previous year. Each of the others has a chance equal to

$$\frac{1 - \dfrac{x}{10}}{9},$$

since the clubs are of equal skill.

Now (a) A's chance of winning next year and the year after

$$= \left(\frac{1}{10}\right)^2.$$

(b) A's chance of winning, losing and then having the same chance as the other eight losing clubs

$$= \frac{1}{10} \cdot \frac{9}{10} \cdot \frac{1 - \dfrac{x}{10}}{9}.$$

(c) A's chance of losing and then having the same chance as the other eight losing clubs

$$= \frac{9}{10} \cdot \frac{1 - \dfrac{x}{10}}{9}.$$

A's total chance $= (a) + (b) + (c)$, and this we know to be $\dfrac{x}{10}$. Solving the resulting equation, we find that A's chance is $\frac{4}{37}$.

Note. The above solution assumes that the total probability of winning, for all the clubs, is unity, i.e. that the cup must eventually be won. It is easily seen that the cup must be won outright. If the chance that any particular club fails to win the cup outright after m trials is $1/n$, where n is greater than 1, then if there be an infinitely large number of sets of trials, the chance that the cup is never won outright by any particular club will not be greater than $\underset{k \to \infty}{\mathrm{Lt}} \left(\dfrac{1}{n}\right)^{km}$ which is obviously zero. In other words, if the contests be continued for a sufficient length of time, the chance that the cup is not won outright is zero, i.e. the cup must be won.

Example 31.

The atoms of a certain radio-active element are continuously disintegrating at the uniform rate of $\frac{1}{300}$ per annum, those atoms that disintegrate thereupon becoming atoms of a different element. What is the average period of years that an atom of the original element will survive as such, and what is the probability that any particular atom will survive that period?

Let the year be divided into n instants.

Then the chance that an atom disintegrates in any one instant is $\dfrac{1}{300n}$

and ,, ,, ,, does not disintegrate ,, ,, $1 - \dfrac{1}{300n}$.

Now let $f(r)$ be the chance that the atom has not disintegrated at the end of the rth instant.

Then $$f(r) = \left(1 - \frac{1}{300n}\right)^r,$$

and the average number of instants required for disintegration is

$$1 + \sum_{r=1}^{\infty} f(r) = 1 + \sum_{r=1}^{\infty} \left(1 - \frac{1}{300n}\right)^r$$

$$= \frac{1}{1 - \left(1 - \dfrac{1}{300n}\right)}$$

$$= 300n, \quad \text{i.e. 300 years.}$$

The chance that an atom survives this period is

$$\underset{n \to \infty}{\text{Lt}} \left(1 - \frac{1}{300n}\right)^{300n} = e^{-1}.$$

EXAMPLES 10

1. Explain how the probability of a compound event, consisting of two constituent simple events, is obtained. Illustrate your answer by examples.

2. The chance of one event happening is the square of the chance of a second event, but the odds against the first are the cube of the odds against the second. Find the chance of each.

3. If three squares are chosen at random on a chess-board, show that the chance that they should be in a diagonal line is $\frac{7}{744}$.

4. A man has three current English coins. Find the chance that he can give change for half a crown.

5. A can hit a target four times in 5 shots; B three times in 4 shots; C twice in 3 shots. They fire a volley; what is the probability that two shots at least hit?

6. A and B stand in a ring with ten other persons. If the arrangement of the twelve persons is at random, find the chance that there are exactly three persons between A and B.

7. The first twelve letters of the alphabet are written down at random. What is the probability that there are four letters between the A and the B?

8. Find the chance of drawing two white balls in the first two draws from a bag containing five red and seven white balls, balls drawn not being replaced.

9. An experiment succeeds twice as often as it fails. Find the chance that in the next six trials there will be at least four successes.

10. If an experiment is equally likely to succeed or fail, find the chance that it will succeed exactly n times in $2n$ trials.

11. Find the chance of throwing ten with four dice.

12. If a die whose faces are numbered from 1 to 6 is thrown four times, what is the probability that the sum of the four throws is 14?

13. A five-figure number consisting of the digits 0, 1, 2, 3, 4 (no repetitions) is chosen at random. What is the chance that it is divisible by 4?

14. Out of a bag containing thirteen balls, six are drawn and replaced, and then seven are drawn. Find the chance that at least three balls were common to the two drawings.

15. If a die is thrown five times what is the probability that a six appears on at least two consecutive occasions?

16. What is the chance that a person with two dice will throw aces exactly four times in six trials?

17. There are m candidates taking an examination paper of n questions of equal difficulty; assuming that a candidate answers a question correctly or not at all, either being equally likely:

   (a) In how many different ways may a paper be answered?

   (b) How many different sets of answered papers are possible?

   (c) What is the chance that a set of papers is handed in in which a particular question is solved by not more than one candidate?

18. Six cards are chosen at random from a pack of 52. Find the chance that three will be black and three red.

19. A card is chosen at random from each of six packs of cards. Find the chance that three will be black and three red.

20. The 26 letters of the alphabet are placed in a bag. A and B alternately draw a letter from the bag, the letters drawn not being replaced. The winner is the one who draws most vowels. A starts and draws a vowel with his first draw. What is his chance of winning?

21. A book contains 1000 pages. A page is chosen at random. What is the chance that the sum of the digits of the number on the page is nine?

22. A bag contains three tickets marked with the numbers 00, 01, 10, and two tickets each marked with the number 11. A ticket is drawn at random eight times, being replaced each time. Find the probability that the sum of the numbers on the tickets thus drawn is 33.

23. If x be one of the first hundred numbers chosen at random, find the probability that $x + \dfrac{100}{x}$ is greater than 50.

24. In a lottery there are 1000 tickets numbered 1 to 1000. Three tickets are drawn. Find the chance that

(1) the three tickets bear consecutive numbers;

(2) two of the three bear consecutive numbers.

25. If m odd integers and n even integers be written down at random, prove that the chance that no two odd numbers are adjacent to one another is

$$\frac{n!\,(n+1)!}{(m+n)!\,(n-m+1)!},$$

m being not greater than $n+1$.

26. The sum of two whole numbers is 100; find the chance that their product is greater than 1000.

27. There are ten tickets, five of which are numbered 1, 2, 3, 4, 5 and the other five are blank. What is the probability of drawing a total of 10 in three trials, one ticket being drawn and replaced at each trial?

28. If two of the first hundred numbers are chosen at random, what is the probability that their difference is greater than 10?

29. A and B have equal chances of winning a single game; A wants two games and B wants three games to win a match. Find the chance that A will win the match.

30. A and B play at a game which cannot be drawn. On the average A wins three games out of five. Show that it is more than 2 to 1 that A would win at least three games out of the first five.

31. A, B, C throw in order, each using three dice. Prove that A's chance of throwing 10 first is $(\frac{8}{13})^2$ and find C's chance.

32. A and B play for a prize. A is to throw a die first and is to win if he throws 6. If he fails, B is to throw and win if he throws 6 or 5. If he fails, A is to throw again and win if he throws 6 or 5 or 4, and so on. Find each player's chance of winning.

33. A and B play for a stake which is to be won by him who makes the highest score in four throws of a die. After two throws A has scored 12 and B 9. What is A's chance of winning?

34. *A* and *B* play a set of games, to be won by the player who first wins four games, with the condition that if they each win three they are to play the best of three to decide the set. *A*'s chance of winning a single game is to *B*'s as 2 to 1. Find their respective chances of winning the set.

35. *A*, *B* and *C* draw in succession from a bag containing four white and eight black balls until a white ball is drawn. What is the probability that the white ball is drawn by *C*? Is his chance improved if each ball is replaced after drawing?

36. Three players of equal skill, *A*, *B* and *C*, play a series of games and the winner of each game scores one point. Each of the three keeps a separate score and the winner of the set is the one who first scores 4. *A* wins the first, *B* the second and *A* the third game. What is then *C*'s chance of winning the set?

37. *A* and *B* play a match of five games. *A*'s chances of winning, drawing and losing any game are in proportion to 3, 2 and 1 respectively. Two points are scored for a win and one for a draw. What is the chance that the match is drawn?

38. *A* and *B* play a match, the winner being the one who first wins two games in succession, no games being drawn. Their respective chances of winning any particular game are $p : q$. Find

(1) *A*'s initial chance of winning;

(2) *A*'s chance of winning after having won the first game.

39. Three players, *A*, *B*, *C*, play under the following conditions. In each turn the chance of success is the same for each of two contestants. *A* and *B* play together for the first turn, the winner plays with *C*, and if he win again he wins the game; if not, *C* plays with the third man and so on until one man has won two turns in succession. Find each man's chance of winning the game.

40. The winner of a game is the one who first scores 4 points, but if both players score 3 points the game continues until one player has scored 2 points more than the other. *A* and *B* play; find *A*'s chance of winning when the score is 2—0 in *B*'s favour, being given that *A* is twice as skilful a player as *B*.

41. *A*, *B*, *C*, *D* each throw two dice for a prize. The highest throw wins, but if equal highest throws occur (thrown by two or more players) the players with these throws continue. *A* throws 10; find his chance of winning.

42. *A* and *B* cut a pack of cards, the player who wins the cut six times to be the winner. *A*, having won four times to *B*'s once, cuts a five. Find the chance that *A* will be a winner.

43. A and B play a match consisting of a maximum of nine games. The chance that any game is won by A, won by B or drawn are equal. A win counts one point and a draw half a point (to each). The match ends when one of the players has a sufficient lead to leave him with an excess of points over his opponent even if the latter were to win all the remaining games. What is the chance that the match ends with the 7th game and not before?

44. A bag contains ten counters, numbered 1 to 10. One counter is drawn and replaced and this operation is repeated until four different numbers have appeared. Calculate the probability that success will be attained with the sixth draw.

45. If n is the product of any 69 integers taken at random, find, to the first significant place of decimals, the value of the probability that n is not a multiple of 5, given that $\log_{10} 2 = \cdot 3010300$.

46. A bag contains counters marked with the digits 2, 4, 6, 8 and the number of times each digit occurs is equal to the value of the digit. Counters are drawn one at a time, each counter being replaced when drawn. What is the chance

(1) that the digit 2 is drawn before the digit 8;

(2) that the sum of the first three digits is 16;

(3) that the first five counters drawn contain at least one of those marked 4 or 6?

47. A and B have each eight pennies. Each tosses his set of pennies. Find to three places of decimals the chance that the number of heads obtained by A exceeds the number obtained by B by at least three.

48. At a certain age 99 per cent. of the persons alive at the beginning of the year will live to the end of the year. Find expressions for the probabilities that out of four persons of that age there will die within the year

(1) exactly 2;

(2) not more than 2;

(3) two specified persons;

(4) two specified persons and no others.

49. If the probability that exactly three lives out of six all aged x survive n years is $\cdot 08192$, find the probability that at least three survive n years.

50. The probability that exactly one life out of three lives aged 20, 35 and 50, will survive 15 years is $\cdot 092$; the probability that all will die

within 15 years is ·006. If the probability that the life aged 20 will survive 15 years is ·9, find the probability that

(1) he will survive 30 years;

(2) he will survive 45 years.

51. Three men, A, B, C, are each aged 30. Given that the probability that a man aged 30 will survive 5 years is ·974 and the probability that he will survive 10 years is ·940, find the chance that between the end of the 5th year and the end of the 10th year from now

(1) one at least will die;

(2) all will die, A dying first and B second.

Find also the chance that A and B will die within this period and C will survive the 10th year.

52. The following table shows the probability that a woman of the age specified will marry in a year:

Age	Probability of marriage
20	·0665
25	·1033
30	·0649
40	·0183

Find the probability that, out of 4 women aged 20, 25, 30, 40 respectively, only one marries within a year.

53. Given that the probability that of three lives aged x one, and one only, will survive n years is 27 times the probability that all will die within n years, find the probability that

(a) at least two will survive n years;

(b) at least one will die within n years.

54. Given the following table, find the probability that of four persons aged 65 at least one will die between ages 75 and 85 and at least one after age 85:

Age	Probability of surviving 10 years
65	One-half
75	One-fifth

55. If m things are distributed amongst a men and b women, show that the chance that the number of things received by the group of men is odd is equal to

$$\frac{1}{2} \cdot \frac{(b+a)^m - (b-a)^m}{(b+a)^m}.$$

56. The sum of two positive quantities is constant and equal to $2n$. What is the chance that their product is less than $\frac{1}{2}n^2$?

57. How many times must a man be allowed to toss a penny so that the odds may be 100 to 1 that he gets at least one head?

58. A coin is tossed $m+n$ times $(m>n)$. Prove that the chance of at least m consecutive heads appearing is $\dfrac{n+2}{2^{m+1}}$. Find also the chance of a run of exactly m consecutive heads.

59. If ten different things be distributed among three persons, show that the chance of a particular person having more than five of them is $\dfrac{1507}{19683}$.

60. If p be the chance that an odd number of aces turn up when n ordinary dice are thrown, show that $1-2p=(\tfrac{2}{3})^n$.

61. A pack of cards has been dealt in the usual way to four players. One player has just one ace; prove that the chance that his partner has the other three aces is $\dfrac{22}{703}$.

62. A bag contains a certain number of balls some of which are white. I am to get a shilling for every ball so long as I continue to draw white only, the balls drawn not being replaced. An additional ball not being white is introduced and I claim as compensation to be allowed to replace every white ball that I draw. Is this fair?

63. There are three sets of cards, red, yellow and blue. Each set contains ten cards, numbered 1 to 10. Three cards are drawn at random. Find the chance that the sum of the numbers on them equals 15:

(1) if the cards are all to be drawn from the red set;

(2) if one card is to be drawn from each set;

(3) if the cards are to be drawn from the three sets mixed indiscriminately.

64. From a bag containing ten red, ten white and ten blue balls one is to be drawn at random and replaced. The operation is to be repeated ten times. Find the chance that at least one ball of each colour will be drawn.

65. Out of $3n$ consecutive integers three are selected at random. Find the chance that their sum is divisible by 3.

66. In a book of values of a certain function there is one error on the average in every m values. Find the number of times, r, a value must be turned up at random in order that you may have an even chance of turning up an erroneous value. Show that when m becomes large the ratio r/m tends to a fixed quantity and find this quantity.

67. *A*, *B*, *C* and five other football teams enter for a competition. The teams are of equal skill and are drawn by lot in pairs before each round, the winners of the previous round entering the next round. Find the chance that in the course of the competition *A* will beat *B*, having first beaten *C*.

68. A street consists of 24 houses numbered 1 to 24, odd numbers on one side, even on the other. Three houses are vacant. Assuming that the houses are all equally likely to be vacant, find the chances:

(1) that the three houses are next to each other;

(2) that all three are on the same side of the street;

(3) that if they are all on the same side the sum of their numbers equals 42.

69. *A* put 10 balls in all, some of which were white, some red, and some black, into a bag, and asked *B* and *C*, neither of whom knew the number of balls of each colour, each to make 1000 draws and note the colour of each ball drawn. *B*'s and *C*'s results were exactly the same, viz.:

White	600
Red	300
Black	100

It subsequently turned out that whereas *B* had returned each ball to the bag after noting its colour, *C* had kept the balls drawn in hand until he had drawn all ten balls and had then returned them to the bag and made another 10 draws, and so on.

What difference does this make to the probabilities of drawing balls of different colour as inferred from the results of the experiment, and what in the circumstances was the probability that *B* and *C* would obtain the same result?

70. Find the chance that the sum of the numbers on three cards drawn at random from an ordinary pack of 52 cards amounts to 21, all the court cards counting as 10. How will the result be altered if an ace can count as 1 or 11?

71. If a coin be tossed 15 times, what is the probability of getting heads exactly as many times in the first 10 throws as in the last 5?

72. A bag contains eight counters numbered 1 to 8. Four are drawn at random. Find the chances that

(1) the sum of the numbers on the four counters amounts to at least 17;

(2) the counters numbered 2 and 3 are among the four;

(3) the four counters contain at least two of the three numbers 3, 5, 7.

73. If $6n$ tickets numbered 0, 1, 2, ... $6n-1$ are placed in a bag and 3 are drawn out, find the chance that the sum of the numbers on them is equal to $6n$.

74. From a bag containing nine red and nine blue balls nine are drawn at random, the balls being replaced. Show that the probability that four balls of each colour will be included is a little less than $\frac{1}{2}$.

75. A looks at a clock at some time between 2 and 5 p.m., all times within the limits being equally likely. He looks again when it strikes the next quarter hour. What is the chance that in the meantime the minute has overtaken the hour hand?

76. Four suits of cards, each suit consisting of 13 cards numbered from 1 to 13, are dealt to four persons. Find the chance that each person's cards contain all the numbers from 1 to 13.

77. There are four sets of calculations on one sheet which have to be made, then checked and finally scrutinized. A and B can calculate only, C and D can calculate or check, and E and F can scrutinize only. No person may check a calculation he has made and all work must be signed. Find the chance that when the sheet is finally completed each name of the above six appears exactly twice.

78. From an ordinary pack of cards a card is drawn and then six other cards at random. Find the chance that the card first drawn is the highest of its suit amongst all the cards drawn.

79. A bag contains thirteen balls of which four are white and nine black. If a ball be drawn r times successively and replaced after each drawing, show that the chance that no two successive drawings shall have given white balls is

$$\frac{16 \cdot 12^r - (-3)^r}{15 \cdot 13^r}.$$

80. The reserved seats in a certain section of a concert-hall are numbered consecutively from 1 to 100. A man sends for five consecutive tickets for one concert and for eight consecutive tickets for another. Find the chance that there will be no number common to both sets of tickets.

81. In a cup draw there were four Southern and four Northern teams, the names being drawn one by one from a bag. Find the following probabilities:

(1) that each one of the four successive pairs consisted of one Southern and one Northern team;

(2) that each one of the four successive pairs consisted of two Southern or two Northern teams;

(3) that the first drawn in at least three of the pairs was a Southern team.

82. A number consists of seven digits whose sum is 59. Find the chance that it is divisible by 11.

83. Two dice are thrown and one of the players will win (a) if the sum be 7 or 11, or (b) if the sum be 4, 5, 6, 8, 9 or 10 and the same sum reappears before 7. Find the player's chance of success.

84. A and B cast alternately with two dice. It is agreed that, on each failure to win, the prize money is to be reduced by 3 per cent. of its value at the previous attempt. A wins if he throws 6 before B throws 7, and B wins if he throws 7 before A throws 6. A starts first. Compare the values of the respective chances of A and B.

85. A bag contains n counters marked 1, 2, 3 ... n. If two counters are drawn show that the chance that the difference of the counters exceeds m (less than $n-1$) is

$$\frac{(n-m)(n-m-1)}{n(n-1)}.$$

Deduce from this result the chance that if two points are taken at random on a line the length between them exceeds half the length of the line.

86. A bag contains two white balls and one black ball. A drawing of two balls is made. If either is black, the two are replaced and another black ball is added. A second drawing of two balls is then made, and again if either is black, the two are replaced and another black ball is added and so on.

What is the chance that if the drawings are continued indefinitely two white balls will never be drawn together?

87. A's chance of scoring any point is $\frac{5}{4}$ of B's. A engages to score 14 in excess of B before B shall have scored 3 in excess of A. Show that A's chance of winning the match is equal to

$$\frac{1-(\frac{4}{5})^3}{1-(\frac{4}{5})^{17}}.$$

88. A and his wife engage in a "mixed doubles" tennis tournament in which each pair of players consists of one member of each sex. There are fourteen other persons, seven of each sex, also entered for the tournament and players are drawn by lot before each round in such a way that any person of one sex may be the partner of any person of the other sex. Only the winners in any one round enter the next round. Assuming that all the players of each sex are equal in skill, find the probability that in the final round A and his wife play together as partners.

89. All that is known about a quadratic equation is that the coefficients are all different and are positive integers less than 10. Find the chance that the roots of the equation are real, all the integral values of the coefficients satisfying the above conditions being equally likely, and zero values of the coefficients being excluded.

90. A pack of cards is dealt in the usual way to four players of whom two and two are partners and the dealer turns up his last card. Denoting by the term "honours" the ace, king, queen, knave of the suit to which the turned-up card belongs, find the chance that each pair of partners shall have two honours.

91. A number taken at random is squared. Find the chances that the following are even numbers:

(1) the digit in the units place of the result;

(2) the digit in the tens place of the result;

(3) the digit in the hundreds place of the result.

92. Before commencing a game of cards four players cut for partners, i.e. the two highest play together and the two lowest together. All suits being of equal value, what is the chance that they will have to cut again?

93. A and B play a series of games to be won by the player who first wins two consecutive games. A's chances of winning, losing or drawing any particular game are $\frac{1}{2}$, $\frac{1}{4}$ and $\frac{1}{4}$ respectively. Find B's chance of winning the match (a) at the outset, (b) when he has just won one game, and (c) when he has just lost one game.

94. A and B have equal chances of winning a single game. A wants n games and B $n+1$ games to win a match. Show that the odds on A are $1+p$ to $1-p$ where $p \equiv \dfrac{(2n)\,!}{n\,!\,n\,!\,2^{2n}}$.

95. Three posts are filled one after another by lot from amongst ten persons (A, B, C, D, and six others), the first by any one of the ten, the second by anyone except A and B, the third by anyone except C and D. What is the chance that A or B or both of them, and C or D or both of them, are chosen? No one can hold more than one post, and in drawing for the second and third posts the barred persons and any person previously chosen are excluded.

96. With a hand of thirteen cards a player is known to hold one ace. What is the chance that he has at least one other ace?

If it is known that the ace he holds is the ace of hearts what is the chance that he has at least one other ace?

CHAPTER XI

ELEMENTARY STATISTICS

1. It is not the object of this book to deal exhaustively with the science of statistics. We shall treat only with the elementary ideas of the subject, and this treatment should be sufficient to enable the student to solve the simpler types of problem that are met with in practical work.

Statistical investigation covers a very wide field and is concerned with the collection, tabulation and summarization of data, the interpretation of the results and the deductions that can be made therefrom. Collection and tabulation must here be taken for granted and the other aspects will be considered to a limited degree only.

2. Elementary definitions.

Suppose that a number of men were selected at random and arranged in order of their heights, and suppose that these men formed a representative and unbiased sample of the particular class under review. We should be able by mere inspection to obtain some idea of the variable characteristic—in this case, height—of the class. For some purposes this might be sufficient, but, in general, this method, namely, the assembling of the men, is quite impracticable. Further, we should probably need records of the experiment, and it is essential therefore to arrange the work so that these records may be readily made.

If we were to represent the men by straight lines proportional to the heights of the men, drawn at equal intervals at right angles to a fixed straight line, and retained the order of magnitude as before, we should be in possession of a permanent record of the heights. An arrangement such as this is termed an *array* and the individual values of the measured characteristic are called *variates*. As an illustration of this pictorial review of a particular characteristic we may consider the following figure, which shows the heights of 42 men, all of whom are under 5 ft. 9 in. For convenience of illustration only the excess of height over 5 ft. is given, and fractions of an inch are ignored.

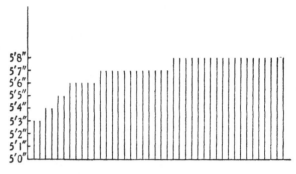

Fig. 6.

An examination of this array shows that there were 2 men whose height was 5 ft. 3 in., 2 whose height was 5 ft. 4 in., and so on. These numbers, which from the diagram are 2, 2, 2, 5, 12 and 19, are known as the *frequencies* with which the heights occurred.

The full sample of which the above is an extract consisted of 100 men for whom the table of frequencies is as under:

Height of man to the nearest inch	Number of cases
5 ft. 3 in.	2
5 4	2
5 5	2
5 6	5
5 7	12
5 8	19
5 9	16
5 10	16
5 11	14
6 0	7
6 1	2
6 2	3
	100

These data can be arranged to advantage in an array, not of variates, but of frequencies, in either of the following forms:

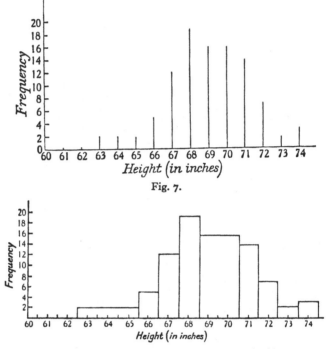

Fig. 7.

Fig. 8. The block diagram in this figure is called a *histogram*.

It should be noted that whereas Fig. 6 represents an array of heights with one scale only, namely height, Figs. 7 and 8 necessitate the adoption of two scales, height and frequency. In these figures we have, in fact, shown values of a variable (frequency) compared with those of the independent variable (height).

3. Reference to the table on p. 255 will show that the figures in the first column are given to the nearest inch. It is obvious, however, that, for example, the 19 men whose heights were stated to be 5 ft. 8 in. were not all exactly of this height. "Heights of 5 ft. 8 in. to the nearest inch" means any height between the limits 5 ft. 7½ in., to 5 ft. 8½ in., and this interval of one inch is called the *class-interval*. The recorded height of 5 ft. 8 in. may be taken as **the**

mid-value of the *class range*. Data may be displayed either in the form given in the table on p. 255, or with the class range indicated by its lower limit, as shown in the following example relating to the age distribution of a body of lives:

Age	Frequency
20·5–	38
21·5–	70
22·5–	82
23·5–	101
24·5–	128
25·5–	175
26·5–	181
27·5–	200
28·5–	181
29·5–	190
	1346

Here the class-interval is one year, and it is often assumed for practical purposes that there were 38 cases of age 21, 70 of age 22, and so on. In many distributions it will be found convenient to use a larger class-interval than a unit interval; examples of various class-intervals will occur later in this chapter.

A set of relative frequencies tabulated according to class ranges is called a *frequency distribution*. Given an ungrouped set of observations it is a matter for careful consideration as to the best form of grouping to adopt in order to obtain a reasonable frequency distribution from which to work.

The following is an important point which may arise in the construction of a frequency distribution. Suppose that in examining the data for a distribution such as that in the above table it was found that there were two persons exactly $21\frac{1}{2}$ years old at the date when the observations were made. In such a case it is the practice to assign one of these to the group $20\frac{1}{2}$–$21\frac{1}{2}$ and the other to the group $21\frac{1}{2}$–$22\frac{1}{2}$, since they may be said to belong equally to each of the groups that they divide. If there had been three of such cases, $1\frac{1}{2}$ would be assigned to the lower age-group and $1\frac{1}{2}$ to the upper group. It may happen therefore that although we are dealing with integral numbers of cases the distribution may show fractional frequencies when the table is completed.

4. Averages.

It will be convenient at this stage to revert to a pictorial representation of an array of variates as exemplified in paragraph 2. In the following example a small sample only has been taken in order that the deductions that may be drawn from the figure may be clearly shown.

The data relate to the ages of a class of 25 students and are given in the following table:

Nearest age	Number of students
18	1
19	2
20	1
21	6
22	3
23	4
24	1
25	1
26	1
27	1
28	4
	25

The array of variates is

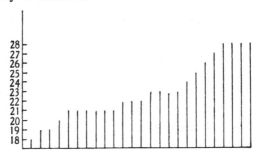

Fig. 9.

There are 25 variates depicted in this diagram in order of magnitude, and since there happens to be an odd number, we can at once single out the middle variate. The middle variate corresponds to an age 22 and is a particular variate of our sample. The statistical name for the middle variate is the *median*, so that the median, or to be more precise the median age, for this distribution is 22 years. If therefore a number of such experiments were made with different samples of similar students we should be in a position to compare one average characteristic of each sample, namely the median age.

If we examine the diagram and table again, we see that the variates which occur with the greatest frequency are those representing the number of students at age 21. We have found the *mode*, or most frequent value, and this again is another average. In this case it happens that the mode is immediately apparent from the table giving the frequency distribution, although the median cannot be deduced without further investigation.

Now an average may be defined as a quantity which typifies the magnitude of the set of variates from which it has been ascertained, and it may occur to the reader that the simplest average that could be found from the given data would be the ordinary arithmetic mean or, if we were using a frequency table, the weighted mean. This is so, and by simple calculation it is evident that the *mean* is 22·8 years.

We thus have three averages:

Mean	...	...	22·8 years
Median	...	...	22 years
Mode	...	...	21 years

and it remains for us to determine which of these averages is the most satisfactory for statistical purposes and, in addition, what use we can make of them.

It should be noted that frequency distributions may be illustrated by curves drawn through the peaks of the ordinates of a frequency diagram such as that in Fig. 7. While the positions of the mean, mode and median are often represented on *frequency curves* by ordinates, it is really not the ordinates but the corresponding *abscissae* which give the values of the mean, etc. Thus, in the frequency curve in Fig. 10 below, the values of the three averages are XA, XB and XC and not the ordinates through A, B and C.

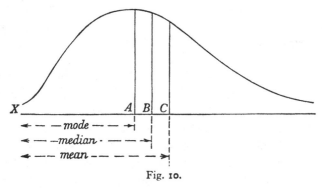

Fig. 10.

5. It is not immediately apparent which particular kind of average is most suitable for any group of observations, and it requires a considerable amount of experience before a student can use these averages to their best advantage. There are, however, criteria which enable us to select the most satisfactory form of average for general adoption. The principal criteria may be stated as follows:

A satisfactory average should be

(*a*) rigidly defined;

(*b*) based on unbiased observations as numerous as possible;

(*c*) relatively stable with fluctuations of sampling; i.e., though different samples might produce slightly different results, the variation from sample to sample should be as small as possible;

(*d*) capable of easy calculation and simple algebraic treatment.

Let us consider the example in paragraph 4. If it had happened that our data included no cases over age 27—i.e. the four cases at age 28 were non-existent—the mean age of the 21 cases observed would be about one year younger than before—about 21·8 years—while the median and the mode would remain unaltered. It appears from this simple example that a few extreme cases more or less may considerably affect the mean, while the median and mode are unchanged. But this possible disadvantage of the mean disappears when larger distributions are under consideration. In point of fact, the mean possesses several advantages over the median and the mode. It is rigidly defined, while the median is somewhat indefinite. Again, the mean can easily be calculated and lends itself to simple algebraical treatment, while, as will be seen later, it is generally impossible to obtain more than estimates of the other two averages. For these reasons the mean is the average that is used to a very great extent in statistical calculations.

6. Calculation of the mean.

Let n be the number of observations, x_r the value of the variate in the rth class-interval and f_r the frequency in the rth class-interval, so that $\Sigma f_r = n$.

Then M, the mean, is simply $\Sigma (f_r x_r)/\Sigma f_r$ or $\frac{1}{n} \Sigma (f_r x_r)$, where the summation extends over all the class-intervals. This evidently gives a weighted mean value of x_r.

The calculation of M can obviously be effected from this formula whatever the size of the distribution and wherever in the range the mean happens to be. If however the values of x are large (such as measurements in a small unit) and the frequencies are also numerous, a change of unit and origin will simplify the arithmetic considerably.

Thus, if a is the value of the temporary origin and δ_r is the deviation of x_r from a, then

$$x_r = a + \delta_r.$$

Now
$$M = \frac{1}{n} \Sigma (f_r x_r)$$

$$= \frac{1}{n} \Sigma [f_r (a + \delta_r)]$$

$$= \frac{1}{n} [a\Sigma f_r + \Sigma (f_r \delta_r)]$$

$$= \frac{1}{n} [an + \Sigma (f_r \delta_r)]$$

$$= a + \frac{1}{n} \Sigma (f_r \delta_r),$$

and if a be suitably chosen, i.e. so that the deviations of x from a are small and of different signs, it is evident that the calculation of $\Sigma(f_r \delta_r)$ is far less troublesome than that of $\Sigma(f_r x_r)$.

Example 1.

Calculate the mean age of wife corresponding to the age-group 60– of husband from the 1921 Census of married couples. (See Chap. X, paragraph 10.)

The first point to note is that the class-interval is five years, so that the age of wife must be assumed to be the mid-value of the range. The data have been tabulated and a glance at the figures suggests that a suitable origin will be the mid-value of the group 55–. The method of calculation in the table is self-explanatory.

Age (mid-value of class range)	Frequency f	Deviation from origin in terms of class-interval δ as unit	$f\delta$
27·5	1	−6	− 6
32·5	2	−5	− 10
37·5	4	−4	− 16
42·5	10	−3	− 30
47·5	21	−2	− 42
52·5	53	−1	− 53
57·5	126	0	−157
62·5	163	+1	+163
67·5	35	+2	+ 70
72·5	6	+3	+ 18
77·5	1	+4	+ 4
	422		+255

Thence

$$\Sigma(f\delta) = 255 - 157$$
$$= 98 \text{ class-intervals}$$
$$= 490 \text{ years,}$$

so that

$$\frac{1}{n}\Sigma(f\delta) = 490/422 = 1\cdot15 \dots$$

$$\therefore \quad M = 57\cdot5 + 1\cdot15 \dots$$
$$= 58\cdot7 \text{ years (say).}$$

An alternative method of obtaining the arithmetic mean, if the class-interval be taken as the unit, is based on a single and double summation of the column of frequencies. Thus, if the origin is taken at one value lower than the lowest value given, the initial value of the variable may be denoted by 1, the second by 2 and so on.

A first summation gives $\Sigma f_r = f_1 + f_2 + f_3 + \ldots + f_{n-2} + f_{n-1} + f_n$.

Summing again from the bottom upwards,

$$\Sigma\,(\Sigma f_r) = 1f_1 + 2f_2 + 3f_3 + \ldots + (n-2)f_{n-2} + (n-1)f_{n-1} + nf_n$$

$$= \sum_{r=1}^{r=n} rf_r.$$

If therefore the original initial value is k, so that the origin is at $k-1$, the mean value is

$$k - 1 + \frac{\Sigma rf_r}{\Sigma f_r}.$$

An example will make this clear.

Example 2.

Find the mean height of the sample of men from the table in paragraph 2.

The lowest value of the height is 63 in. Take the origin at 62 in.

Height in inches	Deviation from origin	f	Σf
63	1	2	100
64	2	2	98
65	3	2	96
66	4	5	94
67	5	12	89
68	6	19	77
69	7	16	58
70	8	16	42
71	9	14	26
72	10	7	12
73	11	2	5
74	12	3	3
		100	700

Then the mean height $= 62 + 700/100 = 69$ in.

In a large group it is often simpler to take the origin at k and the second summation up to the second line from the top. Thus, in this example, the mean height $= 63 + 600/100 = 69$ in.

This method is convenient in actuarial calculations where it is necessary to find the average age of a distribution consisting of comparatively large numbers.

7. Calculation of the median.

The median is the middle variate of the array, and if we were to construct a diagram showing the array of the variates of the observations in, say, the example above, it would be possible to select the middle variate. In practice it is generally impracticable to construct such a diagram, and a reasonable approximation obtained from a table of frequencies is, as a rule, sufficient for most purposes.

Consider, for example, the table in Example 1. There are 422 cases, so that the median will lie between the 211th and 212th cases. Now from the frequency distribution it is seen that up to and including the class range 50–55 there are 91 observations, while if the next group be included there are 217 observations. The median is therefore in this last group of 126 cases. It is reasonable to assume that the first observation in this group has the value of the lower boundary of the class range, the last observation has the value of the upper boundary and the 126 observations increase uniformly within the range. Since we require the age corresponding to a hypothetical case between the 211th and 212th cases, simple proportion will give the median to be

$$55 + \frac{5\,(211 \cdot 5 - 91)}{126},$$

the class-interval being 5 years.

Then the median $\quad = 55 + \dfrac{602 \cdot 5}{126}$

$$= 55 + 4 \cdot 78 \ldots$$

$$= 59 \cdot 8 \text{ years (say).}$$

8. Calculation of the mode.

The mode is the value which occurs with the greatest frequency. Although in a case where the variates proceed by unit variation it may be possible to select at sight the most likely value, this is not practicable where the distribution is one which concerns a continuous variable. Thus in Example 1 all that can be said is that the mode lies in a five-yearly group of which 62·5 is the mid-interval, although an examination of the table might suggest that the required value is nearer the lower limit than the upper one.

In many cases a good approximation to the mode can be found from the following simple formula:

Let M, M_i and M_0 represent the values of the mean, median and mode respectively.

Then
$$M_0 = M - 3\ (M - M_i).$$

In Example 1 the value of the mode according to this formula is

$$M_0 = 58\cdot7 - 3\ (58\cdot7 - 59\cdot8)$$
$$= 58\cdot7 + 3\cdot3$$
$$= 62\cdot0 \text{ years.}$$

It should be emphasized that this relation though often very close is not exact, and is not applicable to all distributions. Other methods have to be adopted in extreme cases, although even then a reasonable approximation may often be obtained by drawing a smooth curve through the statistics.

9. Ogive curve.

When a rough estimate of the median is required it is often useful to use a graphical method. This method is best illustrated by an actual example.

If we take the data from the table on p. 263 we may write them down in an alternative form, thus:

Height of not more than *x* inches *x*	No. of cases
63	2
64	4
65	6
66	11
67	23
68	42
69	58
70	74
71	88
72	95
73	97
74	100

Then, if the numbers so found be plotted against the heights and the points joined by a smooth curve, we have an *ogive* curve.

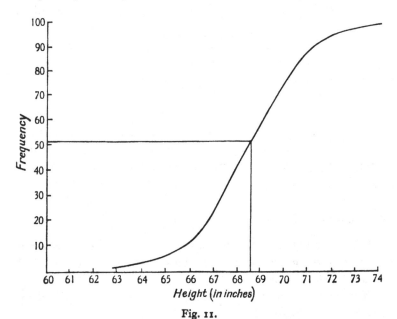

Fig. 11.

An approximate value of the median will be the abscissa corresponding to the ordinate midway between the 50th and 51st cases, i.e. about $68\frac{1}{2}$ inches.

The mode can also be estimated from the ogive, its position being where the slope of the curve is steepest. In many cases however the shape of the curve is such that all that can be said is that the mode lies between certain comparatively wide limits, and in those circumstances no better approximation can be obtained from the curve than is evident from a consideration of the statistics in their original tabular form.

10. Probable value and expectation.

Before we proceed further with the discussion of the mode or most likely value, it will be convenient to refer to another aspect of the mean.

Suppose that there are n counters in a bag, each counter having a value in shillings. Then, if we are given the number of counters of each particular value it is a matter of simple arithmetic to find the average value of a counter. All that we need do is to weight the number of counters having a particular value by that value, add the products and divide by the number of counters.

Example 3.

Find the weighted mean of the following distribution:

No. of counters (x)	9	1	2	5	7
Value of counter (y) in shillings	1	2	3	4	5

$$\text{Total value of counters} = \Sigma xy$$
$$= 9 + 2 + 6 + 20 + 35$$
$$= 72,$$

Total number of counters $= \Sigma x = 24$,

Weighted mean $= \Sigma xy / \Sigma x = 3$ shillings.

We may look upon this problem from another point of view. Suppose that we use the word *prize* to denote the value of a quantity to be attained. In general, the attainment of a prize is contingent upon the happening of some event and may therefore not always be secured. If the amount of the prize is S and it is obtained in pN trials out of a total of N in which the opportunity of obtaining the prize can occur, then the probability of its being obtained is p. Also, the total value of all the prizes is SN and the average value is pS. This average value is called the *expected value* or *probable value*. If we are concerned with the person who is playing for the prize the probable value of the prize is called his *expectation*. In other words, expectation is the product of an expected gain in actual value and the mathematical probability of obtaining such a gain. It may be noted that the gain or prize is not necessarily restricted to financial gain, but may be a number of years of life or a number of heads in a series of throws.

Let us consider the problem above in the light of this definition, and calculate the expectation of a man who is allowed to draw one counter at random from the bag.

The chance that he draws a counter value one shilling $= \frac{9}{24}$;

the chance that he draws a counter value two shillings $= \frac{1}{24}$,

and so on.

His expectation, which is the same as the probable value of his draw, is, therefore,

$$\left(\tfrac{9}{24}\right) 1 + \left(\tfrac{1}{24}\right) 2 + \left(\tfrac{2}{24}\right) 3 + \left(\tfrac{5}{24}\right) 4 + \left(\tfrac{7}{24}\right) 5$$
$$= \frac{9 + 2 + 6 + 20 + 35}{24}$$
$$= 3 \text{ shillings, as before.}$$

It is seen from this example that the difference between weighted mean and expectation lies solely in the order of the operations required to obtain the result. It is sometimes more convenient to treat such a question as one in which the mean is to be calculated, while at other times the second order should be adopted. Thus, in the following questions, the expectation is most easily calculated by introducing the chances of success and failure.

Example 4.

A player throwing an ordinary die is to receive $£(1/2^n)$, where n is the number of throws that he takes to throw the first 6. Find his expectation.

His expectation

$$= \frac{1}{6} £ \frac{1}{2} + \frac{5}{6} \cdot \frac{1}{6} £ \frac{1}{2^2} + \frac{5}{6} \cdot \frac{5}{6} \cdot \frac{1}{6} £ \frac{1}{2^3} + \dots + \left(\frac{5}{6}\right)^r \cdot \frac{1}{6} £ \frac{1}{2^{r+1}} + \dots$$

$$= £ \left\{ \frac{1}{6} \cdot \frac{1}{2} \left(1 - \frac{5}{6} \cdot \frac{1}{2} \right)^{-1} \right\}$$

$$= £ \left\{ \frac{1}{12} \cdot \frac{12}{7} \right\} = £ \frac{1}{7}.$$

Example 5.

A table is divided into six squares numbered 1 to 6. A player places a coin on a certain square. Three dice are thrown. If the number thus backed appears once, twice or thrice, the player receives back his own coin together with one, two or three others respectively of the same value. In any other event he loses his stake. Does the advantage in the long run lie with the player or the "banker"?

(a) The chance that no die shows the number backed $= (\frac{5}{6})^3$.

(b)   ,,   one die shows   ,, $= 3 (\frac{5}{6})^2 \frac{1}{6}$.

(c)   ,,   two dice show   ,, $= 3 \frac{5}{6} (\frac{1}{6})^2$.

(d)   ,,   three dice show   ,, $= (\frac{1}{6})^3$.

The net expectation of the player

$$= (b) + 2 (c) + 3 (d) - (a) = -\tfrac{17}{216},$$

and that of the banker

$$= -(b) - 2 (c) - 3 (d) + (a) = \tfrac{17}{216},$$

so that the advantage lies with the banker in the long run.

For a stake of a shilling it is easily seen that this advantage is just under a penny.

Here it might be contended that as the player is to receive back his own coin in addition to the prize, his expectation should be based on respective receipts of two, three or four units instead of one, two or three units, as appears in the above solution. His expectation on this basis might be argued as being $2 (b) + 3 (c) + 4 (d) - (a)$ or $\tfrac{74}{216}$, which would show a substantial advantage to the player. Further consideration would show, however, that if the return of the stake is treated as a *profit*, then the laying of the stake must be treated as a *payment* to the banker for the privilege of playing and that it is, accordingly, definitely paid away whether the player wins or loses. His expectation then becomes $2\,(b)+3\,(c)+4\,(d)-1 = -\frac{17}{216}$ as before.

11. In connection with mathematical expectation it is interesting to note the celebrated St Petersburg problem, which has been a fruitful source of discussion for nearly two hundred years. Briefly stated, the problem is this: A coin is tossed until head turns up. If head turns up first A is to pay B one unit; if head does not turn up till the second throw B is to receive two units; if not until the third throw four units, and so on. How much must B pay A before the game, in order that the game may be considered fair? That is, what is B's expectation?

The theoretical solution is this:

At the first trial B's expectation is $\quad\frac{1}{2}\times 1 \quad =\frac{1}{2}.$

,, second ,, ,, $(\frac{1}{2})^2\times 2 \quad =\frac{1}{2}.$

....

,, nth ,, ,, $(\frac{1}{2})^n\times 2^{n-1}=\frac{1}{2}.$

B's expectation is therefore $\frac{1}{2}+\frac{1}{2}+\frac{1}{2}+$ ... to infinity, and as this is a divergent series, it appears that B could afford to pay an infinitely large sum before the game starts for his expectation.

Many explanations of this result have been given by eminent mathematicians, notably by d'Alembert, Bernouilli and de Morgan. An interesting account of the problem with an alternative solution depending upon the amount of money that B possesses at the outset is given by Whitworth in his *Choice and Chance*. This solution depends on a somewhat arbitrary assumption, and a more practical limitation of B's expectation arises from the fact that A's resources, however great, must be limited. Poincaré (*Calcul des Probabilités*, p. 42) shows that if A's total assets are 2^p, B's expectation is $1 + \frac{1}{2}p$. For example, if A possesses 2^{30} —which is more than a thousand millions—B's expectation is reduced from infinity to 16, and as Poincaré drily remarks, this is a considerable reduction!

12. It is essential to distinguish between the absolute probability of an event, the average number of times that it may happen over a series of trials and the most probable number of times that it will occur. The *most probable value* (or mode, in a statistical distribution) is the value that occurs with greatest frequency, and in simple examples this value can be easily determined by considering separately the contingency of each event. Thus in a single throw with two dice the numbers that may turn up and the chances of occurrence of these throws are given in the following table:

Possible numbers: 2 3 4 5 6 7 8 9 10 11 12

Chances of occurrence: 1 2 3 4 5 6 5 4 3 2 1 ($\div$36)

The most probable number to be thrown is therefore 7.

Again, in Example 7 on p. 272, a hasty conclusion would be that half the pack (i.e. 26 cards) would have to be turned up before two aces out of the four would appear. This is not so, however. The four aces divide the remaining 48 cards into 5 groups. If a large number of such divisions were made the average number in each of the 5 groups would be $\frac{48}{5}$. The average number of cards which must be turned up before two aces appear is therefore 2 of these groups plus 2 aces, i.e. $\frac{96}{5}+2$ or 21·2, as on p. 272. The solution there given shows that 26 is neither the average number nor the most probable number, and, further, that there is a definite probability associated with each number of cards turned up. At the risk of labouring the point, it must be emphasized that these separate probabilities are only to be realized over a long series of trials.

Example 6.

A purse contains two half-crowns and three shillings; a second purse one half-crown and four shillings. A coin is drawn from the first and placed in the second, and then a coin is drawn from the second and placed in the first. Assuming that the chance of drawing a half-crown is twice that of drawing a shilling, find the most probable value of the coins in the first purse after the second operation.

At the end of the second operation the first purse may contain:

    (i) 2 half-crowns and 3 shillings; or

    (ii) 3   ,,   ,, 2   ,,   ,,

    (iii) 1 half-crown ,, 4   ,,

The respective chances are found thus:

(i) In order to achieve this result, a coin of the same value must be taken from the second purse at the second draw as was placed in this purse as the result of the first draw.

Since the chance of drawing a half-crown is twice that of drawing a shilling, the chance that a half-crown is drawn from the first purse originally is $\frac{4}{7}$. The second purse will then contain 2 half-crowns and 4 shillings, and the chance of drawing a half-crown from this purse is $\frac{4}{8}$. The total chance that a half-crown is drawn on both occasions is therefore $\frac{4}{7} \cdot \frac{4}{8}$!

Similarly, the chance that a shilling is drawn both times is $\frac{3}{7} \cdot \frac{5}{7}$.

The total chance that the coins in the first purse have the same value at the end of the two operations is therefore

$$\tfrac{4}{7} \cdot \tfrac{4}{8} + \tfrac{3}{7} \cdot \tfrac{5}{7} = \tfrac{29}{49}.$$

By proceeding similarly, it can easily be shown that the respective chances under headings (ii) and (iii) are $\frac{6}{49}$ and $\frac{2}{7}$.

The greatest of these values is $\frac{29}{49}$.

The most probable value of the purse after the second draw is the value associated with this fraction, namely 8 shillings.

Note that the probable value of the coins in the purse at the end of the second operation (i.e. the expectation of a person drawing the coins) is

$$[(\tfrac{29}{49} \times 8) + (\tfrac{6}{49} \times 9\tfrac{1}{2}) + (\tfrac{2}{7} \times 6\tfrac{1}{2})] \text{ shillings, or } 7\tfrac{37}{49} \text{ shillings.}$$

In other words, it would be worth while to give about 7s. 9d. for the purse after the second draw.

Example 7.

Cards are dealt one by one from an ordinary pack (without replacements) until two aces have appeared. Find (i) how many cards (on the average) will be turned up, (ii) the most probable number of cards to be turned up.

(i) Since two aces cannot appear until the second trial at the earliest, we have

Chance of success at the second trial $= \frac{4}{52} \cdot \frac{3}{51}$

,, ,, third ,, $= 2 \cdot \frac{48}{52} \cdot \frac{4}{51} \cdot \frac{3}{50}$

,, ,, fourth ,, $= 3 \cdot \frac{48}{52} \cdot \frac{47}{51} \cdot \frac{4}{50} \cdot \frac{3}{49}$

...................................,

and generally

Chance of success at the xth trial $= \dfrac{(x-1)(52-x)(51-x) \cdot 4 \cdot 3}{52 \cdot 51 \cdot 50 \cdot 49}$.

The average number of cards to be turned up will be the sum of the series whose xth term is

$$x \left\{ (x-1)(52-x)(51-x) \frac{4 \cdot 3}{52 \cdot 51 \cdot 50 \cdot 49} \right\}$$

for all values of x from 2 to 50 (since there must be two aces at least in the first 50 cards).

Summing this by ordinary algebraic or finite difference methods, it is found that the average number of cards to be turned up is 21·2.

(ii) The most probable number to be turned up will be the value of x which gives

$$\frac{(x-1)(52-x)(51-x)\,4.3}{52.51.50.49}$$

its greatest value.

The value for $x=r>$ the value for $x=r-1$ so long as

$$(r-1)(52-r)(51-r)>(r-2)(53-r)(52-r),$$

i.e. so long as $\qquad -r^2+52r-51>-r^2+55r-106,$

i.e. so long as $\qquad\qquad 55>3r,$

i.e. r is not greater than 18 (since r must be integral).

The most probable number of cards to be turned up is therefore 18.

EXAMPLES 11

1. Find the mean age of the persons in the following table:

Exact age	20	21	22	23	24	25	26	27	28	29	30
Number of persons	43	68	120	150	150	130	80	90	95	81	70

2. Calculate the mean and median in respect of the following distribution:

Length in inches	No. of cases	Length in inches	No. of cases
57–58	2	65–66	641
58–59	4	66–67	532
59–60	50	67–68	316
60–61	100	68–69	124
61–62	169	69–70	72
62–63	543	70–71	20
63–64	762	71–72	5
64–65	750	72–73	1

3. The infant mortality rates for a certain year in the aggregates of the urban districts of the 61 administrative counties of England and Wales were as follows:

30, 101, 100, 53, 57, 72, 87, 48, 63, 70, 49, 58, 79, 94, 50, 98, 69, 56, 100, 55, 71, 84, 71, 95, 114, 85, 61, 108, 64, 76, 99, 63, 68, 97, 80, 68,

90, 75, 65, 111, 90, 66, 65, 85, 84, 82, 96, 99, 67, 71, 71, 91, 102, 80, 89, 113, 74, 87, 79, 88, 73.

Discuss methods of setting out more clearly the information conveyed by these figures. Plot a frequency diagram and determine graphically the mode.

4. The following table shows the marks obtained by 100 candidates in an examination. Calculate the mean number of marks, and ascertain as accurately as you can the position of the median:

Marks obtained	Number of candidates
1-5	1
6-10	2
11-15	6
16-20	10
21-25	11
26-30	15
31-35	16
36-40	15
41-45	9
46-50	7
51-55	4
56-60	3
61-65	1
	100

5. Estimate the mode from the data in Question 4.

How would your estimate be affected if you were given in addition the following information?

Marks obtained	Number of candidates
25	3
26	2
27	1
28	6
29	3
30	3
31	4
32	4

6. Find, by drawing a frequency curve, the approximate values of the median and mode from the given data:

Value	·5	1·5	2·5	3·5	4·5	5·5	6·5	7·5	8·5	9·5	10·5	11·5
Frequency	11	17	26	38	56	83	120	163	196	181	93	16

How would you check your results?

7. The following are the death rates per thousand per annum of two towns in a certain year:

Ages	Town A			Town B		
	Population	Deaths	Death rate per thousand	Population	Deaths	Death rate per thousand
0–2	3,000	192	64·0	5,000	300	60·0
2–10	10,000	70	7·0	12,000	78	6·5
10–20	10,000	40	4·0	10,000	38	3·8
20–60	32,500	260	8·0	25,000	190	7·6
60 +	8,500	510	60·0	8,000	460	57·5
All	64,000	1072	16·75	60,000	1066	17·77

In each group the death rate of Town A is greater than that of Town B, but the reverse is the case when all ages are grouped together. Explain clearly why this is.

8. The exports of a certain country during a period of 22 years were as follows, in millions:

Year	Exports	Year	Exports	Year	Exports
1904	200	1912	205	1919	207
1905	198	1913	205	1920	208
1906	197	1914	202	1921	200
1907	201	1915	199	1922	195
1908	202	1916	195	1923	193
1909	200	1917	197	1924	200
1910	195	1918	203	1925	208
1911	199	—	—	—	—

A writes to the paper to point out that trade is diminishing and gives the following figures:

Average exports	1909–11	£198
	1915–17	£197
	1921–23	£196

B replies that it is increasing, and gives the following figures:

Average exports	1906–8	£200
	1912–14	£204
	1918–20	£206

Write a short letter commenting upon the letters and pointing out the true significance of the figures.

9. What is the difference, if any, between *weighted mean* and *expectation*? Illustrate your answer by an example.

10. Define carefully *probable value* and *most probable value*.

A purse contains four half-crowns, three pennies and two shillings. Four coins are drawn at random. How many different sums can these amount to, and what is the most probable sum? (Assume that any one coin is as likely to be drawn as any other.)

11. A coin is tossed until both head and tail have appeared twice.

 (1) On the average how many times will the coin have to be tossed?

 (2) What is the most likely number of throws?

 (3) How many throws must a man be allowed if the odds in favour of success are to be 7 : 1?

12. Two persons throw an ordinary die alternately, and the first who throws 6 is to receive eleven shillings; find their expectations.

13. There are eleven tickets in a bag numbered 1, 2, 3, ... 11. A man draws two tickets together at random and is to receive a number of shillings equal to the product of the numbers he draws; find the value of his expectation.

14. A bag contains eighteen exactly similar counters. Ten counters are each of value *a*, four are each of value *b* and the remaining four are each of value 2*b*. A man draws two counters at random. It is equally likely that any counter will be drawn. Find the ratio of *a* to *b*, if the value of the man's expectation is to be 4*a*/3.

15. Each of two bags contains *m* sovereigns and *n* shillings. If a man draws a coin out of each bag, is he more or less likely to draw two sovereigns than if all the coins were in one bag and he drew two coins?

16. Purse A contains six shillings and two sovereigns, purse B seven shillings and one sovereign. Seven coins are transferred from A to B and then seven coins are transferred from B to A. Which purse is now likely to be the more valuable?

17. A bag contains thirteen counters marked with the squares of the first thirteen natural numbers respectively.

(1) A man draws a counter and is to receive the number of shillings equivalent to the number on the counter. Find his expectation.

(2) If the man is allowed to draw three counters and to reject the highest and lowest, find his expectation.

18. A purse contains five half-crowns and four shillings. A pays 5s. 3d. for the right to receive the value of three coins drawn at random. Criticize his bargain, and find the chance that, after two attempts, the second on the same terms as the first, he will be a winner.

19. A bag contains m white balls and two red balls. The balls are drawn from the bag one at a time without being replaced until a red ball is drawn. If 1, 2, 3, ... white balls are drawn, A is to receive $1^2, 2^2, 3^2, ...$ shillings respectively. Find his expectation.

20. A bag contains twenty shillings and three sovereigns. Coins are drawn in succession, one at a time, without being replaced, until two sovereigns have been drawn. What is the probable number of shillings left in the bag?

21. There are ten counters in a bag marked with consecutive numbers. Two counters are drawn from the bag. If the sum of the numbers drawn is odd, a man is to receive that number of shillings; if it is even, he is to pay that number of shillings. Find the man's expectation

(1) if the counters are marked from 0 to 9;

(2) if they are marked from 1 to 10;

(3) if they are marked from 2 to 11.

22. A bag contains a coin of value M, and a number of other coins whose aggregate value is m. A person draws one at a time till he draws the coin of value M. Assuming it is equally likely that any particular coin is drawn, find the value of his expectation.

23. A bag contains twenty white balls numbered 1 to 20 and ten unnumbered red balls. A ball is drawn at random and replaced, six times. Find the probability that

(1) at least three white balls are drawn;

(2) three white and three red balls are drawn;

(3) three red balls and Nos. 1, 2, 3 of the white balls are drawn.

What is the most probable number of white balls drawn, and what is the probability that this number is drawn?

24. A man throws a six-faced die until he gets an ace. He is to receive £1 if he succeeds at the first throw, 10s. if he succeeds at the second throw, 6s. 8d. if he succeeds at the third throw and so on.

Given
$$\log 2 = \cdot 3010300,$$
$$\log 3 = \cdot 4771213,$$
$$\log 2 \cdot 718282 = \cdot 4342945,$$

find the value of his expectation to the nearest penny.

25. *A* and *B* have each two ordinary cubical dice, the faces being numbered from 1 to 6 on each die. They throw simultaneously until the whole of a stake of £100 has been divided on the following conditions:

   (i) If *A* throws 7 before *B* has thrown 2, *A* is to take the balance of the stake then remaining.

   (ii) If *B* throws 2 before *A* has thrown 7, *B* is to take the balance of the stake then remaining.

   (iii) If simultaneously *A* throws 7 and *B* throws 2 the balance then remaining is to be divided equally between *A* and *B*.

   (iv) If at the *n*th throw neither 7 nor 2 has yet been thrown by *A* or *B* respectively, *B* is to take $1/n$ of the balance then remaining, except that this additional benefit to *B* does not operate at the first throw.

Find to the nearest penny the respective expectations of *A* and *B*.
Given $\log 6 = \cdot 7781513$, $\log 41 = 1 \cdot 6127839$, $\log e = \cdot 4342945$.

CHAPTER XII

FURTHER PROPOSITIONS IN STATISTICS

1. In the preceding chapter we have defined three different averages of a distribution, and any one of these three averages may be used to typify the whole distribution. Thus, the *mean* gives an indication of the magnitude of the variates, the *median* tells us the position of the middle variate and the *mode* gives us the most frequent value. But these averages tell us very little about the distribution itself. For example, if the sums assured under whole-life policies were in question and we were given a random sample of 100 such policies, the mean of the sums assured might be £276, the median £265 and the mode £250. From the mean, all that we could gather would be that the average sum assured was £276 out of a total of £27,600; from the median that there were as many policies with sums assured less than £265 as there were policies with sums assured greater than this amount; and from the mode that there were more policies for £250 than for any other individual amount. What we require to know in addition is the extent to which the individual sums assured vary from the particular average. The statistical term for this variation is the *dispersion* of the group.

2. The range.

The range of the distribution—i.e. the difference between the extreme variates—is a simple measure of dispersion. It would help us to some extent if we knew that in the example above the lowest sum assured was £100 and the highest £500; we should then know that the range was £400. This measure is however not of very much value, for it would not add appreciably to our knowledge of the distribution if it happened that there was only one policy for £100 and only one for £500. Another sample which gave the same figures for the three averages might well have a smaller range, say from £150 to £450, notwithstanding that the most important frequencies, at the centre of the sample, were not very different from those at the centre of the first distribution. It is essential therefore that a more accurate and stable measure of dispersion be chosen. The range does not depend upon all the variates and the measure that is likely to be most useful is one which, as far as possible, does satisfy this condition.

3. Mean deviation.

If any particular average were taken and the deviations of the variates from this average were set down, it is obvious that the signs of some of the deviations would be positive and others negative. It might happen therefore that the sums of the deviations would be a small positive or negative quantity, or, in certain cases, zero, notwithstanding that the individual deviations were considerable. Consequently, if regard were had to sign, the algebraic sum of the deviations of the variates from, say, the mean would be of very little help as a measure of dispersion. As a result, in finding the total deviations from an average we ignore the signs of the individual deviations and treat them all as positive. We can then find the *mean deviation*, irrespective of sign.

The mean is the average which lends itself most easily to arithmetical and algebraic treatment, and, as a rule, the mean is chosen as the origin from which to calculate the mean deviation. The mean deviation may, however, be found from any arbitrary origin. The following example gives a simple method for the calculation of the mean deviation from the median.

Example 1.

Calculate the mean deviation from the median of the distribution in Example 1 of Chapter XI.

The median is 59·8 years. Take the same origin as before (57·5) and assume that all the variates are concentrated at the mid-point of the group in which they lie. (See Note on p. 281.)

$M_i - a = 59 \cdot 8 - 57 \cdot 5 = 2 \cdot 3$ years $= \cdot 46$ class-intervals

Age	Frequency f	Deviation from the median in terms of class-interval δ as unit	$f\delta$
27·5	1	6·46	6·46
32·5	2	5·46	10·92
37·5	4	4·46	17·84
42·5	10	3·46	34·60
47·5	21	2·46	51·66
52·5	53	1·46	77·38
57·5	126	·46	57·96
62·5	163	·54	88·02
67·5	35	1·54	53·90
72·5	6	2·54	15·24
77·5	1	3·54	3·54
	422		417·52

Mean deviation from the median $= \dfrac{417 \cdot 52}{422} = \cdot 9894 \ldots$ class-intervals

$$= 4 \cdot 95 \ldots \text{ years.}$$

Note. Strictly speaking, the assumption that all the variates are concentrated at the mid-points of their respective groups should not be made for the group in which the origin lies. In this example, however, since the median is almost at one end of a group the result given above is virtually correct. The extreme cases arise when the mean deviation is required from the middle of a large group. In that event special treatment is necessary for this group.

4. Root-mean-square and standard deviations.

The difficulty that some deviations are positive and some negative would be obviated if the deviations were squared. Then, by summing the squares, dividing by the total number of observations, and taking the square root of the result, a form of mean deviation would be obtained which would be independent of the signs of the individual deviations. This measure of dispersion is called the *root-mean-square deviation*. We shall denote this by the abbreviation r.m.s. deviation.

If s be the r.m.s. deviation and δ_r the deviation of the frequency f_r from the origin, then $s = \{ \Sigma f_r \delta^2{}_r / \Sigma f_r \}^{\frac{1}{2}}$.

The r.m.s. deviation possesses all the qualities of a good measure of dispersion; it is based on all the data, it lends itself to algebraic treatment and, in general, it is less affected by fluctuations of sampling than other measures.

It has been shown that to calculate the mean without the use of a temporary origin may involve a considerable amount of arithmetic. This is even more marked in the case of the r.m.s. deviation. A formula similar to that obtained for the calculation of the mean from a temporary origin can, however, be found for the easier calculation of the r.m.s. deviation.

Let a be a temporary origin and d be the deviation of the mean M from this origin.

Let δ_r be the deviation of observation X_r from a so that

$$\delta_r = X_r - a = x_r + d,$$

where x_r is the deviation of X_r from the mean.

Then
$$f_r \delta_r^2 = f_r x_r^2 + 2f_r x_r d + f_r d^2,$$

$$\Sigma f_r \delta_r^2 = \Sigma f_r x_r^2 + 2d\Sigma f_r x_r + d^2 \Sigma f_r.$$

Now $\Sigma f_r x_r$ is the sum of the deviations, positive and negative, from the mean, and is therefore zero. (See paragraph 6.)

$$\therefore \qquad \Sigma f_r \delta_r^2 = \Sigma f_r x_r^2 + d^2 \Sigma f_r,$$

i.e.
$$\frac{\Sigma f_r \delta_r^2}{\Sigma f_r} = \frac{\Sigma f_r x_r^2}{\Sigma f_r} + d^2,$$

or
$$s^2 = \sigma^2 + d^2,$$

where
$$\sigma^2 \equiv \Sigma f_r x_r^2 / \Sigma f_r.$$

In order therefore to find s we may calculate the sum of the squares of the deviations from an arbitrary origin, so long as we know the deviation of the mean from that origin.

If now the mean is taken as the origin, then $d = 0$, and the r.m.s. deviation is a minimum. In these circumstances, the r.m.s. deviation is called the *standard deviation*. The standard deviation is the measure of dispersion that is most commonly used in statistical investigations, and supersedes for all practical purposes the r.m.s. deviation, which depends on an arbitrary origin.

The recognized abbreviation for the standard deviation is s.d. and its value is generally represented by σ.

Example 2.

Calculate the standard deviation of the distribution in Example 1. The method of calculation is as follows:

Age	Frequency f	Deviation from mean δ	$f\delta$	$f\delta^2$
27·5	1	−6	− 6	36
32·5	2	−5	− 10	50
37·5	4	−4	− 16	64
42·5	10	−3	− 30	90
47·5	21	−2	− 42	84
52·5	53	−1	− 53	53
57·5	126	0	−157	
62·5	163	+1	+ 163	163
67·5	35	+2	+ 70	140
72·5	6	+3	+ 18	54
77·5	1	+4	+ 4	16
	422		+255	750

$$\Sigma f_r \delta_r^2 = 750 \text{ and } \Sigma f_r = 422.$$

Therefore
$$s^2 = 750/422 = 1\cdot777,$$

$$d = \Sigma f_r \delta_r / \Sigma f_r = (255 - 157)/422 = \cdot 232.$$

$\therefore$
$$\sigma^2 = s^2 - d^2 = 1\cdot777 - \cdot054 = 1\cdot723$$

and
$$\sigma = 1\cdot31 \text{ class-intervals}$$

$$= 6\cdot56 \text{ years.}$$

5. The standard deviation gives not only, as already explained, a general idea of the dispersion or spread of the observations, but also a definite numerical limit to the frequency of extreme cases, i.e. those in which the variate is much larger or much smaller than the mean.

We shall prove the following proposition:

In a set of measurements, $x_1, x_2 \ldots x_N$ whose mean is $\bar{x}$, let the s.d. be σ, so that

$$N\sigma^2 = \text{sum of squared deviations} = \Sigma\,(x_r - \bar{x})^2.$$

Then the proportion of cases in which $x - \bar{x}$ (the deviation from the mean) is numerically greater than $\lambda\sigma$ cannot exceed $1/\lambda^2$: i.e. there cannot be more than N/λ^2 cases in which x is either greater than $\bar{x} + \lambda\sigma$ or less than $\bar{x} - \lambda\sigma$.

Suppose that the actual proportion is p, so that there are pN such cases. In each of such cases the squared deviation $(x - \bar{x})^2$ is at least $(\lambda\sigma)^2$, so that the total squared deviations, arising from these cases, is at least $pN\lambda^2\sigma^2$. But this partial total cannot exceed the full total, $N\sigma^2$, derived from all the observations.

Therefore $\qquad\qquad pN\lambda^2\sigma^2 \not> N\sigma^2$

or $\qquad\qquad\qquad\qquad p \not> 1/\lambda^2.$

Thus, if σ is small the observations will be heaped up round the mean, and their "precision" is great; while if σ is large the observations will be widely spread, and their precision is small.

It may be added that in the common case of a frequency distribution (such as that of Example 2) which starts with small values, rises to much larger ones, and then falls to small ones, the actual value of p is usually much under the limit $1/\lambda^2$.

This proposition is a simple case of Tchebycheff's theorem. [Cf. W. F. Sheppard, *J.I.A.* vol. LIII, p. 82.]

6. It is a simple matter to prove that the weighted algebraic sum of the deviations of a variable quantity from the mean is zero.

For, if a be the origin, f_r the frequency of an observation X_r, then $\qquad M = \Sigma f_r X_r / \Sigma f_r$, so that $\Sigma f_r X_r = M \Sigma f_r$.

Also, if δ_r is the deviation of X_r from a,

$$\Sigma f_r X_r = \Sigma f_r\,(a + \delta_r), \quad \text{since } \delta_r = X_r - a,$$
$$= a\Sigma f_r + \Sigma f_r \delta_r,$$

i.e. $\qquad\qquad M\Sigma f_r = a\Sigma f_r + \Sigma f_r \delta_r$

and $\qquad\qquad M - a = \Sigma f_r \delta_r / \Sigma f_r.$

If therefore the mean be taken as the origin, $M = a$ and $\Sigma f_r \delta_r = 0$.

7. We have shown that the r.m.s. deviation is a minimum when measured from the mean. It is instructive to show that the mean deviation is a minimum when measured from the median.

Let the frequency distribution be $f_1, f_2, f_3, f_4, \ldots f_r, \ldots f_n$ with class-interval a, and let $\Sigma f_r = n$. We may illustrate the distribution graphically, thus:

Let d_1 be the mean deviation from the temporary origin X distant c ($< a$) from the beginning of the class range m to $m+1$.

Then $d_1 = \dfrac{1}{n} \{ f_m c + f_{m-1}(a+c) + f_{m-2}(2a+c) + \ldots + f_1(\overline{m-1}a+c)$

$$+ f_{m+1}(a-c) + f_{m+2}(2a-c) + \ldots + f_n(\overline{n-m}a+c) \}.$$

If now the origin is changed to m the mean deviation is d_2, where

$$d_2 = \frac{1}{n} \{ f_m 0 + f_{m-1}a + f_{m-2}2a + \ldots + f_1(\overline{m-1}a)$$

$$+ f_{m+1}a + f_{m+2}2a + \ldots + f_n(\overline{n-m}a) \}.$$

$$\therefore \ d_1 - d_2 = \frac{1}{n} \{ f_m c + f_{m-1}c + f_{m-2}c + \ldots + f_1 c$$

$$- (f_{m+1}c + f_{m+2}c + \ldots + f_n c) \}$$

$$= \frac{1}{n} \left\{ c\sum_1^m f_r - c \sum_{m+1}^n f_r \right\} = \frac{c}{n} \left\{ \sum_1^m f_r - \sum_1^n f_r + \sum_1^m f_r \right\}$$

$$= \frac{c}{n}(2M - n),$$

where $M = \sum_1^m f_r$.

$$\therefore \qquad d_2 = d_1 + \frac{c}{n}(n - 2M),$$

which $< d_1$ if $M > \frac{1}{2}n$, i.e. if the median lies to the left of f_m.

Therefore, if n is even, the mean deviation is constant for all positions of the origin between the $\frac{1}{2}n$th and ($\frac{1}{2}n+1$)th observations, and this value is the least value. If n is odd, d is least when the origin coincides with the $\frac{1}{2}(n+1)$th observation. That is, the mean deviation is least when measured from the median, or if the median is indeterminate, from an origin in the class range in which the median lies.

8. Semi-inter-quartile range.

We have seen that, in an array of variates, the observation which is such that as many observations lie on one side of it as on the other is a particular form of average, i.e., the median, which can be used to obtain a measure of dispersion. There are certain observations other than the median which divide the array and which may also be used to obtain such a measure. The observation which is such that one-quarter of all the observations lie below it in magnitude is called the *lower quartile*, while that observation which is such that one-quarter of all the observations lie above it is called the *upper quartile*. In the example on p. 255 the lower quartile is the height of the (hypothetical) man between the tenth and eleventh man, and is therefore 5 ft. 6 in., while the upper quartile is the height of the (hypothetical) man between the thirtieth and thirty-first man and is therefore 5 ft. 8 in.

The quartiles, like the median, can be estimated by first difference interpolation from frequency distributions, or from a consideration of the ogive curve, and the student will find it a useful exercise to obtain the quartiles from the examples given in this and the preceding chapter.

From the definitions given above we see that if Q_1 and Q_3 are the lower and upper quartiles respectively, one-half the total frequency lies between Q_1 and Q_3. This range, namely $Q_3 - Q_1$, is called the inter-quartile range, and it is an even chance therefore that an observation taken at random will lie within this range.

A simple measure of dispersion, and one which can be calculated with little difficulty, is the quartile deviation, Q, such that

$$Q = \tfrac{1}{2}(Q_3 - Q_1).$$

It is worthy of note that where the distribution is symmetrical, or nearly so, it is generally found that Q is approximately equal to $\tfrac{2}{3}\sigma$.

The quartile deviation is generally called the *semi-inter-quartile range* and is an approximate method of estimating the dispersion of a frequency distribution.

9. Relative measures of dispersion.

The measures of dispersion described in the previous paragraphs are all absolute and relate to the individual distributions only. In order to compare the dispersion between two different distributions we need a measure of relative dispersion. Thus, the mean of a sample of sums assured may be £317 and the standard deviation £10, while the mean of another sample may be \$620 and the standard deviation \$30. It does not follow, however, that the variability in the second case is greater than that in the first. We cannot compare the variability of the two distributions without eliminating the absolute values of the measures of dispersion. To obtain a relative value we express the particular measure of dispersion as a ratio of the average on which the dispersion is based. Thus, to compare two or more standard deviations we calculate the standard deviation as a percentage of the mean, and obtain thereby the *coefficient of variation*. If, therefore, σ is the standard deviation and M the mean, the coefficient is $100\sigma/M$ for each distribution.

The following is a simple example involving the use of the coefficient of variation.

Example 3.

In order to pass a certain examination candidates must obtain at least 40 marks. All successful candidates with less than 50 marks are placed in the third class. The distributions of those who passed in the third class in two successive years being given in the table below, find which was the more consistent set:

Marks	40	41	42	43	44	45	46	47	48	49
No. of successful candidates in the first year	1	—	5	10	4	1	4	5	—	—
No. of successful candidates in the second year	—	—	—	7	—	3	2	6	6	2

The more consistent set may be regarded as the one for which the coefficient of variation is the smaller. (See, however, Note below.)

No. of marks	First year				Second year			
	f	δ	$f\delta$	$f\delta^2$	f	δ	$f\delta$	$f\delta^2$
40	1	-3	-3	9	—	—	—	—
41	—	-2	0	0	—	—	—	—
42	5	-1	-5	5	—	—	—	—
43	10	0	-8	0	7	-4	-28	112
44	4	$+1$	$+4$	4	—	-3	0	0
45	1	$+2$	$+2$	4	3	-2	-6	12
46	4	$+3$	$+12$	36	2	-1	-2	2
47	5	$+4$	$+20$	80	6	0	-36	0
48	—	—	—	—	6	$+1$	$+6$	6
49	—	—	—	—	2	$+2$	$+4$	8
—	—	—	$+38$	—	—	—	$+10$	—
	30	—	30	138	26	—	-26	140

First year: $M = 43 + 30/30 = 44$,

$$\sigma = \sqrt{138/30 - 1} = \sqrt{108/30} = \sqrt{3\cdot6} = 1\cdot897.$$

Coefficient of variation $= 189\cdot7/44 = 4\cdot36$.

Second year: $M = 47 - 26/26 = 46$,

$$\sigma = \sqrt{140/26 - 1} = \sqrt{114/26} = \sqrt{4\cdot3846} = 2\cdot094.$$

Coefficient of variation $= 209\cdot4/46 = 4\cdot47$.

The second coefficient of variation is larger than the first, so that the more consistent set was that in the first year.

Note. Care should be taken in using the coefficient of variation as a measure of consistency. It might not be safe to use it if, for example, given two sets of frequencies, Σf_r and $\Sigma \phi_r$, $f_r = \phi_r + $a constant, for all values of r.

10. Corresponding relative measures for other absolute measures may be formed by dividing by the corresponding averages. The mean deviation $\Sigma (X_r - M_i)/n$ gives a relative measure of $\Sigma (X_r - M_i)/nM_i$, while the coefficient of variation for the quartile deviation may be taken as $\frac{1}{2}(Q_3 - Q_1)/(Q_3 + Q_1)$.

*11. Standard error and probable error.

Before the characteristics of different distributions can be compared by means of calculated statistical measures, certain considerations must be borne in mind. One distribution may be a random sample drawn from a large parent population, and it is to be expected that another sample of the same size would produce results conforming to those of the first sample and of the parent population, were they available. The results may, however, differ. In that case we must find the degree to which they are reliable, or alternatively, to what extent the observed differences arise simply from errors of sampling and errors of chance. Consider, for simplicity, the value of the mean calculated from a sample. This value is one of a distribution of means calculated from all possible samples of the same size, which lie on a frequency curve of which the s.d. is found to be $\sigma'/\sqrt{n}$, where σ' is the s.d. of all the observations in the parent population and n is the number of observations in the sample. In practice σ' is not known, and as an approximation we use σ, the s.d. derived from the sample. In this case, $\sigma/\sqrt{n}$ is known as the *standard error* of the mean.

For reasons connected with the normal curve of error (see p. 290) the *standard error* is often multiplied by ·6745 to produce the *probable error*.

We may explain the use of the probable error in the following manner.

If two values of a variable x (say a and b) are given and it is required to find the chance that a value of the variable selected at random lies between these limits we may construct a distribution curve of unit area, and this curve will be such that the area between the ordinates a and b represents the chance required. Distribution curves may be constructed either from data given for a question in mathematical probability or from statistical data obtained from the results of a series of observations. We may take, for example, the binomial curve. A simple conception of this curve results from calculating by the mathematical definitions the number of heads that turn up when m coins are tossed. The relative frequencies are given by the successive terms of the binomial series $(\frac{1}{2}+\frac{1}{2})^m$, and by plotting the relative frequencies against the number of heads we obtain a bell-shaped curve symmetrical about the mean. When m is very large it can be shown that this curve approximates to a curve known as the *normal curve of error*.

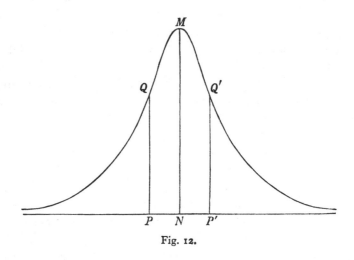

Fig. 12.

In Fig. 12, which is in the form of the normal curve of error, NM is the ordinate through the mean of the means. PQ and $P'Q'$ are the ordinates through points at distances from N such that PN and $P'N$ are equal to the probable error of the means. Then it may be shown that the area of the curve cut off by PQ, $P'Q'$ and PP' is half the total area. Ordinates drawn through distances from N equal to twice the probable error would include most of the curve, while ordinates through three times this distance would include practically the whole curve.

As a result of this property of the normal curve it is usual in practice to say that it is improbable that a statistical measure calculated from a sample will differ from the value which would be obtained from the parent population by more than three times the probable error. Thus, if the difference between two calculated means exceeds three times the probable error of the difference, it

STATISTICS AND PROBABILITY

is assumed that this difference is unlikely to have arisen from errors of sampling, but is due to intrinsic differences in the two samples. The difference is then said to be significant.

12. We have already seen that the calculation of mathematical expectation can be reduced to the determination of the weighted *mean*. Also, if we have to find the value which occurs with the greatest frequency from a consideration of ideal objects—the most probable value—we have a parallel in the *mode* of a statistical distribution. Further, deviations from the mean in a statistical question correspond to deviations from the expectation in a problem in probability.

This parallelism may be extended. Equally likely events have their counterpart in equally likely intervals or ranges. Just as equally likely events are rare in practice, so ranges are seldom equally likely. For example, a simple question in mathematical probability is: "Two clerks are in an office: one goes to lunch between 12 and 1 and the other between 1 and 2. Each takes an hour for lunch. Find the chance that they are not out at the same time." Unless it be assumed that all times between the given limits are equally likely, the problem cannot be solved as it stands. But it can hardly be doubted that, in practice, all such times would not be equally likely—for a variety of reasons. Similarly, in statistical problems there will be certain intervals or ranges which are much more likely to occur than others. Consider, for instance, the case of a lamp filament. The resistance of such a filament cannot be forecast with certainty, and if the resistance is to be, say, 300 ohms, it is more probable that the resistance of a filament made for this purpose will lie between 300 and 310 ohms than between 390 and 400 ohms. Again, the average height of the men in a given community is 5 ft. 7 in. A man chosen at random from the community is more likely to be between 5 ft. 6 in. and 5 ft. 7 in. than between 6 ft. 1 in. and 6 ft. 2 in. Many such examples occur in statistical problems.

19-2

EXAMPLES 12

1. The following table shows the proportion of male births per 1000 births in a certain community. Find the mean and standard deviation of the distribution:

Number of male births per 1000 births	Number of cases
465–	2
477–	6
489–	43
501–	399
513–	176
525–	9
537–	2

2. Calculate the mean age, the median age and standard deviation in terms of year of age from the following data:

Age-group	Number of cases
5–	20
10–	300
15–	860
20–	435
25–	230
30–	150
35–	70
40–	60
45–	35
50–	20
55–	10
60–	7
65–	3

3. Find the values of the upper and lower quartiles.

Value	·5	1·5	2·5	3·5	4·5	5·5	6·5	7·5	8·5	9·5	10·5	11·5
Frequency	22	34	52	76	112	166	240	326	392	362	186	32

4. Estimate roughly the mean wage from the following data:

Median 37s., Quartiles 29·5s. and 40·5s. 6 per cent. of the observations are less than 20s. per week and 3 per cent. are 45s. per week or more.

5. Illustrate by a diagram the following distribution:

Length in in.	0–	1–	2–	3–	4–	5–	6–	7–	8–	9–	10–	11–
No. of cases	1	1·5	2·5	4	5·5	8·5	12	16	20	18	9·5	1·5

Estimate the mode, median and upper and lower quartiles. Calculate the mean, and check approximately the relative values of the mean, mode and median.

6. If in a series of measurements we obtain m_1 values of magnitude x_1, m_2 of magnitude x_2, and so on, and if x is the mean value of all the measurements, prove that the standard deviation is

$$\sqrt{\frac{\Sigma m_r (k - x_r)^2}{\Sigma m_r} - \delta^2},$$

where $x = k + \delta$.

Taking k as 200 apply this formula to obtain the standard deviation of the exports given in the adjoining table:

Year	Exports in £ (millions)	Year	Exports in £ (millions)	Year	Exports in £ (millions)
1904	200	1912	205	1919	207
1905	198	1913	205	1920	208
1906	197	1914	202	1921	200
1907	201	1915	199	1922	195
1908	202	1916	195	1923	193
1909	200	1917	197	1924	200
1910	195	1918	203	1925	208
1911	199				

*7. Given the following statistics, find the probable error of the mean:

Height of man	No. of cases	Height of man	No. of cases
5 ft. 3 in.	2	5 ft. 9 in.	16
5 4	2	5 10	16
5 5	2	5 11	14
5 6	5	6 0	7
5 7	12	6 1	2
5 8	19	6 2	3

What use is made of the probable error? If you measured another body of men and found that the mean height was 5 ft. 7 in., with nearly the same probable error, what conclusion would you draw?

**8. Find the probable error of the mean:

Age-group	Number of cases
15-	5
20-	83
25-	157
30-	162
35-	147
40-	125
45-	105
50-	80
55-	55
60-	40
65-	22
70-	14
75-	4
80-	1

9. Find the average wage, the median and the standard deviation of the following distribution:

Weekly wage	32s. 6d.	37s. 6d.	42s. 6d.	47s. 6d.
Number of cases	4	3	6	10
Weekly wage	52s. 6d.	57s. 6d.	62s. 6d.	67s. 6d.
Number of cases	12	16	13	11
Weekly wage	72s. 6d.	77s. 6d.	82s. 6d.	87s. 6d.
Number of cases	8	8	4	3
Weekly wage	92s. 6d.	97s. 6d.	102s. 6d.	
Number of cases	1	0	1	

10. The scores of two golfers for 24 rounds each are

A 74, 75, 78, 78, 72, 77, 79, 78, 81, 76, 72, 72, 77, 74, 70, 78, 79, 80, 81, 74, 80, 75, 71, 73.

B 86, 84, 80, 88, 89, 85, 86, 82, 82, 79, 86, 80, 82, 76, 86, 89, 87, 83, 80, 88, 86, 81, 84, 87.

Which may be regarded as the more consistent player?

11. A sample of the numbers of persons engaged in a certain occupation is as follows:

Age last birthday	Number
14 and 15	13
16 and 17	35
18 and 19	41
20–	108
25–	176
35–	204
45–	190
55–	65
60–	39
65–	21
70 and over	12

Find the standard deviation.

12. What is meant by the term "Coefficient of Variation"?

During the first 20 weeks of a session the marks of two students taking the course were

X 58, 59, 60, 54, 65, 66, 52, 75, 69, 52, 65, 66, 56, 42, 67, 30, 50, 60, 46, 48.

Y 56, 87, 89, 78, 71, 73, 84, 65, 66, 46, 84, 56, 92, 65, 86, 78, 44, 54, 78, 68.

Which would you consider was the more consistent?

CHAPTER XIII

MEAN VALUE. THE APPLICATION OF THE CALCULUS TO THE SOLUTION OF QUESTIONS IN PROBABILITY

1. It has already been seen that the mean of a number of quantities is simply the arithmetic average, weighted if need be. Thus, if there are n quantities $\phi(a)$, $\phi(a+h_1)$, $\phi(a+h_2)$, ... $\phi(a+h_{n-1})$, then the mean value is

$$\frac{\phi(a)+\phi(a+h_1)+\phi(a+h_2)+...+\phi(a+h_{n-1})}{n}.$$

Suppose that $y=\phi(x)$ is a function of x, and that x has the n successive values a, $a+h$, $a+2h$, ... $a+(n-1)h$. Then the mean value of $\phi(x)$ for these n values from $x=a$ to $x=a+(n-1)h$ is, as above,

$$\frac{\phi(a)+\phi(a+h)+\phi(a+2h)+...+\phi(a+\overline{n-1}h)}{n}.$$

Let $b=a+nh$ so that $nh=b-a$.

Then the mean value $=\dfrac{n}{nh}\overset{r=n-1}{\underset{r=0}{\Sigma}}\phi(a+rh)$

$$=\frac{h}{b-a}\overset{r=n-1}{\underset{r=0}{\Sigma}}\phi(a+rh).$$

If x varies continuously between a and b so that the number of values, n, tends to infinity, the mean value becomes

$$\underset{n\to\infty}{\text{Lt}}\frac{h[\phi(a)+\phi(a+h)+...+\phi(a+\overline{n-1}h)]}{b-a}$$

$$=\frac{1}{b-a}\int_a^b\phi(x)\,dx.$$

It should be noted that, where the function is continuous, the mean value depends on the law governing the selected values. For example, the mean value of the ordinate of a semicircle determined by ordinates passing through equidistant points along the diameter is different from the mean value determined by taking equidistant points along the circumference. It thus appears that the mean value of a continuous function $\phi(x)$ is not a definite quantity but a quantity varying according to the law assumed for the successive values of x.

This point is illustrated in Example 3.

2. This application of the integral calculus enables us to solve many problems involving mean values. The solution of these problems can generally be effected by the use of single integrals, although some of the more difficult questions necessitate the use of double integration. The three following examples illustrate the use of single integrals and, as will be seen, the solutions present little difficulty.

Example 1.

Find (i) the mean value of the ordinate, (ii) the mean value of the square of the ordinate of the curve $y = a \sin nx$ for the range $x = 0$ to $x = \dfrac{\pi}{n}$.

(i) We have to find the sum of the ordinates over the given range divided by the number of ordinates. Since the number of these ordinates will tend to infinity as the distance between them tends to zero, we shall have

$$\text{M.V.} = \frac{\displaystyle\int_0^{\frac{\pi}{n}} y\,dx}{\displaystyle\int_0^{\frac{\pi}{n}} dx} = \frac{\displaystyle\int_0^{\frac{\pi}{n}} a \sin nx\,dx}{\displaystyle\int_0^{\frac{\pi}{n}} dx}$$

$$= \frac{\left[-\dfrac{a}{n} \cos nx \right]_0^{\frac{\pi}{n}}}{\left[x \right]_0^{\frac{\pi}{n}}}$$

$$= \frac{-\dfrac{a}{n} \cos \pi + \dfrac{a}{n} \cos 0}{\dfrac{\pi}{n}}$$

$$= \frac{-\dfrac{a}{n}(-1) + \dfrac{a}{n}}{\dfrac{\pi}{n}}, \text{ since } \cos \pi = -1$$

$$= \frac{2a}{\pi}.$$

(ii) Similarly

$$\text{M.V.} = \frac{\int_0^{\frac{\pi}{n}} a^2 \sin^2 nx \, dx}{\int_0^{\frac{\pi}{n}} dx}$$

$$= \frac{\int_0^{\frac{\pi}{n}} a^2 \tfrac{1}{2} (1 - \cos 2nx) \, dx}{\dfrac{\pi}{n}}$$

$$= \frac{\left[\tfrac{1}{2} a^2 x - \tfrac{1}{2} a^2 \dfrac{1}{2n} \sin 2nx \right]_0^{\frac{\pi}{n}}}{\dfrac{\pi}{n}}$$

$$= a^2 \frac{\pi}{2n} \bigg/ \frac{\pi}{n} = \tfrac{1}{2} a^2.$$

Example 2.

A straight line of length a is divided at random into two parts. Find the mean value of the rectangle contained by the two parts.

Let x be the length of one part; then $a - x$ is the length of the other part. The rectangle contained by the two parts is $x(a - x)$, and we have to integrate this function with respect to x. Also, since x may have any value from o to a, these values will be the limits of integration.

Hence,

$$\text{M.V.} = \frac{\int_0^a x(a - x) \, dx}{\int_0^a dx}$$

$$= \frac{\int_0^a (ax - x^2) \, dx}{\int_0^a dx}$$

$$= \frac{\left[\dfrac{ax^2}{2} - \dfrac{x^3}{3} \right]_0^a}{\left[x \right]_0^a}$$

$$= \frac{\dfrac{a^3}{2} - \dfrac{a^3}{3}}{a}$$

$$= \frac{a^2}{6}.$$

Note. Since we are required to find the mean value of an area, the result must be of the second degree in *a*.

Example 3.

A ship steering a straight course at a uniform speed picked up a stationary object 2 miles away with the beam of a searchlight, the beam making an angle of 45° ahead with the course of the ship. The beam was kept on the object until it made an angle of 60° astern with the course. Calculate the mean distance of the object during this time.

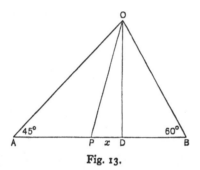

Fig. 13.

Let O be the object and AB the course of the ship. Draw OD perpendicular to AB.

Then the lengths of the various lines in the figure are $OA = 2$, $AD = \sqrt{2}$, $OD = \sqrt{2}$, $DB = \sqrt{2}/\sqrt{3}$ and $OB = 2\sqrt{2}/\sqrt{3}$.

Let P be any position of the ship, distant x from D, so that $OP^2 = 2 + x^2$.

Then S, the sum of all lengths such as OP,

$$= \int_{-\sqrt{2}}^{\sqrt{2}/\sqrt{3}} \sqrt{2 + x^2}\, dx$$

$$= \tfrac{1}{2} \left[x\sqrt{x^2 + 2} + 2 \log (x + \sqrt{x^2 + 2}) \right]_{-\sqrt{2}}^{\sqrt{2}/\sqrt{3}}$$

which, on evaluation,

$$= \tfrac{2}{3} + \sqrt{2} + \log (\sqrt{6} + \sqrt{3}).$$

$$\therefore \text{M.V.} = S \Big/ \int_{-2}^{\sqrt{2}/\sqrt{3}} dx$$

$$= \frac{\frac{2}{3} + \sqrt{2} + \log(\sqrt{6} + \sqrt{3})}{\sqrt{2}\left(1 + \dfrac{1}{\sqrt{3}}\right)}.$$

It will be noted that the variable has been taken as the distance from the point D. If either of the angles POD or OPD had been selected as the variable an erroneous result would have been obtained. This can be seen by a consideration of the argument below.

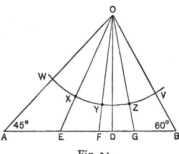

Fig. 14.

The use of the angle at the vertex O as the variable implies that this angle changes uniformly during the progress of the ship. If the ship were sailing along the arc $WXYZV$ of the circle round O, equal variations of the angle at O would correspond to equal distances along the arc, i.e. to a uniform speed of the ship.

The ship, however, is sailing along AB.

If the ship were to sail along AB so that the angles at O altered at a uniform rate, the ship would have to travel from A to E in the same time as from E to F, F to G, and G to B. In that event the ship would not be travelling at a uniform speed along AB.

If the mean value is looked upon as the result of drawing lines from O to the base AB at equal intervals and taking the total length of all the lines divided by the number of lines when this number is indefinitely increased, it is obvious that the result when the lines are drawn so as to divide the base AB into equal parts will not be the same as when they are drawn so as to divide the angle AOB into equal parts.

Similarly when the angle is taken at the base.

3. The use of double integrals.

Consider first a function, $\phi(x)$, involving a single variable x. Then the mean value of $\phi(x)$ between the limits $x=a$ and $x=b$ is

$$\sum_{x=a}^{x=b} \phi(x) \Big/ \sum_{x=a}^{x=b} 1.$$

If there be a function $\psi(x, y)$ of two variables x and y, we may write similarly

$$\text{M.V.} = \sum_{x=a}^{x=b}\sum_{y=\alpha}^{y=\beta} \psi(x, y) \Big/ \sum_{x=a}^{x=b}\sum_{y=\alpha}^{y=\beta} 1,$$

where x and y proceed by small but finite intervals.

If these intervals, say $1/n$ and $1/m$ for x and y respectively, be very small, the numerator and denominator of this fraction will be very large.

Multiply both numerator and denominator by $(1/n \cdot 1/m)$, so that the fraction is

$$\sum_{x=a}^{x=b}\sum_{y=\alpha}^{y=\beta} \psi(x, y) \frac{1}{n}\frac{1}{m} \Big/ \sum_{x=a}^{x=b}\sum_{y=\alpha}^{y=\beta} 1 \frac{1}{n}\frac{1}{m}.$$

Replace the small quantities $1/n$ and $1/m$ by Δx and Δy, and find the limit when Δx and Δy each tend to zero. Then, since the limit of a quotient is the quotient of the limits of the numerator and denominator (provided that the limit of the denominator is not zero), we have

$$\text{M.V.} = \text{Lt} \frac{\sum\limits_{x=a}^{x=b}\sum\limits_{y=\alpha}^{y=\beta} \psi(x, y)\, \Delta y \Delta x}{\sum\limits_{x=a}^{x=b}\sum\limits_{y=\alpha}^{y=\beta} 1\, \Delta y \Delta x},$$

when Δx, Δy each tend to zero,

$$= \frac{\int_a^b \int_\alpha^\beta \psi(x, y)\, dy\, dx}{\int_a^b \int_\alpha^\beta dy\, dx}.$$

The following examples are illustrative of the method of application of double integrals.

Example 4.

A rod of length a is divided at random into three parts. Find the mean value of the sum of the squares on the three parts.

Let OP be the rod of length a. Take any point X in the rod distant x from O, and another point Y distant y from X. The squares on the three segments of the line will be x^2, y^2, $(a-x-y)^2$, respectively.

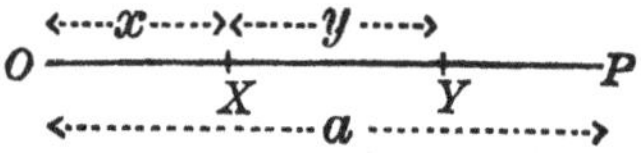

Fig. 15.

Let X be fixed. Then y will vary from 0 to $a-x$, so that the total values of the sum of the squares OX^2, XY^2, YP^2 will be

$$\Sigma\,[x^2+y^2+(a-x-y)^2],$$

where y has every value from 0 to $a-x$.

Now let x vary. The limits of variation of x are evidently from 0 to a. Then

$$\text{M.V.} = \frac{\int_0^a \int_0^{a-x} [x^2+y^2+(a-x-y)^2]\,dy\,dx}{\int_0^a \int_0^{a-x} dy\,dx}$$

$$= \frac{\int_0^a \int_0^{a-x} (2x^2+2y^2+a^2-2ax-2ay+2xy)\,dy\,dx}{\int_0^a \int_0^{a-x} dy\,dx}$$

$$= \frac{\int_0^a \left[2x^2y+\tfrac{2}{3}y^3+a^2y-2axy-ay^2+xy^2\right]_0^{a-x} dx}{\int_0^a \left[y\right]_0^{a-x} dx}$$

$$= \frac{\int_0^a [2x^2(a-x)+\tfrac{2}{3}(a-x)^3+a^2(a-x)-2ax(a-x)}{\int_0^a (a-x)\,dx},$$
$$\frac{\qquad\qquad\qquad -a(a-x)^2+x(a-x)^2]\,dx}{}$$

which becomes, on evaluating the integral,

$$\frac{\dfrac{a^4}{4}}{\dfrac{a^2}{2}}=\tfrac{1}{2}a^2.$$

It is important to note that if the sums of the required values can be obtained by considering separate sets of the values, the *total* sum must be found and divided by the total of the values. For example, if we could best solve a mean value problem by summing $\phi(x)$ for all values of x varying continuously from o to a, and $\psi(x)$ for all values from a to b, then we must write

$$\text{M.V.} = \frac{\int_0^a \phi(x)\,dx + \int_a^b \psi(x)\,dx}{\int_0^a dx + \int_a^b dx}$$

and not

$$\frac{\int_0^a \phi(x)\,dx}{\int_0^a dx} + \frac{\int_a^b \psi(x)\,dx}{\int_a^b dx}.$$

The fallacy in the second expression is easily seen when we consider that $\dfrac{A}{C} + \dfrac{B}{D}$ is not necessarily the same as $\dfrac{A+B}{C+D}$.

Example 5.

Find the mean value of the distance from one corner of a square to any point in the square.

Let $OABC$ be the square. Take any point X in the side OC distant x from O, and draw XM parallel to the side CB to meet the diagonal OB in M. Let Y be any point in XM distant y from X. The length $OY = \sqrt{x^2+y^2}$ and

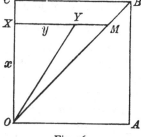

$$XM = OX = x.$$

For a fixed value of x the sum of all values of OY, i.e. of $\sqrt{x^2+y^2}$, will be

$$\sum_{y=0}^{y=x} \sqrt{x^2+y^2},$$

Fig. 16.

since Y may take up all possible positions on the straight line XM. But x may have all values from o to a.

Therefore the sum of the distances from the corner O to any point in the triangle OBC

$$= \int_0^a \int_0^x \sqrt{x^2+y^2}\,dy\,dx.$$

For the sum of the distances from O to any point in the square $OABC$ we must double this. The required mean value is therefore

$$\frac{2 \int_0^a \int_0^x \sqrt{x^2+y^2}\, dy\, dx}{2 \int_0^a \int_0^x dy\, dx}$$

$$= \frac{1}{a^2} \int_0^a x^2 [\sqrt{2} + \log(1+\sqrt{2})]\, dx,$$

on integrating with respect to y and inserting the limits o and x,

$$= \frac{a}{3}[\sqrt{2} + \log(1+\sqrt{2})].$$

4. Application of the calculus to probability.

When we are dealing with problems in probability where the number of cases involved depends upon magnitudes varying continuously over a given range, the method of approach is similar to that outlined above for the solution of mean value problems. The general principle is to take the quotient of the number of favourable ways by the number of possible ways, where all ways are equally likely.

The application of the integral calculus to problems in probability is best illustrated by examples; as a general rule it is sufficient to employ single integrals, although in some instances it is of advantage to use double integration. Many problems can be solved by either method, and examples of both methods are given below.

Example 6.

A line of given length is divided into three parts by two points taken at random. Find the chance that no one part is greater than the sum of the other two.

We shall adopt the method of single integration for the solution of this question.

Let one of the random positions be at P distant x from the end A of the line, and let $AC = CB = \frac{1}{2}a$.

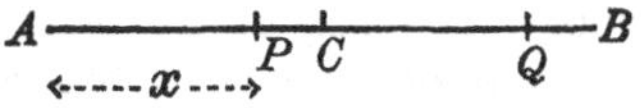

Fig. 17.

(i) Consider the favourable cases in which $AP\,(=x)$ is less than $\frac{1}{2}a$. Take a point Q in the line such that $PQ = \frac{1}{2}a$. Then, for the conditions of the problem to be satisfied, the other random point R must lie in

CQ (otherwise PR or RB will be greater than half the line and consequently greater than the sum of the other two parts AP, RB or AP, PR).

Now P lies in the small part dx between distances $x+dx$ and x
from A, and since P has been taken at random, the chance that it falls
in this small part is $\dfrac{dx}{a}$.

The chance that R lies in CQ is

$$\frac{CQ}{a} = \frac{AQ-AC}{a} = \frac{x+PQ-AC}{a} = \frac{x}{a},$$

since PQ and AC are each $\frac{1}{2}a$.

Therefore the total chance that P falls in dx and R in CQ is

$$\int_0^{\frac{1}{2}a} \frac{x}{a} \cdot \frac{dx}{a},$$

the limits of x being o and $\frac{1}{2}a$.

(ii) Consider the favourable cases in
which $AP\,(=x)$ is greater than $\frac{1}{2}a$.
Then, as above, R must lie in QC,
the chance of which is

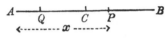

Fig. 18.

$$\frac{QC}{a} = \frac{PQ-CP}{a} = \frac{\frac{1}{2}a-x+\frac{1}{2}a}{a} = \frac{a-x}{a}.$$

Therefore, since the limits of x are now $\frac{1}{2}a$ and a, the chance that P
falls in dx and R in CQ is

$$\int_{\frac{1}{2}a}^a \frac{a-x}{a} \cdot \frac{dx}{a}.$$

The total chance required

$$= \int_0^{\frac{1}{2}a} \frac{x}{a} \cdot \frac{dx}{a} + \int_{\frac{1}{2}a}^a \frac{a-x}{a} \cdot \frac{dx}{a}$$

$$= \frac{1}{a^2}\left[\tfrac{1}{2}x^2\right]_0^{\frac{1}{2}a} + \frac{1}{a^2}\left[ax-\tfrac{1}{2}x^2\right]_{\frac{1}{2}a}^a$$

$$= \frac{1}{a^2}\left(\frac{1}{2}\,\frac{a^2}{4}\right) + \frac{1}{a^2}(a^2-\tfrac{1}{2}a^2-\tfrac{1}{2}a^2+\tfrac{1}{8}a^2)$$

$$= \tfrac{1}{4}.$$

Example 7.

Two points are selected at random on a line of length a. What is the
probability that none of the three sections into which the line is thus
divided is less than $\frac{1}{4}a$?

As an alternative this question will be solved by the use of double integrals.

Let AB be the given line divided into four equal parts at C, D, E. Now if P and Q be the random points, then to satisfy the required conditions neither can be in AC or EB.

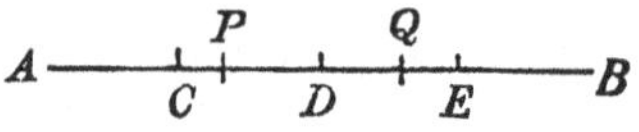

Fig. 19.

Let P be at distance x from A. Then the limits of x will evidently be $\frac{1}{4}a$ and $\frac{1}{2}a$. Let Q be at distance y from A; then Q can take up any position from $\frac{1}{4}a$ along the line from P to the point E. As the origin is at A, the limits of y will be $\frac{1}{4}a+x$ and $\frac{3}{4}a$.

Again, when P is fixed, all possible positions of Q will be from P to B, i.e. y can vary from x to a. Obviously x can vary from o to a.

Then by the unitary definition, the required chance is

$$\frac{\displaystyle\int_{\frac{a}{4}}^{\frac{a}{2}}\int_{\frac{a}{4}+x}^{\frac{3}{4}a} dy\,dx}{\displaystyle\int_{0}^{a}\int_{x}^{a} dy\,dx} = \frac{\displaystyle\int_{\frac{a}{4}}^{\frac{a}{2}}\Big[y\Big]_{\frac{a}{4}+x}^{\frac{3}{4}a} dx}{\displaystyle\int_{0}^{a}\Big[y\Big]_{x}^{a} dx}$$

$$= \frac{\displaystyle\int_{\frac{a}{4}}^{\frac{a}{2}}\big[\tfrac{3}{4}a-\tfrac{1}{4}a-x\big]\,dx}{\displaystyle\int_{0}^{a}(a-x)\,dx}$$

$$= \frac{\Big[\tfrac{3}{4}ax-\tfrac{1}{4}ax-\tfrac{1}{2}x^2\Big]_{\frac{a}{4}}^{\frac{a}{2}}}{\Big[ax-\tfrac{1}{2}x^2\Big]_{0}^{a}}$$

$$= \tfrac{1}{16},$$

on inserting the limits and simplifying.

Note. Each of the above two problems can be solved by the different methods here demonstrated. The two questions are exactly similar, and with the necessary alterations in the limits precisely the same working can be applied.

Example 8.

Two independent events, A and B, must each happen once and once only in the future. The chances of their happening in the interval from

t to $t+dt$ are proportionate to $a^t dt$ and $b^t dt$ respectively, where t is the time elapsed and a and b are constants (positive fractions). Find the chance that the two events happen in the order AB.

Let the chance that A happens at the moment of time dt be $ka^t dt$ and the chance that B happens be $lb^t dt$. Then, since the events must happen, we have

$$\int_0^\infty ka^t dt = 1 \quad \text{and} \quad \int_0^\infty lb^t dt = 1.$$

This gives $\quad k = -\log a \quad$ and $\quad l = -\log b.$

Now the chance that B happens between now and time t from now

$$= \int_0^t lb^x dx.$$

Therefore the chance that B has not happened by that time

$$= 1 - \int_0^t lb^x dx.$$

The chance that A happens at the moment of time dt

$$= ka^t dt,$$

and the chance that A happens at that moment, B not having happened,

$$= \left(1 - \int_0^t lb^x dx\right) ka^t dt.$$

Therefore total chance that the events happen in the order AB

$$= \int_0^\infty \left(1 - \int_0^t lb^x dx\right) ka^t dt,$$

which becomes $\quad \dfrac{\log a}{\log a + \log b}$

on substituting for k and l and evaluating the integrals.

Example 9.

In a certain year A and B were in London for one period only in each case, A for one-third of a year, B for one-quarter of a year. Assuming that in the case of A any one period of one-third of a year and in the case of B any one period of one-quarter of a year is as likely as any other period, find the probabilities that

(1) A was in London the whole of the time that B was;
(2) A and B were not in London at any moment together;
(3) A and B were in London at some moment together;
(4) A came to London before B.

(1) The chance that A arrived in London at point of time between t and $t+dt$ from the beginning of the year is $\dfrac{dt}{\frac{2}{3}}$, since he must have arrived in the first two-thirds of the year.

The chance that B arrived in the one month permissible $= \dfrac{\frac{1}{12}}{\frac{3}{4}} = \dfrac{1}{9}$.

Therefore the chance that A was in London the whole of the time that B was $= \displaystyle\int_0^{\frac{2}{3}} \frac{1}{9} \frac{dt}{\frac{2}{3}} = \frac{1}{9}$.

(2) The chance that A and B were not in London together $= (a)$ the chance that B arrived after A had left $+ (b)$ the chance that B left before A arrived.

For (a) B must have arrived between times $t+\frac{1}{3}$ and $\frac{3}{4}$, i.e. in the space of time $\frac{5}{12} - t$. The limits of t are 0 and $\frac{5}{12}$.

Therefore $\qquad$ chance $= \displaystyle\int_0^{\frac{5}{12}} \frac{\frac{5}{12}-t}{\frac{3}{4}} \frac{dt}{\frac{2}{3}} = \frac{25}{144}$.

For (b) B must have arrived between the times 0 and $t-\frac{1}{4}$, and the chance of this event, namely that B left before A arrived

$$= \int_{\frac{1}{4}}^{\frac{2}{3}} \frac{t-\frac{1}{4}}{\frac{3}{4}} \frac{dt}{\frac{2}{3}} = \frac{25}{144}.$$

Total chance under this head $= \frac{25}{72}$.

(3) This is evidently the complement of (2) and is

$$1 - \tfrac{25}{72} \quad \text{or} \quad \tfrac{47}{72}.$$

(4) If A came to London before B the chance is evidently

$$\int_0^{\frac{2}{3}} \frac{\frac{3}{4}-t}{\frac{3}{4}} \frac{dt}{\frac{2}{3}} = \frac{5}{9}.$$

5. Geometrical solutions.

Many of the above types of question can be solved by the aid of geometry. Since a definite integral represents an area, the ratio of the number of favourable ways to the total number of ways when there is continuous variation between the limits can evidently also be solved by relating the areas enclosed by parts of curves.

These curves or parts of curves may take the form of rectilinear figures, and in this event the problem can often be solved in a simpler manner by the use of geometry than by having recourse to the methods of the calculus.

Consider for instance Example 7 (p. 305):

If the straight line be divided at random into three parts x, y, $a-x-y$, the following must hold to satisfy the conditions of the problem:

$$x+y < a; \quad x, y, a-x-y \text{ each} > \tfrac{1}{4}a.$$

We have
$$x > \tfrac{1}{4}a$$
$$y > \tfrac{1}{4}a$$

and
$$a - x - y > \tfrac{1}{4}a,$$

giving
$$x + y < \tfrac{3}{4}a.$$

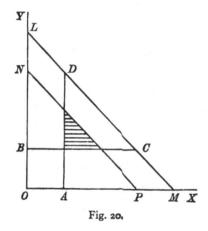

Fig. 20.

Draw the straight lines LM, $x+y=a$ and NP, $x+y=\tfrac{3}{4}a$ and complete the diagram as shown:

$$OM = a = OL; \quad OA = \tfrac{1}{4}a; \quad OB = \tfrac{1}{4}a; \quad AP = \tfrac{1}{2}a.$$

Then the conditions above may be illustrated thus:

$x > \tfrac{1}{4}a$ means that the points must be to the right of AD;

$y > \tfrac{1}{4}a$ means that the points must be above BC;

$x+y < \tfrac{3}{4}a$ means that the points must be below the line NP.

The only points satisfying all these conditions are contained in the shaded area.

Similarly, for the total possible positions governed by the condition $x+y < a$, it will be seen that all possible points lie in the triangle LOM.

The required chance is therefore

$$\frac{\text{Shaded area}}{LOM} = \frac{\frac{1}{2}(\frac{1}{4}a)^2}{\frac{1}{2}a^2} = \frac{\frac{1}{32}a^2}{\frac{1}{2}a^2} = \frac{1}{16}, \text{ as before.}$$

6. We will conclude this chapter by solving a further problem by integral calculus and by plane geometry. The alternative solutions by integral calculus are given in order to show that there may be more than one method of approaching the question, and the geometrical solution is an excellent example of the application of elementary methods to a seemingly difficult problem.

Example 10.

X starts between 2.30 and 3 o'clock to walk at a uniform rate of 4 miles per hour from A through B and C to D. Y starts from D in the reverse direction between 2 and 3 o'clock and walks at a uniform rate of 3 miles per hour. From A to B is 2 miles, B to C 1 mile, C to D 3 miles. What is the chance that they meet between B and C assuming that between the given limits any time of starting is equally likely?

Method (i).

The chance that Y leaves D between t and $t+dt$ past 2 is $\dfrac{dt}{60}$. He arrives at C at t minutes past 3, and at B at $t+20$ minutes past 3. The chance that he meets X between B and C is that X has not reached C by t minutes past 3, i.e. that X has not started before $t+15$ minutes past 2 and that he has reached B by $t+20$ minutes past 3.

If X has reached B by $t+20$ minutes past 3, he must have started by $t+50$ minutes past 2.

In order to meet, X must have started between $(t+15)$ and $(t+50)$ minutes past 2; the earliest time cannot be before 2.30 and the latest after 3.

Therefore if t is 10 or less, X can start at any time between 30 and $t+50$;

$$\text{chance} = \frac{t+20}{30}.$$

If t is 10 to 15, X can start anywhere from 30 to 60;

$$\text{chance} = \tfrac{30}{30}.$$

If t is 15 to 45, X can start anywhere from $t+15$ to 60;

$$\text{chance} = \frac{45-t}{30}.$$

Required probability

$$= \int_0^{10} \frac{t+20}{30} \frac{dt}{60} + \int_{10}^{15} \frac{30}{30} \frac{dt}{60} + \int_{15}^{45} \frac{45-t}{30} \frac{dt}{60}$$

$$= \tfrac{17}{36} \text{ (on evaluating the integrals)}.$$

Method (ii).

The chance that they *miss* is the sum of the chances that Y starts too early and Y starts too late.

(*a*) Y starts too early.

The chances that X reaches B between t and $t+dt$ minutes past 3 is $\dfrac{dt}{30}$.

As Y cannot reach B until 3.20, t must be greater than 20.

Therefore chance that Y is too early $= \displaystyle\int_{20}^{30} \frac{t-20}{60} \frac{dt}{30} = \frac{1}{36}$.

(*b*) Y starts too late.

The chance that X reaches C between t and $t+dt$ minutes past 3 is $\dfrac{dt}{30}$, and the limits of these times are evidently 3.15 and 3.45.

The chance that Y has not arrived at C by t minutes past 3 $= \dfrac{60-t}{60}$.

Therefore chance that Y is too late $= \displaystyle\int_{15}^{45} \frac{60-t}{60} \frac{dt}{30} = \frac{1}{2}$.

Therefore the chance that they *miss* $= \tfrac{1}{36} + \tfrac{1}{2} = \tfrac{19}{36}$.

Therefore the chance that they *meet* $= 1 - \tfrac{19}{36}$

$$= \tfrac{17}{36}.$$

Method (iii).

Let the straight line $ABCD$ (Fig. 21) represent the route.

Draw two straight lines at right angles to AD at A and D respectively and choose a suitable unit on both these straight lines to represent an hour. Then if X starts from A at 2.30 he would cover the distance AD by 4 o'clock; if he starts at 3.0 he would reach D by 4.30. Similarly, if Y starts at 2 o'clock he would reach A by 4 o'clock; if at 3 o'clock by 5 o'clock.

If, therefore, we join these points by the straight lines A_1D_1; A_2D_2 and DA_3; D_4A_4, the rhombus $KLMN$ represents graphically the space of time over which it is possible for X and Y to meet.

Draw BB_1 perpendicular to AD meeting DA_3 and A_2D_2 in b_1, b_2 respectively, and CC_1 perpendicular to AD meeting A_1D_1 and A_2D_2

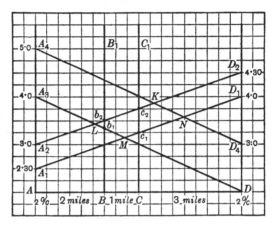

Fig. 21.

in c_1, c_2 respectively. Then the space of time over which X and Y can meet between the points B and C on their journey is represented by the area $b_2b_1Mc_1c_2$.

The required chance $= \dfrac{\text{area } b_2b_1Mc_1c_2}{\text{area } KLMN}$.

By simple geometrical methods the value of this is found to be $\frac{17}{36}$.

EXAMPLES 13

1. There are m posts in a straight line at equal distances of a yard apart. A man starts from any one and walks to any other; prove that the average distance which he will travel after doing this at random a great many times is $\frac{1}{3}(m+1)$ yards.

2. If two milestones be selected on a straight road n miles long, what is their average distance apart?

3. Two quantities are taken at random from o to a; find, by means of the integral calculus, the chance that the greater of the two is less than a given value b.

4. Find the mean value of the reciprocals of all quantities from n to $2n$.

5. A ladder of length l can be safely used, without its being secured, at any angle to the ground between $\dfrac{\pi}{4}$ and $\dfrac{\pi}{3}$. If any angle between these limits is equally likely, find the mean vertical height reached by the ladder in an infinite number of placings.

6. OP is a straight line of length p. A fixed point Q is taken in OP such that $OQ = q$. Two other points are taken at random in OP. Find the chance that they both fall in OQ.

7. A point is taken at random on a given finite straight line of length a. Find the mean value of the sum of the squares on the two parts of the line. Find also the chance of the sum being less than this mean value.

8. A semicircle, APB, stands on a base, AB, of length $2r$. P is a point on the circumference, and AP, BP are joined to form the right-angled triangle, APB. Find the mean value of the area of the triangle:

    (1) if P is a point chosen on the circumference at random;
    (2) if P is fixed by choosing a point N at random in the base AB, and erecting a perpendicular from N, to meet the circumference at P.

9. Find the mean value of the ordinate of a semicircle, the points along the diameter at which the ordinates are taken being equidistant.

10. In two opposite sides of a square, whose side is of length a, points P and Q are taken at random and are joined by the line PQ which thus divides the square into two pieces. Find the mean value of the area of the smaller of the two pieces.

11. Find the mean of the square of the distance of a point within a given square of side $2a$ from the centre of the square.

12. A straight line of length a is divided at random at two points. Find the mean value of the product of the three segments.

13. A point is taken at random within the area bounded by $y = x \log x$, the x-axis and the ordinates $x = 1$, $x = 4$. Find the probability that the distance of the point from the y-axis is less than 2.

14. Three points are taken at random on the circumference of a circle. Find the chance that the sum of any two of the arcs thus cut off is greater than the third.

15. A straight line is divided into three parts by two points taken at random. Find the chance that none of the three parts is greater than five-eighths of the line.

16. There are two clerks in an office, each of whom goes out for an hour for lunch. One may start at any time between 12 and 1 o'clock, the other at any time between 1 and 2. All times within these limits are equally likely. Find the chance that they are not out together.

17. Find the chance that the roots of the equation $x^2 - 2ax + b = 0$ are real, where a and b are positive proper fractions chosen at random.

18. The point M is the centre of a line LMN of length $4a$. Two points P, Q on the line are chosen at random. Find the chance that the sum of the two distances MP and MQ is greater than a.

19. If on a straight line of length $(a+b)$ two lengths a and b are cut off at random, find the chance that the common part does not exceed a length c.

20. In a line AB of length $3a$, a point P is taken at random and then in AP a point Q is taken at random. What is the probability that PQ exceeds a?

21. The sides of a rectangle are taken at random each less than an inch and all lengths are equally likely. Find the chance that the diagonal is less than an inch.

22. Three points are taken at random on the circumference of a circle. Find the probability that they lie in the same semicircle.

23. Two points are taken at random on a given straight line of length a. Prove that the probability of their distance exceeding a given length c $(<a)$ is equal to $\left\{1 - \dfrac{c}{a}\right\}^2$.

24. OA and OB are straight lines of length a at right angles to one another. P and Q are points taken at random in OA and OB respectively. Find the chance that the area of the triangle OPQ is less than $\frac{1}{4}a^2$.

25. A starts to walk from X to Y 3 miles apart at 3 miles per hour. On the journey he unknowingly drops his handkerchief, but discovers his loss when he has covered half the remaining distance. He then proceeds to retrace his steps at 4 miles per hour. B starts on the same journey at 3 miles per hour 5 minutes after the handkerchief is dropped. Find his chance of reaching the place where it was dropped before A does.

Assuming that B picks it up, find the mean distance he would have to carry it to restore it to A if the series of events were to take place a large number of times.

26. Find the mean distance between two points on opposite sides of a square whose side is unity.

MISCELLANEOUS EXAMPLES

1. Find the sum of n terms of the series 1, 2, 4, 9, 19, 36, 62, ...

2. A person writes four letters and four envelopes. If the letters are placed in the envelopes at random, what is the chance that not more than one letter is placed in its correct envelope?

3. Find the mean age and median age of the following distribution:

Age	Population 1,000's	Age	Population 1,000's
20–	382	55–	148
25–	379	60–	115
30–	348	65–	84
35–	316	70–	52
40–	272	75–	26
45–	234	80–	11
50–	194	85–	4

4. Given $u_0 = 1027$, $u_6 = 1212$, $u_{12} = 1469$, $u_{18} = 2014$, explain
   (i) how you would complete the series from u_0 to u_6;
   (ii) how you would proceed if you were asked to complete the series from u_6 to u_{12} supposing that it were unnecessary to find u_1, u_2, u_3, u_4 and u_5.

5. The faces of a cubical die are marked 1, 2, 2, 4, 6, 6. Find the chance that, in ten throws, four 2's, two 4's, four 6's are thrown.

6. Find the tenth term of the series:
   (a) 1, 4, 13, 36, 97, 268, 765, ...;
   (b) 2, 12, 36, 98, 270, 768, ...

7. Show that $\Delta u_x v_x = v_x \Delta u_x + u_{x+1} \Delta v_x$ and hence prove by *mathematical induction* that

$$\Delta^n u_x v_x = v_x \Delta^n u_x + n_{(1)} \Delta v_x \Delta^{n-1} u_{x+1} + n_{(2)} \Delta^2 v_x \Delta^{n-2} u_{x+2}$$
$$+ n_{(3)} \Delta^3 v_x \Delta^{n-3} u_{x+3} + ...$$

8. Explain the mathematical meaning of the word "probability". If the probability of the happening of an event at each trial be p, and n trials are to be made:
   (1) What does pn represent?
   (2) What is the probability that the event will happen at least m times?
   (3) What is the most probable number of times the event will happen?

9. Prove that in the process of obtaining divided differences of the function u_x, given u_a, u_b, u_c, ..., the last divided difference is numerically the same whatever the order of the arguments and the corresponding u's.

10. Show that

$$(1) \quad \Sigma x^m = C + \frac{x^{(2)}}{2!} \Delta o^m + \frac{x^{(3)}}{3!} \Delta^2 o^m + ...;$$

$$(2) \quad \Sigma u_x = C + x^{(1)} u_0 + \frac{x^{(2)}}{2!} \Delta u_0 + \frac{x^{(3)}}{3!} \Delta^2 u_0 + ...$$

11. Two Companies A and B make simultaneous issues each of 1000 bonds. Those of Company A are redeemable by equal drawings spread over 20 years, and those of B by equal drawings spread over 40 years. Find, in the case of two definite bonds, one of each issue:

    (1) the probability that the bond of Company B is redeemed before the bond of Company A;

    (2) the probability that the bond of Company B is redeemed before the bond of Company A and within 15 years of issue.

12. If u_0, u_5, u_{10}, u_{15} be four values of a function at equidistant points, find expressions true to third differences for u_6 and u_8, solely in terms of u_0, u_5, u_{10} and u_{15}.

13. Explain what is meant by the terms *median*, *histogram*, *ogive*, illustrating your answers by rough diagrams.

14. Two throws are made, the first with three dice and the second with two. What is the probability both that the first throw is not less than 11 and that the second throw is not less than 8?

15. Show that the series whose nth term is

$$\frac{(-1)^{n-1}}{8^{n-1}} \frac{1 \cdot 3 \cdot 5 \cdots (2n-3)}{(n-1)!} \Delta^{2(n-1)} u_{x-n+\frac{1}{2}}$$

is equivalent to

$$2 (u_x - u_{x+1} + u_{x+2} - u_{x+3} + ...).$$

16. Obtain the approximate quadrature formula

$$\int_{-\frac{1}{2}}^{1\frac{1}{2}} u_x dx = \tfrac{1}{24} (27 u_0 + 17 u_1 + 5 u_2 - u_3).$$

17. The numbers of members in a Friendly Society were available for the following years:

Year	1922	1923	1924	1925	1928
Number of members	995	998	1003	996	976

It was desired to obtain estimates for the years 1926 and 1927. This was effected on the assumption of a constant fourth difference. Subsequently it was discovered that the numbers for 1926 were actually 1002, and a fresh estimate for the year 1927 had to be prepared. Calculate the original estimates for 1926 and 1927, and find the revised figure for the year 1927.

18. If b and c are positive quantities $(b > c)$ and if $\dfrac{3x^2 - bc}{6x - b - 3c}$ may have any value between b and c, all such values being equally likely, find the probability that x is real.

19. Establish the formula for the difference of a product of two functions,

$$\Delta\,(u_x v_x) = u_x \Delta v_x + v_{x+1}\Delta u_x,$$

and deduce the formula for the sum of a product,

$$\sum_{x=0}^{n-1}(u_x \Delta v_x) = (u_n v_n - u_0 v_0) - \sum_{x=0}^{n-1}(v_{x+1}\Delta u_x).$$

By means of this formula find the value of $\sum_{x=0}^{n-1} x^2$.

20. If $\sum_{x=a}^{a+x} u_x = w_a$ for all integral values of a, prove that, to the third order of differences,

$$u_7 = \cdot 2w_5 - \cdot 008\,(w_{10} - 2w_5 + w_0).$$

Given the following table, find u_7, u_{12} and u_{17}:

a	0	5	10	15	20
$\displaystyle\sum_{x=a}^{a+4}$	·0427	·1467	·2459	·3408	·4317

21. If events A, B, and C are independent of each other, and events E and F are mutually exclusive and are both contingent upon the happening of A, give an expression for the probability that either E or F will happen and that neither B nor C will happen.

22. The equation

$$10x^3 + 3 = 15x$$

has a root between 1 and 2. Obtain it to three places of decimals by inverse interpolation.

23. The following formulae for approximate integration are correct to third differences:

$$\int_{-3}^{+3} u_x dx = \tfrac{3}{4}\,(3u_{-2} + 2u_0 + 3u_2),$$

$$\int_{-3}^{+3} u_x dx = u_{-3} + 4u_0 + u_3.$$

Prove that if these formulae are applied to a function whose fifth differences are constant, the respective errors involved in the approximations are in the ratio $7:18$, and are in opposite directions.

By a combination of the two formulae obtain an expression, correct to fifth differences, for $\int_{-3}^{+3} u_x dx$.

24. Define *standard deviation*. Find the mean and standard deviation of the following distribution:

Length in cms.	No. of cases
10–	2
15–	—
20–	8
25–	11
30–	12
35–	16
40–	25
45–	17
50–	8
55–	1

25. If third differences of u are constant, express u_n in terms of

$$u_0, \quad \Delta u_1, \quad \Delta^2 u_2 \quad \text{and} \quad \Delta^3 u_3.$$

26. If three different whole numbers from 1 to 30 inclusive are chosen at random, what is the probability that their sum is equal to 30?

27. In each of two adjacent sides of a square a point is taken at random. Find the chance that the length of the line joining the two points is between $\tfrac{1}{2}a$ and a, where a is the length of a side of the square.

28. Draw the graph of $y = x^3 - 3x + 1$. By reference to the graph, supplemented by arithmetical trials, find approximately the value of the negative root of the equation $x^3 - 3x + 1 = 0$, correct to two places of decimals.

29. *A* and *B* throw in turn with two dice, *A* having the first throw. *A* is to win either (1) if he throws a double six in his first six throws or (2) if he throws a double six before *B* has a throw scoring 9 or more. Find an expression for *A*'s chance of winning.

30. Find the mean length of a straight line drawn from one of the angular points of an equilateral triangle to a point taken at random in any one of the sides.

31. Find an expression, correct to fourth differences, for the value of $\dfrac{du_x}{dx}$ when $x=1$, in terms of u_{-2}, u_{-1}, u_0, u_1, u_2.

32. Show that, if fourth differences of u are constant,

$$(\tfrac{1}{5}[5]-1)(u_{n+2}-u_2)=\Delta^2 u_{n+1}-\Delta^2 u_1.$$

33. Prove that

$$\int_0^1 \frac{dx}{1+x^2}=\frac{1}{4a}\left(1+\frac{1}{6a}\right)+\sum_{x=1}^{x=a}\frac{a}{a^2+x^2}$$

approximately, where a is a positive integer.

By putting $a=3$, obtain the value of π to three places of decimals.

34. Three numbers are selected at random, one at a time, from the five numbers 1, 2, 3, 4 and 5, repetitions being allowed. Find the probability that the third number selected is not less than the second and the second is not less than the first.

35. By means of the formula (taking $n=10$)

$$\sum_{x=0}^{x=mn} u_{a+x}=n\sum_{x=0}^{x=m} u_{a+nx}-\frac{n-1}{2}(u_{a+mn}+u_a)$$

$$-\frac{n^2-1}{12}\left[\left(\frac{du_x}{dx}\right)_{x=a+mn}-\left(\frac{du_x}{dx}\right)_{x=a}\right]\text{ approx.,}$$

find the approximate value of $\log_{10}\dfrac{50!}{9!}$, given that $\log_{10}2=\cdot3010$, $\log_{10}3=\cdot4771$, $\log_{10}e=\cdot4343$.

36. Given that
$$u_0=\ 16$$
$$u_1+u_2=\ 64$$
$$u_3+u_4+u_5=\ 266$$
$$u_6+u_7+u_8+u_9=1029$$

find the values of u_4 and u_5, on the assumption that $\Delta^3 u_x$ is constant.

37. Through two points taken at random in a diagonal of a square, two straight lines are drawn parallel to one of the sides and to each other.

Find the probability that the area of that part of the square between the two lines is not less than one-third of the area of the whole square.

38. The number of herds of cows in a certain district is as follows:

Number of cows in herd	Number of herds
1–10	311
11–30	538
31–40	227
41–50	199

Estimate the total number of cows in the 550 largest herds.

39. *A* and *B* play a game in which they toss a coin alternately. If the coin turns up head the thrower scores two points; if it turns up tail his opponent scores one point. The winner is the one who first scores at least seven points. *A* has scored four points and *B* two, and it is *A*'s turn to toss the coin. Find the chance that *A* will win the game.

40. In a lottery there have been sold 2500 £1 tickets numbered 0001 to 2500 and 5000 10s. tickets numbered 2501 to 7500, and it is arranged to draw £500 worth of tickets, the holders of which will receive 10 times the face value of their tickets. The following method of drawing the winning tickets has been suggested. Ten counters marked with the figures 0 to 9 respectively are to be placed in a bag. A counter is to be taken at random from the bag and replaced; this is to be done four times and the figures obtained are to be written down in the order in which they are drawn to form a four-figure number. Drawings are to be carried out in this way, the tickets bearing the numbers so drawn to participate in the prize, until £500 worth of tickets have been drawn, subject to the provision that any drawing giving a number to which there is no corresponding ticket or a number which has already been drawn or a number which would cause more than £500 worth of tickets to be drawn is to be ignored.

The following criticisms of the suggested method have been made:

(i) The holders of the 10s. tickets have an advantage over the holders of the £1 tickets, since although the 10s. tickets cost only half as much as the £1 tickets, they have the same chance of being drawn.

(ii) The system by which it is possible for a number to be drawn to which there is no corresponding undrawn ticket produces inequalities in the chances of the various ticket-holders.

(iii) The system of making the drawings is inequitable as it does not ensure that the correct proportions of £1 and 10s. tickets will participate in the prize.

You are asked briefly to consider these criticisms and to advise whether the method is fair in all its aspects.

41. A school contains 330 children, all of whom were born in the eleven years 1920–1930. Four times the total number of children born in any group of five consecutive years is equal to five times the number born in the first and last years of the group *plus* ten times the number born in the middle year of the group. The total number of children born in 1924, 1925 and 1926 is three less than three times the number born in 1925. Find the number born in 1925.

42. Show that

$$\frac{d^3 u_x}{dx^3} = \frac{1}{2h^3} \left(\Delta^3 u_{x-h} + \Delta^3 u_{x-2h} \right)$$

approximately, where h is the interval of differencing.

43. Establish Hardy's formula "39 a"; and use a Hardy formula to find the value of $\int_0^1 (1 + x^2)^{-1} dx$ correct to four places of decimals.

44. A and B play a match of seven games. A's chances of winning, drawing and losing any game are as $5:3:2$. One point is scored for a win and half a point for a draw. Find the chance that the match is drawn.

45. Prove that $u_1 - u_2 + u_3 - \ldots = \frac{1}{2} u_1 - (\frac{1}{2})^2 \Delta u_1 + (\frac{1}{2})^3 \Delta^2 u_1 - \ldots$, where u_n is a real positive quantity which diminishes as n increases, and $\underset{n \to \infty}{\mathrm{Lt}}\, u_n = 0$.

In the series $1 - \frac{1}{3} + \frac{1}{5} - \frac{1}{7} + \ldots$ find the value of $\Delta^r u_n$ and prove that this series is equivalent to the series

$$\frac{1}{2} \left[1 + \frac{1}{3} + \frac{1 \cdot 2}{3 \cdot 5} + \frac{1 \cdot 2 \cdot 3}{3 \cdot 5 \cdot 7} + \ldots \right].$$

46. Use the conception of finite differences to prove that the general term in the recurring series $u_0 + u_1 x + u_2 x^2 + u_3 x^3 + \ldots$ (scale of relation $1 - px - qx^2$) is of the form $Aa^n + Bb^n$, where a and b are functions of p and q, and A and B are constants.

Prove that every series whose coefficients form an arithmetical progression is a recurring series, and that the generating function is

$$\frac{a + (d - a)\, x}{(1 - x)^2},$$

where a is the first term and d the common difference of the progression.

47. A bag contains four black balls and eight white balls. Two balls are drawn at a time and replaced, this operation being performed six times. Calculate the probability that two black balls are not drawn four times consecutively.

48. Obtain a formula for the finite integration of any rational integral function of x and apply it to find the sum to n terms of the series whose rth term is $(r^2+1)(r-2)$.

49. $a_{25:30}=16\cdot311$; $a_{30:30}=15\cdot784$; $a_{25:35}=15\cdot660$;

$a_{35:30}=14\cdot420$; $a_{25:40}=14\cdot824$; $a_{30:35}=15\cdot209$.

Find as accurately as possible $a_{27:32}$.

50. A and B toss a coin in turn, a head counting two and a tail one. The winner is the person who first scores a total of exactly three. If either tosses a head when his score is already two, his score is reduced to one. Calculate A's chance of winning the game if he has the first toss.

51. By successive approximations based on the values of x^3-5x+3 when $x=0$, 1, 2 and 3, find to two places of decimals the smallest positive root of the equation $x^3-5x+3=0$.

52. Two points are chosen at random on the circumference of a circle of radius r. Find the chance that the length of the chord joining them is less than $r\sqrt{3}$.

53. A die whose sides are marked, 1, 2, 3, 4, 5, 6 is thrown five times. Find the probabilities:

(a) that the product of the five throws is 432;

(b) that the sum of the first three throws is exactly three more than the sum of the last two throws.

54. Complete the series u_5 to u_{15} by means of Everett's formula:

x	-5	0	5	10	15	20	25
u_x	61·0	91·4	113·6	134·2	179·4	238·0	296·2

55. The probability that A will die within ten years is ·2 and the probability that A, B and C will all be alive ten years hence is ·42. The probability that at least one of the three will be alive ten years hence is ·985. Find the probability that A and B alone will be living at the end of the tenth year.

56. Explain clearly the meaning of the term *dispersion* in statistics. What are the most usual methods of measuring dispersion? Indicate the advantages and disadvantages of these methods.

57. A and B throw for a certain stake, each throwing with one die; A's die is marked 2, 3, 4, 5, 6, 7 and B's 1, 2, 3, 4, 5, 6. Prove that A's expectation is $47/72$ or $21/31$ of the stake, according as equal throws divide the stake or go for nothing.

58. Let $\phi(x_1)$, $\phi(x_2)$, ..., $\phi(x_n)$ be the values of a function $\phi(x)$ corresponding to n equidistant values of x distributed over the range $b - a$. Define the *mean value* of $\phi(x)$ over this range (i) as a limit, and (ii) as a definite integral.

Extend your definitions to a function $\phi(x, y)$ of two variables x, y for the ranges $b - a$ of x and $\beta - \alpha$ of y. Hence find the mean value of

$$\frac{e^{x+y}}{(e^x + e^{-x})(e^y + e^{-y})}$$

for $0 \leqslant x \leqslant 1$, $0 \leqslant y \leqslant 1$.

59. Four variables x, y, z and u are connected by the equations

$$100y = 1 + 9x^3,$$

$$10z = 2 + 7y^2,$$

$$u = 3 + 5z.$$

If you were told to construct a table showing the value of u (but not the values of y and z) corresponding to each integral value of x from 1 to 20, how many values of u would it be necessary for you to compute by means of the above equations before you could fill in the remaining values by a finite difference method?

Write down the formula by which you would calculate these remaining values.

60. In an examination the numbers of candidates who obtained marks between certain limits were as follows:

Number of marks	Number of candidates
0–19	41
20–39	62
40–59	65
60–79	50
80–99	17

Estimate the number of candidates who obtained fewer than 70 marks.

61. Explain Sheppard's rules.

Use the rules to express u_x in terms of

(i) u_0, Δu_0, $\Delta^2 u_{-1}$, $\Delta^3 u_{-2}$, $\Delta^4 u_{-3}$, $\Delta^5 u_{-3}$, $\Delta^6 u_{-3}$;

(ii) u_0, Δu_{-1}, $\Delta^2 u_{-1}$, $\Delta^3 u_{-1}$, $\Delta^4 u_{-1}$, $\Delta^5 u_{-2}$, $\Delta^6 u_{-2}$.

62. (i) Explain, giving a simple example in each case, the meanings of (a) a probability depending on mutually exclusive events, (b) expectation and (c) probable value.

(ii) If two dice are thrown and six coins are tossed, find the probability that the difference between the numbers shown by the dice is equal to the number of heads shown by the coins.

63. (i) In a straight line AB of length a, two points X and Y are chosen at random. Using a geometrical method, find the probability that XY exceeds a length b (where $b < a$).

(ii) If X is first chosen at random in AB and Y is then chosen at random in AX, explain carefully with the aid of a diagram why a similar method cannot be used and find the probability in this case.

64. The equation $x^3 + 2x - 20 = 0$ has a root between 2·4 and 2·5. Determine the value of this root correct to four decimal places by a method of inverse interpolation.

65. A large army consists of men between ages 20 and 40, the number at age x being proportionate to $a + bc^x$, where a, b and c are constants. If the numbers at ages 20, 30 and 40 are proportionate to 100, 68 and 20 respectively, find, correct to one decimal place, the average age of the men in the army. Given

$$\log_{10} 2 = \cdot 301, \quad \log_{10} 3 = \cdot 477, \quad \text{and} \quad \log_{10} e = \cdot 4343.$$

66. If three whole numbers are chosen at random, what is the chance that their product is a multiple of 27?

67. The winner of a game is the one who first scores four points, with the proviso that if two players score three points, the game continues until one player has scored two points more than the other. A's skill is to B's as 2:1. Find A's chance of winning the game if he owes one point and B receives a start of one point.

68. (i) Prove that $e^x = \left(\dfrac{\Delta^2}{E}\right) e^x \cdot \dfrac{E e^x}{\Delta^2 e^x}$ (interval of differencing h).

(ii) If u_x be a function of the form

$$b_1 x + b_2 x^2 + b_3 x^3 + \dots \text{ to infinity,}$$

show that it can be expressed in the form

$$u_x = \frac{b_1 x}{1-x} + \frac{\Delta b_1 x^2}{(1-x)^2} + \frac{\Delta^2 b_1 x^3}{(1-x)^3} + \dots.$$

69. On March 1st a plant 6 inches high was put into a greenhouse. On March 8th its height was found to be 10 inches, and on March 29th 14 inches. Estimate its height on April 12th

(i) assuming that the height (h) is a rational integral function of the time (t),

(ii) assuming that h and t are connected by a relation of the form $h = a + bt^n$;

and explain why one method should give a better answer than the other in this particular case.

70. The following data are available:

Age x	32	37	42	47	52	57
e_x	35·36	33·25	30·72	27·23	23·16	19·11

It is desired to obtain $e_{57\frac{1}{2}}$ with as little labour as possible, and it is suggested that 18·71 would be a reasonable approximation. Do you agree with this? Give reasons.

From the above data, obtain a value for $e_{44\frac{1}{2}}$.

71. A die is thrown repeatedly until the total of the numbers turned up reaches 5 or more. What is the probability that one of these numbers is a 6?

72. If u_x be a function whose differences, when the increment of x is unity, are denoted by δu_x, $\delta^2 u_x$, $\delta^3 u_x$, ... and by Δu_x, $\Delta^2 u_x$, $\Delta^3 u_x$, ... when the increment of x is n; then if $\delta^2 u_x$, $\delta^2 u_{x+1}$, ... are in geometric progression with common ratio q, show that

$$\frac{\Delta u_x - n\delta u_x}{(q^n - 1) - n(q - 1)} = \frac{\delta^2 u_x}{(q - 1)^2}.$$

73. Prove that, approximately,

$$125u_0 = [5]^3 (u_0 + \Delta u_{-2} - \Delta u_1).$$

74. Two men throw for a guinea, equal throws to divide the stake. A uses an ordinary die, but B uses a die marked 2, 3, 4, 5, 6, 6. Show that B thereby increases his expectation by 5/18ths.

75. A bag contains five counters marked 1 to 5. One counter is drawn at a time and replaced. What is the average number of draws required in order that counter No. 5 may be drawn twice?

76. If
$$u_0 = 6,$$
$$u_{10} = 27,$$
$$u_{20} = 62,$$
$$u_{30} = 111,$$

find the value of x satisfying the equation

$$u_x + u_{10+x} + u_{20+x} = (u_{10-x} + u_{20-x} + u_{30-x}) - 42.$$

77. The goals scored by two teams A and B in a football season were as follows:

Number of goals scored in a match	Number of matches A	B
0	27	17
1	9	9
2	8	6
3	5	5
4	4	3

By calculating the coefficient of variation in each case, find which team may be considered the more consistent.

78. Find $u_{2:2}$ from the following table of $u_{x:y}$, using all the values given:

$$
\begin{array}{c|ccc}
 & \multicolumn{3}{c}{x} \\
 & 0 & 1 & 2 \\
\hline
\begin{array}{c} 0 \\ y\left\{ 1 \right. \\ 2 \end{array} &
\begin{array}{c} 16\cdot25 \\ 15\cdot55 \\ 14\cdot48 \end{array} &
\begin{array}{c} 15\cdot08 \\ 14\cdot58 \\ 13\cdot74 \end{array} &
\begin{array}{c} 13\cdot49 \\ 13\cdot15 \\ \end{array}
\end{array}
$$

79. During a certain month of the year it is reckoned that if at any time the weather is fine the odds are four to one against its breaking up within a week. At the beginning of this month, while it is fine, a gardener applies to his lawn a weed-killer for the success of which it is essential that the weather should remain fine for two days but should break up within fifteen days. Find to two places of decimals the chances that the weed-killer is successful.

80. A match consisting of a maximum of five games is played between A and B. The chances that any game is won by A, won by B or drawn are equal. Each player scores one point for every game he wins and half a point for every game drawn. The match ends as soon as one of the players has a sufficient lead to leave him with an excess of points over his opponent even if the latter were to win all the remaining games. If a large number of such matches were played, what proportion of them would you expect on the average to end with the third, fourth and fifth game respectively, and what proportion would you expect to be drawn?

81. If u_x is a rational integral function of the fourth degree in x, and if $u_0 = u_2 = u_1 + u_3 = u_1 u_3 + 1 = u_4 + 2u_1 = 0$, and u_1 is negative, find for what values of n greater than 4

$$
\epsilon \, (\ldots \ldots) \sum_{1}^{n-1} \ldots \ldots \quad (\ldots \ldots)(\ldots \ldots) \ldots
$$

82. If $f(x)$ is a rational integral function of the third degree in x, and $\phi(x) = f(x) + f(t-x)$, show that $\int_0^t f(x)\,dx$ can be expressed in the form $\sum_{x=0}^{t} f(x) + a\phi(0) + b\phi(1) + c\phi(2)$, where a, b and c are independent of t, and find the values of these constants.

83. Four people A, B, C, D and twelve others are to be seated at random at a round table. Find the chances that:

    (i) these four people are arranged in two separated pairs, A and B together, and C and D together,

    (ii) all four are separated from one another.

84. Explain the difference, if any, between $\Delta_x \Delta_y$ and Δ_{xy}.

Find $a_{44:51}$, given

$$a_{40:50} = 10\cdot894 \qquad a_{40:55} = 9\cdot796 \qquad a_{40:60} = 8\cdot553$$
$$a_{45:50} = 10\cdot591 \qquad a_{45:55} = 9\cdot583$$
$$a_{50:50} = 10\cdot059$$

85. A certain type of tag consists of a "bootlace" with a cylinder at one end into which the tag at the other end fits. If any number N of exactly similar tags be held in the middle so that the cylinder ends hang down at one side and the tag ends at the other:

    (a) what is the chance that if, say, n tags be fitted into n cylinders at random, both ends have been chosen from the same "bootlace", so that n loops are formed?

    (b) if all the N tags be fitted into all the N cylinders, what is the chance that one large loop is formed?

86. Three metal discs are numbered 1, 2, 4 respectively on one side: the other side of each disc is blank. The discs are tossed three times, and the numbers showing up are added. A is to win a stake from B if the total is 8 to 13 inclusive, while B wins if the total is less than 8 or more than 13. Find the odds in favour of B's winning.

87. In a certain town the post office has four telegraph boys who take it in turns to deliver telegrams. If a resident in the town receives telegrams on n separate occasions, what is the chance that they will be delivered by at least three of the telegraph boys?

88. A player throws two dice simultaneously and is to continue throwing them so long as no figure less than a 5 turns up. If two 6's

turn up simultaneously he is to receive a prize amounting to £13 on the first occasion it happens, £13² on the second occasion, £13³ on the third occasion and so on. If two 5's turn up simultaneously he is to receive £3 on the first occasion, £3² on the second occasion, £3³ on the third occasion and so on.

Find the value of his expectation.

89. If interpolated values are found in the interval $x=0$ to $x=1$ from the values u_{-1}, u_0, u_1, u_2, by means of the formula

$$u_x = \xi u_0 + \frac{\xi^2 (\xi - 1)}{2} \Delta^2 u_{-1}$$

$$+ x u_1 + \frac{x^2 (x-1)}{2} \Delta^2 u_0 \quad \text{(where } \xi = 1 - x\text{)},$$

and in the next interval $x=1$ to $x=2$ by the corresponding formula based on the values u_0, u_1, u_2 and u_3, show that:

(1) The given values u_0, u_1 and u_2 will be reproduced by the interpolation.

(2) The two interpolation curves have the same differential coefficient when $x=1$.

(3) The interpolated values for $u_{\frac{1}{2}}$ and $u_{\frac{3}{2}}$ agree with those given by the ordinary third difference interpolation formula based on the same values of u_x.

Given the following values:

$$u_{-5} = 1000, \qquad u_{10} = 2609,$$
$$u_0 = 1403, \qquad u_{15} = 3487,$$
$$u_5 = 1931,$$

complete the table for unit intervals from u_0 to u_{10} by the above formulae and calculate the value of the differential coefficient of the interpolated curves when $x=5$.

90. A bag contains 10 counters numbered 1 to 10 respectively. A counter is drawn at random and replaced in the bag; this is done three times, the numbers on the counters so drawn being added together to give a total. The process is repeated as many times as may be necessary to obtain three totals each of which does not exceed 12, any series of three drawings which produces a total exceeding 12 being ignored.

Find the chance that these three totals will (if arranged in ascending order of magnitude) form an arithmetical progression of common difference 2.

91. Having given the present value of £1 per annum at the end of 20 years at the undermentioned rates of interest per cent.:

Rate per cent.	Present value of £1 per annum
2	16·351433
$2\frac{1}{2}$	15·589162
3	14·877475
$3\frac{1}{2}$	14·212403
4	13·590326
$4\frac{1}{2}$	13·007936

use Everett's formula of interpolation to find the present value of £1 per annum at the end of 20 years at 3·2 per cent. per annum.

92. The estimated distribution of cinema admissions in a certain year was as follows:

Price of admission in pence	Number of admissions in millions
2	13·6
3	74·4
4	52·2
6	272·5
9	164·7
12	193·2
15	53·8
18	91·1
20	47·8

Give a sketch of a frequency distribution, showing the median and the mode.

93. If x is a whole number chosen at random between 1 and 99 inclusive, find the chance that $x(100-x)$ will exceed one-half of its maximum possible value.

94. A floor is ruled with equidistant parallel lines. A rod, shorter than the distance between the lines, is thrown at random on the floor. Prove that the chance that it falls on one of the lines is $2c/\pi a$, where c is the length of the rod and a the distance between the parallels.

95. If in an examination six men are bracketed, the extreme difference between their marks being 6, find the chance that they have all obtained different marks.

96. The xth term of the series $1, 2, 17, 72, 243, 754, \ldots$ is of the form $a + bx + c^x + d^x$. Determine a, b, c, d and find the sum of n terms of the series.

97. A team of eight men is engaged in a practice shoot. Each man's probability of hitting the bull on his target with any one shot is $\frac{2}{5}$. Each man fires one shot; then those who have not hit the bull fire a second shot, and so on, the unsuccessful men at each trial firing again.

What is the minimum number of trials that should be made in order to ensure an even chance of all the men hitting the bull?

98. In a certain game the player throws a ball on to a board containing twelve holes into one of which the ball is bound to fall. It is equally likely to fall into any one of the holes, which are marked $0, 0, 0, 0, 1, 1, 1, 1, 1, 2, 2, 2$ respectively. If it falls into a hole marked 0 it is "lost", but if it falls into any of the others it is returned to the player, who continues to throw the ball until it is eventually "lost", when the game ceases. At each throw the player scores the number of the hole into which the ball falls.

Show that the probability that the player obtains a *total* score of n is the $(n + 1)$th term of a certain recurring series and hence find this probability.

99. A and B both wish to journey from X to Z by tram. A decides to take a tram which travels direct from X to Z in 55 minutes, while B decides to go by a different route, taking first a tram which travels from X to Y in 20 minutes and then another which travels from Y to Z in 30 minutes. Trams run from X to Z, from X to Y and from Y to Z at intervals of 10 minutes, 7 minutes and 7 minutes respectively, but the times of running are not known. If A and B arrive at the same moment at X to wait for their respective trams, find the chance that A arrives at Z before B.

100. If
$$w_{-1} = u_{-7} + u_{-6} + u_{-5} + u_{-4} + u_{-3},$$
$$w_0 = u_{-2} + u_{-1} + u_0 + u_1 + u_2,$$
$$w_1 = u_3 + u_4 + u_5 + u_6 + u_7,$$
$$w_2 = u_8 + u_9 + u_{10} + u_{11} + u_{12},$$

prove that
$$u_2 + u_3 = \cdot 2\,(w_0 + w_1) - \cdot 032\,(\Delta^2 w_{-1} + \Delta^2 w_0).$$

ANSWERS TO THE EXAMPLES

Examples 1.

1. 58. **2.** 30, 42. **3.** 15.

4. 1·9. **5.** 1110. **8.** $6ah^3$.

9. $\frac{1}{6}(-11x^3 + 252x^2 - 1051x + 1344)$. **10.** $abcd \cdot 10!$.

11. $ab^{ca}(b^c - 1)$; $\ ab^{ca}(b^c - 1)^2$; $\ ab^{ca}\dfrac{(b^c - 1)\,[(b^c - 1)^{10} - 1]}{b^c - 2}$.

12. (i) $\frac{1}{2}x(x-1) + k$, (ii) $c^x/(c-1) + k$,

(iii) $3x(x-1)(x-2) + \frac{9}{2}x(x-1) + 3x + k$, where k is a constant.

13. $-\dfrac{2}{(x+2)(x+3)} - \dfrac{3}{(x+3)(x+4)}$;

$\dfrac{4}{(x+2)(x+3)(x+4)} + \dfrac{6}{(x+3)(x+4)(x+5)}$.

14. $\dfrac{2}{x(x-1)(x-2)}$. **15.** -2 or 109.

16. (1) $an!$; (2) $e^{ax+b}(e^a - 1)^n$. **18.** 55. **19.** $a^{2x} + (a^2+1)^2 a^{4x}$.

20. $\frac{1}{4}x(x-1)(x-2)(x-3) + 2x(x-1)(x-2) + \frac{9}{2}x(x-1) + 12x + k$.

21. 2225. **22.** 20. **23.** -161. **24.** 229. **25.** 1261.

28. $x^{(4)} - 6x^{(3)} + 13x^{(2)} + x^{(1)} + 9$; $4x^{(3)} - 18x^{(2)} + 26x^{(1)} + 1$;

$12x^{(2)} - 36x^{(1)} + 26$; $24x^{(1)} - 36$; 24.

29. (i) $(m+1)m(m-1) \ldots (m-n+2)\,a^{m+1}(b/a + x + m)^{(m-n+1)}$;

(ii) $(-1)^n(m+1)(m+2) \ldots (m+n)\,a^{-\overline{m+1}}(b/a - 1 + x)^{(-\overline{m+n+1})}$.

30. $2\cos(x + \frac{1}{2}\alpha)\sin\frac{1}{2}\alpha$; $\sin\alpha/\{\cos(x+\alpha)\cos x\}$; $\alpha - 2\sin(x + \frac{1}{2}\alpha)\sin\frac{1}{2}\alpha$.

31. $6x$; $6/(x+1)^2$. **42.** $\gamma^2 + 4\alpha\gamma = \beta^2$. **43.** $2(x-2)^n - 2(x-3)^n$.

Examples 2.

1. 465. **2.** 441; 653. **3.** 300.

4. 182; 343. **5.** 5414. **6.** 89,920; 89,073.

7. 128. **8.** 94; 396; 662. **9.** 194·3; 279·9.

10. 97,357. **11.** 844; 746. **12.** ·98127.

13. 69,215. **14.** 2·37223. **15.** $-·432$; $-·338$; $-·196$.

16. 30; o. **17.** 14·73658. **18.** 3·708; 3·711.

19. 5281; 6504. **20.** ·5479. **21.** 2153; 1705.

22. 2459; 2424; 2359; 2268; 2153; 2018; 1868; 1705; 1534; 1357; 1180.

23. ·017; ·035; ·052; ·070; ·087; ·104; ·122; ·139; ·157.

24. 23·1234; 23·2039; 23·2914; 23·3865; 23·4898; 23·6019; 23·7234.

26. 1·000.　　　**27.** ·020660; ·020625; ·020628.　　　**28.** 58,835.

29. 1; 2·10; 3·31; 4·64; 6·11; 7·73; 9·51; 11·47; 13·62; 15·97.

31. 117·7; 114·2; 110·5; 106·7; 102·7; 98·6; 94·3; 89·8; 85·2; 80·3; 75·4.

32. ·24928.　　　**33.** Third degree: 275.　　　**34.** 459.

35. $u_2 = 218$; $u_4 = 0$; $u_5 = -19$; $u_x = 1876 - 1429x + 360x^2 - 30x^3$.

Examples 3.

1. 5745.　**2.** 47,983.　**3.** 2·8169.　**4.** 1·7243.　**5.** 2300.　**6.** 460.

7. $-\dfrac{l+m}{l^2m^2}$; $\dfrac{lm+mn+nl}{l^2m^2n^2}$; $-\dfrac{lmn+mnp+npl+plm}{l^2m^2n^2p^2}$.

8. 13·18.　　　**9.** 14·942.　　　**10.** 20·43.　　　**11.** 162.

12. $659 + 22\frac{1}{4}x + \frac{2}{7}\frac{9}{2}x^2 - \frac{7}{12}x^3$.　　　**13.** 32.　　　**16.** 1; 25.

18. 33 and 67 to the nearest integer.　　　　**19.** 37·2.

20. 7·37.　　　　**21.** 130,326.

23. $(x-4)$; $(x-3)(x-4)$; $(x-3)(x-4)(x-7)$; $x(x-3)(x-4)(x-7)$.

24. The $\triangle u$'s are $\underset{3}{\triangle}u_4$; $\underset{3,0}{\triangle^2}u_4$; $\underset{4,3,0}{\triangle^3}u_7$; $\underset{4,3,0,11}{\triangle^4}u_7$.

Examples 4.

1. 33.　　**2.** 6.　　**3.** 47,692.　　**4.** 3251.　　**5.** 16·9216.

6. 2·85805; 2·86305; 2·86157; 2·86155.　　**7.** 2017.

8. 3·5283.　　　**9.** 2196, 2108, 2022, 1939; 1786, 1718, 1657, 1604.

10. ·01625.　　　**11.** ·3165.　　　**12.** 2290·1.　　　**14.** 4·034.

Examples 5.

1. 471·5; 2·7.　　**2.** 13·3.　　　**3.** 2·019...; 2·018....

4. 43·1.　　　**5.** 8·34.　　　**6.** 2·751.　　　**7.** 16·9.

8. 1·1576....　　**9.** 1·2134.　　**10.** 45·70.　　**11.** 1·85.

12. 3·091.　　　**13.** 3·667 per cent.　　**14.** 1·3713.　　**15.** 37·2.

Examples 6.

1. $\frac{1}{6}n(-2n^2 + 27n + 17)$.　　　**2.** $\frac{1}{12}n(n+1)(3n^2 + 7n + 2)$.

3. -4195.　　**4.** $2^{21} + 628$.　　**5.** $3^{n+1} + \frac{1}{2}(n^2 + 7n - 6)$.

6. $\frac{1}{8}\{\frac{1}{2}(3^n - 1) + 5n + \frac{1}{3}n(n+1)(2n+1)\}$.

7. $2^{2k+1} - 2 - \frac{1}{3}k(2k+1)(4k+1)$.　　　**8.** $\frac{1}{8}(n^4 - 10n^3 + 29n^2 + 10n)$.

9. $2n^4 + 16n^3 + 47n^2 + 60n.$ **10.** $2^{19} - 2095.$

11. $\frac{1}{4}(n+3)(n+4)(n+5)(n+6) - 90.$

12. $\frac{1}{4}n(n+1)(n+4)(n+5).$

13. $\frac{1}{12}\{(3n-2)(3n+1)(3n+4)(3n+7) + 56\}.$

14. $\frac{1}{12}n(n+1)(n+2)(3n+13).$

15. $\frac{1}{30}n(n+1)(n+2)(6n^2+57n+137).$

16. $\frac{1}{10}\{(2n+3)(2n+5)(2n+7)(2n+9)(2n+11) - 10395\}.$

17. $\dfrac{n}{4(n+4)}.$ **18.** $\dfrac{n(5n+13)}{12(n+2)(n+3)}.$ **19.** $\dfrac{n(n+1)}{6(n+3)(n+4)}.$

20. $\dfrac{n(3n+5)}{8(3n+1)(3n+4)}.$ **21.** $\dfrac{n(5n+11)}{4(n+1)(n+2)}.$

22. $\frac{1}{18}n(n+1)(n+2)(3n^2+36n+101).$

23. $\dfrac{19}{168} - \dfrac{12n^2+33n+19}{6(3n+1)(3n+4)(3n+7)};\ \dfrac{19}{168}.$

24. $\frac{1}{12}n(n+1)(3n^2+31n+74).$

25. $\frac{1}{4}(n+3)(n+2)(n+1)n;\ \frac{1}{4}n(n-1)(n-2)(n-3).$

26. $3^n - 1 - n.$ **27.** $\dfrac{a^x}{a-1}\left\{x^2 - \dfrac{2ax}{a-1} + \dfrac{a(a+1)}{(a-1)^2}\right\} + C.$

28. $1 - 3(n+1)! + (n+2)!.$

29. $\frac{1}{15}\{(3n-1)(3n+2)(3n+5)(3n+8)(3n+11) + 880\}.$

30. $\frac{1}{8}n(6n^3+16n^2+9n-4).$ **31.** $\frac{1}{24}n(7n^3-34n^2+89n-254).$

33. $\frac{1}{12}n(n+1)(9n^2+17n+4);\ \{2^{n+1}(n^3-3n^2+10n-14)\} + 28.$

34. $\dfrac{2}{3} + \dfrac{4^{n+1}}{3}\left\{\dfrac{n-1}{n+2}\right\}.$ **35.** $\dfrac{11}{768}.$ **36.** $34 - (4n^2+12n+17)/2^{n-1}.$

37. $(x-2)3^x.$ **38.** $\frac{5}{2}(3^n-1) + \frac{1}{12}(42n+17n^2+n^4).$

39. $\dfrac{(n+2)x^n-2}{x-1} - \dfrac{x^{n+1}-x}{(x-1)^2}.$ **40.** $C - \dfrac{12x^3+36x^2+28x+3}{12x(x+1)(x+2)(x+3)}.$

42. $\dfrac{1}{54}\left\{\dfrac{39}{10} - \dfrac{36n+39}{(3n+2)(3n+5)}\right\}.$ **43.** $23.$ **44.** $n^2 2^{n+1}.$

45. $\dfrac{2-(n+1)(n+2)x^n}{1-x} + \dfrac{2x}{(1-x)^2}\{2-(n+2)x^n\} + \dfrac{2x^2}{(1-x)^3}(1-x^n).$

46. $C - 2^{x-2}\dfrac{(x-1)!}{(2x-1)!}.$

47. $\frac{5}{4} + \frac{1}{60}(2n-1)(2n+1)(2n+3)(24n^2+54n+25).$

48. $\frac{1}{4}ax^4 - (\frac{1}{3}a - \frac{1}{3}b)x^3 + (\frac{1}{4}a - \frac{1}{2}b + \frac{1}{2}c)x^2 + (\frac{1}{6}b - \frac{1}{2}c + d)x + C.$

49. $(1-x)^{r+1}.$ **52.** $\dfrac{1}{a-1}\left\{1 - \dfrac{(n+1)!}{(a+1)(a+2)\dots(a+n)}\right\}.$

53. $2^{n-4}n(n+1)(n^2+5n-2).$

Examples 7.

2. $20 \cdot 796875$; $-\frac{1}{64}$.

11. $\cdot 109$.

13. $ke^{ax+\lambda^2 x}$.

10. $\cdot 02455$; $-\cdot 0003$; o.

15. 48; 24.

19. $5 \cdot 254$.

22. $13 \cdot 094$.

23. $5 \cdot 319$.

24. $3 \cdot 9634$.

25. $10 \cdot 389$; $10 \cdot 475$.

Examples 9.

2. $\cdot 9921$.

3. $20 \cdot 4$ miles.

8. $\frac{1}{144}(95u_0 - 50u_1 + 600u_2 - 350u_3 + 425u_4)$.

9. 200 square inches.

11. $\cdot 8571...$; (i) $\cdot 8806...$; (ii) $\cdot 8946....$

12. The second.

13. 29,426.

14. 888.

16. $\cdot 6942$.

22. $\cdot 5236$.

24. $3 \cdot 142....$

25. $1 \cdot 1358....$

26. $\cdot 6931....$

27. $3 \cdot 142....$

Examples 10.

2. $\frac{1}{9}$; $\frac{1}{8}$.

4. $\frac{1}{12}$.

5. $\frac{5}{6}$.

6. $\frac{2}{11}$.

7. $\frac{7}{66}$.

8. $\frac{7}{22}$.

9. $\frac{400}{729}$.

10. $\dfrac{(2n)!}{n!\,n!}\left(\dfrac{1}{2}\right)^{2n}$.

11. $\frac{5}{81}$.

12. $\frac{146}{1296}$.

13. $\frac{5}{16}$.

14. $\frac{679}{865}$.

15. $\dfrac{75^1}{6^5}$.

16. $\dfrac{15 \times 35^2}{6^{12}}$.

17. (a) 2^n; (b) 2^{mn}; (c) $\dfrac{(m+1)}{2^m}$.

18. $\frac{18000}{39151}$.

19. $\frac{5}{16}$.

20. $\frac{773}{1180}$.

21. $\frac{55}{1000}$.

22. $\dfrac{138 \times 56}{5^8}$.

23. $\frac{11}{20}$.

24. (1) $\frac{1}{166500}$; (2) $\frac{997}{166500}$.

26. $\frac{7}{9}$.

27. $\frac{33}{1000}$.

28. $\frac{89}{110}$.

29. $\frac{11}{16}$.

31. $\left(\frac{7}{13}\right)^2$.

32. $\frac{169}{324}$; $\frac{155}{324}$.

33. $\frac{493}{648}$.

34. $\frac{16592}{19683}$; $\frac{3091}{19683}$.

35. $\frac{7}{33}$; $\frac{4}{19}$.

36. $\frac{83}{729}$.

37. $\frac{263}{1944}$.

38. (i) $\dfrac{p^2(p+2q)}{(p+q)(p^2+pq+q^2)}$; (ii) $\dfrac{p(p+q)}{p^2+pq+q^2}$.

39. $\frac{5}{14}$; $\frac{5}{14}$; $\frac{2}{7}$.

40. $\frac{208}{405}$.

41. $\frac{1547}{2304}$.

42. $\frac{711}{832}$.

43. $\frac{380}{2187}$.

44. $\cdot 126$.

45. 2×10^{-7}.

46. (1) $\frac{1}{8}$; (2) $\frac{87}{800}$; (3) $\frac{31}{32}$.

47. $\cdot 105$.

49. $\cdot 98304$ or $\cdot 09888$.

50. (1) $\cdot 72$; (2) $\cdot 504$.

51. (1) $\cdot 099...$; (2) $\cdot 000007...$, $\cdot 001....$

52. $\cdot 2109$.

53. (a) $\cdot 972$; (b) $\cdot 271$.

54. $\frac{173}{648}$.

56. $1 - \dfrac{1}{\sqrt{2}}$.

57. 7.

58. $\dfrac{n+3}{2^{m+2}}$.

63. (1) $\frac{1}{12}$; (2) $\frac{73}{1000}$; (3) $\frac{307}{1000}$.

64. $\frac{6220}{6561}$.

65. $\dfrac{3n^2 - 3n + 2}{9n^2 - 9n + 2}$.

66. $-\dfrac{\log_e 2}{\log_e \left(1 - \dfrac{1}{m}\right)}$; $\log_e 2$.

67. $\frac{1}{54}$.

68. (1) $\frac{5}{506}$; (2) $\frac{5}{23}$; (3) $\frac{3}{44}$.   **70.** $\frac{443}{5525}$; $\frac{503}{5525}$.   **71.** $\frac{3003}{2^{15}}$.

72. (1) $\frac{23}{35}$; (2) $\frac{5}{14}$; (3) $\frac{1}{2}$.   **73.** $\frac{3n}{36n^2 - 18n + 2}$.   **75.** $\frac{7}{66}$.

76. $\frac{(4!)^{13}\,(13!)^4}{52!}$.   **77.** $\frac{1}{90}$.   **78.** ·506....

80. $\frac{979}{1118}$.   **81.** (1) $\frac{8}{35}$; (2) $\frac{3}{35}$; (3) $\frac{17}{70}$.   **82.** $\frac{4}{21}$.

83. $\frac{244}{495}$.   **84.** 3000 : 3007.   **85.** $\frac{1}{4}$.   **86.** $\frac{1}{8}$.   **88.** $\frac{1}{32}$.

89. $\frac{5}{21}$.   **90.** $\frac{325}{833}$.   **91.** (1) $\frac{1}{2}$; (2) $\frac{4}{5}$; (3) $\frac{59}{100}$.

92. $\frac{461}{4165}$.   **93.** (a) $\frac{3}{13}$; (b) $\frac{5}{13}$; (c) $\frac{2}{13}$.   **95.** $\frac{38}{245}$.

96. $\frac{5359}{14498}$; $\frac{11686}{20825}$.

Examples 11.

1. 24·9... years.   **2.** 64·65...; 64·55....   **3.** 77 (approx.).

4. 32·1; 31·6.   **5.** 33–34.   **6.** 7·9...; 9·0....

10. 11; 6s. 1d.   **11.** (1) Between 5 and 6; (2) 4; (3) 7.

12. 6s. 0d.; 5s. 0d.   **13.** 35s. 0d.   **14.** 6 : 1.   **16.** Purse A.

17. (i) 63s. 0d.; (ii) 56s. 0d.   **18.** $\frac{775}{1764}$.   **19.** $\frac{1}{6}m\,(m+1)$.

20. 10.   **21.** (1) 1s.; (2) $1\frac{2}{9}$s.; (3) $1\frac{4}{9}$s.   **22.** $M + \frac{1}{2}m$.

23. (1) $\frac{658}{729}$; (2) $\frac{189}{729}$; (3) $\frac{1}{8075}$: Most probable number is 4; $\frac{240}{729}$.

24. 7s. 2d.   **25.** £43. 14s. 11d.; £56. 5s. 1d.

Examples 12.

1. $M = 509\cdot6$; $\sigma = 8\cdot0$.   **2.** $M = 22\cdot3$; $M_i = 19\cdot5$; $\sigma = 9\cdot2$.

3. 9·2 and 6·2.

4. 35·3s. (if the extreme values are omitted) or 34·7s. (if they are included).

5. $M_0 = 8\cdot6$, $M_i = 7\cdot9$, Quartiles 10 and 6. $M = 7\cdot5$.

6. $\sigma = 4\cdot2$.   **7.** ± ·15 in.   **8.** ·27 year.

9. $M = 60\cdot7$; $M_i = 57\cdot3$; $\sigma = 14\cdot25$.   **10.** B is the more consistent.

11. $\sigma = 14\cdot7$.   **12.** X is the more consistent.

Examples 13.

2. $\frac{1}{3}(n+2)$.   **3.** $\frac{b^2}{a^2}$.   **4.** $\frac{1}{n}\log_e 2$.   **5.** $\frac{6l}{\pi}(\sqrt{2}-1)$.

6. $\frac{q^2}{p^2}$.   **7.** $\frac{2}{3}a^2$; $\frac{1}{\sqrt{3}}$.   **8.** (1) $\frac{2r^2}{\pi}$; (2) $\frac{r^2\pi}{4}$.   **9.** $\frac{\pi r}{4}$.

10. $\frac{1}{3}a^2$.   **11.** $\frac{2a^2}{3}$.   **12.** $\frac{1}{60}a^3$.   **13.** $\frac{8\log 2 - 3}{64\log 2 - 15}$.

14. $\frac{1}{4}$.   **15.** $\frac{27}{64}$.   **16.** $\frac{1}{2}$.   **17.** $\frac{1}{3}$.   **18.** $\frac{7}{8}$.   **19.** $\frac{c^2}{ab}$.

20. $\frac{2}{3} - \frac{1}{3}\log_e 3$. 21. $\frac{\pi}{4}$. 22. $\frac{3}{4}$. 24. $\frac{1}{2} + \frac{1}{2}\log_e 2$.

25. $\frac{19}{24}$; $\frac{19}{48}$ miles. 26. $\frac{1}{3}(2-\sqrt{2}) + \log(1+\sqrt{2})$.

Miscellaneous Examples.

1. $\frac{n}{12}(n^3 - 4n^2 + 11n + 4)$. 2. $\frac{17}{24}$.

3. $40.3...; 37.7....$ 5. $\frac{113}{13122}$.

6. (a) 19,764; (b) 59,156. 11. (1) $\frac{19}{80}$; (2) $\frac{9}{40}$.

14. $\frac{5}{24}$. 17. 977, 961; 1023. 18. $\frac{2b}{3(b-c)}$.

20. .0294; .0492; .0682. 22. 1.109. 24. 38.45; 9.4....

25. $u_0 + n\Delta u_1 + \frac{1}{2}n(n-3)\Delta^2 u_2 + \frac{1}{6}n(n-4)(n-5)\Delta^3 u_3$.

26. $\frac{61}{4000}$. 27. $\frac{3\pi}{16}$. 28. -1.88.

29. $1 - (\frac{35}{36})^6 + (\frac{35}{36})^6 (\frac{29}{36})^6 \frac{18}{103}$. 30. $\frac{1}{2}a + \frac{1}{8}a\log_e 3$.

34. $\frac{7}{25}$. 35. 58.9321.... 36. 86; 121.

37. $\frac{4}{5}$. 38. 20,536. 39. $\frac{47}{54}$.

41. 45. 43. .7854. 44. .109....

47. $1 - \frac{31}{11^5}$. 49. 15.975. 50. $\frac{2}{3}$.

51. .66. 52. $\frac{2}{3}$. 53. $\frac{180}{6^5}$; $\frac{780}{6^5}$.

54. 113.6, 117.0, 120.4, 124.2, 128.8, 134.2, 141.4, 149.4, 158.6, 168.6, 179.4.

55. .14 or .18. 58. $\frac{1}{4}\left[\log\frac{e^2+1}{2}\right]^2$. 60. 196.

62. (ii) $\frac{21}{128}$. 63. (i) $(a-b)^2/a^2$. 64. 2.4695....

65. 28.0. 66. $\frac{17}{81}$. 67. $\frac{448}{729}$.

69. (1) 10 in. (ii) 15.8 in. 70. 29.08.

71. $\frac{2491}{4116}$. 75. 10. 76. 3.

77. B is the more consistent. 78. 12.50.

79. .32. 80. $\frac{2}{27}, \frac{8}{27}, \frac{17}{27}; \frac{17}{81}$. 81. 7, 13.

82. $a = -\frac{5}{8}, b = \frac{1}{6}, c = -\frac{1}{24}$. 83. (i) $\frac{22}{1365}$; (ii) $\frac{33}{91}$.

84. 10.476. 85. $\frac{(N-n)!}{N!}$; $\frac{1}{N}$. 86. 15 : 17.

87. $\frac{1}{4^n}(4^n - 6.2^n + 8)$. 88. 15s.

89. 1403, 1498, 1598, 1703, 1814, 1931, 2054, 2182, 2316, 2458, 2609; 120.6.

90. $\frac{243}{6050}$. 91. 14.606063. 93. $\frac{71}{90}$.

95. $\frac{3600}{30963}$. 96. $\frac{1}{2}\{2^{n+2} + 3^{n+1} - 7n^2 - n - 7\}$.

97. 5. 98. $\frac{3}{13}(\frac{2}{3})^n + \frac{4}{39}(-\frac{1}{3})^n$. 99. $\frac{713}{2940}$.

INDEX

Printed in the United States
By Bookmasters